A Complete Guide to
CAREER
PLANNING

Devajit Bhuyan

career
planning

MOVING ON

KNOWING YOURSELF

EXPLORING YOUR OPTIONS

MAKING DECISIONS

V&S PUBLISHERS

Published by:

V&S PUBLISHERS

F-2/16, Ansari Road, Daryaganj, New Delhi-110002
011-23240026, 011-23240027 • *Fax:* 011-23240028
Email: info@vspublishers.com • *Website:* www.vspublishers.com

Branch : Hyderabad
5-1-707/1, Brij Bhawan (Beside Central Bank of India Lane)
Bank Street, Koti, Hyderabad - 500 095
040-24737290
E-mail: vspublishershyd@gmail.com

Follow us on: **t** **f** **in**

For any assistance sms **VSPUB** to **56161**

All books available at **www.vspublishers.com**

© **Copyright: Author**
ISBN 978-93-815887-7-2
Edition 2013

Printed at : Unique Colour Carton, New Delhi-110020

Dedication

*This book is dedicated to all my friends of school days at
Raha Higher Secondary School &
college days at Assam Engineering College*

Publisher's Note

Preparing for the future may be daunting and overwhelming for many students and families alike, but it doesn't have to be. There are a variety of options that a student can pursue after high school, 10+2 or graduation. Learning about the choices and creating a plan will help a student in the path to success.

You can help yourself and your friends as well navigate the career options you can pursue and prepare for the future by using the book — **A Complete Guide To Career Planning**. Written by well-known author Devajit Bhuyan, who is eminently qualified for writing the most comprehensive book in this genre, backed by more than 28 years of professional experience in the Education Sector, The Complete Guide To Career Planning has all the information you need to plan your future and take control of your career. The book is an effort on the part of the author to develop a comprehensive course on career planning that is worthy to stand with other academic subjects. This comprehensive guide book includes aspects like how to explore career options, plan a career path, and find the right school and colleges for higher studies that will help a student reach his goals easily and convincingly.

This book is indeed a guide to your career planning. It will guide you through the needed steps to choose the right career. This book is a must read for every student in the age group of 15-22 years and their parents and teachers alike.

Contents

Preface

There are already many Career Guide available in the market. Moreover, in today's era of Information Technology and Internet, most of the information are available on the fingertip through click of a mouse. In such an environment is there any need of another career guide? The answer is yes, as most of the career guides available in the market devoted only on giving routine information and could not clear doubts of a vast majority of students. I strongly feel that there is need of a career guide in the form of FAQs (Frequently Asked Questions) which can provide a wider collection of information, as well as a guide to the younger generation and enable them to make their own decision.

The Complete Guide to Career Planning is specially written in the form of question-answer for the students of India and especially for those students, who not only lack in information, but also to migrate to other cities, outside of their home town. In this career guide emphasis is given on basic information required by students/parents for selecting a career or institution for studying a course. As information changes very fast and it is difficult to collect and compile all the information, there may be omission of many information which a student may require. Author shall be highly obliged and glad if the readers point out these shortcomings in the book to be corrected in the next edition.

I have to say that it is due to continuous support from my wife Mitali and daughter Bonu, I could complete this book. At last I thank my publisher; specially Dibya Borah without whose sincere effort this book would had remained as a manuscript.

— Author
Devajit Bhuyan

INTRODUCTION

Q.1 What is Career?

Ans: Career is one of the most important words with which we are all concerned throughout our

means profession or occupation with opportunities for advancement or promotion. Here comes the question as to what is occupation and profession? Occupation means job or employment for earning a livelihood and profession means paid occupation, especially one that requires advanced education and training, e.g. architecture, law, engineering or medicine, etc. So a career is not simply a job or an employment to earn a livelihood. A job or profession or employment can be called a career only when it has an element or opportunity for progress and advancement.

Human needs change progressively. So, in order to call a job or employment as career it must offer adequate opportunities or scope to satisfy or meet those changing needs. So a job or profession

process of upward progression and that is why we never say pulling rickshaw can also be a career. Any occupation or profession to mature into a career must provide good remuneration, social prestige, good health, opportunity for growth and of ultimately happiness in life.

Some people think that earning money for a livelihood is career. However, earning money alone is not a career. After all thieves, robbers or smugglers also earn lot of money. Obtaining a degree is also not a career. One can now see hundreds of young men with too many degrees moving around without any job because they have earned a degree but not the skills or knowledge. To make a career out of an occupation, one must like it; possess the required intelligence and acquire the necessary skills/knowledge. Unless one has the aptitude for a particular profession, success in

Q.2 What are the factors are to be considered before choosing a career?

Ans: The following factors should be considered before choosing a career:

(i) Intelligence: Intelligence includes your I.Q., Social Intelligence and Emotional Intelligence (E.Q.). Total intelligence is more important to be successful in life and career than simply having a high I.Q. There are many cases where an academically brilliant executive,

have required social intelligence and emotional stability.

(ii) Personality: As a person you may be an Introvert or Extrovert. You may be a Dominating personality or Submissive personality. If you are an Introvert, you should not choose a career that needs people with Extrovert nature. You may be too social or you prefer loneliness to do creative work. Only you can judge your personality and decide what is best for you. So always give due importance to your personality factor while deciding on your career.

(iii) Interest: All work is hard work unless you care for it and show interest in it. No amount of

interest in the job is absent. However, it must also be said that excessive interest towards

into account.

(iv) Special Aptitudes: If one is good at art, it would be really sad for him to take up a career where he has to work in a machine shop. M.F. Hussain cannot play better cricket than Sachin Tendulkar nor can Tendulkar sing better than Sonu Nigam.

(v) Physique: All jobs make varying degree of physical demands and the choice should be made after carefully considering all the relevant facts associated with it. So a man with a poor health and heart problem should not take up a career in the mountain brigade of the army.

(vi) Sex: Though legally and socially men and women are equal, but nature has given them different physique and capabilities too. Some careers are more suited to men than women. So this factor should also be kept in mind while choosing a career.

(vii) Age: Some careers need early entry to be successful. Belated entry may lead to frustration due to thwarted ambition and the mental agony of working under much younger people in age.

Q.3 What are the options available to a student after the completion of school education (class X board examination/HSLC)?

Ans: Under the present education system in India, a student completing his/her school education (Metric/HSLC) can opt for Science, Arts (Humanities) or Commerce stream for studies at (10+2) or

in Engineering/Pharmacy/Nursing, etc. Courses are also available in Fine Arts/Applied Arts/ Music/Sports, etc., after school education (10th or Metric).

Once a student completes his Higher Secondary or 10+2 in Science/Arts/Commerce, he becomes eligible for admission to undergraduate courses leading to a Bachelor Degree. Bachelor Degree

To join various courses at Degree level, a student must mandatorily study some subjects at his 10+2 level. For example, if you want to study Medicine (MBBS), you must take the science stream with Physics, Chemistry and Biology at 10+2 level. Similarly, if you want to do Engineering (BE/B. Tech), you must be in the science stream with Physics, Chemistry and Mathematics at 10+2 level.

However, there is rigidity in the Arts and Commerce stream in selecting subjects at 10+2 level, because the career options available after Graduating with Arts or Commerce degree are more or less interdisciplinary. So you must be very careful while selecting subjects of study at 10+2. You should only select those subjects which will lead you to your dream career. Under the present curriculum in science stream, if you opt for subjects like Physics, Chemistry, Mathematics and Biology in your 10+2 level, you can become eligible for most of the professional courses, namely Medicine/Engineering/Agriculture, etc.

Q.4 What are the courses available for a student after completing Higher Secondary (10+2) in science stream?

Ans: The following courses are available for a student after 10+2 in science stream:

B.Sc	: Bachelor of Science (pass/major/honours)
B.Sc	: Bachelor of Science (Computers/computer application)
B.Sc	: Bachelor of Science (applied)
B.ScBEd: Bachelor of Science & Education (integrated)	
B.E-com	: Bachelor of Electronic Commerce
BBA	: Bachelor of Business Administration
BBM	: Bachelor of Business Management
BBS	: Bachelor of Business Studies
BBM	: Bachelor of Bank Management
BCA	: Bachelor of Computer Application
BCS	: Bachelor of Computer Studies
B.A.	: Bachelor of Arts (general and Corporate Secretaryship)
BL/LL.B	: Bachelor of Law (5 years-integrated course)
BHM	: Bachelor of Hotel Management
BHRD	: Bachelor of Human Resource Development
BHRM	: Bachelor of Human Resource Management
BIBF	: Bachelor of International Business and Finance
BIT	: Bachelor of Information Technology
BJ	: Bachelor of Journalism
BMS	: Bachelor of Management Science
BRP	: Bachelor of Public Relation

22.BRS	: Bachelor of Rural Studies	
BSW	: Bachelor of Social Works	
BHS	: Bachelor of Hospitality Science	
BTA/S	: Bachelor of Tourism Administration/Studies	
BEM	: Bachelor of Environmental Management	
BHM/A	: Bachelor of Hospital Management/Administration	
BMIT	: Bachelor of Management and Information Technology	
BD	: Bachelor of Dramatics	
B.Ped	: Bachelor of Physical Education (Health Education and Sports)	
CA	: Chartered Accountancy (Foundation)	
CS	: Company Secretaryship (Foundation)	
BE	: Bachelor of Engineering	
B.Tech	: Bachelor of Technology	
B.Sc(Engg)	: Bachelor of Science(Engineering)	
B.Arch	: Bachelor of Architecture	
BAM	: Bachelor of Ayurvedic Medicine	
BCS	: Bachelor of Computer Science	
BDH	: Bachelor of Dental Hygiene	
BDM	: Bachelor of Dental Mechanic	
BDS	: Bachelor of Dental Surgery	
BFSc	: Bachelor of Fishery Science	
BHMS	: Bachelor of Homeopathic Medicine & Surgery	
BHSc	: Bachelor of Home Science	
BIT	: Bachelor of Information Technology	
B.Tech(NA)	: Bachelor of Technology(Naval Architecture)	
B Text	: Bachelor of Textiles	
B Text(Eng)	: Bachelor of Textiles (Engineering)	
BUMS	: Bachelor of Unani Medicine and Surgery	
BVSc&AH	: Bachelor of Veterinary Science & Animal Husbandry	

BYS	:	Bachelor of Yogic Science
MBBS	:	Bachelor of Medicine & Bachelor of Surgery
B.Des	:	Bachelor of Design
BPT	:	Bachelor of Physio Therapy
BOT	:	Bachelor of Occupational Therapy
BSc(Agri)	:	Bachelor of Science (Agriculture)
BSc(Ag&AH)	:	Bachelor of Science in Agriculture and Animal Husbandry
B Sc(Hort)	:	Bachelor of Science (Horticulture)
B Sc(Nurs)	:	Bachelor of Science in Nursing
BSSc	:	Bachelor of Sanitary Science
BPS	:	Bachelor of Professional Studies
BRSc	:	Bachelor of Rehabilitation Science
B Sc(N&D)	:	Bachelor of Science (Nutrition & Dietetics)
B Sc(HC&M)	:	Bachelor of Science (Health Care and Hospital Management)
BS(Comm)	:	Bachelor of Science (Communication)
B Sc(AHS)	:	Bachelor of Science (Allied Health Sciences)
B Sc(SL&H)	:	Bachelor of Science (Speech, Language & Hearing Science)
B Sc(P&OE)	:	Bachelor of Science in Prosthetic & Orthotic Engineering
B Sc(OT)	:	Bachelor of Science (Ophthalmic Technology)
B Sc(HB)	:	Bachelor of Science (Human Biology)
B Sc(Radghy)	:	Bachelor of Science (Radiography)
B Sc(NM)	:	Bachelor of Science (Nuclear Medicine)
B Sc(RTT)	:	Bachelor of Science (Respiratory Therapy Technique)
B Sc(MT-X)	:	Bachelor of Science (Medical technology − X Ray)
BSLH	:	Bachelor of Speech Language and Hearing
B Sc(MSS)	:	Bachelor of Science (Medical Secretarial Services)
B Sc(OpT)	:	Bachelor of Science (Operation Theatres)
B Sc(MM)	:	Bachelor of Science (Medical Microbiology)
B Sc(HA)	:	Bachelor of Science (Hospital Administration)

The following career oriented competitive examinations are also open after 10+2 in science:

01. National Defense Academy (NDA)
02. Special Class Railway Apprentices Examination
03. Examination by Director General of Shipping for Nautical Science & Marine Engineering

Diploma courses are also available in engineering, paramedical science, hotel management, fashion designing, interior decoration, costume designing, printing technology, pharmacy, nursing and various other vocational subjects.

The above list of courses is only an indicative list and not a complete list. There are many other courses which a student can opt for after (10+2) in science. Some courses, especially engineering/ technology courses require Physics, Chemistry and Mathematics in (10+2) whereas medical/ paramedical/ life sciences require Physics, Chemistry and Biology in (10+2). The interdisciplinary courses are open to all science students.

Q.5 What courses are available to a student after completing Higher Secondary (10+2) in Arts (Humanities) stream?

Ans: The following courses are available for Arts (Humanities) student after Higher Secondary (10+2):

B.A	: Bachelor of Arts(pass/major/ honours)
BFIA	: Bachelor of Financial & Investment Analysis
BT&TM	: Bachelor of Tourism & Travel Management
B.A.BEd	: Bachelor of Arts & Education (integrated)
BSSc	: Bachelor of Sports Science
BBA	: Bachelor of Business Administration
BBM	: Bachelor of Business Management
BBS	: Bachelor of Business Studies
BBM	: Bachelor of Bank Management
BCA	: Bachelor of Computer Application
BRI	: Bachelor of Religions of India
B.A.	: Bachelor of Arts (General and Corporate Secretaryship)
BL/LL.B	: Bachelor of Law (5 years-integrated course)
BHM	: Bachelor of Hotel Management
BHRD	: Bachelor of Human Resource Development
BHRM	: Bachelor of Human Resource Management

BIBF	: Bachelor of International Business and Finance
BPP	: Bachelor of Physical Planning
BJ	: Bachelor of Journalism
BMS	: Bachelor of Management Science
BRP	: Bachelor of Public Relation
BRS	: Bachelor of Rural Studies
BSW	: Bachelor of Social Works
BHS	: Bachelor of Hospitality Science
BTA/S	: Bachelor of Tourism Administration/Studies
BEM	: Bachelor of Environmental Management
BHM/A	: Bachelor of Hospital Management/Administration
BMIT	: Bachelor of Management and Information Technology
BD	: Bachelor of Dramatics
B.Ped	: Bachelor of Physical Education (Health Education and Sports)
CA	: Chartered Accountancy (Foundation)
CS	: Company Secretaryship (Foundation)
BAEd	: Bachelor of Adult Education
BA(EdDeaf)	: Bachelor of Arts(Education of Deaf)
BA(Mus)	: Bachelor of Arts(Music)
BEEd	: Bachelor of Elementary Education
BFA	: Bachelor of Fine Arts
BJ&MC	: Bachelor of Journalism & Mass Communication
BLM	: Bachelor of Labour Management
BVA	: Bachelor of Visual Arts
BYS	: Bachelor of Yogic Science
BMR	: Bachelor of Mental Retardation

This list is only an indicative list and not a complete list. There are many other courses which a arts student can opt after 10+2 in arts.

Competitive Examinations after 10+2 in Arts (Humanities)

01. Defense Services (various wings)
02. Banking/LIC/GIC, etc., (Clerical cadre)
03. SSB/Air Force
04. Indian Railways
05. Inter disciplinary services in central and state government (clerical grades)
06. Clerk's Grade Examination
07. NDA (Army wing)

Q.6   What all courses are available to a student after completing Higher Secondary (10+2) in Commerce stream?

Ans: The following courses are available to students completing Higher Secondary (10+2) in commerce stream:

B.Com	: Bachelor of Commerce(pass/major/honours)
B.Com	: Bachelor of Commerce(Computers/computer application)
B.Com	: Bachelor of Commerce (applied)
B.ComBEd	: Bachelor of Commerce & Education (integrated)
B.E-com	: Bachelor of Electronic Commerce
BBA	: Bachelor of Business Administration
BBM	: Bachelor of Business Management
BBS	: Bachelor of Business Studies
BBM	: Bachelor of Bank Management
BCA	: Bachelor of Computer Application
BCS	: Bachelor of Computer Studies
B.A.	: Bachelor of Arts (general and Corporate Secretaryship)
BL/LL.B	: Bachelor of Law (5 years-integrated course)
BHM	: Bachelor of Hotel Management
BHRD	: Bachelor of Human Resource Development
BHRM	: Bachelor of Human Resource Management
BIBF	: Bachelor of International Business and Finance
BIT	: Bachelor of Information Technology
BJ	: Bachelor of Journalism

BMS	: Bachelor of Management Science
BRP	: Bachelor of Public Relation
BRS	: Bachelor of Rural Studies
BSW	: Bachelor of Social Works
BHS	: Bachelor of Hospitality Science
BTA/S	: Bachelor of Tourism Administration/Studies
BEM	: Bachelor of Environmental Management
BHM/A	: Bachelor of Hospital Management/Administration
BMIT	: Bachelor of Management and Information Technology
BD	: Bachelor of Dramatics
B.Ped	: Bachelor of Physical Education (Health Education and Sports)
CA	: Chartered Accountancy (Foundation)
CS	: Company Secretaryship (Foundation)
ICWA	: Indian Cost and Works Accountants

The above list is only an indicative list and not a complete list. There are many other courses, which a commerce student can opt after 10+2 in commerce.

Competitive examination for job after completing 10+2 in commerce stream:

Defense Services (various wings)
Banking/LIC/GIC, etc. (Clerical cadre)
SSB/Air Force
Indian Railways
Inter disciplinary services in central and state government (clerical grades)
Clerk's Grade Examination
NDA (Army wing)

Q.7 Name the top twenty careers one can opt in present day scenario.

Ans: The Top Twenty Careers (In alphabetical order) are:

Accountancy(CA/ICWA)
Agriculture
Advertising & Public Relation
Biotechnology & Bio-informatics
Civil Services (IAS/IPS/IES /State Civil Services, etc.)
Civil Aviation (Pilot/Air Hostess)

Company Secretary
Defence Services
Engineering
Environmental Science
Fashion Design & Fashion Modelling
Hotel Management, Hospital Management, Event Management
Information Technology & Computer Science
Insurance
Law
Management
Mass Communication (Print Media/TV/Cinema/Radio and other Audio Visual Media)
Medicine (Allopathic/Homeopathy/Ayurvedic/Alternative Medicine, etc.)
Paramedical Science
Travel & Tourism

ACCOUNTANCY

Q.1 What is Accountancy?

Ans:

to users such as shareholders and managers. The communication is generally in the form of

the management. The art lies in selecting the relevant information and presenting it to the user reliably. The principles of accountancy are applied to business entities in three divisions

Oxford English Dictionary (OED) as "the profession or duties of an accountant".

results thereof." Accounting is thousands of years old; the earliest accounting records, which date back more than 7,000 years, were found in Mesopotamia (Assyrians). The people of that time relied on primitive accounting methods to record the growth of crops and herds. Accounting evolved, improving over the years and advancing as business advanced.

Q.2 What does an accountant do?

Ans:

they are employed, or what their specialty might be. Some accountants work for companies or individuals to help manage internal accounts — either personal or business. In this position, an

to identify areas of waste. Accountants may go by different names, depending on where they work and their level of experience. A few names are bookkeeper, controller and comptroller.

Auditors examine the records of companies and individuals to check for compliance with tax laws and to look for any illegal activity.

Q.3 What kind of training does an accountant need?

Ans: The level necessary for accounting training varies. Some junior-level jobs in accounting can be attained through an associate degree. However, many careers in accounting require at least a bachelor degree (B.Com.). Many people who wish to start a career in accounting should consider becoming a Chartered Accountant (CA). The most lucrative accounting jobs usually require a CA/ ICWA, which can be earned by passing a rigorous exam.

Q.4 How can one become a Chartered Accountant?

Ans: The Institute of Chartered Accountants of India (ICAI) is the statutory body established under the Chartered Accountants Act, 1949 to regulate the profession of Chartered Accountants in India. During its 61 years of existence, ICAI has achieved recognition as a premier accounting

professional development, maintenance of high accounting, auditing and ethical standards. ICAI now is the second largest accounting body in the whole world.

Test (CPT) which is designed in the pattern of entry level test for engineering, medical and other professional courses. It is a test of 4 hours duration comprising two sessions of 2 hours each, with a break between two sessions. The test comprises objective type questions with negative marking for wrong options.

Under the existing chartered accountancy scheme of education, training and examination, the requirements for becoming a chartered accountant are as follows:

(CPT) after passing class 10th examination conducted by an examining body constituted by law in India or an examination recognised by the Central Government as equivalent thereto.

(ii) Appear in CPT after clearing the senior secondary examination (10+2 examination), conducted by an examining body constituted by law in India or an examination recognised

day of the month in which examination is to be held, viz., students registered on or before 1st April/1st October will be eligible to appear in June/December examination, as the case may be. However, candidate should pass both CPT and 10+2 before registering for Integrated Professional Competence Course (IPCC).

(iii) Enroll for Group I or Group II or for both Group I and Group II of Integrated Professional Competence Course (IPCC) to become "Chartered Accountant".

(iv) Successful completion of 9 months of study course from the date of IPCC registration.

(v) Successful completion of Orientation Course of one week spanning 35 hours and covering topics,

general commercial knowledge, etc., before the commencement of articled training.

(vi) Successful completion of 100 hours of Information Technology Training (ITT) before commencement of articled training.

(vii) Passing Group I as well as Group II of Integrated Professional Competence Examination (IPCE). Group I comprises four papers and Group II comprises three papers.

(viii) Register as Articled Assistant for a period of 3 years, on passing either Group I or both the Groups of IPCE.

(ix) Register for CA Final Course and prepare for CA Final Examination.

(x) Undergo General Management and Communication Skills (GMCS) (15 days) course while undergoing Final Course and serving the last 12 months of articled training.

(xi) Complete 3 years period of articled training.

(xii) Appear in the Final Examination on completion of the practical training or while serving last 6 months of articled training on or before the last day of the month proceeding the month in which the examination is to be held.

(xiv) Enroll as a member of ICAI and designate as "Chartered Accountant".

the Institute in this regard. The CPT Examination is taken in two parts or sections of two hours each and each examination tests students in two subjects.

Section 1 has questions from the subjects Fundamentals of Accounting and Mercantile Laws.

Section 2 has questions from the subjects General Economics and Quantitative Aptitude.

The CPT Examination has Objective Type questions. Each of the questions would have a problem statement with four possible options from which a student is required to choose the most appropriate. These questions can be of following types:

"Fill in the blanks" type having four alternative answers.

Small paragraph of two-three lines, followed by a question having four alternative answers or Numerical having four alternative answers

Each wrong answer would attract Negative marking.

Q.5 How can one become an Accounting Technician?

Ans:

conducted by a competent body constituted by law in India or an examination recognised by the Central Government as equivalent thereto.

(ii) Appear in CPT after appearing in the senior secondary examination (10+2 examination) conducted by an examining body constituted by law in India or an examination recognised

of the month in which examination is to be held, viz., students registered on or before 1st April/ 1st October will be eligible to appear in June/December examination, as the case may be. However, the candidate should pass both CPT and 10+2 before registering for Accounting Technician Course (ATC).

(iii) Enroll for ATC.

(iv) Successfully complete 9 months of study course from the date of ATC registration.

(v) Successfully complete Orientation Course of one week spanning 35 hours and covering environment, general commercial knowledge, etc.

(vi) Successfully complete 100 hours Information Technology Training (ITT).

(vii) Appear and pass Accounting Technician Examination (ATE) (i.e. Group I of Integrated Professional Competence Examination (IPCE)) comprising four papers.

(viii) Successfully complete one year work experience under a chartered accountant in practice or in industry.

(x) Designate as "Accounting Technician".

Q.6 How can one become a CA after becoming an Accounting Technician?

Ans:

(i) Enrol for Group II of Integrated Professional Competence Course (IPCC).

(ii) Register as an Articled Assistant for a period of 3 years.

(iii) Appear and pass Group II of Integrated Professional Competence Examination (IPCE) comprising three papers.

(iv) Register for CA Final Course and prepare for CA Final Examination.

(v) Undergo General Management and Communication Skills (GMCS) (15 days) course while undergoing Final Course and serving the last 12 months of articled training.

(vi) Complete 3 years period of articled training.

(vii) Appear in the Final Examination on completion of the practical training or while serving last 6 months of articled training on or before the last day of the month preceding the month in which the examination is to be held.

(ix) Enrol as a member of ICAI and designate as "Chartered Accountant".

Q.7 Who is a Cost Accountant?

Ans: A Cost Accountant is a person who offers to perform or perform services involving the costing and related statements. The Institute of Cost and Works Accountants of India is the only recognised statutory professional organisation and licensing body in India specialising exclusively in Cost and

a number of important chapters situated elsewhere in India and abroad.

Q.8 What is the job of a Cost accountant?

Ans: It is one of the most essential management services. It is a fairly new branch, a profession ushered in during the last century. With increase in competition and consequent economic areas of an organisation are the functions of a cost accountant. There is no denying the fact that an organisation's success or failure depends on the quality of information made available to the management. This is where cost accountants' productivity is of vital importance to the company. It is his primary job to ensure that managerial decisions are well within the cost prescriptions. The cost accountant is expected to give a prognosis for projects to be undertaken based on past and

costs will help the cost accountant to prepare budgets for the operation that is planned. In other words, the Cost Accountant can facilitate strategic decisions in respect of diverse economic activities of an organisation where he/she is employed or deployed as a consultant.

Q.9   What is the nature of job of a cost accountant?

Ans: A cost accountant specializes in navigating managerial decisions, stabilising budgets and

include: designing and implementing effective management information and control systems, planning costing systems and methods, inventory control incorporating mathematical models, investment analysis, project management, internal audit, cost audit, diagnosis in the case of sick industries, fund management, pricing planning, interpreting information and data related to business activities and translating them in such a way as to guide the core management into taking the right decisions. The academic requirement is to pass the examination conducted by the Institute of Cost and Works Accountants of India (ICWAI).

Q.10   Why should one study Cost Accountancy?

Ans:
and audit requirement, etc. Similarly, the core area of MBA (Finance) is to understand the art

required to take strategic management decisions in respect of these three activities. Operation

has been designed to equip its students with the modern tools of management so that they are in a position to facilitate the strategic management decisions in respect of the diverse economic activities of an organisation where they are employed or deployed as consultant.

traversing the path of cost control, cost reduction, we have now entered into the arena of cost management. Cost Accountants are the best professionals for this job.

Q.11   What is the Career Chart for Cost Accountants?

Ans:
Higher Secondary (class 10+2) Passed Candidates
Foundation Examination

Intermediate Course (18 months minimum) [Direct admission for graduates (any discipline)]
Final Course (18 months minimum). After passing the Intermediate Examination
Final Examination Passed Candidates with 3 years Practical Experience
Cost Accountants (Members of the Institute)

Q.12   How are the ICWAI examinations held?

Ans: The ICWAI examinations are held in three stages — Foundation, Intermediate and Final. A candidate may appear for the Foundation examination after passing the 10+2 (twelfth standard) examinations and completing coaching either postal or oral. The students are tested in Organisation and Management Fundamentals, Financial Accounting Fundamentals, Economics and Business Fundamentals and Business Mathematics and Statistics Fundamentals .The Foundation

and graduates from other streams .They are generally allowed to register with the institute for the intermediate examination. The institute has made it mandatory for registered candidates to undergo coaching either directly or through correspondence and practical training, before appearing for the examinations.

Q.13   What are the qualities essential for cost accountancy?

Ans:
course academic abilities do top the list alongside. Other equally important requirements are an ability to communicate (both written and spoken) concisely, a keen business sense and the ability to negotiate. The job calls for a high sense of motivation, concentration and determination. Regional councils and other institutes recognised by the Directorate of Studies of the ICWAI conduct these classes. Examinations are held twice in the year. The Cost and Work Accountancy course may be completed over a period of three years.

Q.14   What does the future hold?

Ans: Once a candidate has passed the examination, there are several options for him. He could either serve in an industry or opt for government service. There is plenty of scope in the banking and insurance sectors. There is always the option of practising as a consultant. A third option is to impart teaching at institutes or at universities. Higher academic pursuit for a doctorate is also possible. The ICWAI programme has been recognised by Association of Indian Universities for admission to Ph. D courses in commerce and allied subjects. **The returns:** For

he is employed in.

Q.15   What is the List of Indian Cost and Works Accountant Institutes?
Ans:

the ICWAI, 3, Institutional Area ,Lodhi Road, New Delhi-110 003. Western India Regional Council of the ICWAI, Rohit Chambers, 4th Floor, Janmabhoomi Marg, Fort, Mumbai-400 001, Southern India Regional Council of the ICWAI, 4, Montieth Lane, Egmore, Chennai-600 008. Eastern India

Q.16 What are the employment prospects of a cost accountant in India after completing ICWA?

Ans: There is increasing awareness amongst the business entrepreneurs about the vital contribution made by cost and management accountancy services and professionals in the attainment of business objectives. This has accentuated the demand for cost and management accounting services in all sectors of the economy. Many members of the Institute are holding top management positions, viz., Managing Director, Finance Director, Financial Controller, Chief Accountant, Cost Controller, Marketing Manager, Chief Internal Auditor, CEO, CFO etc. Those managing their own business have

a Cost Accountant can attain the highest ladder of professional success. Realising the importance of the profession of the Cost and Management Accountancy in the economic development of the nation, the Central Government has constituted an all-India cadre known as Indian Cost Accounts Service (ICAS) at par with other Class-I services such as IAS, IFS etc. to advise the government in

Other Academic Staff in Universities and Colleges and Measures for the Maintenance of Standards in Higher Education, 2010 vide its Circular No. F.3-1/2009 dated 30th June 2010.

above area and Principal/Director/Head of the Institution include First Class Graduate and

other requirements including qualifying NET/SLET/SET as the minimum eligibility condition for recruitment and appointment of Assistant Professors.

Further Academic pursuits:

1. A member of ICWAI can get enrolled as a member of IMA USA.
2. Recognised by the Academic Councils of many Universities in India for the purpose of admission

   registration as M.Phil. and Ph.D candidates in commerce and allied disciplines.

   ICWAI introduces a new CIMA Professional Gateway examination (available from May 2009) for ICWAI students who have successfully completed the whole of the ICWAI professional

   tests of professional competence and ultimately CIMA Membership.
4. MOU between Indira Gandhi National Open University (IGNOU): ICWAI and IGNOU have entered into an MOU on 11th July, 2008 to offer specialised B.Com and M.Com Programmes for ICWAI students. The Students can simultaneously study the specialised B.Com (Financial & Cost Accounting) programme with ICWAI Foundation/Intermediate Course and specialised M.Com (Management Accounting &Financial Strategies) with ICWAI Final Course.

Q.17 What is equivalent of ICWAI qualification with International academic standard?

Ans: The minimum requirement of entry in the ICWAI Course is Graduation. A candidate himself for Ph.D course in Commerce and allied areas. The Final Examination of the Institute of Cost and Works Accountants of India (ICWAI) has been recognised by AIU in

Those who are known as **"Cost Accountants"** in India are called **"Management Accountants"** all over the world

Q.18   When is one eligible for Membership of ICWAI?

Ans: One is eligible for Membership of ICWAI:

> After passing of Final course and completion of practical training as provided under the regulations.
>
> Initially one is admitted as an Associate Member and can use the descriptive title "AICWA" after his/her name to indicate that he/she is an Associate Member of the Institute.
>
> Letter 'FICWA' after his/her name to indicate that he/she is a Fellow Member of the Institute.

Q.19   How can I become Chartered Financial Analyst?

Ans:

called the Chartered Financial Analyst programme has been brought into being by the Institute of

course enjoys wide recognition all over the country.

Q.20   What does a CFA do?

Ans: Financial analysts provide guidance and analysis to businesses and people to assist with

certain investment decisions. They use their results to create reports to present and provide recommendations on which investments a business or individual should buy or sell. Financial analysts usually concentrate on a certain region, industry, or product type. They evaluate current trends in business practices, competition, and products of their area of specialisation. They are required to be up-to-date on new policies or regulations that can affect the investments they are looking after. They must also watch the economy to see how it will affect earnings.

climb up the corporate ladder to higher executive levels. The areas where a CFA can use his skills

India and for the international scene), investment management, security evaluation, project planning, venture capital management and credit rating among other things. A CFA will be responsible for decisions in the above mentioned areas. His or her decisions will be based on quantitative techniques of analysis of relevant data. The training provided by the ICAFI will enable a CFA to know what to look for, where to look for it and how to analyze whatever data he or she has obtained. The work performed by a CFA can be extremely challenging and rewarding in terms of both professional and monetary satisfaction.

Q.21 What is the procedure for the completion of the CFA Course?

Ans:

three-year postgraduate programme. This programme can be studied through correspondence. It is conducted by the Institute of Chartered Financial Analysts of India (ICFAI). And on completion of the course one can become a member of the ICFAI. The admission to this course is based on an entrance exam. This examination basically tests a candidate's aptitude for the course. The

Q.22 What is the eligibility for the CFA course?

Ans: The CFA course is opted for by both students and employed executives. Fresh graduates

attempts to test a candidate's verbal skills and quantitative reasoning abilities.

Q.23 What are the course contents of CFA?

Ans: The foundation module of the course is aimed at familiarising candidates from disciplines

management accounting, essentials of tax planning, basic guiding principles of investment, basics

module of the course. The others who take the foundation course can appear for the qualifying exam of the foundation module three months after enrolment.

The preliminary level: This level, also known as the second module, is divided into two groups

Group A. A candidate can take an exam in these papers six months after enrolment. There is only one paper in Group B: quantitative methods and economics. A candidate can take an exam in this paper twelve months after enrolment.

The Inter level: This level, referred to as the third module, is divided into two groups: Group C and Group D. Group C has two papers — one on economic legislation and the other on management accounting. Exams for papers in this group can be taken six months after passing the preliminary level. Group D also has two papers: one on security evaluation and the other on project appraisal planning and control. Exams for this group can be taken twelve months after passing the preliminary level.

taken six months after passing the inter level. Group F has two papers in investment management

this group can be taken one year after passing the inter level. Candidates at this level are also given practical training by placing them with reputed organisations.

Q.24   What are the employment prospects for CFA?

Ans: Employment opportunities are a plenty in sectors such as banking, insurance, corporate sector,

Bank of India (IDBI), the Industrial Finance Corporation of India (IFCI) and the Indian Railways recognise the CFA programme and employ trained CFAs. Besides these, a trained CFA can go into business as an

Q.25   Where can one study CFA course?

Ans: Some of the Colleges/Institutes offering CFA Courses are: Birla Institute of Technology and Science, Pilani; Narsee Monjee Institute of Management, Mumbai; International Management Institute, New Delhi; SP Jain Institute of Management and Research, Mumbai; Xavier Institute of Management, Bhubaneshwar; ICFAI Business School, Plot No. 5, Equity Tower, Sanghi Nagar, DP Road, Aundh, Pune 411007; ICFAI Business School, Building No. 71, Nirlon Complex, Off Western Express Highway, Goregaon (E), Mumbai

ICFAI Business School, ICFAI House, Near GNFC Info Towers, Sarkhej — Gandhinagar Highway, Bodakdev, Ahmedabad 380054; The ICFAI University, 52, Nagarjuna Hills, Hyderabad 500082; ICFAI Business School, 12, Thiruveedian Street, Off Cathedral Road, Opp. Stella Maris College, Chennai 600086; ICFAI Business

Q.26   Who is an auditor? What does an auditor do?

Ans:
Audit is an important part of accounting that evaluates a person, organisation, process, system, product, or project to determine the validity and reliability of information. Auditors are trained professionals that carry out these duties. Auditors help ensure that organisations are running the way they are supposed to, the taxes are properly paid, and the public records

major corporations, business, small companies, the government, and individual clients. There are two types of auditors, internal and external. Internal auditors are company employees that are hired to evaluate and assess the internal control system of the organisation. They directly present their reports to upper management or the board of directors. Internal auditors can also have specialty titles such as compliance, environmental, and information technology auditors.

Q.27   What kind of training does an auditor need?

Ans: Auditors typically need at least a bachelor degree in accounting (B.Com), business, or other

and work experience. Some employers prefer auditors to have a master degree in accounting (M.Com) or business administration (MBA-Finance & Accounting) with accounting concentration.

complete continuing education courses to renew their licenses. Other auditors stay abreast on their skills by attending seminars and conferences.

Q.28 What are the career prospects in auditing?

other professions — an increase of 18 percent between 2006 and 2016!. This growth will be driven by the increase in the number of business enterprises, corporate governance regulations,

Job prospects are expected to be favourable for auditors who have received advanced education

Q.29 What does an internal auditor do?

desired goals and improve the operations, internal controls, and risk management. Internal auditors are trained professionals who perform a variety of internal auditing activities for their

check for fraud, waste, and mismanagement activities and make sure records are accurate. They

compliance with government regulations and corporate policies. Internal auditors also evaluate

preventing and investigating any form of fraud. Internal auditors also help management assess the effectiveness of controls based on real-time data.

Q.30 What kind of training does an internal auditor need?

with a master degree in business administration. Many prospective internal auditors complete

internal auditors. New auditors work with experienced professionals completing simple tasks and move on to more advanced duties as they gain skills and experience. Many internal auditors gain

and passing a four-part examination. Internal auditors must also complete annual continuing

Q.31 What are the prospects for a career as an internal auditor?

Ans: Employment growth potential of internal auditors is expected to grow faster than the average growth in all others professions; it is projected to increase 18 percent from 2006 to 2016. The increase in new businesses and changes in legislation will drive the growth in jobs. Prospects

job openings will arise from the need to replace internal auditors who retire, transfer, or leave

Q.32 Who is a Financial Advisor? What does a financial advisor do?

provide advice and guidance to individuals and businesses in making investment decisions and

their recommendations to their clients. They help their clients identify and achieve their short-

recognises problem areas, makes improvement recommendations, and chooses the suitable investments that will meet the client's goals.

Q.33 What kind of training does a financial advisor need?
Ans:

designation. The requirements include at least a bachelor degree, 3 years of related work experience, abiding by the code of ethics, and passing a comprehensive examination.

Q.34 What are the prospects for a career as a financial advisor?
Ans:
professions, increasing 41 percent from 2006 to 2016. Financial advisors are expected to be among the 10 fastest growing professions. Job growth will be driven by the millions of people

Q.35 What does a credit analyst do?
Ans:
business, or organisation is worthy of credit. Credit analysts are trained professionals that analyze a variety of data and issues for many different clients to determine if credit can be awarded.

Credit analysts process many different variables to determine if applicants are worthy of credit. They work for a variety of clients such as individuals applying for credit cards and companies seeking

contacting employer and credit bureaus, and conducting research to collect an applicant's credit history. They create credit reports that give applicants a breakdown of their credit score. They determine how likely clients are to repay their loans and the accrued interest. Credit analysts

thoroughly understand the credit requirements of their employer and take those requirements into account when reviewing credit applications. They present their decisions either directly to

Q.36 What kind of training does a credit analyst need?

Ans: Credit analysts typically need at least a bachelor degree in accounting (B.Com), business,

to gain practical experience. Credit analysts must keep up to date on the current market trends

attend workshops, conferences, and seminars.

Q.37 Who is a Financial Consultant? What does a financial consultant do?

Ans:

investment. Financial planners are expected to have a big picture viewpoint of their client's or

the expertise to know how much money to invest and where to invest it. For businesses, this also
means knowing how to develop business deals with other companies to bring additional revenue

solely on buying, selling or both, depending on the nature of the position.

Q.38 What kind of training does a financial consultant need?

Ans:

Financial

Q.39 What does a stock broker do?

Ans: Stock brokers sell securities to retail investors, who are the majority investors. Since
there are so many securities, retail investors must work with a stock broker instead of trading

broker then passes on the information to a trader of the securities company. The stock trader

Q.40 How can one become a stock broker?

Ans: Stock brokers should have a bachelor degree. Most have a bachelor degree in accounting, brokers regularly attend training seminars and conferences to stay up to date with new services and

1. Begin to prepare for your career in high school by taking courses in mathematics, economics and business. And with even a small starting sum, you can manage your own stock portfolio (in a parent's name if you are under 18) to learn about different investments and their return.
2. Join an investment club, which compares different investment opportunities, analyzes results and jointly invests its funds.

    business (B.Com/BBA/BA/B.Sc. etc).

5. Expect a competitive work environment after being hired. Firms often hire a plethora of recent college graduates with the expectation that a large percentage will 'wash out' during the gruelling early months of training and building a clientele.

    business while writing your resumé. A professional, aggressive image is crucial at the interview, where prospective employers will be evaluating your tenacity along with your business savvy.

Also if you want to be registered as a broker then you should register with SEBI. The Securities &

conditions namely:
(a) He holds the membership of any stock exchange;
(b) He shall abide by the rules, regulations and bye-laws of the stock exchange or stock exchanges of which he is a member;
(c) In case of any change in the status and constitution, the stock broker shall obtain prior permission of the Board to continue to buy, sell or deal in securities in any stock exchange;
(d) He shall pay the amount of fees for registration in the manner provided in the regulations; and
(e) He shall take adequate steps for redressal of grievances of the investors within one month of the date of the receipt of the complaint and keep the Board informed about the number, nature and other particulars of the complaints received from such investors.

Q.41 What are the various Stock Broking Courses offered in India and scope of jobs after taking such courses?

Ans: Some of the stock broking courses offered in India are:

Postgraduate Diploma in Capital Market and Financial Services
Postgraduate Diploma in Fundamentals of Capital Market Development
Chartered Financial Analyst Equity Research

Eligibility Criteria for Stock Broking Course:

sub-broker, the aspirants need to have a pass in standard 10+2.

As to qualify as a stock broker, students will require to register themselves with the stock exchange. To become a member, the aspirants must appear for an admission test and clear it successfully. Subsequently, aspirants will have to undertake training for a certain period. Some of the entrance

Job Scope after Stock Broking Courses:

There are many organisations in India as well as overseas that take in students of stock broking. Investment Firms of India are one such place that employs stock brokers. Because of the undergoing

handsome money.

Some Job Types:

Accountants
Capital Market Specialists
Economists
Equity Analysts
Finance Managers
Financial Advisers
Financial Analysts
Financial Planners
Independent Agent
Investment Advisor
Investment Planners

AGRICULTURE

CHAPTER **2**

Q.1 What is Agricultural Science?
Ans:

production of quality food at the farm and in the agricultural-food industry linked to farming.

Closely related to biological science, it uses the principles of biology, chemistry, physics and mathematics to solve the problems related to agriculture. Agricultural science includes research and development on production techniques; improving agricultural productivity in terms of quantity and quality; transformation of primary products into end consumer products and prevention and correction of adversities. Major areas of specialisation within agricultural science are food science, plant science, soil science and animal science.

Agricultural science professionals specialize in agricultural production and livestock. They play an important role in maintaining the nation's food supply. Some of the major tasks performed by them involves improving the quality and quantity of farming; improving crop yield with less labour; conservation of soil and water; controlling pests and weeds more safely and effectively, etc. In short, Agricultural scientists engage in research to discover and promote effective,

Q.2 How can one pursue a course in Agriculture?
Ans: Various universities and colleges in India offer Under-graduate, Post-graduate, Diploma and Doctorate courses in agricultural science. The minimum eligibility for B.Sc Agricultural Science is 10+2 or equivalent with science subjects at minimum 50 percent marks. Duration of the course is 4 years and the admission to most of the institutions is based on merit or performance in the entrance examination conducted by the concerned institute/ university or on the basis of marks obtained in the ICAR Examination. B.Sc or B.Tech degree in relevant subject is needed for the 2-year Master's degree programmes. In M.Sc. Agricultural science several specialisations are offered in the branches like agronomy, plant physiology, seed technology, soil science and soil conservation, sericulture, animal husbandry and dairy, horticulture, water conservation, farming system management, agricultural botany, agricultural biotechnology, agricultural chemistry, agricultural Economics, agricultural marketing management and so on.

disciplines. Several institutes offer P.G Diploma courses in agriculture and those having a bachelors degree with an extensive knowledge base in agricultural science can also opt for these courses.

Admission to all the courses in Agricultural science is conducted through an Entrance Examination, conducted by the concerned institute/ university. Indian Council of Agricultural Research (ICAR), New Delhi conducts an entrance examination separately for graduate and postgraduate courses. Eligibility requirement for the exam is 12th pass in science / agriculture with 50 percent marks, for graduate level courses, and 60 percent marks in B.Sc/B.Sc (Agriculture) for postgraduate level courses. Certain institutes also admit students on the basis of the marks obtained in the ICAR examination. The ICAR also provides fellowship for students of postgraduate courses and

postgraduate level.

Indian Agricultural Research Institute (IARI), Delhi; Indian Veterinary Research Institute, Izatnagar;

are some of the major institutes which conduct their own entrance examinations.

Apart from conventional courses such as B.Sc in agriculture, horticulture, forestry and home science, the Agriculture universities also offer technology oriented courses – B.Tech in food process engineering, Energy and environmental engineering, Bio-technology, and Bioinformatics.

Q.3   What are the qualities/attributes required to become a successful agricultural professional?

Ans: To be a successful agricultural professional, an aspirant must have a good grounding in science, and must be familiar with crops, pastures, soil types, agricultural and horticultural chemicals, etc. They should possess a keen and analytical mind; a high level of concentration; an aptitude for research; ability to work as part of a team and abundant physical stamina to put in long hours of work and patience.

Other essential attributes are good observation skills, communication skills, organising skills, written and oral skills and the ability to give presentations besides knowledge of common

and chemical processing. This profession demands hard work and high level of patience along with many years of study.

Q.4   What are the various areas of specialisation in the field of Agricultural Science?

Ans: Among the various specialisations within Agricultural Science, the broad areas are food science, plant science, soil science and animal science.

Food Science:
improved ways of preserving, processing, packaging, storing and delivering foods. Food science professionals/ scientists analyse food content to determine levels of vitamins, fat, sugar or protein; or search for substitutes for harmful or undesirable additives and preservatives.

Plant Science or Horticulture:

production of crops. Entomology is the study of insects and their relationship to plants. Plant breeding includes Forestry, Floriculture, etc.

Soil Science: Soil science is the study of the physical, chemical and biological composition of soils; its impact on plant growth and how various types of soils respond to things such as fertilizers, crop rotation, etc.

Animal Science:

genetics, reproduction, and growth of domestic farm animals. Animal scientists examine and grade livestock food products, purchase of livestock, or work in technical sales or marketing.

science, ecology; agricultural engineering, bio-systems engineering; biotechnology; genetic engineering; microbiology, etc.

Q.5 What are the career prospects/employment opportunities for a graduate in Agriculture?
Ans:

government and private concerns will provide a regular income. Agriculture professionals can seek

Industry Sector; Agricultural universities and various agricultural service organisations. Their work

agricultural journalism, etc. are some of the areas offering good career potential.

Graduates in agricultural science are employed as agricultural managers/ inspectors in farm

breeding centres. Many of these positions can be in areas that support the marketing and distribution of agricultural commodities as well as in the production sector of agribusiness operations. They can also set up their own business in primary economic sectors such as farming,

Union Public Service Commission (UPSC) and State Public Service Commissions recruit postgraduates

Depending on their areas of specialisation, postgraduates with doctoral degree can get employed in the agricultural universities as plant pathologist, agronomist, economic botanist, agro-meteorologist, research engineer, associate professor, etc. Reserve Bank of India, State Bank of India and the nationalised banks offer openings for postgraduates in agriculture and allied entrance examination conducted by the Public service commission/concerned department. International Crops Research Institute for the Semi-Arid-Tropics (ICRISAT) with its head quarters

Q.6   What is Agricultural Economics? How can one become an Agricultural Economist?

Ans:

enormous career opportunities. Agriculture covers farm management, businesses and industries that manufacture agricultural machinery, industries that buy and process farm products, banking

products, so on and so forth.

The study of economic principles, with emphasis on applications to the solution of farm, agribusiness and agricultural industry problems in relation to other sectors is known as Agricultural

agricultural economics looks at all elements of food production and applies rational thought and planning across the board. Right from crops, livestock, land usage and soil content, all aspects of farm life are examined including their mutual relations and the way and means strengthen them.

economists. Agricultural economists manage farms and other agricultural industries by applying business concepts and problem-solving techniques. Agricultural economists also predict trends in markets for farm products. They closely observe and explain changes in the market. An agricultural economist would monitor crops, prices, animal health, equipments, imports and exports, weather cycles, buying patterns, and new methods of production.

A career in agricultural economics is ideal for those who enjoy agricultural business and have a knack for calculation and economical theory. Agricultural economics combines the technical

agribusinesses, farms and ranches.

Students who wish to pursue a career in agricultural economics should possess a strong base in botany, physics, chemistry and mathematics. Various agricultural universities and colleges in India offer Under-graduate, Post-graduate, Diploma and Doctorate courses in agricultural economics.

Q.7   What is ICAR?

Ans: The Indian Council of Agricultural Research (ICAR) is an autonomous organisation under the Department of Agricultural Research and Education (DARE), Ministry of Agriculture, Government of India.

Formerly known as Imperial Council of Agricultural Research, it was established on 16 July 1929 as a registered society under the Societies Registration Act, 1860 in pursuance of the report of the Royal Commission on Agriculture. The ICAR has its headquarters in New Delhi. The Council is the apex body for co-coordinating, guiding and managing research and education in agriculture

and 47 agricultural universities spread across the country this is one of the largest national agricultural systems in the world.

The ICAR has played a pioneering role in ushering Green Revolution and subsequent developments in agriculture in India through its research and technology development that enabled the

times (marine 5 times and inland 17 times), milk 6 times and eggs 27 times since 1950-51, thus making a visible impact on the national food and nutritional security. It has played a major role in promoting excellence in higher education in agriculture. It is engaged in cutting edge areas of science and technology development and its scientists are internationally acknowledged

The Education Division of ICAR undertakes planning, development, coordination and quality control for higher education in agiculture for the entire country and strives to maintain and upgrade quality and relevance of higher agricultural education through partnership and efforts of the components of the ICAR-Agricultural Universities (AUs) System comprising State Agricultural Universities (SAUs), Deemed to be universities (DUs), Central Agricultural University (CAU) and Central Universities (CUs) with Agriculture Faculty. The Division has a National Academy of Agricultural Research Management (NAARM) at Hyderabad to facilitate capacity building at the National Agricultural Research System (NARS) in research and education policy, Planning and management and a National Centre for Agricultural Economics and Policy Research. (Visit www.icar.org.in)

Q.8   What is Horticulture?

Ans: Horticulture is the science and art involved in the cultivation, propagation, processing

branch among the plant sciences because it not only involves science and technology, but also incorporates art and principles of design.

Horticulture, as an industry, is divided on the basis of crop and plant use. For instance, horticulture can be divided into two groups including edible plants and aesthetic plants [meaning those grown for their beauty]. The branch of horticulture which deals with the production, storage, processing, and marketing of vegetables, such as sweet potatoes, lettuce, peppers, and sweet corn, is called olericulture. The science and practice of fruit production is called pomology. Pomological crops include apples, oranges, blueberries, and strawberries. Floriculture is the

grown covers, and vines used in exterior landscapes. Landscape horticulture entails the design, construction and maintenance of landscapes for homes, businesses and public areas [municipal buildings, highway right-of-way, rest areas, public/private golf courses, city/state/federal parks,

Q.9 What are the career scopes in the field of Horticulture?

Ans:

above. The Department of Horticulture offers three distinct areas of concentration in the Plant and Soil Systems curriculum to cater to the personal needs of the students. The main options are *Ornamental, Olericulture* and *Pomology*. The areas offer many opportunities for eager and aggressive graduates. Entrepreneurial and professional employment opportunities exist in areas of nursery crop production industry, installation and maintenance of outdoor/indoor landscapes, in wholesale and retail sales. Many students interested in this option undergo internships nationwide

or crop consultants. The *Turfgrass Management Option* trains students to manage golf courses, *turfgrass* management specialists often command some of the highest salaries available in professional agriculture. The *Science Option* is for students interested in teaching and/or research in horticulture. Most students taking this option pursue an advanced degree.

Horticulture is more or less a smaller version of agriculture. While agriculture deals with cultivation on a large scale, Horticulture is about gardening that too, on a smaller scale. The name 'Horticulture' is derived from the Latin terms 'hortus' (garden) and 'cultura' (cultivation) which means garden cultivation. Horticulture is the Science and art of gardening which is associated

tuber crops, medicinal and aromatic plants. Plants play a major role in everyday life, from the fruits and vegetables we eat, to the trees that make our parks and streets beautiful, through

cultivation of plants, is of great importance in an agrarian economy like India. Horticulture is an applied science, relying upon many other disciplines such as chemistry, physics, engineering, art, meteorology, economics, entomology, botany and many more. Horticulturist uses the basic

cultivation, crop production, preparation of soil, plant breeding and genetic engineering, plant biochemistry and plant physiology. This branch of agriculture supplies food products to man, feed to animals and many raw materials of plant origin to numerous industries (food, mixed-feed, textile, pharmaceutical, and perfume industries). Hence, Horticulture is closely associated with animal husbandry. It includes vegetable growing, fruit growing, viticulture (science of grape

fastest growing area of horticulture.

Horticulture is the best choice for those who love outdoors and greenery. Horticulture industry

Horticulturists work and conduct research in various areas of horticulture, to improve crop yield, quality, nutritional value, and resistance to insects, diseases, and environmental stresses. Now practice of engaging people in various therapeutic horticultural practices for the improvement of their mental and physical well-being. Horticultural Therapists use horticultural activities and

Q.10   What are the educational opportunities/courses available in Horticulture?

Ans: The level of education that you need depends upon the type of horticultural occupation

undergraduate level. Candidates who have passed 10+2 in Science stream (class 12th) with physics, chemistry and mathematics/biology/agriculture as the subjects can opt for Bachelors degree in Horticulture as a separate discipline or as a subject of B.Sc Agriculture Science. The

in Horticulture are eligible for M.Phil.

For admission to Ph.D Programme different agricultural universities exercise different modes of admission. Most of the State Agriculture Universities and ICAR Institutes conduct Entrance Examinations for Ph.D admissions. Horticulture courses include subject areas of plant propagation, plant materials, tissue culture, crop production, post-harvest handling, plant breeding, pollination management, crop nutrition, entomology, plant pathology, economics, and business.

Q.11   What is Horticulture Therapy?

Ans:
in conjunction or liaison with other professionals such as psychologists, occupational therapists, physicians and social workers. Horticultural Therapists treat those who have physical disabilities,

illnesses, and elderly people. Programmes can also be developed for the rehabilitation of offenders or those suffering from drug or alcohol abuse. With more and more people opting for

provide attractive business opportunity to horticultural nursery/gardens.

Q.12   What is Floriculture?

Ans:

plants, seed and bulb production, micro propagation and extraction of essential oils. Though the agro climatic conditions, versatile human resources, etc., offer India a unique opportunity for judicious employment of existing resources and exploration of avenues yet untouched.

Development Authority) is the registering authority for such units.

Besides, there is scope to work as consultant, landscape architect, etc., with proper training. One can also work as entrepreneur and offer employment to others. In addition to these careers which

horticultural therapists. Such jobs require practitioners to deal directly with clients.

Q.13 What are the courses available in the field of Floriculture?

Ans: Floriculture is not available as a subject at the undergraduate/degree level. Those who wish

Agriculture degree) after which they can opt for an M.Sc in Horticulture at the postgraduate level.

companies as supervisors, farm or estate managers, handling large-scale production of a variety

Q.14 What is the career prospect in field of Dairy Industry?

Ans: Dairy Industry is one of the leading industries that plays a dynamic role in India's agro-based economy. Dairy farming includes breeding and care of milk yielding cattle, procuring milk and processing of milk into a variety of dairy products. Dairy products are a major exporting industry and earn considerable foreign exchange for the country. In 1946, the foundation of Anand Milk Union Ltd (AMUL) led to the development of a better organised dairy industry and gave momentum to education in dairying in India.

processing and distribution of dairy products. The main jobs are in production and processing.

Production process includes the collection of milk, breeding of high yielding cattle and taking care of the animals. Dairy Scientists are supposed to take care of the production aspect of the industry. They conduct experiments to determine the effects of different kinds of feeds and environmental conditions on the quantity, quality and nutritive value of milk produced. They also research on breeding to improve dairy breeds, feeding and management of dairy cattle.

Q.15   How can one pursue a course in Dairy Science/Dairy Technology?

Ans: Traditionally dairy technology is a part of veterinary and animal husbandry courses. These courses were and still offered by Agricultural Universities as part of the B.VSc. (Bachelor of Veterinary Science and Animal Husbandry) course. Now there are several institutes offering exclusive diploma, undergraduate and postgraduate courses in Dairy Technology. Many general universities also offer dairy science as vocational subject at the B.Sc level. Dairying is also available as a vocational subject for the 10+2 level education.

A dairy technology course comprises three basic areas like Dairy Engineering which deals with only the technological aspects of the product; Dairy Chemistry which covers the products,

Bacteriology which maintains products standards. Therefore the role of a biotechnologist is very important.

Courses in dairy technology are available at the diploma, graduation, postgraduate and doctoral levels. The diploma and degree courses in dairy technology require candidates who have passed the 10+2 examination, with Chemistry, Physics, Mathematics and English or Physics, chemistry, Biology or Agriculture with a minimum aggregate of 50 percent marks. The diploma courses of two years duration include Indian Dairy Diploma (IDD) and National Dairy Diploma (NDD). This is a base course for BSc / B.Tech dairy degree and gives basic knowledge on breeding, feeding of animals, their health care, farm management, planning a farm, milk products, dairy chemistry, bacteriology, book keeping, etc. At the graduation level, the course is usually called B.Tech./B.Sc. in Dairy technology or Dairy Science. After graduating in dairying, candidates can opt for further studies and specialisation through a Master's programme in Dairying (M.Tech in Dairy Technology/ M.Sc Dairy Science), or related areas such as animal genetics and breeding,

and preservation.

Dairy Technology is a challenging career which offers enormous prospects for trained professionals. There are now more than 400 dairy plants in the country and many Dairy equipment manufacturers.

in dairy farms, cooperatives, rural banks, milk product processing and manufacturing industries. Quality control departments also recruit dairy technologists. A large number of dairy technologists also start their own business such as small-scale milk plants, creamery, ice-cream units, etc., or work as consultants. A consultant, however, needs several years of work experience in dairy farms to emerge successful. There are also opportunities in teaching as well as Research and development. The latter is a growing area and crucial for the dairy industry.

Q.16   What is Sericulture?

Ans: The word 'Sericulture' is derived from the Greek word 'Sericos' meaning 'Silk' and the English word 'Culture' meaning 'Rearing'. Sericulture is the art and technology of raising silk worms for production of raw silk yarn. Sericulture is a farm based, labour intensive and commercially attractive economic activity falling under the cottage and small scale sector. As a cottage industry, it provides ample work for the women in rural areas. This agro-based industry playing an eminent role in the rural economy of India, is not limited to just worms, but includes all activities related to them, like mulberry cultivation and even post-cocoon technology. It requires both technical know-how as well as specialisation. Innovative researches have turned sericulture into an industry and now it has become a major cash crop of the country. The sericulture industry is unique for more than one reason.

It is based on agricultural output, viz., cocoons. It is a cottage-based and labour intensive in nature. Sericulture refers to the conscious, mass-scale rearing of silk producing organisms to obtain silk. Mulberry Sericulture involves the cultivation of mulberry to produce leaf rearing of silkworm to convert leaf to the cocoon, reeling of the cocoon to obtain silk yarn and weaving to convert the yarn to Fabric. The industry comprises reeling, silk preparatory and weaving,

besides garment manufacturing. China and Japan were the two main producers of silk yarn, together producing over 50 per cent of the total world production each year but now Japan has been relegated to the third position ever since India doubled its production of silk. The trends in international silk production suggest that sericulture has better prospects for growth in the developing countries rather than in the developed countries. The principal silk consuming countries are India, USA, Canada, Germany, France, Italy, Denmark, Sweden, Netherlands, Switzerland, Japan, Austria and Australia. India is home to a vast variety of silk because of a

commercially traded varieties of silks namely mulberry, tropical tasar, oak tasar, *eri* and *muga*. Among the silk producing countries, India tops in the production of tropical tasar and *eri* silk.

Socio-economic studies have shown that sericulture needs less investment, small land holdings and higher returns. It also offers best career options to both job seekers as well as entrepreneurs. The export of silk products has shown a steady growth and export earnings have also increased during the last decade. Being one of the largest exporters of silk, chances for boost in

job seekers.

Q. 17 What are the courses available in the field of Sericulture?

Ans: To become a Sericulture Graduate one has to pass the four year degree course from Sericulture College of State Agricultural Universities or Silk Institutes of various Universities. There are two types of degrees — B.Sc. (Sericulture) and B.Sc. Silk Technology (Sericulture).

HSC (10+2) with subjects such as Biology and Chemistry. There are also post-graduates courses for which a basic degree in sericulture is essential. The course duration for degree course is four years while the same for post-graduation is two years.

B.Sc (Sericulture) and B.Sc Silk Technology (Sericulture) involve courses on Silk Worm Rearing and Grainage, S/W Breeding and Genetics, Silk Reeling and Spinning, Silk Grading and Testing, Seed Technology, Arboriculture and Moriculture, Diseases and Pests of Silk Worm and Food Plants,

Production Planning and Exterision, Costing and Management, Silk Weaving Technology, Silk Dyeing and Printing Technology.

The fourth year syllabus includes practical experience for setting up Sericulture Farm/Silk Reeling Unit/Weaving and Dyeing-Printing Mill, etc. Candidates who have passed B.Sc. Sericulture/Silk Technology can apply for M.Sc. Sericulture/Silk Technology courses.

Q.18   What are the career opportunities in Sericulture?

Ans: Sericulture, in recent times, has begun to offer a wide variety of employment and entrepreneurship options. Most importantly, every state in India has a sericulture department to

silk carpets has been on the rise constantly.

All this has created additional avenues for Sericulturists. Sericulture is quite popular in Southern India and is now available as a career option in Northern India too. With research institutions devising new technological processes, Sericulture is being recognised as a mainstream profession.

sericulture units, agriculture sector banks, etc. One can get jobs in Central Government agencies

Candidates with M.Sc sericulture can apply for the post of lecturer, professor and lab assistant.

nationalised as well as private banks. They can work as a manager in Sericulture Farm, Grainage, Silk Reeling (Filature), Silk weaving mill, Dyeing, Printing and Spinning mill, etc., as well as in various schemes run by the central government like SGSY, Welfare Dep't. Scheme Run by NGO's like Pradan, Vikash Bharati, etc.

Sericulturists can also set up their own enterprises or start ups in silk retailing, weaving,

demand, especially to provide guidance in setting up sericulture farms.

Q.19   What is Fisheries Science and what is its scope?

Ans:
inland and sea or other aquatic species. This industry covers catching, processing, marketing and

aquatic organisms in fresh water, brackish water and any marine environment. Fisheries aim at developing and maintaining sea wealth. Fisheries are estimated to provide protein to 16 percent of the world population and India holds the seventh position in the world as regards to the value brackish water and freshwater aquaculture. Given India's vast natural resources and abundance in entrepreneurial class and skills, this profession is turning very lucrative to the Indian economy.

the much needed technically competent extension personnel for transfer of technology. It helps a

Q.20 How can one study a graduate level course in Fisheries Science?
Ans:

colleges of state agriculture universities. The eligibility criteria for B.FSc is 10+2 with biological science as one of the subjects. The B.FSc course prepares a candidate with basic knowledge in all the

For admission to various Central Institute of Fisheries Education in the country, candidates have to appear for an all India level common entrance test conducted by ICAR (Indian Council of Agricultural Research), New Delhi.

After completing B.FSc., one can study M.FSc (Masters of Fisheries Science), which is of 2-year duration. After getting a professional degree in Fisheries Science, one can go for research-oriented activities.

B.FSc. students are trained in a wide variety of subjects such as aquaculture (inland and

have a research oriented mentality. Dedication to work, devotion, hard working, patience, a curious and inquisitive mind are essential for this course. Quick thinking and ability to come

science is directly or indirectly related to a business sector.

Q.21 What are the career opportunities in the field of Fisheries Science?
Ans:

Opportunities are also available in government agencies, State Departments of Agriculture and organisations such as the Central Marine Fisheries Research Institute (CMFRI). Recruitments to these institutions are done through the State Public Service Commissions. For those having

Fisheries Technology (CIFT) and the National Fisheries Development Board as research assistant, biochemist, biologist, technicians, etc.

Development Authority (MPEDA), Fisheries survey of India (FSI), NIO, WHO, etc. They can also

well as private banks. Job prospects are also available in private sector in aquaculture farms,

products and ornamental dishes are potential areas of self employment and entrepreneurship

Recruitment to these positions is done by the Agricultural Scientists Recruitment Board (ASRB) through a nation-wide competitive examination followed by a personal interview

and processing sectors in gulf and African countries.

Q.22 What is Tea Management and what are the career prospects in tea industry?

Ans: Tea is one of the most refreshing and popular beverages of the world. India being the world's

Though not a very well-known career option, jobs in this area can be interesting.

There are a variety of jobs one can specialise in tea industry. The jobs put together are known as tea management. Tea tasting is one of the highly specialised areas of work. Other areas are that of researchers, plantation managers, tea brokers, consultants, etc.

Work in the Tea industry includes plantation work, processing, auctioning, branding, marketing and research. Plantation work involves nurturing tea plants in the plantations which includes preparing the soil, applying the appropriate fertilizers, choosing the right variety best suited for the prevailing conditions and supervising the pinching and plucking of the leaves. Processing work involves the crushing, tearing and curling of the leaves, which takes place in the factories. The tea is then packed and dispatched to auction centres. The various samples of tea from different plantations are tested, blended and branded by the tea tasters in the auction centres. Tea brokers who have a background in planting, tasting and a knowhow of market trends, auction

used for blending varieties of tea, the tea taster's verdict is still considered the ultimate test for determining the quality of tea. In India, best tea growing areas are Assam, Darjeeling and Nilgiris. Several varieties of tea can be grown in one garden. As tea is a seasonal plant, the same leaves from the same bush, plucked in different seasons, have different bouquets. Each of these varieties requires different ways of handling.

Q.23   What are the qualifications required to become a professional in the tea industry?

Ans: Even though a basic education is enough to get into the tea industry and pick up the requisite skills on the job, a degree in Agricultural Science or a B.Sc. in Botany, Food Sciences, Horticulture

or marketing are recruited for marketing jobs.

New recruits are absorbed as Assistants at the plantation industry. After gaining requisite experience and competence, an assistant can get promoted to the level of Assistant Manager, and then Manager of a tea garden. Most assistants expect to become managers after putting in 12-15 years of service.

The prospective tea tasters who are selected get trained on the job. Besides natural talent, vigorous training for a number of years is essential to become a professional tea taster and then a tea tasting manager. Besides acquiring skills in tasting, they need to work on their managerial and marketing capabilities too.

Any person opting for a career in the tea sector must have an interest and liking for outdoor

to handle labourers will be additional assets for plantation/ factory managers. One must also possess demonstrable initiative, knowledge about the tea market and an alert mind on the changing market forces, and willingness to undertake strenuous work. One should also possess fair knowledge about the topography and geographical location of the tea estate. Tea tasters need to have keen taste buds and clean sensitivities. They should refrain from smoking, drinking and exercise control over the intake of spicy foods.

Those planning to become brokers should be level headed and disciplined and be able to strike a good rapport with producers and buyers. Since India is one of the leading producers of tea in the

companies and tea gardens. Tea broking Houses, Tea associations and the Tea Board of India also offer lucrative positions. An experienced tea planter can move into tea brokerage or tea tasting or take up a job in a tea broking house. Senior professionals can branch off into consultancy to offer professional advice. Those academically inclined can get into research positions available at many tea plantations.

Q.24   Who is a Plantation / Factory Manager?

Ans: Tea gardens are manned by Managers who are assisted by Assistant Managers and junior assistants depending on the size and requirement of the gardens. Their work involves supervision of all plantation work involved from planting to plucking, processing to packing and transport of tea to auction houses. New entrants are taken as Assistants at the plantation level. Experience is the deciding factor in the appointment of a manager. It is a long wait as it usually takes 12 to 15 years. The Indian Institute of Plantation Management, Bangalore offers a training programme on the relevant subject under the Indian Commodity economy.

Q.25   Who is a Tea Taster?

Ans:
of tea and help to brand the varieties according to the quality. Most tea companies employ tea

tasters for ensuring quality standards, and preparing blends. Tea tasting is typically learnt on the job. Tea tasters have to develop the expertise to distinguish between the taste and aroma of different varieties of tea. They must also need to develop managerial as well as marketing skills. Tea tasters should keep their sensitivities clean and keep instincts for smoking, drinking and intake of spicy foods under check. The drawbacks can damage the digestive system especially at peak seasons when one has to taste as many as 200-300 cups of tea a day and result in stains on the teeth which has to be removed periodically. Tasters are hired by manufacturing companies, brokers as well as buyers. In a manufacturing company, the taster's task is to detect defects in the production process by looking at the colour and size of the leaves and determine if they

if needed. They also have to coordinate with gardens, look after import and exports, advise researchers on commercial factors like taste, economic viability and maturity of tea, etc. In the

In buying houses, besides ensuring quality, the tasters have to be in the know of what's happening in both the domestic and international markets. Many youngsters opt for this profession because of the extra ordinary nature of the work and high pay.

Q.26   Who is a Tea Broker?

Ans: Tea brokers act as intermediaries between the planter-producer and the buyer, and must be up-to-date with market trends and international prices. A background in tea industry and a keen tea tasting ability are important requisites in becoming a broker. At the auction centres, the tea samples are listed and evaluated by tea brokers. There are broking houses in the country where the brokers test the various samples of tea, coming from different tea gardens. Those planning to become brokers should be level headed and disciplined and capable of striking a good rapport with producers and buyers.

Q.27   What is Food Technology?

Ans: Food technology is a science in which food science is applied in the manufacturing and preservation of food products. It is basically the application of science and technology to the treatment, processing, preservation and distribution of food. The term 'Food Technology' is wide ranging; it deals with developing new methods and systems for keeping food products safe and immune from the threat of natural phenomena like bacteria. Food Technology in simpler terms is the application of food science in manufacturing safe, wholesome and nutritious food products. Food being the basic need of every human being, food technology is directly concerned with

Maybe from the time that Louis Pasteur developed the process of Pasteurisation — the process of heating milk and milk products to prevent food spoilage to destroy disease producing organisms.

Q.28   What is the scope in Food Technology?

Ans: India is one of the largest producers of consumable foods stuffs. Therefore the importance and scope for preserving food and its processing is increasing. As a result, new technology in food processing and preservation has become the need of the hour. The health and well being of people everywhere not only depends on good agricultural yields but also on reliable storage, successful processing and safe handling of all types of food. Food processing industry is one of the most technology-intensive industries covering a range of food products. They include basic or primary foods, such as wheat and rice products, sugar, oil and pulses, etc., and the processes to convert them into edible forms. The research and development in food technology has led

comprising various processes such as quality management, primary and secondary processing, preservation, packaging and labelling of various products such as confectionery products, dairy

Nowadays, there is an ever increasing demand for packaged, processed and ready to eat foods. This requires continuous research and innovation to preserve food stuff for long periods without losing its nutritious content. Therefore Food technologists are involved in a wide variety of activities associated with delivering nutritious food. They study the chemical, physical and microbiological makeup of the food. The food is processed, preserved, packaged and stored

Food processing companies need food technology personnel in different sections like Production, Quality Assurance, R&D (Research and Development), etc. Specialised jobs include Product Development Manager who is into devising food products according to the needs of the consumers and effectively putting those products in an innovative way. You can work as a Sensory scientist

more. Food technologists work in research laboratories or R&D sectors to develop new products, test current ones, and control the overall food quality.

In private as well as public sectors, lucrative job opportunities are open for Food technologists. In

the purchase, storage, transport and distribution of food grains and other food items, Modern Food Corporation which markets bread, fruit juices, edible oils, soft drink concentrates, North-Eastern Agricultural Marketing Corporation which markets and process fruits and vegetables, etc. Major companies in private sector include Amul, Cadbury, Britannia, Metro Diary, Hindustan

Indian candidates do get a preferential treatment for these jobs.

There are many lucrative jobs open to food technologists, such as Quality Assurance Manager, Laboratory Supervisor, Production Manager and Food packaging manager.

Production Managers/Supervisors: They are responsible for the entire processes in the manufacturing of a product, right from the purchase of raw materials to the production of the

Quality Assurance Managers/Supervisors: They are responsible for ensuring the quality of food throughout the whole production process. This also includes the quality of raw materials,

Laboratory Supervisors/Technicians: They carry out or supervise quality tests, such as microbiological and chemical analyses, before any product is released.

Food Packaging Managers/Technologists: They are responsible for the research and development

Research Scientists: They are responsible for the continuing research and development programmes within the industry. Research scientists are employed in a wide variety of projects with Government, Food Research Institutes and Food companies.

Product Development Managers/Technologists: They are responsible for the improvement of the existing food products as well as the development of new products.

Lecturers and Advisers: They work in a range of posts in the Government sector and in Universities, as college lecturers or advisory and inspection jobs.

Q.29 What Educational qualification is required for entering the field of Food Technology?

Ans: The general criterion for admission to undergraduate food technology course is 10+2 in science related subjects. A Postgraduate course will require the student to complete his graduation in

The courses cover various aspects like food science, food biotechnology, food analysis, microbiology, food preservation techniques, genetics and food packaging, marketing and advertising, food logistics management, operations management, etc.

Other useful qualities required for aspiring food technologists are – a sense of responsibility; ability to work well on their own as well as part of a team; effective communication skills and a discerning approach to food items. A genuine interest in science, high standards of cleanliness, commitment, enthusiasm and motivation are other attributes required for this job. A high level of accuracy is also very essential to be a good food technologist.

Training in Food technology gives adequate exposure to the knowledge in the quality analysis of raw materials; packaging standards and methodology; health and hygiene parameters; processing techniques; storage and food value; and methodologies for extracting useful byproducts from industrial and domestic waste. It can be said that the future of the food industries is in the hands of Food technologists.

Q.30 What is Botany and who is a Botanist?

Ans:
disciplines such as agricultural sciences and forestry are based on the basic science of Botany. Botany studies the structure, growth, reproduction, metabolism, development, diseases and chemical properties and evolutionary relationships between different groups of plants. It encompasses the study of more than three hundred thousand species of plants ranging from ground-hugging mosses to giant redwood trees.

and industry. Their work affects agriculture, agronomy (soil and crop science), conservation, forestry, and horticulture. In general, Botanists study the development and life processes of plants. In a broader sense, a botanist studies and conducts research on various aspects of the plant physiology, plant pathology, plant fossils, mycology (study of fungi) and so on. Overall, botanists study the behaviour of plants from the chromosome level to the reproduction process. Botanical studies have helped in the development of many medicines and drugs which are extracted from

which provide natural raw materials like cotton, rubber, paper, silk, vegetable oils, etc.

Q.31 What are the Educational opportunities in Botany?

Ans: Botany is one of the preferred choices of study among the science students. But it is necessary that the students who study Botany must have interest in plants and enjoy working in that environment. Minimum requirement for a career as botanist is a bachelor's degree. However for higher degrees you require to specialise in one of the many areas of Botany.

Courses are offered at bachelor level, master level and doctoral level. For bachelor course, the basic requirement is 10+2 in science. After graduation, one can go for postgraduate and then doctoral course. Bachelor course is of 3 years and the postgraduate course has 2 years of duration. You need to study for an additional two to three years to obtain a doctoral degree. After doctoral degree, one can work at the administrator level or teach at the institutes, or do

the area of interest. Each area of specialisation concentrates on a particular subject necessary to know about the plant.

Q.32 What are the specialisations available in the field of Botany?

Ans: Various Specialisations as botanists are that of:

Plant Taxonomists:
taxonomists are botanists who work to identify, describe, classify and name plant species. Plant

physical activity as well as environments that are unsafe or uncomfortable. Plant taxonomists usually work in herbariums, botanical gardens and research institutes.

Plant Ecologists: Plant ecologists are botanists who work to understand the relationship between plant and the world in which they live. In other words, Ecologists study the connection between plants, animals and their physical environment. They examine the environmental factors such as rainfall, population, pollutants, temperature and altitude that regulate plant growth. In some cases, ecologists may be exposed to unsafe or unhealthy working conditions. For example, when plant materials have to be studied after an environmental disaster, the condition in which they have to work may not be safe or healthy. Plant ecologists are employed by government regulatory

Plant Morphologist: Plant morphologists study the manner in which cells are arranged in a plant to give it a form. To determine the cellular arrangement of plant they study how different plants transport and conduct food and water. They work generally in research laboratories.

Plant Cytologist: Botanists who study plant cells are known as cytologists. They study the structure, function and life history of plant cells. Cytologists study minute particles of plant tissue with the help of microscopes. They are concerned with the physical arrangement of DNA in a particular species of plants. They also study the cells concerned with reproduction as well as

laboratories and pharmaceutical industry.

Plant Physiologist: A plant physiologist studies the internal functions and processes of plants. Plant processes include growth, respiration, cultivation, excretion, reproduction and various other functions. They develop an understanding of the biological, chemical and physical processes that are basic to plant life, so that they can regulate and control plant growth. Plant physiologists play an important role in agriculture where drought-resistance, crop production, nutritional value, quality of food crops, germination as well as the storage of seed and the production of fruit are

Ethno Botanist: Ethno botany is the study of the relationship between plants and people. 'Ethno' is the study of people and 'botany' is the study of plants. Ethno botanists study relationships

production. Ethno botanists study the different ways in which people make use of plants, whether

botanists develop new products for food, herbal, and pharmaceutical companies and sometimes assist in managing biological resources. Ethno botanists mainly hold research positions for companies in the pharmaceutical, cosmetic and alternative health product industries, as well as universities and government health agencies.

Mycologist:
industry. Fungi often live in symbiosis with plants and play an important role in the ecology of the environment. They cause decay in food and other natural products and they are also important in

collecting specimens and performing research in laboratories.

Plant Geneticists: A plant geneticists are botanists who study plant heredity and plant variation. Plant geneticists study the origin and development of inherited traits. Plant geneticist works to improve breeding methods to ensure that future plant generations possess the desired traits. Geneticists are employed by both government and private forestry organisations to work on programmes for the improvement of trees for cultivation.

Palynologist: Palynology is a highly specialised branch of systematic science and it involves the

Palynology is the study of fossil and living-pollen, spores, similar plant structures, etc. Palynologist's services are also used in forensic medicine and criminology because it is possible to identify pollen on clothes, shoes and the body.

Palaeobotanist: The Palaeobotanist studies plant fossils and must have an interest in rocks and geology. Palaeobotanists and Palynologists are employed in archaeological museums where they are responsible for the study and research of plant fossils. Palaeobotany is a branch of paleontology or paleobiology.

Plant Pathologist: Plant Pathologists study the nature, cause and control of plant diseases as well as the decay of plant products. They attempt to isolate disease-causing agents and study the habits and life cycles of various plants. They work mainly in research laboratories.

Weed scientist: Weed scientists study the different types of weed as well as mechanical, chemical

makes it possible to understand why weeds invade certain areas and to make predictions.

Q.33   What are the job prospects in the field of Botany?

Ans: Job prospects for botanists are generally good. Challenging positions will be available for well-trained botanists. Career options are available not only in India but abroad also. Careers in botany offers individual freedom; varied work; pleasant surroundings; inspiring coworkers; and travel opportunities. If you like nature and outdoors, you might enjoy a career as botanist. Job opportunities usually depend on educational training and experience. Candidates with advanced

The major employers of plant biologists are educational institutions, central and state agencies and industries. Almost all colleges and universities offer courses in plant science and there are faculty positions for botanists who have different specialties. In addition, educational institutions employ botanists as researchers and administrators. Plant scientists also work in the State Departments, Botanical Survey of India, and Environmental Protection Agency, etc. Drug companies, oil industry, chemical industry, lumber and paper companies, genetic research industry, botanical gardens, nurseries, fruit growers, food companies, archaeological museums, fermentation industries all hire men and women trained in botany. The demand for botanists is increasing in areas such as medical plant research, plant diseases, plant breeding and plant genetics. Some botanists work in administration and marketing for biological supply houses, seed

through leading newspapers and employment news.

Q.34   What is Veterinary Science? What jobs are dealt with by Veterinary Doctors?

Ans: Veterinary Science is the science of diagnosing, treating and curing the diverse types of diseases in birds and animals. The subject broadly covers the study of animal physiology, treatment and prevention of diseases among animals. The basic principles of this specialised branch of study

a vet is much bigger than that of a general physician or a surgeon. It involves not only taking care

treatment, Vets perform surgery, prevent spreading of diseases in animals by administering timely vaccination and medicines and give advice on pet-care and farm animals.

Their activities also include Animal husbandry – animal breed improvement by 'selection breeding'

through animals; thus protecting the public from exposure to diseases carried by animals, wildlife conservation, poultry management and health care, livestock insurance and rural development.

Broadly a veterinary doctor has a major role in the conservation of livestock and domestic animal wealth.

Veterinary doctors deal with the treatment, care and handling of domestic pets, livestock, and animals in the zoo, laboratory, sporting animals or animals with the government's animal husbandry departments. They take up exclusive practice of either large animals such as cattle including horses, pigs, sheep; poultry, etc., or small animals which are mainly household pets including dogs, cats, birds, etc., or both. The approach varies with different animals. The vets must be familiar with the many breeds of pets or livestock and the characteristics of each so that

Q.35 How can one become a Veterinary Doctor?

Ans: To practice as a veterinarian it is essential to have a Bachelor's degree in Veterinary Science (B.V.Sc.). To be eligible for the Bachelor's in Veterinary Science and Animal Husbandry (B.V.Sc & AH) course, a candidate should have passed the class 12 examination with science subjects such as Physics, Chemistry and Biology.

Admission to most veterinary colleges is conducted on the basis of an entrance examination conducted by the concerned universities. The Veterinary Council of India conducts an 'All India

in the veterinary colleges of all states; in about 36 colleges the jurisdiction of Indian Veterinary council Act, 1984 extends. This Entrance exam is usually held in the month of May each year. For admission to Masters degree programme an All India Entrance Examination is conducted by the Indian Council for Agricultural Research (ICAR).

skills through theoretical and practical training in various disciplines such as anatomy, physiology, biochemistry, nutrition, livestock management and production, production technology, pathology, microbiology, pharmacology, genetics and breeding, gynaecology, surgery, medicine and animal

six months is internship.

The internship includes three months' training at the Teaching Veterinary Clinical Service

on a rotation basis. Veterinary students undergo a one-month practical training in livestock production and management at animal farms, then one-month training in poultry production and management and another one-month's training in livestock products' technology and other services. Apart from learning to treat animals, training is also provided in dairying and poultry sciences. Generally after doing B.VSc, most candidates go on to do a post graduation, namely a Master in Veterinary Science. The Postgraduate course in Veterinary Science (M.V.Sc.) is a 2 year course and the candidate has the option to specialise in areas like medicine, surgery, anatomy, bacteriology, biochemistry, cardiology, dermatology, microbiology, molecular biology, anaesthesia, gynaecology, pathology, toxicology, virology pharmacology, etc. For jobs in the research and teaching areas, a post-graduate degree in veterinary science and animal husbandry for animals. A good vet must read the signs from the animal's behaviour and diagnose the ailment. As the animals cannot describe the problem, vets have to diagnose it skillfully. Vets must also be able to handle emergencies and work in physically disagreeable conditions, or in rural areas where working hours may be long and irregular, and working conditions uncomfortable. Working

moody behaviour and should instinctively gauge the animal's condition. A vet should have the ability to put the animals at ease, to do teamwork, have powers of observation and self reliance, adaptability, indifference to the occasionally disagreeable conditions of work. He needs to be extra sensitive and patient.

Q.36   What are the employment opportunities for Veterinarians?

Ans: Veterinary science offers a large spectrum of avenues for work. Consequently the demand for Veterinary doctors is increasing tremendously. Veterinarians can choose to work with the government animal husbandry departments, poultry farms, dairy farms, sheep and rabbit farms, race clubs, stud farms, private and government veterinary hospitals and clinics. Wildlife sanctuaries, Zoological parks and Aviaries are also employers for veterinarians.

The Army and the Border Security Forces also employ veterinarians for the care and treatment of their mounted regiments having horses, mules, camels and dogs. Private practice is another option to consider. Teaching is yet another option for experienced professionals who are recruited

Besides regular practice, vets can also take up research work, either on their own or in association with the government bodies such as ICAR (Indian council for Agricultural Research). Pharmaceutical industries appoint veterinary scientists in their research and development divisions for the research and development of drugs, chemicals and bio-products particularly antibiotics and vaccines both for human and animal use.

Q.37   How can one take a career in Poultry Production/Poultry Farming?

Ans: In India Poultry production has been a primitive practice. Today this science has evolved so

producer of poultry meat in the world. Indian poultry sector is advancing rapidly. A candidate can choose the career of poultry specialist in research, education, business, government and public sector and poultry industry.

In Poultry Science, experts train students on how to raise and manage healthy chickens, turkeys, and ducks for eggs or meat. Students learn to apply principles of biology and chemistry to develop productivity. They study animal nutrition and food science. Poultry science education provides a valuable contributor to human health.

Students must passed 10+2 with Physics, Chemistry, and Biology (PCB) for completing B.V.Sc and AH degree (Bachelor of Veterinary Science and Animal Husbandry). After graduation, most of the students enroll in postgraduate programmes, M.V.Sc (Master of

Veterinary Science). The M.V.Sc is a two-year course and the candidate can choose optional subjects to specialise in different areas. Various courses in poultry science are Evaluation of Live Poultry, Introduction to HACCP (Hazard Analysis and Critical Control Points System), Avian

Turkey Production, Commercial Egg Production, Incubation and Hatchery Management, Feed Mill Management and Feed Formulation, Poultry Breeding.

Typical work in a poultry farm involves various tasks related to:

Management of the Farm
Breeding and rearing Chicks
Preventing, diagnosing and controlling disease
Feed formulation and analysis
Administration and Personnel Management
Marketing
Finance

A variety of jobs can be taken up in various Hatcheries, Veterinary Hospitals, Pharmaceutical companies, feed miller and feed production companies and feed analysis laboratories.

one can set up own poultry farms. A large number of entrepreneurs in the country have taken up these types of ventures and have become quite successful too.

ADVERTISING & PUBLIC RELATION

CHAPTER 3

Q.1 What is Advertising?

Ans: "Advertising: The science of arresting the human intelligence long enough to get money from it." — Stephen Leacock

"Advertising is legalised lying." — H.G. Wells

"Advertising is the art of convincing people to spend money they don't have for something they don't need." — Will Rogers

To put it simply, advertising is salesmanship. It can make the difference between business success and

At the very least, it seeks to persuade someone who is in the market for a given product or service to consider a particular brand. The business of advertising involves marketing objectives and artistic ingenuity. It applies quantitative and qualitative research to the creative process. It is the marriage of analysis and imagination of marketing professional and artist. Advertising is art and science, show business and just plain business, all rolled into one. And it employs some of the brightest and most creative economists, researchers, artists, producers, writers, and business people in the country today.

Q.2 How was Advertising Developed?

Ans:

All good advertising includes some basic steps before it appears in public:

It assesses the competition.

It determines who the target audience is, and how and why it chooses the products it does.

It sets goals and a budget: what the advertising should achieve and how much must be spent on achieving those goals.

It determines the media: what vehicle (television, newspapers, magazines, outdoor) will best reach the target audience to be effective.

It creates a message: what pictures, words, and music will best attract and appeal to the

An advertiser usually hires an advertising agency to help him to identify prospective customers, create the advertising, and buy the broadcast (television, radio) time and print space (magazine, newspaper, and outdoor) to carry the advertising work so that the consumers can see it.

Q.3 What are the career prospects in Advertising and qualifications required?

Ans:

for sure, with the opening of large number of agencies. Be it the companies, the religious or voluntary organisations or the personalities, brands, products or services, advertising is

the process of building a relationship between the consumer and the product; it is a means to inform and educate the mass, promote products and services and optimise the process of sale. With a very high pay package, fame and glamour, it is an ideal profession for someone with a creative bent of mind.

Several new areas are coming up and developing in advertising, thereby creating job opportunities or many. Whether it is areas like event management wherein events are managed and marketed

marketing targeting a particular section of people, a career in Advertising is surely challenging and most sought after these days!

Eligibility Criteria:

formal management or mass communication or advertising. For jobs in market research, media planning and client servicing, preference is given to the MBA holders.

The minimum eligibility criterion for pursuing post graduation in advertising, one must possess a graduation degree from a recognised university in any discipline with at least 50% marks. Admission to advertising programmes is based on an entrance examination followed by an interview. Some institutes of advertising in India also provide BA courses in advertising. Students to this course need to qualify their 12th standard. Advertising Agencies generally prefer those individuals who have a creative bend of mind; who can think independently but work well in teams. If you are interested in pursuing a career in advertising, you must be highly goal driven and work well under time pressures. Since this industry is very competitive, you must be willing to give your best at all times to make a successful career.

writing, creativity, the capability to translate different types of ideas into the visual format, etc., are a must-have. One must possess an insight into the wants, need and interests of people from different background and culture. Some other essential skills and attributes required for

importantly the mental strength to take criticism and withstand high pressure. One should be sociable and must possess a calm temperament. The media and the market researchers must

should be able to make the advertisement very appealing to people.

Q.4 What are the Career Options in Advertising?

Ans: Advertising agencies handle a broad range of marketing tasks requiring people with experience and ability in overall management and specialised skills. In all agencies, the jobs usually fall into

Account Management

The responsibility of the account manager is to be the client's representative at the agency, and the agency's representative at the client's organisation. It is his or her job to get the best

means knowing how to handle people at the agency so that they give the client their best effort

The effective account manager develops a thorough knowledge of the client's business, the consumer, the marketplace and all aspects of advertising, including creative, media, research, and commercial production. As team leader and strategist, the account person must communicate the client's needs clearly to the agency team, plan effectively to maximise staff time and energy,

account person must be able to foster productive communication between client and agency

for the client and the agency.

Entry-level positions

Successful candidates must have strong general business skills: the ability to write and speak effectively, demonstrated leadership experience, a capacity for statistical analysis, and developed organisational skills. Candidates should have a bachelor's degree and, in some cases, a master of business administration. A degree in advertising or marketing is not a prerequisite.

Career Opportunities

An entry-level position in account management usually leads to account executive and then to more senior positions, with responsibility for more than one account and for the work of several account executives.

Job Title	Job Description
Director of Account Services	Responsible for mgmt. of the department. Responsibilities include budgets, costs, resource allocation. Provides strategic leadership. Top level client contact with usually 20+ years relevant industry and advertising expertise.
Account Director	Responsible for leadership and overall management of the Client relationship on one large or multiple accounts. Drives long-term business building, oversees Account team management. 15+ years of industry and advertising experience.
Management Supervisor	the Agency's senior management on a day-to-day basis. Typically reports to the Account Director, with 10+ years experience.
Account Supervisor	Provides strategic recommendations and manages all Company/Agency resources to ensure the Client's marketing needs are met. Reports to Account Director, with 7+ years of industry experience.

Account Executive	Manages/coordinates Client projects and may take an active role in all disciplines from planning to completion. Effectively executes strategies, problem-solves, and develops solid business relationships, with 3+ years of experience.
Assistant Account Executive	Provides Client service support to ensure that all assignments are executed timely and accurately. Assists in the daily operations of Client projects internally. Essentially an account executive "in training".

Account Planning

Essentially, account planners make sure the consumer's perspective is fully considered when advertising is developed. The account planner works to continually focus and re-focus the agency's strategic and creative thinking on the consumer, helping the team—particularly the creative—understand what "turns the consumer on". They study how consumers actually make use of marketing communications. Using that knowledge, they help the agency "break out" into new ways of communicating about products and services. They offer not only consumer insight, but a plan of action for approaching marketing communications challenges. The account planner's primary tool is research: consumer psychology and behaviour, brand-sales history, competitive sales and customer information, consumer demographics, and much more. They use this information to determine how the agency can leverage a brand's strengths in a strategic and creative approach.

Career Opportunities

Most account planners have academic backgrounds in Liberal Arts, and certainly exposure to

tend to have in common is the ability to interpret and synthesize information, generating useful insights that can be readily understood and acted upon by others.

Job Title	Job Description
Exec. Account Planning	Responsible for management of the global/national/ regional/local account planning department. May be an integral member of new business team, with 15+ years of planning expertise.
Dir. Account Planning	Responsible for the management of one or more Client groups. Responsible for developing ad strategy and creative brief and bring a strong consumer focus to all decisions based on 10+ years of expertise.
Account Planning Mgr.	Oversees day-to-day activity on assigned accounts, may include training and development of staff. 7+ years of experience.
Account Planning Supervisor	Responsible for applying consumer understanding to creative problems on assigned accounts. Partners with other departments to ensure the quality of the creative brief. 5+ years industry experience.
Account Planner	Manages all research pertaining to strategy and creative development. Provides insight to Clients regarding consumer preference, with 3+ years of experience.
Assistant Account Planner	Responsible for assisting the planners in applying consumer understanding to creative problems.

Creative

The creative department of an advertising agency is responsible for developing the ideas, images, and words that make up commercials and ads. While many people in the agency contribute to the process, the invention and production of advertising is mainly the responsibility of copywriters and art directors.

Entry-level positions

Junior or Assistant Copywriter: The junior copywriter assists one or more copywriters in editing and proofreading ad copy, writing body copy for established print campaigns, and developing merchandising and sales promotion materials. With proven ability and experience, assignments might include generating ideas for product or company names and writing dialogue for TV commercials and scripts for radio ads. Although a bachelor's degree is not required, most agencies look for candidates with proven intellectual ability and emotional maturity. Degrees in English, journalism, or advertising and marketing can be helpful.

Junior or Assistant Art Director: The junior art director assists one or more art directors in preparing paste-ups, rough lettering, and layouts for print ads and television storyboards,

television commercials. A successful candidate will have strong visual conceptualisation skills and good basic drawing and design ability.

Career Opportunities

Job Title	Job Description
Chief Creative Director	Overall responsibility and accountability for the management of the total creative function of the agency. Establishes the 'creative tone' and pace of the agency, based on 15+ years of experience.
Creative Director	Responsible for the quality of all creative work produced by the agency for all clients. Maintains standards of creative excellence. Typically has 15+ years of experience.
Assoc. Creative Director	Supervises and guides the total creative effort of one or more creative groups. Insures creative compliance with clients' goals. Usually has 10+ years of expertise.
Creative Supervisor	Integrates art, copy, and production functions and guiding overall creative effort of assigned general advertising creative groups on one or more accounts. 8+ years of experience.
Copywriter	Responsible for generating concepts/ideas and highly targeted copy on one or more accounts. May adapt to changes in format, media and/or Clients' strategies. 2+ years of experience.
Art Director	Responsible for the visual creation of general advertising campaigns on one or more accounts. Coordinates the design and reproduction of the copy with the art and production staff. 2+ years of expertise.
Illustrator	Prepares a variety of illustrations for one or more accounts. May design, select layout materials, prepare interpretive drawings from written plans. 2+ years of experience.

Media

The media department of an advertising agency is responsible for placing advertising where it will reach the right people at the right time and in the right place...and do so in a cost-effective way. Planning and buying media at an advertising agency is exciting and challenging because ways of communicating are constantly changing and becoming more complex. Such technological advances as cable television and the internet, or videotext make an impact on what media is available for advertising and how viewership is calculated. A recent increase in the number of specialty publications enables more precise targeting of consumers. It is the responsibility of the media department to develop a plan that answers the question: how can the greatest number of people in the target group be reached often enough to have the advertising message seen and remembered — and, at the lowest possible cost?

Entry-level position

Assistant Media Planner: The typical assistant media planner reports to a media planner and gathers and studies information about people's viewing and reading habits, evaluates editorial content and programming of various media vehicles, and about media vehicles, and becomes thoroughly familiar with media data banks and information sources. To accomplish these tasks

Career Opportunities

Job Title	Job Description
Executive Media Director	Oversees management of media planning, including budgets, costs, resource allocation and strategic leadership. Plays lead role in new business and acts as a
Executive Media Buying Director	Responsible for management of the media buying and/or operations. Handles sensitive Company/Agency negotiations. Involved in policy-making decisions, based on 20+ years of media expertise.
Group Media Director	Leads overall management of one large and/or multiple Clients setting strategic direction and driving long-term business. Holds accountability for budgets and planning. 15+ years of experience.
Media Buying Director	Represents Company/Agency's senior management on a day-to-day basis and is involved with negotiations. 15+ years of experience.
Associate Media Director	Responsible for the overall service of assigned accounts and media teams. Approves the development and execution of media strategy, communications plans while maintaining cost controls. 7+ years expertise.
Media Supervisor	Provides strategic recommendations and analysis. Manages media planners to ensure Client's marketing needs are met. 4+ years of media experience.
Media Planner	Responsible for developing, executing and managing media plans best suited to meet established Client requirements and objectives. May supervise, train, delegate assistant media planners. 1+ years expertise.

Interactive Marketing

If you have ever visited a company's website, you have been part of how interactive marketing is changing the relationship between advertiser and the audience.

An important point to understand is to realise that with traditional marketing vehicles, companies

out the company's website and decides how long they will stay. They can tailor the experience to their own needs. This is why interactive marketing is the fastest growing phenomena in the media and marketing world.

Career Opportunities

of design, marketing, and computer programming. Agencies need designers and programmers, as well as strategists who understand how marketers can use interactive media creatively and effectively. The advantage in job-hunting in this area is to those who have a strong knowledge of computers and the digital realm, and are on top of the daily changes in digital technology and its capabilities.

Q.5 Where can one study BA in Advertising in India?

Ans: The following Institutes/colleges offer B.A. degree in Advertising:

College / Institute	State	Eligibility	Course Duration
Nizam College, Gunfoundry, Hyderabad	Andhra Pradesh	Class XII	3 years
Government College for Women, Begumpet, Hyderabad	Andhra Pradesh	Class XII	3 years
Loyola Academy College, Alwal, Secunderabad	Andhra Pradesh	Class XII	3 years
	Andhra Pradesh	Class XII	3 years
JB College, Jorhat, Dibrugarh University	Assam	Class XII	3 years
Gaya College, Gaya	Bihar	Class XII	3 years
Patna Women's College, Bayley Road, Patna	Bihar	Class XII	3 years
N.B. Gurbachan Singh Memorial college, Sohna, Gurgaon	Haryana	Class XII	3 years
BVV Basaveshware Commerce College, Bagalkot		Class XII	3 years
		Class XII	3 years
MLB Arts and Commerce Autonomous College, Rani Durgavati Vishwavidhalaya, Gwalior	Madhya Pradesh	Class XII	3 years
Women, Rani Durgavati Vishwavidhalaya, Jabalpur	Madhya Pradesh	Class XII	3 years
Government Mahakoshal Arts and Commerce Autonomous College, Jiwaji University, Jabalpur	Madhya Pradesh	Class XII	3 years
Department of Communication Journalism, Gokhale Education Society, Nashik	Maharashtra	Class XII	3 years
Siddharth College of Arts and Science, Mumbai University, Anand Bhavan, Dadabhai Naoroji Road, Mumbai 400001	Maharashtra	Class XII	3 years
Somaiya College of Arts, Mumbai University, charni Road, Near Bhartiya Vidya Bhavan, Mumbai	Maharashtra	Class XII	3 years
Jai Hindi College of Arts and JT Lalwani College of Commerce, Mumbai	Maharashtra	Class XII	3 years
Anand Bhawan, DadabhaiNaoroji Road, Mumbai	Maharashtra	Class XII	3 years
Smt. MMP Shah College of Arts and Commerce, Mumbai	Maharashtra	Class XII	3 years

Manipur University, Canchipur, Imphal	Manipur	Class XII	3 years
Jamia Mallia Islamia, Jamia Nagar, New Delhi 110025	Delhi	Class XII	3 years
Delhi	Delhi	Class XII	3 years
Janaki Devi Mahavidyalya, University of Delhi, New Delhi	Delhi	Class XII	3 years
	Delhi	Class XII	3 years
Vivekanand College, University of Delhi, New Delhi	Delhi	Class XII	3 years
Delhi College of Arts and Commerce, New Delhi	Delhi	Class XII	3 years
GGDSD college, Punjab University, Chandigarh	Punjab	Class XII	3 years
	Rajasthan	Class XII	3 years
University	Tamil Nadu	Class XII	3 years
PSG College of Arts and Science, Bharathiar University, Coimbatore	Tamil Nadu	Class XII	3 years
Ethiraj College for Women, University of Chennai, Chennai	Tamil Nadu	Class XII	3 years
Chennai Christian college, Chennai	Tamil Nadu	Class XII	3 years
Bareilly College, Rohilkhand University, Bareilly	Uttar Pradesh	Class XII	3 years
North Bengal	West Bengal	Class XII	3 years
	West Bengal	Class XII	3 years
	West Bengal	Class XII	3 years

Q.6 Where can one get employment after completing a course in Advertising?

Ans: You can get a job in any one of the following:

In private advertising agencies

Different advertising departments in the public and private sector companies

In several media houses

In the advertising sections of journals, magazines, newspapers

In the commercial sections of television or radio

In market research organisations, etc.

Q.7 What is Public Relation and what are the jobs performed by Public Relation specialist?

Ans: Public relations, abbreviated as PR, primarily concerns enhancing and maintaining the image

politicians.

Associations, held in Mexico City, in August 1978, was "the art and social science of analysing trends, predicting their consequences, counseling organisational leaders, and implementing planned programmes of action, which will serve both the organisation and the public interest."

publics. Public relations provides an organisation or individual exposure to their audiences using topics of public interest and news items that provide a third-party endorsement and do not direct payment. Common activities include speaking at conferences, working with the media, crisis communications, social media engagement, and employee communication.

degree to which its targeted publics support its goals and policies. Public relations specialists serve as advocates for businesses, governments, universities, hospitals, schools, and other organisations, and build and maintain positive relationships with the public. As managers recognise the growing importance of good public relations to the success of their organisations, they increasingly rely on public relations specialists for advice on strategy and policy of such programmes.

Public relations specialists handle organisational functions such as media, community, consumer,

mediation; or employee and investor relations. However, public relations is not only telling the organisation's story. Understanding the attitudes and concerns of consumers, employees, and various other groups is also a vital part of the job. To improve communications, public relations specialists establish and maintain cooperative relationships with representatives of community, consumer, employee, and public interest groups and those in print and broadcast journalism.

Informing the general public, interest groups, and stockholders of an organisation's policies, activities, and accomplishments is an important part of a public relations specialist's job. Their work keeps management aware of public attitudes and concerns of the many groups and organisations with which they must deal. Public relations specialists prepare press releases and contact people in the media who might print or broadcast their material. Many radio or television special reports, newspaper stories, and magazine articles start at the desks of public relations specialists. Sometimes the subject is an organisation and its policies towards its employees or its role in the community.

Often the subject is a public issue, such as health, nutrition, energy, or the environment. Public relations specialists also arrange and conduct programmes for contact between organisation representatives and the public. For example, they set up speaking engagements and often

and plan conventions. In addition, they are responsible for preparing annual reports and writing proposals for various projects.

public affairs specialists, or communications specialists keep the public informed about the activities

Energy keep the public informed about the proposed lease of offshore land for oil exploration.

A press secretary for a member of Congress keeps constituents aware of their elected representatives' accomplishments. In large organisations, the key public relations executive, who is often a vice president, may develop overall plans and policies with other executives. In addition, public relations departments employ public relations specialists to write, do research, prepare materials, maintain contacts, and respond to inquiries. People who handle publicity for an individual or who direct public relations for a small organisation may deal with all aspects of the job. They contact people, plan and do research, and prepare material for distribution. They may also handle advertising or sales promotion work to support marketing.

Q.8   What qualifications are essential to enter the field of Public Relation?

Ans:

degree combined with public relations experience, usually gained through an internship, is considered excellent preparation for public relations work. The ability to write and speak well is essential. Many entry-level public relations specialists have a college major in public relations,

worked in electronic or print journalism. Other employers seek applicants with demonstrated

In 1998, over 200 colleges and about 100 graduate schools offered degree programmes or special curricula in public relations, usually in a journalism or communications department. In addition,

in Journalism and Mass Communications is the only agency authorised to accredit schools or departments of public relations. A common public relations sequence includes courses in public relations principles and techniques; public relations management and administration, including organisational development; writing, emphasising news releases, proposals, annual reports, scripts, speeches, and related items; visual communications, including desktop publishing and computer graphics; and research, emphasising social science research and survey design and implementation. Courses in advertising, journalism, business administration, political science, psychology, sociology, and creative writing also are helpful, as is familiarity with word processing and other computer applications. Specialties are offered in public relations for business,

Many colleges help students gain part-time internships in public relations that provide valuable experience and training. The Armed Forces can also be an excellent place to gain training and experience. Membership in local chapters of the Public Relations Student Society of America or the International Association of Business Communicators provides an opportunity for students to exchange views with public relations specialists and to make professional contacts that may help

television or radio station provides valuable experience and material for one's portfolio.

Creativity, initiative, good judgment, and the ability to express thoughts clearly and simply are

skills are also important. People who choose public relations as a career need an outgoing

a team. Some organisations, particularly those with large public relations staffs, have formal training programmes for new employees. In smaller organisations, new employees work under company activities, scan newspapers and magazines for appropriate articles to clip, and assemble information for speeches and pamphlets. They may also answer calls from the press and public, work on invitation lists and details for press conferences, or escort visitors and clients. After gaining experience, they write news releases, speeches, and articles for publication or design

Promotion to supervisory jobs may come as public relations specialists show they can handle

assistant or account assistant and be promoted to account executive, account supervisor, vice president, and eventually senior vice president. A similar career path is followed in corporate public relations, although the titles may differ. Some experienced public relations specialists

The Public Relations Society of America accredits public relations specialists who have at

(5 hours written, 1 hour oral). The International Association of Business Communicators also

relations specialists. Those who meet all the requirements of the programme earn the Accredited Business Communicator designation. Candidates must have at least 5 years of experience in a

of work samples demonstrating involvement in a range of communication projects and a thorough understanding of communication planning. Employers consider professional recognition through

job market.

Public Relations Society of India (PRSI), the national association of PR practitioners was established in 1958 to promote the recognition of public relations as a profession and to formulate and interpret to the public the objectives and the potentialities of public relations as a strategic management function. The society functioned as an informal body till 1966 when it was registered

management of the Public Relations society of India is vested in the National Council, consisting of representatives elected by all the regional chapters. The members of the society are public relations practitioners from Multinationals, Government; Public and Private sector; Academics and PR consultants.

Q.9 What are the courses available in Public Relations?

Ans: The course in Public relation includes mainly public relations principles and techniques, public relations management and administration which includes proposals, annual reports, scripts, speeches, organisational development, writing, research, emphasising social science research and survey design and implementation, etc. The main courses available in PR are:

Degree Course in Public Relations.
Diploma in Communication, Journalism and Public Relations.
Diploma in Public Relation.
Diploma in Public Relations and Corporate Communication.
M.A. Public Relations.
Master's Degree in Journalism and Public Relations.
Postgraduate Diploma in Event Management and Public Relations.
Postgraduate Diploma in Journalism, Public Relations and Advertising.
Postgraduate Diploma in Public Relations.
Postgraduate Diploma in Public Relations and Advertising.

The criteria for joining public relation courses is bachelors degree in any discipline preferably with mass communication, social sciences, liberal arts and humanities. The duration of most of Diploma courses of public relation is 1 year and Master's courses are 2 years. The admission to

are generally three to six months duration.

Q.10 Which are the best institutions to study a course in Public Relation?

Ans:

1. Two-year full time postgraduate diploma in Communication Management with option for majoring in Public Relations, Corporate Communication and Event Management in the second year at Symbiosis Institute of Mass Communication (SIMC), Pune

2. MA in Advertising and Public Relations (MAAPR) at the Makhanlal Chaturvedi National University of Journalism, Bhopal

3. Two year full time MA in Advertising and Public relations at the School of Broadcasting and Communication, Mumbai

4. One year full time Diploma in Public Relations and Corporate Communications at the Xavier Institute of Communications (XIC), Mumbai

5. One year postgraduate diploma in Advertising and PR — started in 1981 at the Indian Institute of Mass Communication (IIMC), New Delhi

Some of the other institutes and colleges in India offering PR courses are:

The Advertising Academy, New Delhi.
Centre for Image Management Studies, Noida (Uttar Pradesh).
Easygyan, Lucknow (Uttar Pradesh).
Dr. B.R. Ambedkar Open University, Hyderabad (Andhra Pradesh).
Meteor Institute of Digital Design Studies (M.I.D.D.S.), Thane (Maharashtra).
Veer Narmath South Gujarat University, Surat (Gujarat).
National Academy of Event Management and Development (N.A.E.M.D.), Maharashtra.
Barkatullah University Institute of Open and Distance Education, Bhopal (Madhya Pradesh).
Indira Gandhi National Open University, New Delhi.

Nalanda Open University, Patna (Bihar).

Ashok Inlead School of Hospitality, Gurgaon, (Haryana).

Aligarh Muslim University, Aligarh (Uttar Pradesh).

Indian Institute of Journalism, New Delhi.

Indian Institute of Public Relations, New Delhi.

Q.11 Where can one study a course on Public Relation in Delhi?

Ans: Some of the institutions offering courses in Public Relation in Dellhi are:

Name of Course	Name of the Institute	Eligibility	Duration
Relations	Centre for Mass Media Studies, YMCA, Jai Singh Road, New Delhi - 110002	Graduation	8 weeks
and Event Management/ Marketing	Delhi School of Communication E Agnel School Bldg, Gautam Nagar, New Delhi - 110049	Class XII	6-8 weeks
Diploma in Public Relations	New Delhi Polytechnic for Women, South Extension, New Delhi	Class XII	1-2 years
PG Diploma in Public Relations	Institute of Management, Delhi	Graduation	1 year
PG Diploma in Public Relations	Indian Foundation of Public Relation Education and Research, New Delhi	Graduation	1 year
PG Diploma in Public Relations	Indian Institute of Mass Communication, Shaheed Jeet Singh Marg, JNU Campus, New Delhi - 110067	Graduation	1 year
PG Diploma in Public Relations	Indian Institute of Public Relations, B-9, Shivalik, New Delhi	Graduation	1 year
PG Diploma in Public Relations	Institute of Advertising and Communication, New Delhi	Graduation	1 year
PG Diploma in Public Relations	National Institute of Advertising, New Delhi	Graduation	1 year
PG Diploma in Public Relations	Sardar Patel College of Communication and Management Bhartiya Vidya Bhavan, New Delhi — 11001	Graduation	1 year
PG Diploma in Public Relations	School of Communication, EMPI, New Delhi	Graduation	1 year
PG Diploma in Public Relations	South Delhi Polytechnic for Women, Behind Lady Shri Ram College, Lajpat Nagar, New Delhi - 110024	Graduation	1 year

Q.12 What is Corporate Communication?

Ans: Corporate communication is an essential aspect of communication, which needs to be

communication collectively refers to the communication processes that are meant for corporate or business purposes. Corporate communication refers to the communication within corporate organisation (internal communication) as well as the communication between different corporate entities (external communication). Corporate communication can make use of different types of mass media.

Internal Corporate Communication: Internal corporate communication means communication within a particular company. Some of the commonly used tools for internal communication can include business meetings, conferences, interviews, presentations or print media like brochures, newsletters, memos, or business letters. Corporate communication is used for making announcements, taking decisions and in general for sharing information, views and opinions within an organisation.

Corporate communication is a great way to create conducive atmosphere for increasing the productivity of the organisation. Factors like work hierarchy come into picture during internal corporate communication. Depending on the direction of communication, internal corporate

referring to communication within peers and vertical referring to communication within different hierarchies in the organisation.

External Corporate Communication: External corporate communication process includes communication of the corporate organisation with its current/potential investors, customers and other corporate entities. The external corporate communication process includes elements like advertising, marketing and public relations. The external communication is responsible for the way the company portrays itself to the entire corporate world. Thus, external corporate communication is instrumental in creating the brand image or brand identity. The advertisement campaigns and promotional events can be included in external corporate communication as well. Television ads, newspaper ads, radio jingles, promotional

external corporate communication.

The responsibilities of a Corporate Communicator include:

> Supervise the status of the Corporate Communication organisation.
> Develop, execute and evaluate corporate strategy.
> Ensuring effective two-way Internal Corporate Communications.
> Taking the lead on media handling, proactively placing good news stories, dealing with enquiries and producing media releases.
> Developing links with other departments, which enhances the smooth functioning.
> Corporate Communication Planning.
> Leading public relations, including customer services.
> Playing a key role in issue management and planning.
> Ensuring that other health organisations are kept fully briefed on developments, plans and any incidents in your organisation.
> Producing high quality information service.
> Advising senior colleagues on strategic communications and related issues.
> Engaging in business promotion campaigns.

Typically, the following skills would be necessary for a communications role :

Ability to work equally well both on your own and within a team.

Ability to write, speak and brief others clearly.

Ability to assess and select appropriate communications routes for different messages and audiences.

Ability to remain calm under pressure.

Ability to recognise sensitive situations and act appropriately.

Ability to work well with others at all levels both within and outside your company.

Ability to gain the trust and respect of senior colleagues.

Ability to provide creative input to projects.

Ability to think strategically.

Above all, corporate communicator represents the corporation's voice, its reputation, integrity and the images it projects of itself on a global and regional stage populated by its various audiences and stakeholders

Q.13   What is Reputation Management?

Ans: Reputation Management, also known as directory management, is the process of tracking an entity's actions and other entities' opinions about those actions; reporting on those actions and opinions; and reacting to that report creating a feedback loop. All entities involved are generally people, but that need not always be the case. Other examples of entities include animals, businesses, or even locations or materials. The tracking and reporting may range from word-of-mouth to statistical analysis of thousands of data points. A number of enterprise reputation management software solutions exist in the international market. These software services are typically designed to connect organisations to their stakeholders, track the orchestration of stakeholder engagement and analyse, measure and manage the results.

The reputation management can be separated into three different categories.

Building: This type of reputation management has to do with building the reputation for a business that is just getting started. It includes building a good reputation to maintaining it for your business.

Maintenance: Reputation management meant to just keep a company's good image superior in the public eye is called maintenance. This is meant for companies that are already established, and have a good reputation already.

Recovery: If your business has got a bad reputation for any reason, then the recovery portion of reputation management is for you. Brick Marketing works to hide the bad reputation with good marketing and self-promotion.

Online Reputation Management is a very labour intensive process. Any approach that is subtle and yet effective will take time, at least three months, before any progress is really seen. This includes many different strategies, which include social media such as:

Blogging — Blogs that are updated every day

Directory listings — Listing a website in directories using optimised keywords

Direct reviews — Hiring someone to write good reviews of the company on websites

Online publicity — Syndicated article writing, links, and banners

Social networking — Posting pages on MySpace.com and Facebook.

BIOTECHNOLOGY & BIOINFORMATICS

Q. 1   What is Biotechnology?

Ans: Biotechnology is an interdisciplinary science including not only biology, but also subjects like mathematics, physics, chemistry and engineering. It is a blend of various technologies applied together to living cells for production of a particular product or for improving upon it. Its use and

products, textiles, etc.), medicine, nutrition, environmental conservation, animal sciences, etc.,

The nature of work of biotechnologists, being interdisciplinary, requires working together with

where biotechnology studies are applicable are as follows:

1. **Medicine and Healthcare:** Biotechnology's application in this area has helped in the development of various medicines, vaccines and diagnostics. The remarkable development

   diagnosis, medicines and vaccinations for diseases which once thought were incurable are no more a cause of worry, which has been a blessing for humankind.

2. **Industrial Research and Development:** Both the government and the private sector employ biotechnologists. They conduct research and development work, for increasing productivity, improving energy production and conservation, minimising pollution and

   like chemical processes, genetic engineering, textile development, cosmetic development etc.

3. **Agriculture and Animal Husbandry:** Indian economy is very much dependent on agriculture and biotechnologists have made major advancements in this area. Over the years, the agricultural output has been improving, owing to the improvements in the quality of seeds, insecticides and fertilizers. The latest technologies such as micro propagation and tissue culture have further helped agriculturists to overcome problems like soil imbalances, genetic breeding and crop diseases. Biotechnologists are also encouraging a shift from chemically prepared fertilizers and insecticides to bio-chemicals and bio-insecticides.

Biotechnology's intervention in the area of animal husbandry has improved animal breeding. Numerous kinds of genetically engineered, high yielding animal breeds have come up which have increased the output of dairy products as well as the meat products. India, in fact, has become the largest milk producer in the world

4. **Environment:** Environmental biotechnology has become another area of extensive work due to the dangers brought about by increasing levels of environmental pollution. A

    biotechnologist spans from checking industrial air pollution levels, treatment of industrial waste to recycling of sewage sludge.

determination, perseverance, imagination, innovation, ability to work for long hours, originality, and team-spirit are some of the important essentials for becoming a successful biotechnologist.

Q.2   What are the courses available in Biotechnology?

Ans: After 10+2 in science stream a student can opt for a course in B.Tech in Biotechnology or B.Sc. in Biotechnology. Also the student can opt for any other graduation course in Bio-science or engineering course and then opt for Biotechnology at P.G. level. The P.G. courses are:

M.Sc. Biotechnology

M.Sc. (Agriculture) Biotechnology

M.V.Sc. (Animal) Biotechnology

M.Tech. Biotechnology, M.Sc./M.V.Sc. Veterinary Biotechnology

M.Sc. (Marine) Biotechnology

Medical Biotechnology

M.Tech. in Biomedical Engineering/Biotechnology.

Depending upon the aptitude and necessity, more advanced courses such Ph.D and Post-Doctoral Research in Biotechnology can also be pursued.

Q.3   What is Agricultural Biotechnology?

Ans: With increase in population and concern about the quality of food, the bio-agriculture has gained focus in the recent past in India. The farmers in India are looking at the GM (Genetically

investments and also increase productivity.

The farmers are now getting a premium for the organic product. With this, they are able to export their product at a much higher price. Lot of research initiatives is also being undertaken

getting approvals from government for exploiting the technologies for the betterment of farmers and obtaining decent returns.

GM Seeds: The challenge of producing more food grains to feed the ever increasing population of India that has already crossed one billion mark with less resources has bought companies like Mahyco, Monsanto, Syngenta, ProAgro, Advanta to invest in GM crops. It was in 2002 a joint venture between Mahyco and Monsanto called Mahyco-Monsanto Biotech Ltd got the green signal from the Government of India for the commercial production and sale of Bt cotton (Bollgard) in six southern states of India.

A lot of awareness campaigns had to be conducted to reach out to the farmers and brief them

which are also tolerant to drought, cold, salinity and other harsh environments. This was to

Bio-fertilizers, Bio-pesticides: In addition to GM seeds, the farmers are also looking at bio-

Bt, viruses like NPV, and GV, as well as neem-based pesticides. To meet the increasing demand, the industry has to scale up investments in bio-fertilizers and bio-pesticides. Conservative estimate shows that 10 percent savings through the use of bio-fertilizers will result in an annual saving of 1.094 million tons of nitrogenous fertilizers costing around Rs 550 crore.

Bio-fuel: Looking at the opportunity in bio-fuel sector, the central government has taken an initiative to promote this sector in a big way. The total consumption of ethanol-blended petrol is expected to be 4.6 million tons per year. This sector not only helps sugarcane farmers, as cane is used as raw material for production of ethanol, but also helps in building up the oil security apart

India imports about 70 percent of its requirement of crude oil.

Q.4   What is Green Biotechnology?

Ans: Green biotechnology which is more commonly known as Plant Biotechnology is a rapidly

into economically important plant species, resulting in crop improvement and the production of novel products in plants. Use of environment friendly and cost effective alternatives to industrial chemicals such as bio fuels, bio fertilizers and bio pesticides are not only resulting in enhanced crop output, improvement in health and safety standards, these new products are also leading to less environment pollution and use of green technology. The ever increasing demand of agricultural produce has given

Today plant biotechnology encompasses the following main areas of research and application:

Plant Tissue Culture: It is the technique that allows to produce whole plants from minute amounts of plant parts like the roots, leaves or stems or even just a single plant cell under laboratory conditions. An advantage of tissue culture is rapid production of clean planting materials. Examples of tissue , pyrethrum and citrus.

Plant Genetic Engineering:
one organism to another to create new, improved crops, animals or materials. Examples of genetically engineered crops include cotton, maize, sweet potato, soy beans, etc.

Plant molecular marker assisted breeding: It is a technique that uses molecular markers to select a particular trait of interest such as yield. A molecular marker is a short sequence of DNA that is tightly linked to the desirable trait such as disease resistance; the selection then leads to the desirable trait. E.g. maize that is tolerant to drought and maize streak virus.

Bio fertilizers and Bio Pesticides: Increasingly farmers are using bio-fertilizers and bio-pesticides

ill effects for crops. As per Conservative estimates, a 10 percent saving through the use of bio-fertilizers will result in an annual saving of 1.094 million tons of nitrogenous fertilizers costing around Rs 550 crore.

Hybridisation: Increasingly plant scientists exploit the characteristic feature of better yielding

some offspring from the progeny of a cross between two known parents would be better than the parents themselves. Many hybrid varieties of several crop species are being grown all over the world today. An example of this is the hybrid tomatoes that we eat commonly.

Q.5 What is White Biotechnology or Industrial Biotechnology?

Ans: White or more commonly known as Industrial biotechnology is used to produce all kinds of products used in daily life — ranging from bread and cheese to biodiesel to microbial strains and bio catalysts. It also involves fermentation and enzymatic processes that are fast becoming

applications by virtue of being cost effective and more environment-friendly.

White biotechnology is a prime example of interdisciplinary cooperation. Its technology pool is generated from diverse areas such as chemistry, molecular biology, genetics, microbiology, chemical engineering, agriculture science, informatics, computer engineering and process engineering. New insights, in particular in genome research and systems biology, are currently giving great impetus to white biotechnology revolutionising the whole industrial application and processes and thereby resulting in greater economies.

Use of biotechnology in industrial application is also leading to introduction of environment-friendly methods and processes in various industries such as the food, textile, mining, cosmetics and paper industries. Currently only 5 percent of chemical products are produced

Chemical Industry" had predicted an increase of 10 to 20 percent in 2010 with further prospects for future growth. This is expected to give good sound bytes to green peace volunteers.

There exist more than 3,000 different known enzymes of which only 150 to 170 are used commercially. Therefore, a huge research potential is waiting to be exploited. Other challenges include the optimisation of methods and the enzymes involved. Washing agents are probably the best-known example of the biotechnological use of enzymes.

twice the energy as compared to when enzymes are used. Enzymes also render the entire

a reduction of energy and water consumption of up to 50 percent. White biotechnology is

Products such as bio-fuels like biodiesel, bio-plastics, etc., have a promising future and have

It gives a boost to the research initiatives, leads to greater industrial output and enhanced

more environment-friendly and less polluting. Needless to say that more and more funds will

the process.

Q.6   What is Red Biotechnology?

Ans: Red Biotechnology is about working for human health and improving lifestyle using the applications and advancements in technology and innovation. In medicine, biotechnology has become an integral part in diagnostics, gene therapy, clinical and contract research and trials, bioactive therapeutic, stem cell research, genetic engineering and in the development and production of new drugs for treating various life threatening diseases. Increased use of combination vaccines, such as DPT with Hepatitis B, Hepatitis A and injectable polio vaccine, besides several veterinary and poultry vaccines are examples of biotechnology application in medicinal arena.

Tissue engineering, which deals with tissue implantation following the cultivation of cells on

skin, tissue-engineering products predominantly service the orthopedics markets through the supply of cartilage, bone and spinal disc replacements. Increased application of biotechnology in the areas of cancer research and treatment of Parkinson's disease by discovering mutations and

Biochips are also developing as important tools in the further development of individualised medicine. Biochips are miniaturised analytical tools that are used in diagnostics. They enable the rapid analysis of a patient's individual genetic make-up. They accelerate the development of new drugs, enable the early diagnosis of diseases, the adaptation of drug dosage to the patients' individual requirements and hence the reduction of the number of unwanted side effects. It is also known that certain substances are only effective in some patients because of their particular genetic disposition.

percent of all cancer patients. It is possible to genetically determine whether a particular patient belongs to the group of patients for whom the drug is effective. Another study has shown that patients react differently to dosages of anti-depression drugs and beta blockers for keeping hyper tension in check depending upon their metabolism level and genetic disposition. Molecular genetics has shown that it is possible to determine the best possible drug dose or to clarify whether a particular drug is actually effective. It is, of course, also

of patients. All this leads to tremendous research potential and industrial application for a market which is ever growing. Needless to say that red biotechnology has great application not only for the growth of the industry but is also useful for a more philanthropic purpose — to use the technology to alleviate human sufferings and enhance the quality of life.

Q.7 What is Blue Biotechnology?

Ans: Blue Biotechnology is concerned with the application of molecular biological methods to marine and freshwater organisms. It involves the use of these organisms, and their derivatives, for purposes such as increasing seafood supply and safety, controlling the proliferation of noxious water-borne organisms, and developing new drugs.

Q.8 What is the prospect of Biotechnology in India?

Ans: Biotechnology is the sunrise industry and perhaps one of the fastest emerging sectors in the new generation Indian economy, resulting in tremendous growth in research initiatives and jobs creation. The vast base of intellectual prowess and well-developed skill sets, R&D facilities and cost advantage all tend to make India as one of the most promising markets in the world and offer great opportunities

also trying hard to frame and modify the policy framework so as to make India a vibrant hub of biotechnology research and infrastructure development centre.

Biotechnology in India can be divided into three broad areas — Medicinal sector relating to improved human and animal health care and drug research, agricultural sector leading to introduction of new crops and improved plant produce and industrial arena leading to establishment of new economy companies and industries.

The core competence of Indian biotech industry exists in the following areas and sectors:

Growth of fermentation-based products
Use of plant and animal parts for extracting value added products of high purity
Use of cell and microbial culture techniques
Plant breeding techniques and animal breeding technology based on molecular methodology
Plant cell/tissue culture, etc.
DNA technology of plants and animals
Isolation of plants and animal products
Bioprocess engineering
Gene manipulation of microbes and animal cells

of US$3 billion by 2010 and the bioinformatics market will touch US$2 billion. Indian companies have become providers of biotech information to clients around the world. Sequencing of genes and delivering genomic information for big pharmaceuticals companies is the next boom industry. India has the potential to become one of the prime forces in the development and manufacture of genomic drugs with right climate and well directed research efforts and initiatives.

At present, there are about 190 biotech companies in India. The Indian Biotech Scenario India comprises a large market for biotech based products. However, most of these products are

by *capitalmarket.com*, the Indian biotech industry is expected to touch Rs. 4,40,000 crores in 2020.

The current demand for Biotech Products in India according to the Technology Information

Forecasting and Assessment Council (TIFAC) report includes: Fermentation based products in vaccines.

DMA products and antibiotics among healthcare products.

Alcohol, organic acids, enzymes, amino acids, baker's yeast and other industrial products.

risen to around 850. India's biotech-industry is small compared to its pharmaceutical industry (about 16,000 small and large drug manufacturers). Biotech in India began during the mid-

Government of India established the Department of Biotechnology (DBT) within the Ministry of Science and Technology. Several small biotech companies have been established since then.

Q.9   What is Biological Engineering or Bioengineering?

Ans: Biological engineering, biotechnological engineering or bioengineering is the application of concepts and methods of physics, chemistry, mathematics, and computer science to solve problems in life sciences, using engineering's own analytical and synthetic methodologies and also its traditional sensitivity to the cost and practicality of the solution(s) arrived at. In this context, while traditional engineering applies physical and mathematical sciences to analyse, design and manufacture inanimate tools, structures and processes, biological engineering uses the same sciences, as well as the rapidly-developing body of knowledge known as molecular biology, to study many aspects of living organisms.

Biological Engineers or bioengineers are engineers who use the principles of biology and the tools of engineering to create usable, tangible, economically viable products. Biological Engineering employs knowledge and expertise from a number of pure and applied sciences, such as mass and heat transfer,

It is used in the design of medical devices, diagnostic equipment, biocompatible materials, renewable bio-energy, ecological engineering, and other areas that improve the living standards of societies. In general, biological engineers attempt to either mimic biological systems to create products or modify and control biological systems so that they can replace, augment, or sustain chemical and mechanical processes. Bioengineers can apply their expertise to other applications

bioprocess engineering, and bio-catalysis.

The Main Fields of Bioengineering may be categorised as:

Bioprocess Engineering: Bioprocess Design, Biocatalysis, Bioseparation, Bioinformatics, Bioenergy

Genetic Engineering: Synthetic Biology, Horizontal gene transfer.

Cellular Engineering: Cell Engineering, Tissue Culture Engineering, Metabolic Engineering.

Biomedical Engineering: Biomedical Technology, Biomedical Diagnostics, Biomedical Therapy, Biomechanics, Biomaterials.

Q.10   What is Bioinformatics?

Ans: Bioinformatics is the application of computer technology to the management of biological information. Computers are used to gather, store, analyze and integrate biological and genetic information which can then be applied to gene-based drug discovery and development. The need for Bioinformatics capabilities has been precipitated by the explosion of publicly available genomic information resulting from the Human Genome Project. The science of Bioinformatics, is a hybrid course borne of the synthesis of molecular biology with computer science, is essential

molecular targets for drug discovery. In recognition of this, many universities, government

computational biologists and bioinformatics computer scientists. Such groups are key to unraveling the mass of information generated by large scale sequencing efforts underway in laboratories around the world.

The terms — bioinformatics and computational biology are often used interchangeably. However bioinformatics precisely refers to the creation and advancement of algorithms, computational and statistical techniques, and theories to solve formal and practical problems posed by or inspired from the management and analysis of biological data.

biological problem using computers, carried out with experimental and simulated data, with the primary goal of discovery and the advancement of biological knowledge. In the last few decades,

the increasingly rapid sequencing of large portions of the genes.

This deluge of information has necessitated the careful storage, organisation and indexing of

called Bioinformatics. The simplest tasks used in bioinformatics concern the creation and maintenance of databases of biological information. Nucleic acid sequences (and the protein sequences derived from them) comprise the majority of such databases. While the storage and or organisation of millions of nucleotides is far from trivial, designing a database and developing an interface whereby researchers can both access existing information and submit new entries is only the beginning.

Q.11   What are the employment opportunities in the field of Biotechnology?

Ans: Biotechnology is ranked second, as a growth sector, after the multimedia industry on the basis of employment potential. Bulk of the biotechnologists is employed in research and development, departments of institutions and industries involved in biotechnological work. From the production of antimicrobial agents, reagents and consumables to the marketing of instruments used in biotechnological applications and research, the opportunities for biotechnologists are on the increase. Biotechnologists work extensively in the production departments of these industries. Generally Biotechnology students coming from engineering stream are given preference for production jobs.

Biotechnologists work in industries producing food, chemicals, bio-processed products, etc. They are involved in research in genetics, biochemistry and biochemical engineering and all areas where these processes are implied. Industrial R&D covers areas such as chemical processes, increase in productivity, waste and pollution management. Some industries employ biotechnologists in their marketing department to develop business in the sector where their product would be most required.

They also help to identify biotechnological development opportunities for the industry in India and abroad. A steep rise in employment is envisaged in environmental biotechnology. Spending to the tune of US$600 billion by the turn of the century will open up vast avenues in this sector, as biotechnologists are expected to resolve crisis related to marine life, depletion of the atmosphere, etc. In the area of drugs and pharmaceutical there are new ventures both in the government and private sectors coming up to provide for the latest R&D facilities as the sector envisages a global market share of almost Rs 35,000 crores. Pharmaceutical industries are offering lucrative pay packets to biotechnologists, microbiologists, molecular biologists and biochemists.

Government labs such as CDRI in Lucknow are constantly employing research workers/scientists. The private sector placements are in both technical and managerial positions. The management

management. In academics, biotechnologists (Doctorates) can work in departments of marine biotech, biomedicine, earth sciences, biomedical engineering, agricultural and environmental biotechnology, etc.

Industries employing biotechnologists: Hindustan Lever, Thapar group, Indo American Hybrid Seeds, Bincon India Limited, Bivcol, IDPL, Indian Vaccines Corporation, Hindustan Antibiotics, Sun Pharma, Cadila, etc.

Laboratories and Institutes employing Biotechnologists: The Centre for Cellular and Molecular Biology, National Botanical Institute, National chemical laboratory, Tata Energy Research Institute, Central Aromatic, Plants Institute, Indian Institute of Science, Agricultural Research Institute, CSIR, National Environment Research Institute-Nagpur, National Institute of Immunology-New Delhi, CDRI- Lucknow, IIT-Mumbai, Delhi.

Q.12   Where and how can one take a Master Degree course in Biotechnology?

Ans:

1985. Since 1985, it was running as the Special Centre for Biotechnology (CBT) under the joint sponsorship of the University Grants Commission (UGC) and the Department of Biotechnology (DBT), Ministry of Science & Technology, Govt. of India. To begin with, it was started to initiate Biotechnology education programme with an impetus to generate a workforce that could turn into a substantially trained pool to meet the country's demands. Considering the growth of Biotechnology at an international level, its applications in general spheres of life and the

Council of JNU resolved to elevate the status of the Special Centre for Biotechnology to that of a School of Biotechnology (SBT) in 2006. Over the years, Biotechnology programme at JNU has established itself as a leading academic programme both from the teaching and research point of view. The faculty of the School is internationally recognised for their contribution to basic and applied aspects of Biotechnology research.

JNU conducts a Combined Entrance Examination for admission to 2-Year M.Sc. Programme in Biotechnology on behalf of following participating Universities. The Entrance Examination is held during the month of May at centres all over the country.

1. University of Allahabad, Allahabad
2. Annamalai University, Tamil Nadu
3. Banaras Hindu University, Varanasi
4. University of Burdwan, Burdwan

6. Devi Ahilya Vishwavidyalaya, Indore
7. Goa University, Goa
8. Gulbarga University, Gulbarga
9. Guru Jambheshwar University of Science & Technology, Hisar
10. Guru Nanak Dev University, Amritsar
11. Himachal Pradesh University, Shimla
12. HNB Garhwal University, Garhwal
13. University of Hyderabad, Hyderabad
14. University of Jammu, Jammu
15. Jawaharlal Nehru University, New Delhi

17. University of Lucknow, Lucknow

19. M.S. University of Baroda, Vadodara
20. University of Mysore, Mysore
21. University of North Bengal, Siliguri
22. Pondicherry University, Pondicherry
23. University of Pune, Pune
24. R.T.M. Nagpur University, Nagpur
25. Sardar Patel University, Gujarat
26. Tezpur University, Tezpur (Assam)
27. T.M. Bhagalpur University, Bhagalpur
28. Utkal University, Bhubaneswar
29. Veer Bahadur Singh Purvanchal University, Jaunpur
30. Visva-Bharati University, Santiniketan

Q.13 What is Department of Biotechnology or DBT?

Ans: The setting up of a separate Department of Biotechnology (DBT-www.dbtindia.nic.in), under the Ministry of Science and Technology in 1986 gave a new impetus to the development of the

the department has promoted and accelerated the pace of development of biotechnology in the country. Through several R&D projects, demonstrations and creation of infrastructural

achievements in the growth and application of biotechnology in the broad areas of agriculture, healthcare, animal sciences, environment, and so on.

The impact of the biotechnology related developments in Agriculture, Healthcare, Environment and Industry, has already been visible and the efforts are now culminating into products and processes. More than 5000 research publications, 4000 post-doctoral students, several technologies transferred

Department of Biotechnology (DBT) has been interacting with more than 5,000 scientists per year in order to utilise the existing expertise of the universities and other national laboratories.

A very strong peer review and monitoring mechanism has been developed. There has been close interaction with the State Governments particularly through State S & T Councils for developing biotechnology application projects, demonstration of proven technologies, and training of human resource in States and Union Territories.

Programmes with the states of Gujarat, Rajasthan, Madhya Pradesh, Orissa, West Bengal,

evolved. Biotechnology Application Centres in Madhya Pradesh and West Bengal have already

community of the country through a number of technical task forces, advisory committees and

programmes and activities.

areas of modern biology and biotechnology has given rich dividends. The proven technologies at

technology transfer to industries and close interaction with them have given a new direction to biotechnology research. Initiatives have been taken to promote transgenic research in plants with emphasis on pest and disease resistance, nutritional quality, silk-worm genome analysis, molecular biology of human genetic disorders, brain research, plant genome research, development, validation and commercialisation of diagnostic kits and vaccines for communicable diseases, food biotechnology, biodiversity conservation and bio-prospecting, setting up of micro-propagation parks and biotechnology based development for SC/ST, rural areas, women and for different States.

Necessary guidelines for transgenic plants, recombinant vaccines and drugs have also been

in terms of new innovations and applications would form a major research and commercial endeavour for socio-economic development in the next millennium.

Q. 14   What is BTIS?

Ans: Biotechnology Information System (BTIS) is a National Bioinformatics Network.

Implementation of Biogrid of India: Research in biotechnology, which is highly knowledge and capital intensive area, has generated a deluge of information in this decade. To make use of this information effectively there is a need for high speed and large bandwidth network. Towards this end, the Department has successfully established a high-speed and high-bandwidth network in the form of Virtual Public Network (VPN) named as BIOGRID INDIA. Eleven nodes have been

resource development and R&D in bioinformatics, dissemination of biotechnology information to researchers in the country. The nodes are interconnected through 2mbps dedicated leased circuit line at each location and 4Mbps Internet bandwidth shared from the central server by all the nodes. The BIOGRID allows exchange of database and softwares which have been created/ acquired by the individual centres/nodes of BTIS.

This resource-sharing helps in enhancing the value and usefulness of the BTIS — the only true resource sharing network in India. The Department of Biotechnology, Government of India, is also supporting long-term teaching programmes on bioinformatics. Therefore BIOGRID will be useful in sharing teaching materials; to deliver lectures through video conferencing-virtual classrooms besides synergising research in biotechnology and bioinformatics.

In the second and third phase, the remaining centres and DBT institutions are envisaged to be covered under the faster network. The mirror sites of internationally recognised genomic databases such as GDB, Protein Data Bank (PDB), Plant Genome Data Banks, Databases of European Bioinformatics institute (EBI) and public domain bioinformatics software packages are also available on the BIOGRID. The advantage of mirroring these databases in India is to provide unhindered mining of high quality data from well-established primary and secondary information sources. Commercial softwares essential to carry out research and training in bioinformatics will also be made available through BIOGRID. The network will act as a knowledge pathway for discoveries in biotechnology and bioinformatics.

Development of Databases/Resource Directories:
are currently available on the BTISnet. Each centre is responsible for developing a database

For example, a major database on animal viruses developed by the centre at University of Pune has been recognised by the Microbial Strain Data Network, CODATA, a Committee of International Council of Sciences on Data for Science & Technology and other international bodies.

Strengthening of Biocomputing Facilities: A national facility has been established at IIT Delhi towards the development of In-silico drug development using bioinformatics applications. The Facility was dedicated to the nation by then Minister for S&T, Prof. Murli Manohar Joshi. During this occasion, the software of gene to drug developed by IIT Delhi was released by then MoS for S&T Bachi Singh Rawat. The facility is being networked through Biogrid India to use the computer power and softwares at IIT Delhi by the Biogrid nodes remotely.

R&D Activities: The bioinformatics centres are being extensively used for intensive research by the hosts and neighbouring institutions. The acknowledgements to BTIS centres in more than 500 research articles published in high quality peer reviewed journals points out the usefulness of this activity. In addition, scientists at bioinformatics centres have carried out research in gene analysis, protein structure prediction and engineering, modelling, macromolecular assembly, evolutionary biology developing tools for peptide vaccine, metabolic pathways engineering, new tools for data mining, etc.

International Cooperation: Cooperation with India has been sought by several countries in this a UNDP/FAO/UNIDO sponsored initiative, a referral centre has been set up as part of the Apex Bioinformatics centre in DBT to maintain regional information on various aspects of the FARM programme, viz., Farming systems, Watershed Management, Agro-forestry, Integrated Pest Management, Safe Pesticides, Biotechnology & Biodiversity and People's Participation. Through the initiatives of DBT, network connectivity had been established at national focal points in China, India, Indonesia, Philippines, Thailand and Vietnam. DBT also coordinated a meeting of

biotechnology amongst the SAARC member-countries. Another international cooperation with Weizmann Institute of Science (WIS), Israel has been initiated as part of international cooperation in Bioinformatics sponsored by UNESCO. Under this programme, India will host a regional node in Bioinformatics along with other regional nodes proposed in China, Poland and Turkey.

node in bioinformatics with particular emphasis to extend the regional cooperation to the SAARC countries. Cooperation on bioinformatics with Govt. of Malaysia has recently been approved and the same with Maldives is under active consideration.

Training/Workshops/Long term courses in Bioinformatics: A number of workshops and training programmes were conducted on the use of computers and databanks in modern biology and biotechnology. Considering the importance of the subject, some institutions and university Departments have introduced Bioinformatics course in their existing Post-graduate programmes in Biotechnology. DBT has introduced a long-term academic course in Bioinformatics leading to

and Pondicherry University, Pondicherry. There had been a sudden increase in the demand of such professionals by small size gene-hunting companies. Many of the larger pharmaceutical companies are now seeing real value in gene mapping and sequence data and have started attracting experts from academia. In light of these developments, the efforts started by DBT are likely to be rewarding towards generation of employment opportunities.

Q.15 Where can one study B.E./B.Tech in Biotechnology?

Ans: Some of the institutions offering B.E./B.Tech in Biotechnology in India are:

01. Anna University, Chennai
02. Acharya Institute of Technology, Solladevanahalli, Chikkabanawara Post, Bangalore North, PIN: 560090

04. Anil Neeruknoda Institute of Science & Technology Sangivalasa, Bheemunipatnam, Visakhapatnam Dist. (AP)
05. Al-Ameer College of Engineering & Technology Gudilova, Anandapuram (M), Visakhapatnam (AP)
06. Audhishankara College of Engineering & Technology Vindhur, Gudur, Nellore Dist. (AP)
07. Bapuji Institute of Engineering & Technology, Shamnur Road, Davangere-577004

09. Bapatla Engineering College G.B.C Road, Bapatla, Guntur Dist. (AP) Ph : 08643-224244

15. Godavari Institute of Engineering & Technology Chaitanya Nagar, NH-5, Rajahmundry. (AP)
16. Gandhi Institute of Technology & Management (GITAM) Gandhi Nagar, Rushikonda, Visakhapatnam. (AP)
17. Gokaraju RangaRaju College of Engineering & Technology Bachupally, Miyapur, R.R. Dist. (AP)

19. Joginpally B.R. Engineering College Yenkapally, Moinabad, R.R. Dist. (AP)

22. MITS, 85 New Colony, Rayagada-765001, Orissa
23. MS Ramaiah Institute of Technology, MSR Nagar, Bangalore-560054

25. Madanapally Institute of Technology & Science Angallu, Madanapally, Chittoor Dist. (AP)
26. Mallareddy Engineering College Gundla Pochampally, Medchal, R.R. Dist. (AP)
27. Nagarjuna College of Engineering & Technology Hosahalli Village, Vijayapura, Hobli Bangalore-562110
28. New Horizon College of Engineering Varthur, Hobli, Bangalore-560087

30. PA College of Engineering, Banktwal Taluk, Mangalore-574153

32. RV College of Engineering, Mysore Road, Bangalore-560059
33. Sapathagiri College of Engineering, Hesaraghatta Main Road, Bangalore-560057
34. Shri BVV Sangha's Basaveshwar Engineering College, Nijalingappa Road, Bagalkot-587102
35. Shri Devi Institute of Engineering. & Technology, Maralenahally, Sira Road, Tumkur-572106
36. Sri Jayachamarajendra College of Engineering, Manasagangothri, Mysore-570006
37. Sri Indu College of Engineering & Technology Ibrahimpatnam, R.R. Dist. (AP)
38. St. Martins Engineering College Dhoolapally, via Hakimpet, Secunderabad. (AP)
39. Srinidhi Institute of Science & Technology Yamnampet, Ghatkesar, R.R. Dist. (AP)
40. Sri Vidya Niketan College of Engineering Sree Sai Nagar, Rangampet, Tirupathi, Chittoor Dist. (AP)
41. The Oxford College of Engineering, Hosur Road, Bangalore-560068

43. Vagdevi College of Engineering Bollikunta, Warangal.
44. Vellore Institute of Technology, Vellore-632014 (Tamil Nadu)
45. University Institute of Engineering & Technology, Sector-14, Punjab University, Chandigarh
46. Govt. Engineering College, Raipur Chhattisgarh-492 010
47. Raipur Institute of Technology S. South Avenue, Choubey Colony, Raipur, Chhattisgarh-492 001
48. Delhi College of Engineering, Shahbad-Daulatpur, Bawana Road, Delhi-110042
49. Netaji Subash Institute of Technology, Ajad Hind Fauj Marg, Sector-3, Dwarka, New Delhi-110045

Rajkot-360 005, Gujrat
51. Ambala College of Engineering & Applied Research, Devsthali, Ambala-Jagadhari Highway, Po-Sambhalkha, Ambala, Haryana-133101
52. Career Institue of Technology & Management, Sector-43, Aravalli Hills, Surajkund-Bhadkal Road, Faridabad, Haryana-121001
53. C.R.State College of Engineering, Murthal, Sonepat, Haryana-131039
54. N.C. College of Engineering, Balana, Israna, Distt. Panipat, Haryana-132107
55. Birla Institute of Technology, Mesra, Ranchi-835 215

57. Mohandas College of Engineering & Technology, Anad Village, Nedumangad,

59. Sree Buddha College of Engineering, Pattoor P.O., Padanilam, Noornad, Alappuzha Dist.-

60. Sree Chitra Thirunal College of Engineering, Pappanamcode, Thiruvananthapuram-695 018

005

Datia-475 661, Madhya Pradesh

234

65. Thadomal Shahni Engineering College, 32nd Road, T.P.S.-Iii,, Bandra, Mumbai-50

Rayagada

Rayagada, Orissa-765001
68. Shri Rajiv Gandhi Institute of Technology, R.S. No. 25,26&27, Pondy - Cuddalore East Coast

69. Shaheed Udham Singh College of Engineering & Technology, Tangori, Mohali

70. Thapar Institute of Engineering & Technology, Bhadson Road, Patiala

Rajasthan-303905
72. Maharishi Arvind Institute of Engineering & Technology, Sector-7, Madhyam Marg, Mansrovar, Rajasthan

Tehsil-Sangarner, Jagartpura, Rajasthan-302017

Tehsil-Sangarner, Jagartpura, Rajasthan-302017
75. Sobhasaria Engineering College, Gram-Gokulpura,, Sikar, Rajasthan-332001

Village, Mannargudi Taluk, Tiruvarur Dist., Tamil Nadu
77. Adhiyamaan College of Engineering, Dr. Mgr Nagar, Hosur, Pin-635 125, Dharmapuri Dist., Tamil Nadu

Virudhunagar Dist., Tamil Nadu
79. Arunai Engineering College, Mathur, Tiruvannamalai, Pin-606 603, Tiruvannamalai Dist., Tamil Nadu

Sathyamangalam, Pin-638 401, Coimbatore Dist., Tamil Nadu
81. Bharathidasan Institute of Engineering & Technology, Bharathidasan University, Tiruchirapalli Dist., Tamil Nadu
82. G.G.R. College of Engineering, Perumugai, Chennai-Bangalore High Way, Vellore, Pin-632 004, Tami Nadu
83. Jeppiar Engineering College, Jeppiaar Nagar, Old Mammallapuram Road, Chennai, Pin-600 119

Pin - 637 209, Tamil Nadu

CampusS.P.G.C. Nagar, Virudhunagar, Pin-626 011, Madurai Dist., Tamil Nadu

89. Mepco Schlenk Engineering College, Amathur Post, Sivakasi, Pin-626 005, Tamil Nadu
90. National Institute of Technology, Tiruchirapalli, Pin-620 015, Tamil Nadu
91. P.S.G. College of Technology, Peelamedu, Coimbatore, Pin-641 004, Tamil Nadu
92. P.S.R. Engineering College, Appayanaickenpatty, Sevalpatty, Sivakasi, Pin-626 140, Tamil Nadu
93. Periyar Maniammai College of Technology For Women, Periyar Nagar, Vallam, Thanjavur, Pin-613 403, Tamil Nadu
94. Prathyusha Engineering College, Aranavayal, Pin-602 025, Thiruvallur Dist., Tamil Nadu

95. Rajalakshmi Engineering College, Rajalakshmi Nagar, Thandalam, Chennai, Pin-602105, Tamil Nadu
96. Shri Andal Alagar College of Engineering, No.6, Namandur Village, Gst Road,
97. Sree Sastha Institute of Engineering & Technology, Chembarambakkam, Pin-602 103, Thiruvallur Dist., Tamil Nadu
98. Sri Nandanam College of Engineering & Technology, Molagarampatti, Tirupattur, Pin-635 601, Vellore Dist. Tamil Nadu
99. Sri Venkateswara College of Engineering, P.B.No.3, Pennalur, Sriperumbudur, Pin-602 105

100. St. Joseph's College of Engineering, Jeppiaar Nagar, Old Mamallapuram Road, Chennai-600 096, Tamil Nadu

    Pin-630 551, Sivagangai Dist., Tamil Nadu
102. St. Peter's Engineering College, Avadi, Chennai-600 054, Thiruvallur Dist., Tamil Nadu

    Tamil Nadu

    Vellore Dist., Tamil Nadu
105. Vivekananda College of Engineering For Women, Elayampalayam, Tiruchengodu, Pin-637 205, Namakkal Dist., Tamil Nadu
106. College of Engineering Technology, Lodhipur Rajput, Delhi Road, Moradabad-244 001
107. College of Engineering & Technology, LILM Academy For Higher LILM Academy For Higher

    Budhnagar
108. Faculty of Engineering & Technology, Raja Balwant Singh College, Bichpuri, Agra-283 105
109. IMS Engineering College, Nh-24, Delhi-Hapur Byepass Road, Adhyatmik Nagar, Ghaziabad-201 009
110. Motilal Nehru National Institute of Technology, Teilarganj, Allahabad-211 004
111. Meerut Institute of Engineering & Technology, Baghpat Road Bypass Crossing, P.O.: Malyana, Meerut-250 002
112. S.D. College of Engineering & Technology, Sahawali, Jansath Road, Muzaffarnagar-251 001
113. Saroj Institute of Technology, Ahmamau, Arjunganj, Sultanpur Road, Lucknow-226 006
114. Haldia Institute of Technology, P.O. Hatiberia, Haldia, Pin-721657

116. Institute of Technology & Marine Engineering Vill-Jingha, P.O—Amira, P.S.Diamond Harbour, Dist Sought Pargana, West Bengal

Q.16 Where can one study Biotechnology course in Delhi?

Ans: Colleges/Institutes offering Biotechnology courses in Delhi are:

Degree / Course	College / Institute	Eligibility
BSc. Biochemistry	University of Delhi, Delhi — 11007	Class XII with Physics, Chemistry and Biology
BSc. Biochemistry	Shivaji College, University of Delhi, Delhi	Class XII with Physics, Chemistry and Biology
BSc. Biochemistry	Deshbandu College, University of Delhi, Delhi	Class XII with Physics, Chemistry and Biology
BSc. Biochemistry	Venkateshwara College, University of Delhi, Delhi	Class XII with Physics, Chemistry and Biology
BSc. Biochemistry	Daulat Ram College, University of Delhi, Delhi	Class XII with Physics, Chemistry and Biology
BSc. Biochemistry	Amity Institute of Biotechnology, RBEF, E-27, Defence colony, New Delhi — 110024	Class XII (50%) or equivalent with Biology as a subject
BSc. Biochemistry	Gargi College, University of Delhi	Class XII with Physics, Chemistry and Biology
BSc. Biochemistry	Institute of Home Economics, University of Delhi	Class XII with Physics, Chemistry and Biology
BSc. Biochemistry	Ram Lal Anand College, University of Delhi	Class XII with Physics, Chemistry and Biology
BSc. Biochemistry	Swami shradhanand College, University of Delhi	Class XII with Physics, Chemistry and Biology
BTech. Biotechnology	All India Institute of Medical Sciences, New Delhi	Class XII with Physics, Chemistry and Biology
MSc. Bioinformatics	Amity Institute of Biotechnology, RBEF, E-27, Defence Colony, New Delhi — 110024	BSc.
MSc. Biochemistry	University of Delhi, Delhi 110007	BSc.
MSc. Microbiology	University of Delhi, Delhi 110007	BSc.
MSc. Genetics	University of Delhi, Delhi 110007	BSc.
MSc. Biophysics	University of Delhi, Delhi 110007	BSc.
MSc. Plant Molecular Biology	University of Delhi, Delhi 110007	BSc.
MSc. Biotechnology	Jawaharlal Nehru University, New Mehrauli Road, New Delhi	BSc. in Physics/Biology/Agriculture/ Pharmacy/ Veterianary Science/ BE
MSc. Agricultural Biotechnology	Jawaharlal Nehru University, New Mehrauli Road, New Delhi	BSc. in Physics/Biology/Agriculture/ Pharmacy/Veteriinary Science/BE
MVSc. Animal Biotechnology	Jawaharlal Nehru University, New Mehrauli Road, New Delhi	BSc. in Physics/Biology/Agriculture/ Pharmacy/Veteriinary Science/BE
MTech. BioTechnology	Jawaharlal Nehru University, New Mehrauli Road, New Delhi	BSc. in Physics/Biology/Agriculture/ Pharmacy/Veteriinary Science/BE
MSc. Biotech Industrial Training	Jamia Hamdard University, Hamdard Nagar, New Delhi	BSc./BTech., MSc./Mtech. in Biotechnology
MSc. Biotech Industrial Training	Biotech Consortium India Ltd. G-6, NDSE Part-I,New Delhi	BSc./BTech., MSc./Mtech. in Biotechnology

MTech. Biotechnology	All India Institute of Medical Sciences, New Delhi	BSc./BTech.
MTech. (Integrated) Biotechnology	Indian Institute of Technology (IIT), New Delhi	Class XII with Physics, Chemistry and Mathematics
MTech. (Integrated) Biotechnology	Guru Gobind Singh Indraprastha University, New Delhi	Class XII with Science
PG Diploma in Bioinformatics	Jawaharlal Nehru University, New Mehrauli Road, New Delhi	BSc./BTech.
Ph.D Biotechnology	Jawaharlal Nehru University, New Mehrauli Road, New Delhi	Bachelor's in Beterinary and Fisheries Sciences
Post-Doctoral Research	Department of Biotechnology, Ministry of Science and Technology, New Delhi	MSc./MTech./Ph.D
Research (Ph.D)	All India Institute of Medical Sciences, New Delhi	MSc./MTech.

5

CIVIL SERVICES

Q.1   What is Civil Service?

Ans: Civil Services constitute all non-military departments of the government machinery, which run State Administration. The Central and the State Civil Servants ensure that the constitutional guarantees and entitlements are brought within the reach of every citizen. In the present era of market economy Civil Services has lost some of its sparkle, nonetheless it still ranks high as a career option among young students. The power and social status along with job security that a civil servant enjoys is unimaginable anywhere else. Besides the lure for power and perks the service provides enough scope for a dynamic person with zeal and desire to bring qualitative changes in the functioning of the government and even opportunities which could ameliorate the lives of millions of Indians.

bestowed with immense administrative powers and their main tasks were preservation of law and order, dispensation of justice and collection of taxes. However today civil servants operate within the framework of a democratic welfare state, with focus on development and progress. Therefore, unlike many other occupations civil service is more of a vocation than a job.

The Civil Services Examination conducted by the Union Public Service Commission (UPSC) selects candidates for various central services, including for the most coveted cadres of Indian Administrative Service (IAS), Indian Police Service (IPS) and Indian Foreign Service (IFS).

IAS and IPS are All India Services created under article 312 of the Constitution. The creation of such services provides safeguards for national unity and ensures uniformity of the administrative system throughout the country to maintain the minimum common administrative standards. Candidates selected for these two services are appointed to different state cadres and as and when required they also move to Central Government jobs on deputation. The remaining services are categorised in two Central Services, Group A, and Group B. The Group 'A' services are:

Indian Railway Accounts Services (IRAS)
Indian Railway Personnel Service (IRPS)
Indian Railway Protection Force (IRPF)
Indian Postal Service

Indian Audit & Accounts Service (IA &AS)

Indian Defense Accounts Service (IDAS)

Indian Civil Accounts Service (ICAS)

Indian Revenue Service (IRS)

The Indian Information Service (IIS)

Indian Ordnance Factories Service (IOFS)

Indian Defense Estate Service (IDES)

The Indian P &T Accounts & Finance Service

Assistant Commandants in Central Industrial Security Force

The Group B Services for which recruitment is made through civil services are the following:

Customs Appraisers' Service Group B

The Delhi, Andaman and Nicobar Islands, Lakshadweep, Daman & Diu and Dadra & Nagar Haveli Civil Service Group B

The Delhi, Andaman and Nicobar Islands, Lakshadweep, Daman & Diu and Dadra & Nagar Haveli Police Service Group B

Pondicherry Civil Service Group B

A graduate in any discipline from a recognised university or institution, between 21-28 years of age as on 1st August of the examination year, is eligible to sit for the Civil Services Examination.

The UPSC conducts the combined Civil Services Exam in three phases comprising preliminary exam, mains and interview or the personality test, and the entire cycle well over a year to complete. The

carries 150 marks. The second paper, called `optional' is on the subject chosen by the candidate and carries 300 marks. Preliminary examination basically eliminates all those who are not serious or well prepared. The success rate of preliminary exam is less than 10%.

Main exam is held around November/December every year and consists of eight papers of conventional type carrying 300 marks each. Two of these are language papers, one in English and the other in any recognised Indian language chosen by the candidate. Qualifying in both these papers is compulsory, however marks obtained in them is not added in the total score, in other

Third and the fourth papers are on general studies and carry 600 marks. The rest of the four papers are on two optional subjects, carrying total marks of 1200. Results of the Mains are declared by February/March and those who qualify make it to the third stage of the selection process, i.e.

the Personality Test. The interview or the personality test carries 250 marks and is held around April/May. Final results are declared by June and successful candidates are allotted different

also taken into account while allocation of service. Those who are at the top of the merit list get IAS, IPS, IFS and so on and so forth.

Q.2 Who can appear in Civil Services Examination and when it is conducted?
Ans:

Application Form for Civil Services (Mains) Examination. Age limit: 21-30 years as on 1st August of

of Examination: November/December of previous year; Conduct of Examination: May.

Q.3 What is the Scheme of Civil Services (Preliminary) Examination?
Ans: The Preliminary Examination consists of two papers of objective type (multiple-choice questions) carrying a maximum of 450 marks. The Question Papers (Test Booklets) are set in English & Hindi. Paper — I: General Studies, 150 Marks. Paper — II: One of the optional subjects to be selected from the prescribed optional subjects, 300 Marks.

Q.4 What subjects one can opt for preliminary examination?
Ans: Any one subject from: Agriculture, Mathematics, Animal Husbandry & Veterinary Science, Mechanical Engineering, Botany, Medical Science, Chemistry, Philosophy, Civil Engineering, Physics, Commerce, Political Science, Economics, Psychology, Electrical Engineering, Public Administration, Geography, Sociology, Geology, Statistics, Indian History, Zoology, Law.

Q.5 What is the scheme of Civil Services Final Examination?
Ans: **Paper-I:** One of the Indian Languages to be selected by the candidate from the 18 languages included in the VIIIth Schedule to the Constitution (Qualifying Paper), 300 Marks

Paper-II: English (Qualifying Paper) 300 Marks

Paper-III: Essay 200 Marks

Papers IV & V: General Studies (300 Marks for each paper) 600 Marks

Papers VI, VII, VIII & IX: Any two subjects (each having 2 papers) to be selected from the prescribed optional subjects (300 marks for each paper) 1200 Marks

Total Marks for Written Examination: 2000 Marks

Interview Test: 300 Marks

Grand Total: 2300 Marks

Q.6 What subject one can opt in the civil services final examination?
Ans: You can opt any one subject from: Agriculture, Management, Animal Husbandry & Veterinary Science, Mathematics, Anthropology, Mechanical Engineering, Botany, Medical Science, Chemistry, Philosophy, Civil Engineering, Physics, Commerce & Accountancy, Political Science & International

Relations, Economics, Psychology, Electrical Engineering, Public Administration, Geography, Sociology, Geology, Statistics, Indian History, Zoology, Law.

Q.7 What are the Optional Subjects (Literature) for Civil Services Main Examination?

Ans: The optional literature subjects are: Arabic, Gujarati, Manipuri, Sanskrit, Assamese, Hindi, Persian, Urdu, French, Marathi, Punjabi, German, Malayalam, and Russian.

Q.8 What books and periodicals one should read for general studies?

Ans:

Monorama Year Book
CSR Year Book
Hindustan Year Book
Yojana/planning commission reports
Civil services chronicle/civil service today
Employment News
Competition Success Review
India Today
Front Line
Business World
The Economic Times
The Hindu/The Times of India/The Hindustan Times

Q.9 What books one should study for opting History?

Ans: For Preliminary:

IGNOU Booklets on Indian History
R.S. Sharma: Ancient India (NCERT)
Satish Chandra: Medieavel India (NCERT)
Bipin Chandra: Modern India (NCERT)
D.N.Jha: An outline of Indian History

R.S.Sharma: Material Culture & Social Formation; Social & Economic Perspective in Ancient India
Romila Thapar: History of India, Vol-I
A.L.Basham: The Wonder that was India
Bipin Chandra: Freedom Struggle (NBT)
Sumit Sarkar: Modern India 1885-1947
Gazetter of India, Published by the Publication Division
S.A.A.Rizvi: The Wonder that was India, Vol-II

For Main Examination

Ancient History:

IGNOU Booklets of Ancient India
R.S.Sharma: Material Culture & Social Formation; Ancient India
Romila Thapar: Ashoka & Decline of Maurya; History of India, Vol-I
A.L.Basham: The Wonder that was India
Devbhuti: Harshvardhan

Medieval History:

IGNOU Booklets on Medieval India
Satish Chandra: Medieval India (NCERT)
S.A.A.Rizvi: The Wonder that was India, Vol-II
U.N.Dey: Some Aspects of Medieval Indian History

Modern History:

IGNOU Booklets on Modern India
Bipinchandra: India's Struggle for Independence
Sumit Sarkar: Modern India 1885-1947
B.L.Grover: Modern Indian History

World History:

L.Mukherji: A Study of European History (1453-1815); Europe since French Revolution
Ralph & Burns: World Civilisation

Q.10 What books one should study to opt for Sociology?

Ans: For Preliminary Examination:

T.B. Bottomore : Sociology
Francis Abraham & John Henry Morgan: Sociological Theory
M.Haralombos: Sociology-Themes & Perspective
MacIver & Page : Sociology
Alex Inkeles: What is Sociology?
M.N.Srinivas: India-Social Structure
Yogendra Singh: Modernisation of Indian Tradition
G.Duncan Mitchell: A New Dictionary of Society

IGNOU Booklets
Rao's Study Materials

For Main Examination:

Paper One:

T.B.Bottomore: Sociology (Blackie & Sons)

Francis Abraham & John Henry Morgan : Sociological Theory (Macmillan)

Anthony Giddens: Capitalism & Modern Social Theory-An Analysis of the Writings of Marx, Durkheim & Max Weber (Cambridge Univ Press)

M.Francis Abraham: Modern Sociological Theory – An Introduction (Oxford Univ Press)

M.Haralombos: Sociology-Themes & Perspective (Oxford University Press)

Paul B.Horton & Chester L.Hunt: Sociology (McGraw Hill)

Jonathan H.Turner: The Structure of Sociological Theory (Rawat, Jaipur)

Ales Inkeles: What is Sociology? An Introduction to the Discipline (Prentice Hall)

IGNOU Booklets

Rao's Study Materials

Paper Two:

(Manohar, Delhi); Social Change in India (Haranand)

S.C.Dubey: Understanding Change – Anthological & Sociological Perspectives (Vikas); Tradition & Development; Indian Society (NBT)

M.N.Srinivas: India-Social Structure (Hindustan, Delhi); Caste in Modern India & Other Essays (Media Promoters & Publishers, Mumbai)

Wilbert E. Moore: Social Change (Pentice Hall)

Rau's Study Material

IGNOU Booklets

Q.11   What books one should study to opt for Public Administration?

Ans:

S.R.Maheswari: Indian Administration; Public Administration

Prassad & Prassad: Administrative Thinkers

Mohit Bhattacharya: Public Administration

A.R.Tyagi: Principles of Public Administration

Padma Ramachandran: Public Administration In India

Journal of the Indian Institute of Public Administration (IIPA, New Delhi)

Ignou Booklets

For Main Examination:

Paper One:

A.Avasthi & S.Maheswari: Public Administration

Prasad & Prasad: Administrative Thinkers (Sterling)

Mohit Bhattacharya: Public Administration Structure, Process & Behaviour (World Press,

O.G.Sathl: Public, Personnel Administration (Oxford)

Paper Two:

D.D.Basu: Introduction to the Constitution of India
S.Maheswari: Indian Administration; Local Government in India (Orient Lomgman)

Journal of the Indian Institute of Public Administration
IGNOU Booklets

Q.12   What books one should study to opt for Geography?

Ans:

Physical Geography: R.N.Trikha
Physical Geography: Savinder Singh
Principles of Geography, VIL-I&II: NCERT
Human & Economic Geography: Leong & Morgan
Geographical Thought: Majid Hussain
Practical Geography: R.L.Singh
Practical Geography: NCERT
Human Geography: Majid Hussain
Population Geography: R.C.Chandana
World: A Regional Geography: L.D.Stanp
India — Economic & Commercial Geography (C.B.Memorial)
India: Gopal Singh
India — General Geography: NCERT
India — Resource & Regional Geography: NCERT
Urbanisation in India: Ram Chandran

Q.13   What books one should study to opt for Psychology?

Ans:

James C.Coleman: Abnormal Psychology & Modern Life (Foresman & Company)

(Tata McGraw Hill)

Ernest R.Hilgard, Richard C.Atkinson & Rita L.Atkinson: Introduction to Psychology (Oxford & IHB New Delhi)
Calvin S. Hall & Gardener Lindzey: Theories of Personality (Wiley Eastern)
David C.Mc Clelland: The Achieving Society (Feffer & Simons)

Durganand Sinha, R.C. Tripathi, Girishwar Mishra: Deprivation — Its Social Roots and Psychological Consequences (Concept Publishing Co.)

Robert A. Baron: Psychology (Pentice Hall)

Wood Worth & Sckoshberg: Experimental Psychology (Oxford & IHB)

Joseph B. Cooper & James L. Mc Gaugh: Integrating Principles of Social Psychology

Janak Pandey: Psychology in India — The State of the Art (Vol-I); Personality & Mental Processes (Vol-II); Basic & Applied Psychology (Vol-III); Organisational Behaviour & Mental Health (Sage, New Delhi)

Usha Alim Psychology (Study Centre, N. Delhi)

NCERT Books (Class-XI & XII)

Indian Journal of Psychology, Indian Psychological Review, Journal of Education & Psychology

Upsc Study Material for Psychology (Jawahar Publication, New Delhi)

Q.14   What books one should study to opt for Political Science?

Ans:

Introduction to Political Theory: O. P. Gauba

A Grammer of Politics: H. J. Laski

Substance of Politics: A. Appadorai

Political Theory: Ray & Bhattacharya

Political Though: C. L. Wayper

Introduction to the Indian Constitution: D. D. Basu

Theories of Development and Underdevelopment: Chilcote

Rao's Study Materials

Q.15   What other examinations are conducted by UPSC?

Ans: The following examinations are conducted by Union Public Service Commission (UPSC):

   (i)   Combined Medical Services Examination [CMS]
   (ii) National Defence Academy & Naval Academy Examination [NDA]
   (iii) Indian Forest Service Examination [IFS)
   (iv) Special Class Railway Apprentices Examination [SCRA]
   (v)   Geologists' Examination [GEOL]
   (vi) Combined Defence Services Examination [CDS]
   (vii) Indian Economic Service Examination [[ES]
   (viii) Indian Statistical Service Examination [ISS]
   (ix) Engineering Services Examination [ENGG]

Q.16   What is Indian Forest Service (IFS) and how can one become an IFS Officer?

Ans: The Indian Forest Service (IFS) is the Forestry service of India. It is one of the three All India Services of the Indian government, along with the Indian Administrative Service and Indian Police Service; its employees are recruited by the national government but serve under the state governments or Central Government. The Indian Forest Service was created in 1966 for protection, conservation, and regeneration of forest resources.

1864, the British Raj established the Imperial Forest Department. In 1866, Dr. Dietrich Brandis, a

was organised subordinate to the Imperial Forest Department in 1867. The British colonial government also constituted provincial forest services and executive and subordinate services similar to the forest administrative hierarchy used today.

The modern Indian Forest Service was established in the year 1966, after independence, under the

development of the IFS. India has an area of 635,400 square km designated as forests, about 19.32 percent of the country. India's forest policy was created in 1894 and revised in 1952 and again in 1988.

Recruitment to the Forest Service is made through the Indian Forest Service Examination conducted by UPSC annually. Entry is open to candidates who hold a Bachelor's degree with at least one of the subjects namely, Animal Husbandry & Veterinary Science, Botany, Chemistry, Geology, Mathematics, Physics, Statistics and Zoology or a Bachelor's degree in Agriculture or Forestry or Agricultural Engineering from a recognised University or equivalent and who are between the ages of 21 and 30 as on July 1 of the year of the examination. Upper age limits are less restrictive for scheduled castes and scheduled tribes and Other Backward Classes (SC/ST/OBC).

essay-based examination is conducted in July and is conducted in English. Each paper is of

optional science subjects from a list of 14 subjects, which includes among them four branches of engineering (Mechanical, Chemical, Civil, and Agricultural). The level required for the optional subjects is at least of the Honours degree level.

Candidates who qualify the written examination appear for an Interview, where they are questioned on academics; current affairs; basic knowledge of forest-related issues and policies and the status of their implementation; knowledge of the geographical features, forest cover, wildlife, and economic and cultural issues of one's community.

Selected candidates are sent for foundation training at the Lal Bahadur Shastri National Academy

Gandhi National Forest Academy at Dehradun, with training on forest and wildlife management, soil conservation, surveying, Scheduled Tribes, and handling weapons.

the state to which he or she is assigned. There is a probationary period of four years during

appointed to the Senior Time Scale and are entitled to be posted as the Deputy Conservators of

Ranks of the Indian Forest Service are as follows:

> Assistant Conservator of Forests
> Deputy Conservator of Forests
> Conservator of Forests (CFs)
> Chief Conservator of Forests (CCFs)
> Additional Principal Chief Conservator of Forests (Addl.PCCFs)
> Principal Chief Conservator of Forests (PCCF) — highest post in a State
> Director General of Forests — highest post at Centre, selected from amongst the senior-most PCCFs of states

Q.17 What is Combined Medical Services (CMS) Examination? What job one can get through Combined Medical Services Examination?

Ans: UPSC conducts Combined Medical Services (CMS) Examination every year to recruit medicos into a variety of central Government organisations and services such as the Indian Railways, Indian Ordnance Factories Health Services, Central Health Services, Municipal Corporation of Delhi and so on.

The combined medical services examination is conducted in the month of January in accordance with the Rules published by the Ministry of Health & Family Welfare (Department of Health) in the Gazette of India in August of every year.

The Examination is held for the recruitment to the following posts:

2. Assistant Divisional in Indian Ordnance Factories Health Service.
3. Junior Scale Posts in Central Health Services.

Eligibility Criteria: Eligibility Criteria for appearing in Combined Medical Services (CMS) Exam are as follows:

Age limits: Below 32 years as on 1st January of the year of Examination. The upper Age-limit

time.

such candidates who qualify the written part of the examination will be required to submit proof

rotating internship is also eligible for admission to the examination but on qualifying the written examination he will be appointed only after he has completed the compulsory rotating internship.

the form, an acknowledgement card and an envelope for sending the application is obtainable from any other agency. This form can be used only once and for only one examination. Candidates must use the form supplied with the Information Brochure only and they should in no case use photocopy/reproduction/unauthorised printed copy of the Form. Since this form is electronically

The examination is held generally in the month of June. Blank application forms and other particulars are published in the Employment News generally in the month of December of previous year. A candidate seeking admission must apply to The Secretary, Union Public Service Commission, Dholpur House, New Delhi-110011. Last date for the submission of applications is third week of February. Further details are available on the UPSC website: www.upsc.gov.in

Q.18   What is Special Class Railway Apprentice (SCRA)?

Ans: The SCRA scheme was started in 1927 by the British, to select a handful of most intelligent Indians to assist them in their Railway Operations, after training at their Railway's largest

were required to appear in the Mechanical Engineering Degree Examination held by Engineering Council (London).

been hotly contested, with as many as 1 to 1.5 lakh candidates taking the entrance examination, now conducted by UPSC, for about 10 seats. That translates into an astonishing ratio of 1 selection per 10,000 applicants. The scheme has continued to draw the country's best talent

Many of the Institute's alumni have won international accolade for having achieved excellence in their chosen careers, which include inventors, academicians, entrepreneurs, and high-ranking

The examination comprises written test in Mathematics, Physics, Chemistry, English Language,

for an interview, which is followed by a medical examination. The standard of syllabus is that of Class XII (CBSE equivalent).

The notice for the SCRA entrance examination, along with form and syllabus, is brought out by the UPSC around the months of June-July. According to the new rules issued by the Ministry of Railways, the exam is now conducted once in every two years.

The selected candidates undergo a four-year rigorous training programme in Mechanical Engineering, for which the Institute has a Memorandum of Understanding with BIT, Mesra, Ranchi. The semester system of BIT, Mesra is followed, with workshop training sessions during the holidays at BIT, Mesra.

privelege passes and PTOs.

After successful completion of four years of training, the candidates join as Indian Railway

satisfying career.

Q.19 What is Geologists Examination?

Ans: UPSC holds a competitive Examination named Geologists Examination for recruitment to the posts of:

Category I (i) Geologist (Junior), Group A (ii) Assistant Geologist, Group B in the Geological Survey of India.

Category II (i) Jr. Hydrogeologist, Group A (ii) Assistant Hydrogeologist, Group B in the Central Ground Water Board (CGWB) at selected centres in India.

Candidates selected under category I are appointed on probation for two years. During this period they have to undergo training and pass test or examination prescribed by the competent authority. Candidates under category II are also appointed on probation for two years.

Educational requirement: Master's degree in Geology or Applied Geology or Marine Geology or Mineral Exploration or Hydrology from a recognised University, or Diploma of Associate ship in Applied Geology of Indian School of Mines, Dhanbad or Master's degree in Mineral Exploration or Master's degree in Hydrogeology. Age: 21-32 years on January 1 of the year of examination.

Plan of Examination: The examination shall be conducted according to the following Plan:

Part I - Written examination

Part II - Interview

Written examination: Subjects of written examination and marks allotted to each is as follows:

Sl. no	Subjects	Marks
1	General English	100
2	Geology Paper I	200
3	Geology Paper II	200
4	Geology Paper III	150
5	Hydrogeology	150

subjects mentioned above. Candidates competing for posts under category I only need to appear in subjects at (1) to (4) above and candidates competing for posts under category II only will be required to appear in subject (1), (2), (3) and (5) above. The Examination in all the subjects will be of conventional (Essay) type. The Question Papers are set in English only. The standard of the paper in General English will be such as maybe expected of a science graduate. The papers on geological subjects will be approximately of the M.Sc. degree standard of an Indian University and questions will generally be set to test the candidate's grasp of the fundamentals in each subject.

Interview: The object of the interview is to assess his suitability for the posts for which he has competed. Special attention will be paid in the Personality Test to assess the candidate's capacity for leadership, initiative and intellectual curiosity, tact and other social qualities, mental and physical energy, powers of practical application, integrity of character and aptitude for adapting

Q.20   What is Indian Economic Service (IES) and Indian Statistical Service (ISS) Exam?

Ans: Indian Economic/Statistical Services Exam is conducted by the Union Public Service

Service (IES). Indian Economic/Statistical Services Exam is generally conducted in the month of November. Out of several careers offered by the Government Sector, Indian Economic/Statistical Service offers a very attractive opening to graduates in Economics and Statistics. Selected candidates are placed in the planning commission, planning board, ministry of economic affairs,

required.

Indian Economic Service (IES) is Central Government Services, which is involved in economic planning and analysis through state boards, planning commission and other government owned bodies in the country. Out of several careers offered by the Government Sector, it is an attractive opening to post-graduates in Economics. Selected candidates are placed in the Planning Commission, Labour Bureau, Central Electricity Authority, Economic Advisers to many ministries, Forward Market Commission, Tariff Commission, Planning Board, National sample

highly specialised service where the appointees are giving critical inputs in the policy making

agencies of the United Nations (UN).

A candidate for Indian Economic Service must have obtained a degree with Economics or Statistics as a subject and a candidate for the Indian Statistical Service must have a degree with Statistics or Mathematics or Economics as a subject from any of the Universities incorporated by an Act of the Central or State Legislature in India or other educational institutions established by an Act of Parliament or declared to be deemed as Universities under Section 3 of the Universities Grant

age of 21 years and must not have attained the age of 28 years on the 1st January of the year of examination. The upper age limit may be relaxed in respect of the Scheduled Castes, Scheduled Tribes, Other Backward Classes and such other categories of persons as may from time to time

The subjects of written examination for IES are as follows. Viva voce of such candidates as may be called by the Commission, carrying a maximum of 200 marks.

Sl. No.	Subject	Max. Marks
1	General English	100
2	General Studies	100
3	General Economics- I	200
4	General Economics- II	200
5	General Economics-III	200
6	Indian Economics	200

The subjects for ISS written examination are as follows:

1	General English	100
2	General Studies	100
3	Statistics- I	200
4	Statistics- II	200
5	Statistics- III	200
6	Statistics-IV	200

Q.21 What is Engineering Services Examination and who can appear in it?

Ans: The Combined Engineering Services Examination is conducted by UPSC every year for recruitment to the four categories of Engineering services:

(a) Civil Engineering

(b) Mechanical Engineering

(c) Electrical Engineering

(d) Electronics & telecommunication Engineering.

The following are the services/posts to which selection is made in the four categories:

Category I – Civil Engineering (Services/Posts):

(i) Indian Railway Service of Engineers

(ii) Indian Railway Stores Service (Civil Engineering Posts)

(iii) Central Engineering Service

(iv) Military Engineer Services (IDSE – Building and Roads Cadre)

(v) Military Engineer Service (Surveyor of Works Cadre)

(vi) Survey of India Service, Group 'A' (Civil Engineering Posts)

(vii) Central Water Engineering Service (Civil Engineering Posts)

(viii) Assistant Executive Engineer (Civil) in P & T Building Works (Group `A') Service

(ix) Central Engineering Service (Roads), Group `A'

(x) Assistant Executive Engineer (Civil) in Border Roads Engineering Service Group `A'

(xi) Indian Ordnance Factories Service (Engineering Branch)

(Civil Engineering Posts).

Category II – Mechanical Engineering (Services/Posts):

(i) Indian Railway Service of Mechanical Engineers

(ii) Indian Railway Stores Service (Mechanical Engineering Posts)

(iii) Central Water Engineering Service (Mechanical Engineering Posts)

(iv) Central Power Engineering Service (Mechanical Engineering Posts)

(v) Indian Ordnance Factories Service (Engineering Branch) (Mechanical Engineering Posts)

(vi) Indian Naval Armament Service (Mechanical Engineering Posts)

(vii) Military Engineer Service (IDSE — Electrical and Mechanical Cadre) (Mechanical Engineering Posts)

(viii) Central Electrical & Mechanical Engineering Service (Mechanical Engineering Posts)

(ix) Assistant Executive Engineer (Elect. & Mech.) (Mechanical Engineering Posts) Border Roads Engineering Service, Group 'A'

(x) Assistant Manager (Factories). Department of Telecom (Telecom Factories Organisation)

(xi) Central Engineering Service (Roads) Group `A' (Mechanical Engineering Posts)

(xii) Assistant Executive Engineer Group `A' (Mechanical Engineering Posts) in the Corps of E.M.E., Ministry of Defence

(xiii) Indian Inspection Service Group 'A' (Mechanical Engineering Posts)

(xiv) Indian Supply Service Group' A' (Mechanical Engg. Posts). Group `B' Services/Posts

(xv) Assistant Engineer Group 'B' (Mechanical Engineering Posts) in the Corps of E.M.E., Ministry of Defence.

Category III — Electrical Engineering (Services/Posts):

(i) Indian Railway Service of Electrical Engineers

(ii) Indian Railway Stores Service (Electrical Engineering Posts)

(iii) Central Electrical & Mechanical Engineering Service (Electrical Engineering Posts)

(iv) Indian Ordnance Factories Service (Engineering Branch) (Electrical Engineering Posts)

(v) Indian Naval Armament Service (Electrical Engineering Posts)

(vi) Central Power Engineering Service (Electrical Engineering Posts)

(vii) Assistant Executive Engineer (Electrical) in P &T Building Works (Group 'A') Service

(viii) Military Engineering Service (IDSE — Electrical and Mechanical Cadre) (Electrical Engineering Posts)

(ix) Assistant Manager (Factories), Department of Telecom (Telecom Factories Organisation)

(x) Assistant Executive Engineer Group `A' (Electrical Engineering Posts) in the Corps of E.M.E., Ministry of Defence

(xi) Indian Inspection Service Group 'A' (Electrical Engineering Posts)

(xii) Indian Supply Service Group `A' (Electrical Engg. Posts). Group `B' Services/Posts

(xiii) Assistant Engineer, Group `B' (Electrical Engineering Posts) in the Corps of E.M.E., Ministry of Defence.

Category IV — Electronics and Telecommunication Engineering (Services/Posts):

(i) Indian Railway Service of Signal Engineers

(ii) Indian Railway Stores Service (Telecommunication/ Electronics Engineering Posts)

(iii) Indian Telecommunication Service

(iv) Engineer in Wireless Planning and Coordination Wing/ Monitoring Organisation; Ministry of Communications (Deptt. of Telecommunications)

(v) Indian Broadcasting (Engineers) Service

(vi) Indian Ordnance Factories Service (Engineering Branch) (Electronics Engineering Posts)

(vii) Indian Naval Armament Service (Electronics Engineering Posts)

(viii) Central Power Engineering Service (Telecommunication Engineering Posts)

(ix) Survey of India Service Group 'A' (Electronics and Telecom. Engineering Posts)

(x) Assistant Manager (Factories), Deptt. of Telecom (Telecom Factories Organisation)

(xi) Indian Inspection Service, Group `A' (Electronics Engineering Posts)

(xii) Indian Supply Service; Group `A' (Electronics Engineering Posts)

(xiii) Assistant Executive Engineer Group 'A' (Electronics Engineering Posts) in the Corps of E.M.E., Ministry of Defence.

(xiv) Assistant Engineer Group 'B' (Electronics Engineering Posts) in the Corps of E.M.E., Ministry of Defence.

The IES paper is divided into two sections. The candidates have to qualify in the written examination followed by a Personality test. The written examination is again divided into three

200 marks. The second part will be a paper on Relevant Trade. It consists of two papers. The duration of each paper is 60 minutes. It carries 200 marks each. The third one is the conventional paper having two parts. It again carries 200 marks. The duration for each paper is 180 minutes.

crack. Those who wish to qualify should start their preparation at the earliest. The portions to be covered are very large. It requires a lot of time and a very calm mind to prepare for the test. One of the methods would be to prepare a timetable and follow it accordingly. Another method would be to join an entrance coaching centre. It will be very helpful as these centres will focus on the portions very well and prepare the students to face the entrance. But one should also put in a lot of hard work from his/her side to qualify for the exam. Revising the daily portions is a very good method to memorise the important points. Students can also practice previous years

be called for a personal interview. This interview carries 200 marks.

Age: A candidate must have attained the age of 21 years and must not have attained the age of

age may be relaxed in respect of Scheduled Castes, Scheduled Tribes, Other Backward Classes

The upper age is also relaxable up to 35 years for departmental candidates.

(i) Degree in Engineering from a University or

(ii) Pass in A and B of the Institution Examinations of the Institution of Engineers (India); or

(iii) Degree/diploma in Engineering from such foreign University/College/Institution or

(iv) Pass in Graduate Membership Examination of the Institute of Electronics and Telecommunications Engineers (India); or

(v) Pass in Associate Membership Examination Part II and III/Sections A and B of the Aeronautical Society of India or

(vi) Pass in Associate Membership Examination (Sections A and B) of the Institution of Mechanical Engineers (India) or

(vii) Pass in Graduate Membership Examination of the Institution of Electronics and Radio Engineers, London held after November, 1959; Provided that a candidate for the posts of Engineer, Group 'A', in Wireless Planning and Coordination Wing/Monitoring Organisation, Ministry of Communications, Indian Broadcasting (Engineers) Service and Indian Naval

Communication, Electronics, Radio Physics or Radio Engineering as a special subject.

6

CIVIL AVIATION

Q.1   What is Civil Aviation?

Ans: Aviation refers to all activities involving the operation of Aircraft. Aviation courses in India deal with Flying Operation (jobs performed by Pilots), Aircrew (such as Air Hostesses), Aircraft,

economics of airport. Civil Aviation courses (as opposed to the Indian Air Force, i.e. the air wing of the Indian armed forces) are necessary for those wishing to work in government or regulatory bodies of aviation or those planning to work as aviation consultants. All aviation courses in India are supposed to comply with the rules laid down by the Director General of Civil Aviation (DGCA). Careers in the aviation industry are much sought after as they are very well paid. Not too many people go in for careers in aviation as the courses are very expensive. However, those who can

the course.

Q.2   What is the nature of work in aviation industry and what should be the personality of a student joining the aviation industry?

Ans: The nature of work is different for different types of workers in the aviation industry. Whereas being a pilot or an air hostess is most advertised, there are other equally lucrative career options in the aviation industry. The aviation courses focus on some aspects of the work such as

marketing and management, transportation of perishable cargo, ticket reservation, regulation

instruction, cockpit resource management, federal regulation and the federal laws on aviation,

The nature of the work, entails, persons occupying posts such as pilot, air hospitality attendants

faced by air hospitality attendants is that the passengers misbehave with them. Air hospitality attendants need to have a strong personality to deal with such problems in a strong manner and rebuke the passengers without becoming excessively rude. As for the technical staff and for almost all jobs in the aviation sector, one must be able to work at different times of the day. One may have to work night shifts and sometimes spend more than 24 hours without sleep. Pilots,

as there is a lot of minute observation and immediate response required in such technical posts and these are also positions of great responsibility as the lives of the passengers depends on the proper functioning of the air plane which is ensured by the minute and thorough work of those involved in such work.

Q.3 What jobs are available in the Aviation Industry?

Ans: The following jobs are available in the aviation industry (the list is indicative only):

Aero Engineer	Executive Positions	Operations
Aerodynamics	Fabricator	Other
	Finance	Painters
Aircraft Interiors	Fitters	Paint sprayers
Aircraft Mechanics	Flight Simulator	Pilots
Airline Customer Service	Freight	PR
Airline Management	Graduate	Quality and Safety
	Helicopter Pilot	Research
Airport Baggage	Hotel	Rotary
Airport	Human Resources	Sales and Purchasing
Airworthiness Engineer	Instructors	Security
Apprentice	IT	Sheet Metal Worker
Aviation Design	Landing Gear	Software Systems
Aviation Materials	Logistics	Space
Aviation Planning	Machinist	Technical Author
Aviation Welding	Maintenance Base	Technician
Avionics Electronics	Maintenance Line	Testing
Cabin Crew	Management	Tooling
Communication	Manufacturing	Training
Composites	Marketing	Trimmers
Electrician		VVIP

Q.4 What are the Educational qualifications/trainings required to enter the aviation industry?

Ans:

Flight Attendant Courses
Commercial Pilot training
Aircraft Maintenance

Air hostess Courses
Ticketing and Travel in Aviation
Aviation Safety

Operations and Research
Cargo Management
Avionics

Civil Aviation courses offer technical, theoretical and practical knowledge about aircraft components and their maintenance. Training is given to students with real time controllable devices that are used in Aircraft to utilise their knowledge in a more practical way.

Q.5 Which are the jobs in the Government sector in Civil Aviation Industry?

Ans: Some of the jobs in Government sector of civil aviation are:

Assistant Gliding Instructor
Assistant Pilot Instructor
Pilot Instructor In-charge
Chief Flying Instructor
Helicopter Pilot
Science Lecturer
Mechanical Lecturer
Chief Lecturer
Principal Lecturer
Aircraft Maintenance Engineers
Airport Service Staff
Chefs
Cargo pilot
Flight engineer
Flight operations support personnel

Q.6 What is DGCA (Directorate General of Civil Aviation)?

Ans:

dealing with safety issues. It is responsible for regulation of air transport services to/from/within India and for enforcement of civil air regulations, air safety and airworthiness standards. It is also responsible to co-ordinate all regulatory functions with International Civil Aviation Organisation

Q.7 What are the duties, functions and responsibilities of DGCA?

Ans: The duties, functions and responsibilities of DGCA are:

1. Registration of civil aircraft
2. Formulation of standards of airworthiness for civil aircraft registered in India and grant of

   examinations and checks for that purpose

   services operating to/from/within/over India by Indian and foreign operators, including

8. Conducting investigation into accidents/incidents and taking accident prevention measures including formulation of implementation of Safety Aviation Management Programmes
9. Carrying out amendments to the Aircraft Act, the Aircraft Rules and the Civil Aviation Requirements for complying with the amendments to ICAO Annexes, and initiating proposals for amendment to any other Act or for passing a new Act in order to give effect to an international Convention or amendment to an existing Convention
10. Coordination of ICAO matters with all agencies and sending replies to State Letters, and taking all necessary action arising out of the Universal Safety Oversight Audit Programme (USOAP) of ICAO

    training, AME training or any other training related with aviation, with a view to ensuring a high quality of training

12. Granting approval to aircraft maintenance, repair and manufacturing organisations and their continued oversight
13. To act as a nodal agency for implementing Annex 9 provisions in India and for 2 coordinating matters relating to facilitation at Indian airports including holding meetings of the National Facilitation Committee
14. Rendering advice to the Government on matters relating to air transport including bilateral air services agreements, on ICAO matters and generally on all technical matters relating to civil aviation, and to act as an overall regulatory and developmental body for civil aviation in the country

    agencies and interaction with ICAO for provision of more air routes for civil use through Indian air space and collaborating with the environmental authorities in this matter, if required

17. Promoting indigenous design and manufacture of aircraft and aircraft components by acting as a catalytic agent

18. Approving training programmes of operators for carriage of dangerous goods, issuing authorisations for carriage of dangerous goods, etc.

Q.8 Which are the Public Sector companies in Civil Aviation Sector in India?

Ans: Some of the Public Sector Companies (PSU) working in civil aviation sector are:

Airport Economic Regulatory Authority

Indira Gandhi Rashtriya Uran Akademi

Pawan Hans Helicopters Limited

Airports Authority of India

National Aviation Company of India Limited and its following subsidiaries

IAL Airport Services Limited

Vayudoot Limited

Airlines Allied Services Limited

Air India

Air India Engineering Services Limited

Air India Air Transport Services Limited

Air India Charters Limited

Hotel Corporation of India Limited

Q.9 Who is a Pilot? What are the duties of a Pilot?

Ans:

(aviateur in French) was in 1887, as a variation of 'aviation', from the Latin avis (meaning bird), coined in 1863 by G. de la Landelle in Aviation Ou Navigation Aérienne (Aviation or Air Navigation). The term aviatrix (aviatrice in French), now archaic, was formerly used for a female aviator. The term aviator is often applied simply to pilots, but can be extended to include aviation navigators,

These include the route to be taken and height maintained and also includes meteorological information. Pilots have to do complex calculations of take-off and landing and they have to work out the fuel needed for distance to be travelled and height and weight to be maintained.

and dedication. The job requires a lot of hard work, stamina, alertness of mind, adaptability

possessing these qualities, the persons willing to take up this as profession, should be calm, pleasant, compassionate, understanding and technically sound.

Q.10 How can one become a Pilot in India?
Ans:

place.

Student's Pilot Licence
basic mathematics knowledge of the aircraft, engines and aerodynamics. Minimum passing marks

these courses is nearly INR 100,000.

Private Pilot Licence: It is the second stage. It consists of practical and theory examinations. The

paper tests the student's knowledge about aircraft engines, air navigation, aviation meteorology and seamanship. The theory paper is conducted by DGCA. The training period is nearly two years depending upon the availability of instructors. The cost is nearly INR 2,00,000- 5,00,000. It does

Commercial Pilot Licence:

part consists of subjects like Air Regulations, Aviation Meteorology, Air Navigation, Technical Planning and Communications in Radio and Wireless Transmission. An additional requirement here is in terms

of the Air Force Unit and the DGCA. The medical clearance has to be taken before the lapse of three

After getting CPL, you can work as a trainee co-pilot for 6-8 months with any airlines and thereafter

tests have to be cleared almost thrice a year or more depending on the license category and age of the pilot. The highest among the category of licenses is the Air Transport Pilot License (ATPL) which

medical and other tests every six months.

Q.11 How can one become a Helicopter Pilot?
Ans: Helicopter pilots need to have Commercial Helicopter Pilots License (CHPL). This license can be acquired by two stages. The Private Helicopter License (PHPL) is granted after 40 hours of

security/protective agencies.

Q.12 Where can one start flying training to become a Pilot?

Ans:
DGCA website for validity/expiry of approval):

2. The Bombay Flying Club Juhu Aerodrome, Juhu, Mumbai-400 049, Maharashtra
3. Andhra Pradesh Aviation Academy, Hyderabad Old Airport, Hyderabad-500 011, Andhra Pradesh

5. The Gujarat Flying Club, Civil Aerodrome, Harni Road, Vadodara - 390 022 (Gujarat)
6. Government Aviation Training Institute, Old Terminal Building, Biju Patnaik Airport, Bhubaneswar, Orissa
7. Bihar Flying Institute, Patna Airport, Patna - 800 014, Bihar
8. The Madhya Pradesh Flying Club Ltd., Devi Ahilyabai Holkar Airport, Civil Aerodrome, Bijasan Road, Indore-452005 (MP)
9. The Madhya Pradesh Flying Club Ltd., Civil Aerodrome, Bhopal (MP)

11. Haryana Institute of Civil Aviation, Civil Aerodrome, Hissar-125 001 (Haryana)
12. Haryana Institute of Civil Aviation, Civil Aerodrome, Pinjore (Haryana)
13. Nagpur Flying Club Pvt. Ltd., Dr. Babasaheb Ambedkar International Airport, Sonegaon Aerodrome, Nagpur, Maharashtra
14. Amritsar Aviation Club, Amritsar International Airport, P.O. Rajasansi, Amritsar-143101, Punjab
15. Patiala Aviation Club, Civil Aerodrome, Sangrur Road, Patiala, Punjab
16. The Madras Flying Club Ltd., Gate No.6 Old Airport, Meenambakkam, Chennai-600027, Tamil Nadu
17. Banasthali Vidyapith Gliding & Flying Club, Banasthali University, P.O. Banashali Vidyapith, Dist. Tonk, Rajashtan — 304022

19. Chimes Aviation, Dhana Airstrip, Sagar, Madhya Pradesh
20. Orient Flight School, 40, G.S.T. Road, St. Thomas Mount, Chennai-600016, Tamil Nadu
21. Ahmedabad Aviation & Aeronautics Ltd., AAA Hangar, Old Terminal Airport, Ahmedabad-380003,
22. Gujarat Amber Aviation Pvt. Ltd. Civil Aerodrome, Pant Nagar, Uttarakhand
23. Yash Air, Datana Air Strip, Dewas Road, Ujjain (MP)
24. Sha-Shib Flying Academy Guna Airport, Guna (MP) 473001
25. Sai Flytech Aviation Pvt. Ltd., Chakarbhata Airport, Bilaspur, Chattisgarh-492101

27. Ambitions Flying club Pvt. Ltd., MS-10, NH-91, Dhanipur Airport, Post Panethi, Aligarh, UP-202 001

28. Pioneer Flying Academy Pvt. Ltd., Aligarh, Uttar Pradesh

30. HAL Rotary Wing Academy, Prototype Hangar, HAL Gate No-30, Vimanpura, Bangalore-560017,

32. Academy of Carver Aviation Pvt. Ltd., Plot P-50, MIDC Airport, MIDC, Baramati-413133 Pune, Maharashtra
33. Alchemist Aviation Pvt. Ltd., Sonari Aerodrome, Jamshedpur, Jharkhand
34. National Flying Training Institute Pvt. Ltd. Gondia, Maharashtra
35. Wings Aviation Pvt. Ltd., 1-11-256/B, Plot No.108, Adjacent Airport Road, Begumpet, Hyderabad (AP)

   Mumbai-Agra Road, Shirpur, Dist.-Dhule-425 405 Maharashtra
37. Birmi Flying Academy Pvt. Ltd., Hangar No.2, Civil Aerodrome, Sangrur Road, Patiala-147001
38. Chetak Aviation Academy, Mile Stone-10, NH-91, Aligarh Airstrip (Dhanipur), Post-Panethi, Aligarh, UP-202001
39. Rainbow Flying Academy Pvt. Ltd., Near ATC Tower, Hangar No.1, Surat Airport, Surat, Gujarat

Q.13 Who is an Air hostess? How can one become an Air hostess?

Ans: One of the important aspects of travel by Air concerns with making the journey of the passengers trouble free, comfortable and safe. It is in this respect that the job of air hostess

hostesses. To become an air hostess one needs good presentable personality as well as pleasing manners and the art of conversation with passengers. air hostess is a pretty exciting career choice for young girls as the perks are many. Along with good pay, the perks include free travel, meeting different people and stay at the best hotels in the town. The basic job of air hostess is

regulations. The job of an air hostess although alluring, is also very demanding as it requires a huge amount of calmness and patience. Encountering different kind of people can have its own affects. A person needs to condition herself to maintain the smiling and happy face even when they personally do not feel like it, but the advantages outweigh the pain.

Eligibility:

   Management or Tourism)
   Age — below 25 years, different airlines may have slightly higher age limits. The preferred age limit is from 18-21 years

   Height — should be more than 157.5 centimeters
   Marital status — unmarried
   Eyesight — normal eyesight of 6/6 uncorrected visions in each eye

Basic requirement:

    Able to interact comfortably with strangers maintaining calm under duress

    Excellent health and ability to speak clearly

    Pleasant personality and attractive appearance

    Good degree of common sense along with lots of physical stamina to work in adverse conditions

Selection procedure:

    Initial screening test followed by a written examination

    Round 2 — Group discussion and personal interviews

    Selections and training period — Recruited as trainees, with training period of 2-3 months

Salary: The salary is paid commensurate with the experience. A fresher commands a salary in

domestic aviation sector. Foreign airlines are better paymasters. Reputed international airliners pay an average of nearly 1.5 Lac Rupees with senior Air hostesses getting above 3 Lac Rupees apart from lucrative perks and packages.

Top recruiters:

private sector and Indian Airlines as the public carrier. Singapore Airlines, British Airways, Virgin Atlantic, Qatar Airways, Fly Emirates are the top recruiters in the international airlines category.

Training: There are different kinds of Air hostess training modules available. One can go for a short-term Air hostess training course lasting not more than 3-6 months or courses lasting a year or more. The training modules include overall personality development and few technical skills.

Q.14   Where can one get a job of Air hostess in India?

Ans: You can apply for job of air hostess in any one of the following Airlines in India:

    Air India

    Air India Domestic/Alliance Air

    GoAir

    Indigo Airlines

    Jagson Airlines

    Jet Airways

    Paramount Airways

    Pawan Hans

    SpiceJet

Q.15   Who is an Air Traffic Controller (ATC)? How can one become an ATC?

Ans:

space and along pre-determined routes of arrival and departure to and from airports around the world. They are also responsible for providing advice and information useful for the safe and on the ground for all maneuvers right till the end of his journey. The ATC tells the pilot when to

ensure adequate separation between aeroplanes. The controller is at constant communication with pilots and his job is of paramount importance in preventing collisions and ensuring an

the destination, clearing the pilot to land and telling him how to taxi his aeroplane to the parking slot so that his passengers can disembark safely at the end of the journey.

While there are internationally agreed standards and procedures to be followed to accommodate the aircraft movements in a safe and orderly manner, on the ground and sometimes, within spilt seconds, ATCs have to visualise quickly and solve in real time problems involving calculating differential speeds and rates of climb and descent of aircraft and issuing clearances to provide safe separation between aircraft at any given time. A large number of details have to be remembered and factored into every decision. A simple oversight or miscalculation or a single

shouldered can be awesome, as the margin for error is zero. Few jobs involve the unremitting effort, focus and concentration required of a controller.

by established and stable teams. Although the ATC is usually alone when he takes decisions, he is part of a large team which coordinates with other sectors and other control centres. While mapping the future course of various aircraft which may converge or diverge over the navigational aid, ATCs have to talk and understand aircraft transmissions and issue appropriate instructions,

aircraft are recorded continuously on tape and any instructional error is traceable by replay, a tremendous strain on the individual. You therefore need to have a good, clear diction, which can

As English is the expected language for radio communications in most parts of the world,

require good eyesight, hearing and a good, logical and mathematical mind. You must also have a strong sense of responsibility, the ability to stay alert, work under constant pressure, and of

are with the Airports Authority of India, selection is made on the basis of the ATC entrance examination; a medical examination and an aptitude test. You can apply for the entrance test after a degree in engineering, Electronics/ Telecommunication/ Radio Engg/ Electrical/ or a Master's degree in Electronics. Preference is sometimes given to CPL holders/candidates with basic knowledge of computers, keeping in view the technological changes that are taking place in test and a personal interview.

Those selected are sent to the Civil Aviation Training College, Allahabad, for a year-long training

so on. Once recruited, all the costs for training are borne by the Airports Authority of India. While the Airports Authority of India (AAI) is the main employer of civilian ATCs, in India, there are some jobs with companies such as Hindustan Aeronautics Limited, and some small private airports. The

and advisory services to Pilots of Military and Civil Aircraft.

Q.16 What are the basic educational qualifications (degrees) needed to apply for the civil ATC entrance exam?

Ans: Engineering degree (BE/B.Tech) in Electronics/Tele Communication/Radio Engg./Electrical with specialisation in Electronics with 1st class (60%) Or M.Sc degree or its equivalent with Wireless Communication, Electronics, Radio Physics or Radio Engg. as a special Subject or Equivalent with 1st Class.

Q.17 What is the age limit required to apply for the civil ATC entrance exams?

Ans: Lower age limit is 21 years, while the upper age limit is 27 years

Q.18 What are the selection criteria of ATC?

Ans: The selection is made on the basis of:

Written test

Voice test
Personal Interview

Standard reservation policy applies for SC/ST/OBC/Ex-Servicemen. No reservation for Physically Handicapped candidates.

Q.19 What are the negative and positive aspects of this profession?

Ans: **Negative:** High stress, Shift duties, Extra work load, Non availability of leaves, Lack of Social life due to strange shift pattern and no standard festivals' leaves, very high professional risk

Positive: Challenging environment, split second decision making, independent decisions, Work is not to be carried home.

Q.20 What are the various ranks that an ATC officer can climb through?

Ans:

Junior Executive
Assistant Manager

Manager

Senior Manager

Assistant General Manager

Deputy General Manager

Joint General Manager

General Manager

Executive Director (ATM)

Member (ATM) in AAI Board

Q.21 How can one join the aviation industry in the area of technical/engineering domain?

Ans:

1. Aeronautical & Avionics engineering
2. Aircraft Maintenance Engineering

Aeronautical Engineering: The modern air vehicles undergo stern atmospheric, pressured, temperature and structural loads conditions on its various components. The technologies that come into play are aerodynamics, avionics, material science and propulsion which collectively are called Aerospace engineering. Aerospace engineering deals with the variegated branches in aeronautical and astronomical engineering. Out of which aeronautical engineering seem to have tremendous scope both in India as well as abroad. These institutes provide the best of faculty, Equipments, Labs and make sure that the students get a professional niche among their global peers.

Some of the good Aerospace/Aeronautical Engineering colleges/schools in India are:

1. IIT (Indian Institute of Technology), Mumbai
2. Indian Institute of Aeronautical Engineering, Dehradun
3. Indian Institute of Technology, Chennai, Tamil Nadu
4. Institute of Aviation Technology, Haryana
5. Institute of Information Technology & Management's Aeronautical Engineering, Pune, (Maharashtra)
6. Indian Institute of Aeronautics, Delhi
7. Punjab Engineering College, Chandigarh
8. School of Aviation Science and Technology, Delhi Flying Club, New Delhi
9. Hindustan Institute of Aeronautics, Bhopal, Madhya Pradesh

Eligibility: To be an aeronautical engineer one must have a graduate degree (BE/BTECH) or at least a Diploma in aeronautics which most of the polytechnics offer. The criteria is 10+2 with a minimum of 60 percent. For better scrutinising, universities have started conducting an Entrance exam. The IITs have their Joint Engineering Exam (JEE) and other institutes conduct their autonomous entrance exams, with the state and national level exams for the government and regional engineering colleges.

Aircraft Maintenance Engineers: With the boom of myriad airplanes coming to India, the need for Aircraft maintenance engineers (AME's) is going to amplify like anything. The Aircraft Maintenance Engineers play a stellar role in Aviation sector as they are the ones who ensure that the aircraft is in a perfect condition before take-off.

An Aircraft Maintenance Engineer needs to be completely focused on safety as the casual attitude can pose a danger to the lives of people on board. The Aircraft Maintenance Engineer has to

possible cost. The Engineering and Maintenance department of an airline performs scheduled and unscheduled tasks, leading to restoration of the expected airworthiness. Aircraft Maintenance Engineer job includes diagnostic and mechanical duties covering maintenance, repair, trouble

Aircraft Maintenance Engineer, at times, has to work under stringent conditions, tough deadlines

have perseverance.

Eligibility for Aircraft Maintenance Engineering: To be designated as an aircraft maintenance engineer, one has to approve license from the Director General of Civil Aviation (DGCA), government of India. Currently there are 37 DGCA approved training institutes in the country which stipulate students and prepare them for the DGCA License Exam. The Aircraft Maintenance License is issued to the candidates who have successfully cleared the exam. The minimum eligibility to get a place in the leading AME training schools is 10+2 or its equivalent degree with 50 percent marks in Physics, Chemistry, and Maths in the aggregate.

Some of the approved AME Training Schools in India are:

1. Aeronautical Training Institute Lucknow(UP)
2. Alpine Institute of Aeronautics, Dehradun,Uttrakhand

   Camp, Lucknow
4. Budha Institute of Engineering and Aeronautics, Nagloi, New Delhi — 110041
5. Centre for Civil Aviation Training, Dwarka, New Delhi
6. College of Aeronautical Engineering and Technology, Meerut
7. Falcon Institute of Aircraft Maintenance Engineering, Lucknow, UP

9. Indian Institute of Aeronautical science, Rothak Road, Multan Nagar, New Delhi

Q.22 What are the jobs available after completing Aircraft Maintenance Engineering course?

Ans: Some of the jobs available after completing AME course are:

Flight and Ground Instructors: The Flight Instructors give training to the Pilots on some systems and are mainly with engineering background. On the other hand, the Ground Instructors are from operations background. Flight Instructors are usually senior Pilots who are employed within the airline. They usually perform line duties as they are not released due to shortage of pilots.

Flight Dispatchers:

Factor Facilitators: The Factor Facilitators give training to the cockpit and cabin crew on resource management. They also undertake joint sessions of cabin crew, engineers and cockpit crew on working together.

Aviation Psychologists: The Aviation Psychologists assess the attitudes of the Pilots through psychometric tests. They also guide the young cabin crew to overcome the problems faced by them at their job.

Aviation Doctors: The Aviation Doctors conduct a rigorous medical check-up of the Pilots and other employees as per the norms of Aviation Medicine and the Central Medicine Establishment, both run by the Air Force. The airlines have to look their slots months' in advance due to high rush of employees from different airlines.

Q.23 What is Airport Operations Management? What are the duties of an Airport Operation Manager?

Ans: In a rapidly changing environment, airports have to adapt to economic downturns, technological changes, market changes, airline commercial deregulation, and the worldwide trend to convert airports from government organisations to more business-like entities. These

In these challenging times, coupled with emerging competition from other airports and other modes of transportation, it is of utmost importance that airports recruit and provide employees and managers with the best available knowledge and skills. Duties include coordination between

applying knowledge of weather information.

Jobs of an Airport Operations Manager are as follows:

and aircraft operation.

to upline controlling agencies.

planning publications, operations publications, charts and maps, and weather information.
Monitor the arrival, parking, refuelling, loading, and departure of all aircraft.
Maintain air-to-ground and point-to-point radio contact with aircraft commanders.
Train operations staff.

functions.

planning.

Coordinate with agencies to meet aircrew requirements for billeting, messing, refuelling, ground transportation, and transient aircraft maintenance.

and departure times.

Post visual display boards and status boards.

equipment to perform duties.

Q.24 What are Baggage Jobs and what qualities are required to become a baggage handler in airport?

Ans: Baggage jobs are menial jobs in an airport and baggage jobs can be quite stressful and it is important that the baggage handler is able to quickly and correctly sort baggage to minimize delays and to ensure that everybody gets their correct luggage. Baggage handler jobs are certainly

Baggage Handler Working Conditions:

A baggage handler needs to be physically strong because they will be expected to lift heavy loads for extended periods of time. Apart from strength, agility is also fairly important because baggage handler jobs involve working in the cramped conditions of an aero plane cargo hold.

Baggage handler jobs often require shift work because an airport will be active 24×7. Working nights, holidays, weekends and overtime is commonplace in baggage jobs. Depending on the airport, some baggage handler jobs have working hours of 12 hours at a time in a condensed week.

To be a baggage handler, the individual needs to be able to cope with working at height because the cargo ramp and the aero plane itself could be 20+ft off the ground. All baggage handler jobs require a uniform, hi-visibility clothing and hard hats.

Those with baggage handler jobs are expected to work outside in all conditions ranging from the cold and windy weather of January to the heat of July and August and the baggage handler needs to be able to deal with this. During the summer months, an aero plane's cargo hold can get very hot.

The baggage handler needs to be able to work calmly but quickly under pressure as large volumes and baggage and freight can come at once which needs sorting and routing to the correct place (either baggage collection or to an aeroplane). All baggage jobs form part of a team and the ability to work and communicate well with people in the other baggage handler is essential.

Everybody who applies to baggage handler jobs will be subjected to a medical examination as well as stringent background security checks due to the nature of baggage jobs and the proximity of the baggage handler to the aero plane moments before takeoff.

7

COMPANY SECRETARY

Q. 1   I want to know in detail about Institute of Company Secretaries of India (ICSI)

Ans: The Institute of Company Secretaries of India (ICSI) is constituted under an Act of Parliament, i.e. the Company Secretaries Act, 1980 (Act No. 56 of 1980). The ICSI is the only recognised professional body in India to develop and regulate the profession of Company Secretaries in India.

of Company Secretary (CS) to a candidate qualifying for the membership of the Institute. It was in 1960 that the Company Law Board started a course in Company Secretaryship leading to the award of Government Diploma in Company Secretaryship. As the number of students taking up the Company Secretaryship started growing, the Government promoted on 4th October, 1968, Institute of Company Secretaries of India under Section 25 of the Companies Act, 1956 for taking over from the Government the conduct of Company Secretaryship examination.

The Institute of Company Secretaries of India (ICSI) has since been converted into a statutory body w.e.f. 1.1.1981 under the Company Secretaries Act, 1980. The Institute of Company Secretaries

practice. The number of current students is over 2,30,000.

and Mumbai. The Institute has four Regional Councils and under their jurisdiction are Chapters as provided in the link below:

Membership of ICSI has been recognised for appointment to various superior posts and services under the Central Government.

of the Central Government. Pursuant to section 383A of the Companies Act, 1956, companies having a paid-up share capital of Rs 5 crore or more, as prescribed by the Central Government, are statutorily required to appoint a whole-time Company Secretary.

The Company Secretary (CS) plays a major role in corporate sector. Company Secretary is an

integrate and cooperate with various other functional heads in a company. A member of the ICSI can the Company Secretaries Act,1980.

Q.2   How can one become a Company Secretary?

Ans: The Institute of Company Secretaries of India (ICSI) is a premier National Professional body established by an Act of Parliament to develop and regulate the Profession of Company Secretaries.

ICSI imparts training in Company Secretaryship by Distance Learning (by correspondence) enabling students to qualify as Company Secretaries. The Institute provides "Course Material" for all the subjects at the time of Registration. There is also provision for Optional Oral Coaching classes.

with it a high level of job satisfaction.

Stages to become a Company Secretary

The students who would like to join the Course after 10+2 have to undergo three stages to pursue the Company Secretaries Course, i.e.

    Foundation Programme
    Executive Programme
    Professional Programme

In addition, the student has to undergo Practical Training for about 15 months, which a student may opt to start after passing the Executive Programme. The Student who would like to join the Course after passing the Graduation has to undergo two stages of the Company Secretaryship, i.e.

    Executive Programme
    Professional Programme

Besides, the student has to undergo Practical Training for about 15 months. Foundation Programme which is of 8 months duration can be pursued by 10+2 pass students of Arts, Science or Commerce stream. Executive Programme can be pursued by a Graduate of all streams except Fine Arts. Professional Programme can be pursued only after clearing the Executive Programme of CS Course.

Training: A student has to undergo 15 months Management Training in Companies sponsored by the Institute after passing the Executive or Professional Programme or under the guidance of a Company Secretary in Practice.

After qualifying the Professional Examination and successful completion of training, a candidate is admitted as an Associate Member of the ICSI and can use the letters ACS after his/her name, i.e. Associate Company Secretary.

Q.3   What is the role of a Company Secretary?

Ans: Behind great corporate progress there is a strong backbone — the Company Secretary (CS).

and corporate governance, a Company Secretary serves as the vital link between the company, its:

Board of Directors

Shareholders

Government and other Agencies

The Company Secretary is:

An expert in corporate laws, securities laws & capital market and corporate governance

Chief advisor to the board of directors on best practices in corporate governance

Responsible for all regulatory compliances of company

Corporate planner and strategic manager

Q.4 When can one take admission in CS course?

Ans: Admission to the CS Course is open throughout the year. Examinations are held twice a year in June and December. Cut off dates for admission to CS course are:

For Foundation Programme	31st March for appearing in December Examination in the same year
	30th September for June Examination next year
For Executive Programme	28th February for December Exams in the same Year
	31st August for June Exam next year

Q.5 What are the employment opportunities of a Company Secretary (CS)?

Ans:

opportunities to practice as an Independent Professional

Companies with a paid-up share capital of Rs.2 crores or more are compulsorily required to appoint a full time Company Secretary who is a Member of ICSI

All companies seeking listing on Stock Exchange are required to appoint a whole time company secretary

Membership of the Institute is recognised for appointment to superior posts and services under Central Government.

Self-Employment/Practising Company Secretaries

go in for Independent Practice.

Every company having a paid-up share capital of Rs. 10 lakhs or more but less than Rs. 5 crores is required to engage the services of a Company Secretary in Whole-Time Practice

Pursuant to Clause 49 of the Listing Agreement, Practising Company Secretaries have been

as stipulated in the Clause.

The CS Course is:

recognised by the various Universities for admission to Ph.D Course

appointment of Lecturers in Commerce & Management

Q.6 Where can one get detail information about CS course?

Ans: You can get detail from ICSI HEADQUARTERS, 'ICSI HOUSE' 22 Institutional Area, Lodi Road, New Delhi 110 003.

E Mail: info@icsi.edu, Website: www.icsi.edu

For further details regarding admission, etc., please contact / write to

Director (Student Services)

The Institute of Company Secretaries of India

C-37, Sector 62, NOIDA 201 309 (U.P.), E-Mail: dss@icsi.edu; ss_fond@icsi.edu

Q.7 Who are eligible for exemption from appearing in the Foundation Examination?

Ans:

recognised by the Council of the ICSI with the approval of the Central Government as equivalent thereto, is exempted from passing the Foundation examination

> A degree or master's degree in Corporate Secretaryship or Commerce
>
> Pass in the Final examination of the Institute of Cost and Works Accounts of India(ICWAI) or the Institute of Chartered Accountants(ICAI) of India or any other Accountancy Institution in India or abroad recognised as equivalent thereto by the Council: or
>
> A degree or master's degree in any discipline other than Fine Arts.

A candidate who is eligible for exemption from the Foundation examination stated above can seek registration as student. Such a candidate before becoming eligible for undergoing coaching for the Intermediate examination is required to undergo satisfactorily a course of postal or oral tuition for those subjects of the Foundation examination which he had not studied at the graduate or post-graduate level, after registration as a student.

DEFENCE SERVICES (Navy, Army, Air Force)

Q.1   I want to join Indian Army as an officer. What are the benefits and advantages of joining Army as an Officer?

Ans:

The Indian Army promises both professional and personal growth at every stage of the career. Opportunities to upgrade through various courses are abundant. The adventure and extra-curricular activities in the Army ensure an all round development essential in today's world. An

Apart from attractive pay and perks, Army offers you the best in Life Style, even better than all

ample opportunities to indulge in adventure and sports, Army has it all. In fact you are paid to lead a healthy life in a healthy environment. Facilities like subsidised housing, free medical for self & family, canteen facilities, group insurance cover, soft loans for house and/or vehicle and above all the feeling of belonging to a family (Army) which cares for you, are the perks of the Army which no other organisation provides.

Q.2   What is Permanent Commission in Indian Army?

Ans: A Permanent Commission means a career in the Army till you retire. For a Permanent commission you have to join the National Defence Academy or the Indian Military Academy.

The National Defence Academy, Pune: You can take the NDA entrance exam right after class XI. Clear the UPSC exam and pass the medical tests, and you're in NDA. Three years in NDA and you will be a

cultivate new interests. There are 31 extra-curricular activities to choose from. You have aero-

Indian Military Academy, Dehradun: Indian Military Academy is yet another cradle of leadership.

Entry if you come on merit. The other entries are 10+2 Tech Entry where you apply after your 12th Exams. University Entry Scheme is for those who wish to apply for Army in Pre-Final/Final

IMA in the Technical Graduate Course. The selection procedure is same as for IMA (Direct Entry) accepting that there are no written exams. The duration of training is 1 ½ years for IMA (DE),

after commissioning) and one year for all other entries. The IMA trains you to lead from the front. You are trained in all aspects of combat and tactics using technology and other modern tools and technologies. The IMA has excellent facilities for all-round development. You can go for adventure sports like river rafting, Para jumping, rock climbing, trekking and mountaineering. From the IMA, you're commissioned as a "Lieutenant" in the Indian Army, to go out into the world and live up to the IMA motto — "Valour & Wisdom".

Q.3   What is Short Service Commission in the Indian Army?

Ans:
years. At the end of this period you have two options. Either elect for a Permanent Commission or opt out. Those not selected for Permanent Commission have the option of a 4 years extension. They can resign at any time during this period. A Short Service Commission empowers you with analytical thinking, planning skills, administrative and organisational abilities. Qualities which will make you an invaluable asset for any organisation that you join after the Army and there are opportunities to side step to an alternate career for which Army will also help you.

Q.4   What is the selection process of Short Service Commission?

Ans: The selection process is a written exam followed by the SSB interview and medicals. For Technical (Engineering) graduates it is direct SSB interview and medicals. If you have done NCC

candidates undergo a medical examination. The duration of training is 49 weeks. Once selected

provides you with opportunities to broaden your perspective and widen your horizon. Whether it's skeet-shooting, golf, riding or angling, at OTA you can do it all.

Q.5   Can women join Indian Army as Short Service Commission Officer?

Ans:
Commission and prove to the world and when it comes to courage and leadership, you are second

to apply. After the written exam, there is the SSB interview followed by a medical examination.

Q.6   How can one join NDA?

Ans: Eligibility Criteria

appearing for above examination can also apply.

Unmarried male candidates only

Age between 16½ to 19 years

Nationality: A candidate must be either:

A citizen of India, or

A subject of Bhutan, or

A subject of Nepal, or

A Tibetan refugee who came over to India before 1st January, 1962, with the intention of permanently settling in India, or

A person of Indian origin who has migrated from Pakistan, Burma, Sri Lanka, the East

and Zambia, Malawi, Zaire and Ethiopia and Vietnam, with the intention of permanently setting in India

Provided that a candidate belonging to categories (ii), (iii), (iv) and (v) above shall be a person in

eligibility will not, however, be necessary in the case of candidates who are Gorkha subjects of Nepal.

Admission Form

About a year before the commencement of a course, a brief notice appears in the leading daily

entrance examination to be held by the UPSC six months later at Agartala, Ahmedabad, Aizwal, Allahabad, Bangalore, Bareilly, Bhopal, Mumbai, Calcutta, Chandigarh, Cochin, Cuttack, Delhi,

Sambalpur, Shillong, Shimla, Srinagar, Tirupati, Trivandrum, Udaipur and Vishakhapatnam.

Q.7   How to Apply?

Ans: A candidate seeking admission to the examination must apply to the Secretary, Union Public Service Commission (UPSC), Dholpur, House, New Delhi-110011, on the application form published in newspapers. The candidates may utilise the original form published in newspapers or in "Employment

application form and the Attendance Sheet neatly typewritten on white paper (foolscap size) in double space typed on only one side of the paper. There is no objection to candidates using printed/ Application Form and Attendance Sheet, if available, from private agencies as long as the format is exactly the same as published in the advertisement. Candidates who have appeared for the previous examinations will not be considered. The envelope containing the application should be superscribed in bold letters as "APPLICATION FOR NATIONAL ACADEMY EXAMINATION" .

Selection Procedure

The process of selecting cadets for the National Defence Academy is split into three phases:

A written examination held by UPSC.

(Intelligence and personality test).

A medical examination by a Service Medical Board.

Scheme of the Examination

The subjects of the written examination, the time allowed and the maximum marks allotted to each subject are as follows:

Subject	Code	Duration	Max Marks
Mathematics	01	2 1/2 hours	300
General Ability	02	2 1/2 hours	600
Total			900

The papers in all the subjects will consist of objective type questions only. The question papers (Test Booklets) will be set in English only.

Q.8 What is the eligibility for 10+2 Technical Entry Scheme in Indian Army?

Ans: Age:
70% and above to apply); Duration of Training: 5 Yrs (1 Yrs IMA & 4 Yrs CTWS); Permanent Commission after 4 Years.

Q.9 What is Military Academy (IMA) and how can one join IMA?

Ans: "The integrity of a nation depends, among other factors, primarily upon its military capability to defend itself against aggression. History is replete with examples of nations either having disappeared or having undergone great misery and humiliation through their inability and failure to defend themselves militarily."

national interests over everything else; safeguarding and protecting the territorial integrity is amongst its primary preoccupation, without which the well-being of the country is inconceivable. In the past, the Indian Army has always risen to the occasion and has delivered the goods irrespective of the nature of duties it was called upon to perform, thereby earning the trust and faith of the countrymen. The success of the armed forces especially the Indian Army is intrinsic

highly disciplined, thoroughly motivated and deeply committed to serve the Nation with honour and dignity. The valediction of the Academy is evident from the bountiful sagas of bravery, valour

The Indian Military Academy was established in the year 1932. During the course of our struggle for independence, a section of Indian leadership realised the necessity of a military institution conforming to the requirements of a sovereign India. Their concerted efforts resulted in the Montague Chelmsford Reforms Committee that enabled 10 Indians to undergo training for

Table Conference in London in 1930 recommended the establishment of an Indian Sandhurst. As a follow up action, a committee was set up under the chairmanship of Field Marshal Sir Philip Chetwode, Baronet GCB, GCSS, CCMA, DSO, the then Commander-in-Chief of India, to work out the modalities for establishment of the proposed Indian Sandhurst. The Committee, in Jul 1931, recommended the establishment of a Military Academy for induction of 40 Gentlemen Cadets from the princely states. The training span was initially envisaged for three years but later reduced to two and a half years.

The Indian Military Academy presently has the following entries:-

1. Regular Course: Comprising Cadets ex-National Defence Academy and ex-Army Cadet College Wing (Siachen Bn) and Direct Entry Scheme (for Graduates in Arts/Sc/Commerce through CDS and SSB)
2. Tech Graduates Course (for BE graduates/PG students with Science and Humanities. They appear for the SSB tests only)

4. Tech Entry Scheme (for candidates who have passed or are appearing in +2)
5. SCO Course (for in service soldiers) (Army only)

The duration of training is one year except for the Direct Entry Scheme, for which it is one and a half years. Graduates opting for Direct Entry (between 19-24 age group) are required to qualify

through the Services Selection Boards. Army cadets from NDA and ACC join after completing three year degree course at respective training establishments. The technical graduates, who are engineering graduates/PG candidates, are not required to write a written examination but need to be selected by respective SSBs. On successful completion of training at IMA, all entrants receive Commissioned rank of Lieutenant. However, UES and TGC (with BE) entries get two years ante-date seniority over their course mates. This is to compensate for the extra time they spend to earn the Engineering degree before commissioning. With the ante-date seniority, opportunities

Candidates selected for 10+2 Technical Entry Scheme (TES) are inducted for one years' basic military training at IMA. This is followed by a four years' degree course in Engineering from College of Military Engineering (CME) Pune or Military College of Telecommunication Engineering (MCTE) Mhow or Military College of Electronics and Mechanical Engineering (MCEME) Secunderabad at Government expense. However, on completion of three years of training they return to the IMA for receiving the commission in the rank of a Lieutenant. Thereafter they return to their technical institutions as Lieutenant to complete fourth year of their degree course.

Q.10 What are the eligibility criteria to join Indian Military Academy (IMA)?

Ans: **Age: 19 to 24 yrs;** Graduation from Recognised University; **Duration of Training:** 1½ Years; Selection through CDSE examination by UPSC.

Q.11 What are the career opportunities in non-officer category in the Indian Army? What are the eligibility criteria and selection procedure?

Ans: Recruitment in the Army is broad based. Every male citizen, irrespective of caste, class, religion and domicile, is eligible for recruitment in the Army, provided he meets the age, educational, physical and medical standards. Recruitment in the Army is carried out through an open rally system. The recruitment programme is published in local newspapers, two weeks prior to the conduct of the rally by the concerned ZROs. The process of screening and enrolment is as follows: -

(a) Checking of documents
(b) Physical measurements

(d) Medical examination
(e) Written examination
(f) Preparation of merit list
(g) Enrolment and Dispatch of selected candidates in order of merit to Centres

Bring the following original documents along with three Photostat copies of each, duly attested: -

Xth/XII th Class marks sheet

For Soldiers in the (GD) Category, the following have been granted dispensation:
(a) Class X Simple Pass.

(ii) Uttarakhand State — Batwari Tehsil of Uttarkashi Distt, Okhimath Tehsil of Rudraprayag Distt and Joshimath Tehsils of Chamoli Distt.
(iii) Rajasthan State — Jaisalmer and Barmer Distts and Shergarh, Osian and Phalaudi Tehsils of Jodhpur Distt.

(v) Punjab State — Candidates from Punjab who are domiciled within the aerial distance of

(vi) Class/Community-

(ab) Rawat from Ajmer, Rajasmad, Bhilwara, Udaipur and Chittor Districts from Rajasthan.

(ad) Sikh (M&R).
(b) To Class VIII.

(ii) Uttarakhand State — Berinag, Didihat, Dharchula and Munsiari Tehsils of Pithoragarh Distt.
(iii) Sikkim State.
(iv) Andaman & Nicobar Group of Islands.

(v) Lakshadweep — Minicoy Group of Islands.

(vi) NE States — All pers incl tribals except Arunachal Pradesh (incl tribals).

(viii) Class/Community — Gorkhas (Nepalese and Indian) and Adivasis.

(c) To Class V.

(ii) Arunachal Pradesh — including tribals.

A candidate should have robust physique and good mental health. Chest should be well developed having minimum 5 cms expansion; should have normal hearing with each ear and good binocular vision in both eyes. He should be able to read 6/6 in distant vision chart with each eye. colour

of natural healthy gum and teeth, i.e. minimum 14 dental points; should not have disease like deformity of bones, hydrocele and varicocle or piles.

Physical Fitness Tests (PFT)

To determine the Physical Fitness, the following tests carrying 100 marks are held :-
  (a) 1 Mile Run
  (b) Pull Ups
  (c) Balance
  (d) 9 Feet Ditch

Marking system is as follows :-
  (a) 1 MILE RUN
     (i) 5.40 Mins and below 60 Mks
     (ii) 5.41 Mins to 5.50 48 Mks
     (iii) 5.51 Mins to 6 .05 36 Mks
     (iv) 6.06 Mins to 6.20 24 Mks
  (b) PULL UPS
     (i) 10 and above 40 Mks
     (ii) 9 — 33 Mks
     (iii) 8 — 27 Mks
     (iv) 7 — 21 Mks
     (v) 6 — 16 Mks

Medical Standards
  (a) A candidate should have robust physique and good mental health.
  (b) Chest should be well developed having minimum 5 cms expansion.

(c) Should have normal hearing with each ear and good binocular vision in both eyes. He should be able to read 6/6 in distance vision chart with each eye. Colour vision should be CP-III.

   points.
(e) Should not have diseases like deformity of bones, hydrocele and varicocle or piles.
(f) Should recognise red and green colours.

Common Entrance Examination (CEE) is conduct on last Sundays of each month for recruitment of Soldiers. It comprises following two papers:
   (a) Paper-I — Compulsory for all soldier categories

PAPER-I

It generally comprises questions on IQ/Numerical ability general knowledge and current affairs. Duration of papers is 60 minutes. Total marks 100; Pass Marks 32.

PAPER-II

Paper II (Sol Tech) — 50 marks. It generally comprises Physics, Chemistry and Maths. Duration - 30minutes, Pass marks-16.

Duration — 30 minutes, Pass Marks-20.

Paper-II (Sol Nursing Assistant) — 50 marks. It generally comprises Chemistry, Botany & Biology, Duration — 30 minutes, Pass marks-16.

Note:

Q.12 How can one join the army as an officer in Crops of Signals?
Ans:

National Defence Academy after clearing Higher Secondary Examination with Science subjects. Indian Military Academy after graduation in Science subjects.

As a technical entry after securing a degree in Electronics. This entry starts with an ante date seniority of two years over the above entries. 10+2 Scheme: This new scheme is for students clearing 10+2. The selected students undergo 6 months training in IMA, followed by four years B.Tech in Electronics & Communication from MCTE, Mhow. All expenses are paid by the Govt. To be eligible for this entry, the candidates should have secured at least 70% aggregate in PCM in 10+2 examination.

On 1 October 1967, the School of Signals was re-designated "Military College of Telecommunications Engineering" (MCTE) in keeping with the advanced technical training being imparted in the Institution, and the Wings were renamed Faculties. With the introduction of computers for management and switching in the Army, a new wing called the Computer Technology Wing was

of the Ministry of Defence to train them as programmers and system analysts. In view of the

periodic intervals.

It is now commanded by a Lieutenant General and has several Faculties for imparting training

Technology and Conceptual Studies. The college set up a Faculty of Electromagnetic Compatibility

technical courses run in the college are in three levels — Diploma, Graduate and Postgraduate level. The Graduate level courses are recognised by the Jawaharlal Nehru University, New Delhi for the grant of a Bachelors degree in Engineering. The Postgraduate Course is recognised by DAVV University, Indore.

Q.13 What is Territorial Army (TA) and how can one join the Territorial Army?

Ans: The English raised the Territorial Army in 1920 through Indian Territorial Act of 1920 and it comprised two wings namely — 'The Auxiliary Force' for Europeans & Anglo-Indians and 'The Indian Territorial Force for Indian Volunteers. After Independence the Territorial Army Act was passed in 1948

Army. The Territorial Army initially had various types of units such as Armed Regt (TA), Infantry Battalion (TA), Air Defence (TA), Med Regt (TA), Engineers Field Park Coy (TA), Signal Regiment (TA), EME Workshop (TA), Coast Battery (TA), ASC GT Coy (TA), ASC Compo Pl (TA), AMC Field Ambulance (TA), by 1972 these units have either been disbanded or converted to Regular Army except Inf Bn (TA).

The Territorial Army is part of Regular Army and its present role is to relieve the Regular Army from static duties and assist civil administration in dealing with natural calamities and maintenance of essential services in situations where life of the communities is affected or the Security of the Country is threatened and to provide units for Regulars Army as and when required. Presently the Territorial Army has strength of approximately 40000 persons comprising Departmental TA units such as Railway, IOC, ONGC, Telecommunication and General Hospital and the non Departmental

The TA units were actively involved in 1962, 1965 and 1971 operations. The "Terriers" have also

in the North East in a most active manner. Departmental units came to the aid of the civil authorities during Industrial unrest and natural calamities, most famous being the earthquake in Latoor (Maharashtra), Uttarkashi in Garhwal Himalaya and the Super Cyclone in Orissa. The Ecological units have arrested man made environmental degradation by planting 2.5 crore trees over 20,000 hectare of land in Mussoori Hills & Pithoragarh (UP), Bikaner & Jaisalmer (Rajasthan) and ravines of Chambal in Madhya Pradesh.

JOINING TA AS OFFICER

Eligibility: Age - 18 to 42 years; Education — Graduation

Process:
advertisements published in leading national newspapers and The Employment News in June-July

and December-January each year. Applications are to be sent to the concerned TA Group Headquarters. After processing of applications, the eligible candidates are called for Preliminary

candidates are granted commission by the President of India.

given the credit of their previous commissioned service on joining the Territorial Army.

JOINING TA AS JCO

Eligibility:
as JCO only)

Ex-JCO's or their equivalent of three services, may also join Territorial Army as JCO's.

Commands and from Area/Sub Area Headquarters. Forms duly completed to be sent to the Unit where commission is sought.

then interviewed by the Sub Area/ Area Command Headquarters. The application of the recommended candidate will then be processed at the Addl. Directorate General of Territorial Army, Army Headquarters.

JOINING TA AS JAWAN:

Eligibility: Age - 18 to 42 years; Education - Matriculation (dispensation for lower Education

designated dates for tests as per laid down procedures. Selected candidates have to go through

Q.14   How can one apply to join the Indian Air Force (IAF)?

Ans: You can begin your Air Force joining process, by sending your application to the relevant branch. IAF will scan your application, and based on merit, will call you to one of their selection boards. Candidates short-listed after the initial selection procedure, will go through a rigorous training regimen at one of the Air Force training establishments. After which they are given a

the advertisement inviting applications in the leading newspapers and the Employment News. After you spot the relevant ad, you should send your application in the format mentioned in the advertisement, before the last date of receiving of application.

Q.15   What are the eligibility criteria for joining Indian Air Force as an Officer?

Ans: Flying Branch:
Air Force. You are trained either as a Fighter pilot, or a Helicopter pilot, or a Transport pilot and

are a part of various peace and wartime missions. As an engineer, you enter the Flying branch through the Air Force Academy.

Air Force Academy

The Air Force Academy is one of the most prestigious training establishments of the Indian Air Force. Here you are trained and prepared for your responsibilities as a pilot.

The following are the three modes of entry for engineers to join the Flying branch:

Combined Defence Services Examination (CDSE)

You can take the Combined Defence Services Examination (written test conducted by UPSC) to join the Flying branch of the Indian Air Force. Men can join the Air Force through this mode of entry and will be given a Permanent Commission. For applying through any of the entry points

Age: 19 to 23 years; Marital Status: Single; Nationality: Indian; Gender: for men only.

Graduate (3-Year Course) in any discipline from a recognised university (with Physics and Mathematics at 10+2 level)/BE/B Tech (Four Year Course). Final Year students can also apply, provided thay do not have any backlog. No Percentage Bar for CDSE entry.

National Cadet Corps Special Entry (Through CO NCC Unit / DG NCC)

the Flying branch of the Indian Air Force. Men can join the Air Force through this mode of entry and will be given a Permanent Commission.

criteria:

Age: 19 to 23 years; Marital Status: Single; Nationality: Indian; Gender: for men only.

Graduate (Three Year Course) in any discipline from a recognised university who have attained minimum 60% marks in aggregate in all papers put together and have Physics and Mathematics at 10+2 level OR BE / B Tech (Four Year Course) from a recognised university with minimum 60% marks in aggregate in all papers put together. Final year students can also apply, provided they do not have any backlog and should have minimum 60 percent marks in aggregate up to the previous year/semester.

Flying (Pilot) Short Service Commission (For Men & women) with term of engagement of 14 Years with no further extension.

Service Commission in Flying branch is for 14 years with no further extension.

eligibility criteria:

Age: 19 to 23 years 19 to 25 Years for CPL Holders (Issued by DGCA (India); Marital Status: Single; Nationality: Indian; Gender: This is applicable to both men and women.

A Graduate (Three Year Course) in any discipline from a recognised university who have attained minimum 60% marks in aggregate in all papers put together with Physics and Mathematics at 10+2 level OR BE / B Tech (Four Year Course) from a recognised university with minimum 60% marks in aggregate in all papers put together. Final Year students can also apply, provided they do not have any backlog and should have minimum 60 percent aggregate marks up to the previous year/semester. Upper age limit for Candidates holding valid and current Commercial Pilot Licence issued by DGCA (India) is relaxed up to 25 years.

GROUND DUTY

Meteorological Branch

Permanent / Short Service Commission:
in the Meteorology Branch. Handling the latest satellite imagery and state-of-the-art monitoring

Age: 20 to 25 years; Marital Status: Single; Nationality: Indian; Gender: This is applicable to both Men and Women.

Postgraduate degree in any Science stream / Mathematics / Statistics / Geography / Computer Applications / Environmental Science / Applied Physics / Oceanography / Meteorology / Agricultural Meteorology / Ecology & Environment / Geo-physics / Environmental Biology. All candidates should have scored a minimum of 50 percent marks in aggregate in all papers of Post-Graduation put together and should have studied Maths and Physics in Graduation with minimum of 50 percent marks in both subjects.

TECHNICAL BRANCHES

equipment in the world.

You can apply for the Technical Branch via any of the two schemes listed below:

Direct Entry Scheme: After you have completed your engineering, you can join the Technical Branch through the Direct Entry Scheme. Both Men and Women can use this mode of entry to apply to the Indian Air Force.

University Entry Scheme (UES)

Eligibility Criteria: Aeronautical Engineering (Electronics) & Aeronautical Engineering (Mechanical)

Permanent Commission (for Men) / Short Service Commission (for Men & Women)

Aeronautical Engineering (Electronics)

As an Aeronautical Engineer in the Electronics stream, you will be responsible for the communication and signals required on the Air Force station. You will also be in-charge of the execution of preventive maintenance and servicing of aircraft. With further in-service training, you could also move to the repair and overhaul divisions of the Indian Air Force.

criteria:

Age: 18 to 28 years; Marital Status: Candidates below the age of 25 years should be Unmarried; Nationality: Indian; Gender: Applicable to both men and women.

Candidates applying for Aeronautical Engineer (Electronics) Branch would be eligible if they have

and a minimum of 60 percent marks in aggregate in all papers put together from a recognised university OR cleared section A and B examination of Associate Membership of Institution of Engineers (India) OR cleared section A and B examination of Aeronautical Society of India OR graduate membership examination of the Institute of Electronics and Telecommunication Engineers by actual studies

All the candidates should have studied at least eight subjects out of the list of eighteen subjects

(1) Physics / Engineering Physics
(2) Mathematics / Engineering Mathematics
(3) Engineering Graphics / Engineering Drawing
(4) Electrical Engineering / Electrical Technology
(5) Control Engineering
(6) Microprocessors
(7) Digital Electronics / Basic Electronics
(8) Computer Networks
(9) Information Technology
(10) Network Theory Design
(11) Telecommunication Systems
(12) Electronic Circuit Design
(13) Radar Theory
(14) Switching Theory
(15) Instrumentation
(16) Microwave Engineering
(17) Antenna and Wave Propagation
(18) Electronic Devices

Aeronautical Engineering (Mechanical)

After you join the Indian Air Force as an Aeronautical Engineer in the Mechanical stream, you could be placed at a position that requires you to be involved with preventive maintenance and servicing of aircraft or of common user and specialist application vehicles. You could also be

Age: 18 to 28 years; Marital Status: Candidates below the age of 25 years should be Unmarried.

Nationality: Indian; Gender: Applicable to both men and women.

Candidates applying for Aeronautical Engineer (Mechanical) Branch would be eligible if they have

in all papers put together from a recognised university OR Cleared section A and B examination of Associate Membership of Institution of Engineers (India) OR Cleared section A and B examination of Aeronautical Society of India

All the candidates should have studied at least eight subjects out of the list of eighteen subjects

(1)   Physics / Engineering Physics
(2)   Engineering Maths / Mathematics
(3)   Engineering Drawing / Graphics
(4)   Automotive Engineering / Plant Engineering / Industrial Engineering
(5)   Engineering Mechanics / Strength of Material
(6)   Aerodynamics
(7)   Thermodynamics and Applications / Heat Power Engineering
(8)   Heat and Mass Transfer

(10) Fluid Mechanics / Turbo Machines
(11) Flight Mechanics
(12) Machine Drawing / Machine Design
(13) Mechatronics
(14) Material Science / Metallurgy
(15) Vibrations
(16) Workshop Technology / Manufacturing Technology / Production Engineering
(17) Hydraulics and Pneumatics
(18) Aircraft Structures

University Entry Scheme (UES)

Permanent Commission (For Men only)

B Tech degree course in the relevant streams of engineering as mentioned above and must have secured minimum of 60% marks in aggregate up to the last semester for which results have been declared, at the time of applying / AFSB testing. There must be No backlog / arrears of papers of previous semesters. On completion of degree, minimum 60 percent of marks in aggregate in all papers put together are mandatory.

Age: 18 to 28 years; Marital Status: Candidates below the age of 25 years should be Unmarried.

Nationality: Indian; Gender: Applicable for Men only.

Q.16   What is the procedure for selection of officer in the Indian Air Force (IAF)?

Ans:
thorough. You can be a part of Air Force family going through this process and proving your mettle.

> **Step1:** Receipt of Applications and Written Test.
>
> **Step2:**
>
> **Step3:** Conducting of Medical Examinations.
>
> **Step4:** Preparing All India Merit List.

Step1: Receipt of Applications and Written Test

The selection procedure begins immediately after you send your application forms. All application

If you seek entry into the Flying Branch through the NDA or CDSE, your applications need to be sent to UPSC, New Delhi. UPSC conducts a written test twice a year in April & August (NDA) and April & September (CDSE). Advertisements for the examinations are released about six months in advance. Qualifying in these exams take you to step two.

into Flying Branch through DG NCC / CO NCC Unit. Based on recommendations of DG NCC, they are directly called for SSB interview.

If you apply for Flying branch (SSC), Technical branch (PC/SSC) and Ground Duty branches (PC/SSC), you are required to send your application to Concerned Command HQs (as per details mentioned in the advertisement) for Air Force Common Admission Test (AFCAT). All applicants whose applications are received by due date are called for AFCAT at one of the examination centres.

If you have successfully cleared Step 1, you will receive a call letter to report to any one of the Air Force Selection Boards located at Dehradun, Varanasi and Mysore. At the Air Force Selection

Boards, you undergo a number of psychological tests, an interview and group tests, which are

The Psychological Tests are written tests that are conducted by a Psychologist.

The Group Tests are interactive indoor and outdoor tests. IAF expect active physical participation from you.

These tests will be explained to you in detail before they are conducted at the Selection Board.

The following is the schedule for OLQ Tests:

Day 1: Pilot Aptitude Battery Test

Day 2: Psychological Tests

Day 3: Group tests

Day 4: Group tests

Day 5: Interview

Day 6: Conference

Pilot Aptitude Battery Test (PABT) is a unique test. It is aimed at assessing a candidate's aptitude to be trained as a pilot. PABT is being used as an independent selection device to

viz., Instrument Battery Test (INSB), Sensory Motor Apparatus Test (SMA) and Control Velocity Test (CVT). Instrument Battery Test (INSB) is a paper pencil test and other two are machine tests. The Instruments Battery Test (INSB) comprises two parts. This test assesses assimilation

panel of an aircraft.

The candidates who score the minimum laid down criteria are subjected to the machine test. The machine test includes Sensory Motor Apparatus Test (SMA) and Control Velocity Test (CVT). These tests measure the psychomotor co-ordination skill of the individual. These tests are conducted on a single day and administered only once in life time.

At the conference held on the last day, all the assessors, i.e. the Psychologist, Ground Testing

and subsequently moves to the next step.

Step3: Conducting of Medical Examinations

If you have applied for the Flying branch and are found suitable by the Selection Board, you would be sent to the Air Force Central Medical Establishment, New Delhi or the Institute of Aerospace Medicine, Bengaluru for a thorough medical examination. If you have applied for the Technical or Ground Duty Branches and are found suitable, you may be asked to return home and await a call for a medical examination or be sent directly for the medical examination.

Step4: Preparing All India Merit List

An All India Merit List is compiled on the basis of your performance at the AFSB and subject to

would issue joining instructions to join Air Force Academy for the training.

Q.17 What all Training Courses one has to undergo after joining Air Force as an Officer?

Ans:

to practice what you have been trained for, but also get a chance to grow and continuously hone

> Flying Training
> Technical Training
> Non-Technical Training
> Miscellaneous Courses
> Security Training
> Meteorology Training
> Medical Courses

Flying Training: After you join the Indian Air Force, it is ensured that you increase your expertise

The following are some training programmes organised for the Flying Branch:
> Ab-Initio Pilots Course
> Transport Conversion Course

> Test Pilot Course
> Flight Test Engineer Course
> Pilot Attack Instructors Course
> Fighter Combat Leader Course

Ab-Initio Pilots Course (Common for Fighter, Transport and Helicopter Streams)

Designed to train newly inducted cadets, this training programme is conducted to impart basic

specialising on Fighter, Helicopter and Transport aircraft.

Transport Conversion Course:

to operate as pilot-in-command on a transport aircraft. This course provides support to enable

Force can become a Flying Instructor. The objective of this course is to teach the methodology of imparting Flying Instructions on basic trainer aircraft. On completion of training, an experienced pilot is capable of preparing cadets for the Flying branch of the Indian Air Force.

Test Pilot Course: After relevant experience, a pilot can become Test Pilot. The purpose of this course

other related systems. The course provides pilots the necessary expertise to support evaluation and

Flight Test Engineer Course (Fixed/Rotary Wing /Avionics/Instrumentation): This course is aimed

and precision.

Pilot Attack Instructors Course: Select pilots of the Fighter Stream take the Pilot Attack Instructors Course. The objective of the course is to introduce them to details of air-launched weapons and their effective employment.

Fighter Combat Leader Course: This course is targeted at veteran pilots of the Fighter Stream to train them in the art and science of aerial combat in a multi-aircraft scenario. The course curriculum also includes a wealth of information about air weapons and strike tactics. This course

Q.18 What is the prospect of career growth as an officer in Indian Air Force?

Ans:

Branch becomes the head of the family, i.e. The Chief of Air Staff. The exact rank structure for

given charge of men and affairs.

Flight lieutenant (Flt Lt): Beginning the climb to the top, Flight Lieutenant is the next rank in the Indian Air Force Hierarchy. Equivalent to a Captain in Army and Lieutenant in Navy, a Flight Lieutenant takes on junior level supervisory responsibilities and is posted as a Pilot, or an

Squadron Leader (Sqn Ldr): Taking on bigger responsibilities under his wings, the Squadron Leader undertakes many tasks. Equivalent to a Major in Army and Lt. Commander in Navy, the Squadron Leader is the operational in-charge of a squadron's role. He is a senior level supervisor and takes

Wing Commander (Wg Cdr): Gearing up for the higher grounds the Wing Commander takes on additional responsibilities. He is equivalent to Lt. Col in Army and Commander in Navy and is

HQs/Command HQs.

Group Captain: Taking charge of men and management, the Group Captain heads large Air Force Stations. Equivalent to Colonel in Army and Captain in Navy, he may command a medium-sized Air

Station or hold key Staff Appointments at the Air HQs/Command HQs.

Air Commodore: The chosen few make it to this position. An Air Commodore is equivalent to

or Staff Appointments (senior level) at Air HQs/Command HQs.

Air Vice Marshal: Only the daring few can climb this high in the Air Force Hierarchy. An Air Vice-Marshal is equivalent to Major General in Army and Rear Admiral in Navy. He is responsible for

Assistant Chief of Air Staff at Air HQ.

Air Marshal: Just one step below the top of the ladder, the Air Marshal commands a lot of power. He is equivalent to Lt. Gen. in Army and Vice Admiral in Navy. He is posted as the Commander-in-Chief (C-in-C) at Command HQs, or as the PSO at Air HQs or Command HQs.

Air Chief Marshal
Chief Marshal heads the Air Force family and is responsible for all strategic and tactical decisions, regarding the Indian Air Force in the times of peace and war

Q.19   What is AFA?

Ans: Air Force Academy (AFA), the premier training centre of the Indian Air Force, is the cradle of

The training at this academy is designed to foster the spirit of camaraderie and promote healthy

every cadet and strives to graduate Air Warriors worthy of the Indian Air Force.

The mission of AFA is to inspire and transform outstanding young men and women into courageous, dynamic, intellectual and cultured young Air Warriors; motivated to lead one of the leading aerospace forces of the world in service to the nation.

The training at the Air Force Academy is designed to inculcate moral values, leadership qualities, sense of honour and duty, mental and physical prowess, a spirit of adventure and the will to win, in the Flight Cadets. This is achieved by training in character building, discipline, military and academic subjects, physical exercise, drill, sports and adventure activities. The underlying theme of activity at the Academy is camaraderie and team spirit and a commitment to excellence. Duty, honour, integrity and self esteem are stressed upon during each stage of training; because these are important abstract qualities to be imbibed by every Flight Cadet. The curriculum and syllabi keep pace with current doctrines and technological developments, allowing the cadets at the same time to imbibe the basic principles / tenets of the military profession.

A need was felt for a long time to establish a permanent Air Force Academy at one place, not back as 1953, with an aim to bring together, at one place, the training of all fresh entrants into

and Secunderabad was acquired from the government of Andhra Pradesh. The location was considered ideal, as satellite bases for advanced training were available at Hakimpet and Bidar

In common with all great institutions, the Academy too, had a humble beginning. In contrast with the present aura of grandeur, one fondly remembers the eventful days in April 1970 when

shared their not-so-enviable accommodation with scorpions, snakes and mosquitoes that showed scant regard for both rank and status.

The Air Force Academy formally came into being when the then President of India Dr Zakir
was a vision

Q.20   I want to know about AFTC?

Ans: Air Force Technical College (AFTC) was established on 4 Jul 1949 with Gp Capt J Beaumont,

Force (RAF). Judged by their civil attire and gentle behaviour it was conjectured that some of

whole of Asia which trained aeronautical engineers.

the entire staff comprised foreigners. By 1956, the staff was completely Indianised. In Dec 1962, owing to the national emergency, the Apprentices' Training Scheme was suspended and

i.e. Aeronautical Engineering (Mechanical) and Aeronautical Engineering (Electronics). With the passing out of No. 51 DEO course in Nov 1972, ab-initio training of Aeronautical Engineers' Course in AE (M) and AE (L) braches was started in Jan 1972.

The Aim of AFTC is to educate and train engineers from various disciplines on current technologies of aircraft, weapon and support systems held in the IAF as also to impart qualities of military leadership, managerial skills, values and ethos of an Air Warrior to enable them to function effectively as Aeronautical Engineers and contribute to growth of knowledge through research

Q.21   How can one join Indian Air Force as a non-officer?

Ans:
through All India Selection Tests and Recruitment Rallies. All India Selection Tests are conducted at the Airmen Selection Centres (ASCs) located all over India as per schedule whereas the

Recruitment Rallies are conducted from time to time in selected areas/regions of particular States/Union Territories of the country.

All India Selection Tests: Advertisements are published in Employment News/Rozgar Samachar inviting the applications for All India Selection Tests (STs). In response to the advertisement, eligible male Indian Citizens are to forward application to the:

President,
Central Airmen Selection Board,
Post Box No. 11807,

The Board sends admit cards to eligible and shortlisted candidates to appear in the Selection Tests.

Recruitment Rallies: Recruitment rallies are conducted at select places within the country from time to time. Rally advertisements are published with the details of eligibility conditions, selection programme and rally venue in local/regional newspapers circulated in the region/area of the rally. For rally recruitment, eligible candidates are to report to the rally venue on the day of test with the requisite documents as published in the advertisements. Further procedures will be briefed to the candidates at rally venue by the team of selections. Candidates while

Sheets and other related documents as mentioned in the advertisement. These documents will

Written Test: Candidates are tested in English, Physics & Mathematics for Group 'X' (Technical) trades and in English & Reasoning and General Awareness (RGA) for all Group 'Y' trades. Written Test is objective type and question paper is bilingual (English & Hindi), except English paper. Written test is based on CBSE syllabus of AISSCE. Candidates for Group 'Z' (Musician) trade are

are to qualify in each paper/test separately.

Physical Fitness Test (PFT): Candidates passing the written tests are to undergo Physical Fitness Test (PFT). The PFT for all trades excluding Indian Air Force (Police) & Indian Air Force (Security)

completed in 30 minutes & 15 minutes respectively. Candidates completing PFT earlier will be awarded additional marks on a sliding scale.

Interview:
Interview is normally conducted in English. Working knowledge of English is thus essential.

Trade Allocation Test (TAT): Candidates of Group 'X' (Technical) trades who qualify in interview are to undergo Trade Allocation Test for bifurcation into Mechanical and Electronics stream.

Air Force (Belgaum).

Medical Examination: Candidates who are recommended in the interview will be medically examined by the Recruitment Medical Team as per Indian Air Force medical standards. Medical

power as stated in Medical Standards given in detail on this site.

All India Select List (AISL) & Enrolment: Candidates who are passing the Written Test, completing PFT, recommended for interview and undergone Medical Examination are arranged in All India Select List (AISL). The inclusion of names of the candidates in the AISL depends upon the performance of the candidates in the Selection Test. Candidates are enrolled in the Indian Air Force as per the existing vacancies. Enrolment is for an initial period of 20 years and extendable up to the age of 57 years.

Training: The candidates on enrolment are routed to Basic Training Institute (BTI), Belgaum,

duration. After successful completion of training, the airmen will be deployed on ground based jobs as per their allotted trades.

Q.22   What are the eligibility criteria to join Indian Air Force as an Airman?
Ans:

GROUP	AGE* (See note below)	EDUCATIONAL QUALIFICATION	TRADE ELIGIBLE FOR
Group 'X'	17-22 Years	Candidates should have passed Intermediate/ 10+2 with pass marks in Mathematics and Physics with a minimum of 50% marks in overall aggregate. OR Should have passed a 3 year Diploma course in Engineering (Mechanical/ Electrical/ Electronics/Automobile/Computer Science/ Instrumentation Technology/ Information Technology) with at least 50% marks from a Govt. recognised Polytechnic Institute.	Technical Trades
Group 'Y'	17-22 Years	Candidates should have passed Intermediate/ 10+2 with science, arts, commerce subjects or equivalent vocational courses with minimum 50% marks in aggregate. Vocational courses conducted Universities (AIU) only are eligible.	All Group 'Y' Trades (Except Musician Trade)
Group 'Y'	17-25 Years	Passed Matriculation/ 10th class passed or equivalent with minimum pass marks from any Govt recognised school/Boards, should be least one musical instrument of the following: Trumpet /Bass/ Violin/ Saxophone/ Clarinet/ Euphonium /Jass- Cello/ Contra Bass (String Bass).	Musician Trade

Regional Newspapers released from time to time.

Q.23   What are the ranks in IAF for airmen?
Ans: Aircraftman - AC

Leading Aircraftman - LAC

Corporal - CPL

Sergeant - SGT

Q.24 Where are Airmen selection centres located?

Ans: Airmen Selection Centres:

1 Airmen Selection Centre Ambala Cantt- 133 001 Tele : 0171- 2634980 Extn.4410 Email : coascamb@dataone.in	8 Airmen Selection Centre, 413 Air Force Station, Tambaram Chennai-600 046 Tele : 044-22395553 Extn:3359 Email : ascafstam@dataone.in
2 Airmen Selection Centre Race Course Camp New Delhi — 110 003 Tele: 011-23010231 Extn. 7652 Email : 2asc@bol.net.in	9 Airmen Selection Centre, Near Rajadhani College, Baramunda, Bhubaneswar-751003 Tele: 0674-2561336 Email : co9asc@yahoo.co.in
3 Airmen Selection centre 402 Air Force Station, Chakeri, Tele: 0512-2451730 Extn.4603 Email : co3asc@yahoo.com	10 Airmen Selection Centre, Air Force Station Bihta, Patna Bihar — 801 103 Tele : 06115-253551-54 Extn. 4340 Email : 10asc@bsnl.in
4 Airmen Selection Centre (Near Palta Gate) Air Force Station Barrackpore, West Bengal — 743 122 Tele: 033-25921251 Extn.6391 Email : co4asc@yahoo.co.in	11 Airmen Selection Centre Borjhar Guwahati- 781 015 Tele : 0361-2842720 Extn.333 0361-2843385 Email : elevenasc@rediffmail.com
5 Airmen Selection Centre Old Pali Road Jodhpur- 342 011 Tele: 0291-2511516 Extn. 2110 Email : co5asc@yahoo.co.in	12 Airmen Selection Centre 404 Air Force Station, Bowenpally Secunderabad-500 011 Tele : 040-27753551 Extn: 267 Email : co12asc@rediffmail.com
6 Airmen Selection Centre 411 Air Force Station, Cotton Green, Mumbai-400 033 Tele: 022-23714963 Extn. 251 Email : co6asc@rediffmail.com	14 Airmen Selection Centre VII/302-B, Vayu Sena Road, Tele : 0484-2427010 Email : co14asc@rediffmail.com
7 Airmen Selection Centre No.1 Cubbon road, Bangalore-560 001 Tele : 080-25328199 Email : co7asc@dataone.in	15 Airmen Selection Centre IInd Floor, Phase-II, Rajiv Gandhi Parisar, 35 Shyamala Hills, Bhopal - 462 002 Tele : 0755 - 2661955 Email : 15ascbhopal@gmail.com

Q.25 What are the advantages of choosing Indian Navy as a Career option?

Ans: The Indian Navy will give you all the training you need and help you make the most of what you have — your talents, your skills, your spirit and your aspirations. Are you in search of a challenge — are you young and bright, just out of school or university, have wide personal interests and hobbies, prepared to work hard and expect far more from your career than a remunerative pay packet? You need a challenge — a job that grows with you and provides variety and excitement. That is what precisely the Navy offers you. The Navy offers an extraordinary range of exciting career opportunities together with the chance to travel widely, meet new people and to enjoy the warmth and camaraderie that is so special to this service.

If you join the INDIAN NAVY you are choosing more than just a job. Indian Navy offers a unique way of exploring your life and provides ample opportunities to exploit your potential in every sphere of life. Indian Navy provides a level of security and comfort that is almost unheard of in civilian life. For many people, the greatest attraction of a career in the Indian Navy is the variety of opportunities to make your career challenging. You can face the challenges and develop methods to exploit the full potential in you. A job in the Navy offers you a chance to exploit your true potential as a professional — by learning new skills, acquiring unrivalled experience in the process of applying those skills, and making the most of Navy advancement. In the Indian

unparalleled career potential, and the lifestyle of freedom and personal growth that you have been waiting for. In the Navy where you can build a career that thrives. Here your individual thoughts, ideas and skills are given an opportunity to shine. Whether you are looking to build

you do it.

Q.26 What are the different options available to join as an officer in Indian Navy?

Ans:
ship. It means you will be a vital part of the complex system that manages the ship and also uses the ship as an instrument of tactical warfare. You will learn to have a good understanding of your ship's capabilities and limitations and be able to turn them to your advantage. It is for this reason

can specialise in any of the following:-

  (a) Gunnery & Missiles
  (b) Navigation and Direction
  (c) Anti-Submarine Warfare
  (d) Communications
  (e) Pilot
  (f) Observer
  (g) Submarine
  (h) Hydrography
  (j) Diving

Armament Inspection and Logistics.

are responsible for collecting information required for making the nautical charts used by the Indian Navy and other Navies around the world.

Navy by various agencies. While they ensure the quality, safety and reliability of naval armament and stores, they are also responsible for in-house research and development leading to indigenisation.

security and vigilance needs of the Navy.

submarines and take part in amphibious warfare, search and rescue, casualty evacuation, etc.

For those with a yearning for the skies, navy needs observers who act as

an opportunity to participate in all facets of naval operations.

If you enjoy the challenge of new frontiers, meet the medical standards and possess an exceptional record, this is the specialisation for you. These new hi-tech war machines

and a high standard of habitability. In peace time, one major responsibility of the submarines is to train for war as effectively as possible in the knowledge that will contribute to its prevention. If you successfully complete the rigorous training, which is conducted at Visakhapatnam, you will be the proud possessor of the 'Dolphin Badge' and a member of a very elite arm of the Navy.

defence of Indian Navy maritime assets. This is yet another elite and challenging task with specialisation in the parent professional arm and further sub-specialisation such as gunnery, Navigation, Anti-submarine warfare or else logistics, hydro, Aviation, etc., are available for one

course.

and community of several hundred people. These personnel have to be fed, clothed and paid, whatever may be the ship's role. A modern warship has also to be constantly supplied with fuel, water and spares for the vast array of sophisticated equipment and machinery. At sea or on shore

organisation. It is a job that requires exceptional managerial skills and the ability to deliver under pressure.

Q.27 What is the selection procedure to join Indian Navy?

Ans:

and Regional news papers/dailies. Selection for all Permanent Commission entries, except 10 + 2 NDA and Naval Academy entry and NCC Special entry (Graduate) is through a written examination conducted by the UPSC, followed by an interview by the Service Selection Board (SSB). There is no written examination for the Short Service Commission entries. These applications are shortlisted as per the criteria laid down by the Naval Headquarters, Directorate of Manpower Planning & Recruitment. Selection is through merit alone. It is mandatory that all degrees and educational

Degrees/marksheets must be original or attested by appropriate authorities, as asked for in the advertisement. No compromise/relaxation will be made on this issue. All candidates desirous of

sports, swimming and extra-curricular activities is desirable. Women are granted Short Service Commission (SSC) in Naval Architect, Law, Logistics, ATC, Aviation (Observer) & Education Branches. The government has also given approval for Permanent Commission (PC) in Education, Law and Naval Architect branch on completion of SSC tenure depending upon merit and vacancy.

FOR FURTHER DETAILS, CONTACT:

The Directorate of Manpower Planning & Recruitment,
Naval Headquarters, Sena Bhawan,
New Delhi-110011.

Q.28 What are the eligibility requirements to join Indian Navy?

Ans:

Type of Entry	Unmarried Men / Women	Age Limit	
EXECUTIVE BRANCH			
National Defence Academy (NDA) (Through UPSC)	Men	16½ - 19	10+2 or equivalent with Physics & Maths
(10+2) Indian Naval Academy, Ezhimala (Through UPSC)	Men	16½ - 19	10+2 or equivalent with Physics & Maths
Graduate Special Entry Scheme (GSES) Indian Naval Academy, Ezhimala (Through UPSC)	Men	19 - 22	B.Sc (Physics & Maths) or BE

NCC Special Entry Indian Naval Academy, Ezhimala	Men	19 - 24	B.Sc (Physics & Maths) or BE with Naval Wing
PC Naval Armament Inspection Centre	Men	19½ - 25	A degree in Electronics / Elect / Mech Engg or Postgraduate degree in Electronics or Physics
PC Law Cadre	Men	22 - 27	A degree in Law qualifying for enrolment as an Advocate under the Advocates Act 1961 with minimum 55% marks
PC Logistics cadre	Men	19½ - 25	A First Class degree in B Com/ BA (Economics)/ MBA/ BBA/ BBM/ MCA/ BCA/ BSC(IT)/ BTech/ BE(any discipline including civil Engineering)/ B Architecture/ ICWA/ Charetered Accountancy/ A graduate degree with Postgraduate/ Degree in Materials Management with minimum 60% aggregate marks from a recognised university.
SSC Executive General Service	Men	19½ - 25	BSc./MSc with Physics & Maths with Min 55 % marks. BE/ BTech in any discipline with min 55 % marks. B.Sc(Physics &Maths) holding NCC Naval in Op Research/ Quantitation Methods with min 75% marks. Graduate/ Postgraduate in Maths with STAT or Probability with min 75% marks.
SSC Hydroraphy	Men	19½ - 25	BSc./MSc with Physics & Maths with Min 55 % marks. BE/ BTech in any discipline with min 55 % marks. B.Sc(Physics &Maths) holding NCC Naval in Op Research/ Quantitation Methods with min 75% marks. Graduate/ Postgraduate in Maths with STAT or Probability with min 75% marks.
SSC -ATC	Men & Women	19½ - 25	Ist Class Science Graduate with Physics / Maths/Electronics or MSc with Physics/Maths/ Electronics with min 55% marks.
SSC Law Cadre	Men & Women	22 - 27	A degree in Law qualifying for enrolment as an Advocate under the Advocates Act 1961 with min 55% marks
SSC Logistics Cadre	Men & Women	19½ - 25	1st Class degree in BA (Economics), BCom, BSc(IT), CA/ ICWA, Catering Technology or BCA/ MCA, or B.E/ B.Tech in Mechanical, Marine, Electrical, Electronics, Civil, Computers, IT, Architecture or Graduate with PG Diploma in Material Management.
SSC Pilot	Men	19-23	Graduate in any discipline with minimum 60% marks from a recognised University/ Institution with Maths & Physics at 10+2 level.
SSC Observer	Men & Women	19-23	Graduate in any discipline with minimum 55 % marks from a recognised University/ Institution with Maths & Physics at 10+2 level.
SSC Naval Armament Inspection cadre	Men	19½ - 25	A degree in Electronics/ Elect/ Mech Engg or Postgraduate degree in Electronics or Physics or Postgraduate in Electronics or Physics

Q.29 What are the options in Engineering Branch, Electrical Branch & Education Branch of Indian Navy?

Ans: ENGINEERING BRANCH:

for keeping all these Hi-tech systems serviceable. Opportunities exist to work in gigantic naval dockyards and indigenous production units. In no other career is an engineer exposed to such a wide spectrum of opportunities and to keep abreast of modern developments. An Engineer

You can also join in the Naval Architecture Cadre of the Engineering Branch. The Indian Navy today employs the largest pool of trained Naval Architects in India. A Naval Architect is involved in design, construction, quality control, repair and new construction work of naval vessels. With the Navy going for more and more sophisticated warship production within the country, the Corps of Naval Architects offers excellent opportunities to keep abreast of the advancement in ship building technology and implement your innovative ideas.

ELECTRICAL BRANCH:

distribution system. In addition, complex missile systems, underwater weapons, radar and radio communication equipment form major part of a warship's equipment. A majority of these are either computer-based or computer aided and incorporate the latest trends in electronics

sharpen their skills, the Navy offers excellent opportunities for post-graduate courses in India/ abroad to deserving candidates.

EDUCATION BRANCH:

of technical subjects of all branches of the navy and also for general education. An Education

Q.30 What are the options available in Indian Navy as Sailor Entry?

Ans: The Indian Navy, as one of the three wings of Indian Armed Forces has kept pace with ever changing advanced technologies and operates and maintains highly sophisticated ships, submarines and aircraft. The propulsion machinery, weapons, sensors and equipment on board these weapon platforms are operated and maintained by sailors, who are imparted with requisite training at various intervals during their service. The initial basic training is given at INS Chilka,

over the country. Prior to release from service sailors are also given pre-release courses to enable them to settle down in civil life. Sailors in the Navy are liable to serve anywhere in India, on board ships and Submarines or abroad as deemed necessary by the service

The Branch and Trade structure which is allotted to Sailors are as follows:

Executive Branch: Modern ships, submarines and aircraft of the Indian Navy are highly sophisticated and technologically advanced platforms. As a sailor of the executive branch, you will be involved with operating the state-of-the-art weapons, navigational systems, communication sets, diving equipment, etc. Your duties will also involve the maintenance of the equipment you will be operating. Duties of the sailors from the executive branch include a thorough training in the art of seamanship operating weapon and sensors, look-out duties and boat work. Besides these

Antisubmarine warfare, Navigation and Direction, Diving, Survey, Physical Trainer, Regulating, Logistics and Communication.

Electrical Branch:
system. As an electrical sailor you have the responsibility of upkeep and maintenance of all electrical, electronics and weapons equipment of the Navy. Their jobs on board ships and submarines are as good as supplying and maintaining power to a mini township.

Engineering Branch: The sailor of this branch are technicians and highly trained mechanics who pride themselves on keeping propulsion and auxiliary system running smoothly be they engines, the weapon system, the aircraft or the machinery systems. As an Engineering branch sailor you will operate and learn to keep all this equipment serviceable. The sailors of this branch are also

You will form part of the special class of men, upon whose judgment, foresight, coolness and skill, the ship and those on board depend for safety. You will be trained and made ready to grasp

you in sound position for post-retirement settlement. Sailors of this branch have the option to join the submarine also.

Aviation Branch: This branch comprises specialist sailors who are trained to maintain and handle different type of aircraft operating in the Navy — whether on board ship or ashore. They also handle highly sophisticated aviation stores and do other precision jobs for which they get special allowances

Submarine Branch: Those who yearn for the exclusive challenge of operating below the surface of the oceans in the highly technical, powerful submarines — join this elite branch. Such sailors have to meet high professional and medical standards. They are entitled to the special Submarine Allowance and Perks.

Medical Branch: Professionals who are trained in a wide range of medical skills to care for the sick and the injured with the full backup of the naval hospital services. They have the opportunity to

Operation Room Assistant and Blood Transfusion, etc.

Q.31 What are the eligibility criteria for joining Indian Navy as Artificer Apprentice?

Ans: Age: The applicant should be of the age between 17-20 years (i.e. he should not be less than 17 or more than 20 years on the date of enrolment).

Nationality: Applicant should be a resident Indian. The Gorkhas, subjects of Nepal, are also eligible for applying for AA recruitment.

Marital Status: Applicant should be an Unmarried male.

(a) 1st Condition: Applicant should have passed Class 12th or equivalent with subjects of Physics, Chemistry and Mathematics.

of entry into Indian Navy may vary and the same is promulgated in the advertisement in Newspapers and the website www.nausena-bharti.nic.in.

Physical Standards:

This capability is tested at the examination venue on qualifying in written examination and is termed as Physical Fitness Test (PFT). Qualifying in Physical Fitness Test is mandatory. PFT will consist of 1.6 km run which is to be completed in 07 minutes, 20 Squats (Utthak Baithak) and 10 Push ups.

Medical Standards:

(a) Medical examination will be conducted by authorised Military Doctors as per medical standard prescribed under current regulations applicable to the sailors of Indian Navy on entry. The detailed guidelines for medical standards are laid down in the Navy Orders (SPL) 01/1999 by IHQ MOD (Navy).

(b) Physical traits include minimum height of 157 cm with proportionate body weight depending on the age and height of the candidate. He should also have proportionate chest with minimum expansion capability of 05 cms.

(c) Candidate should possess good mental and physical health, should be free from any disease

vein, etc. He should not have any type of infection in the ears. Candidates are advised to get their ears cleaned for wax and tartar removed from teeth before appearing for the written test followed by PFT and Medical examination.

(d) Candidate should possess Colour perception standard of CP II and Eyes Visual standards should meet the under-mentioned prescribed standards for both the conditions that is with glasses and without glasses.

Without glasses		With glasses	
Better Eye	Worse Eye	Better Eye	Worse Eye
6/12	6/12	6/9	6/12

recruitment for the same entry in Navy need not apply.

Training:

INS Chilka followed by 8 weeks sea training. Thereafter four years training in technical training

Diploma in Electrical/Mechanical/Aeronautical Engineering which is recognised by the Govt of India for purposes of employment in Central /State Govt.

Initial Engagement: The beginning of engagement of sailor with the Indian Navy is subject to sailor is 20 years. However, engagement (i.e. service) period is extendable with maximum limit being till the attainment of 57 yrs of age, which, in turn, depends on the rank attained and satisfactory performance by the sailor while in the service.

Q.32   What is the procedure to join Indian Navy in the SSR & MR category?

Ans: Advertisements for recruitment of Senior Secondary Recruit (SSR), Matric Recruit (MR),

in the Employment News and all leading National/Regional Newspapers in Dec/Jan and Jun/Jul every year.

Application Form

The application form is published in the important Newspapers which may be used. The form in the prescribed format may be typed on plain paper or downloaded from Indian Navy website. The application forms will be available on Navy site from the date of advertisement for the respective batch and type of entry. Candidates applying for more than one type of entry are required to

entry. Choice of entry is to be clearly indicated on the application form. You can apply only for one entry between MR Cook / MR Steward/ NMR Topass in a batch. All applications for AA and SSR, MR, MUS, NMR are to be addressed to the authority promulgated. Application sent through agent will not be accepted. Applications are received only through Ordinary Post. Applications received through speed post/ registered post or couriers are rejected.

Documents Required

in the sequence as given below:-

at the top right corner and one spare recent Passport size photos with the candidate's name written on the reverse attached along with the form (In the absence of recent photograph candidate will not be allowed to appear in the examination).

applicable.

envelope and one envelope without stamp is to be submitted along with the application form. (White colour envelope for AA entry and brown colour for SSR/MR/NMR entry). On top of the envelope containing the application the Type of Entry, name of District, Percentage in exam and name of Exam passed is to be clearly written.

Short-listing of application is done on the basis of higher education and percentage of marks.

Eligible shortlisted candidates are sent Call-Up letters, indicating date, time and place for examination as scheduled. The shortlisted candidates can also download their admit card from this website.

Written Exam: Written exam is conducted at the designated centre on the promulgated date and time. The question paper will be bilingual (Hindi & English) and of objective type. The question

60 minutes duration. In case of Non-Metric entry the question paper will comprise two sections,

required to pass in all sections and in aggregate. The syllabus for each type of entry is given in the download section.

Physical Test:
Baithak) and 10 Push-ups. Candidates undergoing PFT will do so at their own risk. The results of the Written Test are generally declared on the same day. Those who qualify Written Test are permitted to undergo PFT and only those who qualify PFT are taken for Medical Examination.

Medical Test: Entry level Medical standards are different for different entries. Medical examination is be conducted by authorised military doctors as per medical standard prescribed

Military hospital within a maximum period of 21 days. No further review/ appeal are permissible.

in a Military Hospital on payment of Rs.40 by Military Receivable Order (MRO) in the Government

the designated Military Hospital will NOT be considered. This whole process is generally completed on the same day but it may also take 3-4 days time depending on the service requirements or due to unforeseen contingencies.

Merit List:
prepared at IHQ MOD (Navy), New Delhi depending upon the numbers to be inducted. Out of this list the centre wise select list of candidates will be displayed in the respective Recruitment Centres.

How Musicians are recruited in Indian Navy?

for Musician sailors as per schedule promulgated. The preliminary screening and Medical examination would be carried out at the following Naval Recruitment Establishments (NREs) by a team nominated by DOM.

(d) INS Circars, Visakhapatnam
(e) INS India, New Delhi

of Theory of Music and actual practical skill on any Musical Instrument. The candidates applying

both of Western and Indian Origin. The applicant should be of the age between 17-21 years (i.e. he should not be less than 17 or more than 21 years on the date of enrolment). Applicant should have passed 10th class examination and should be able to exhibit an aptitude for music. The

examination venue on qualifying in written examination and is termed as Physical Fitness Test (PFT). Qualifying in Physical Fitness Test is mandatory. PFT will consist of 1.6 km run which is to be completed in 7 minutes, 20 Squats (Utthak Baithak) and 10 Pushups.

9

ENGINEERING

Q.1 What is Engineering?

Ans:

medical equipment, as well as the processes for cleaning up toxic spills and systems for mass transit. In other words, engineering is the process of producing a product or system.

According to Oxford Advanced Learner's Dictionary, Engineer is a person who designs, builds or maintains engines, machines, bridges, railways, mines, etc., and engineering is the practical

services such as roads, bridges, etc., electrical apparatus, chemicals, etc. Engineering is the work, science or profession of an engineer.

In 1982, the Annual Report of ABET (Accreditation Board of Engineering and Technology) of USA

sciences gained by study, experience and practice is applied with judgment to develop ways to

knowledge. IT has become an essential part of our lives, and thus should not be seen as an end

Q.2 Who should study Engineering?

Ans: Only those who excel in science and love to innovate new gadgets/instruments/ equipments,

Tech. degree is not enough. Engineering is a lifelong education and engineers shall continue to keep abreast of the technology and contribute towards technology advancement. A solid foundation of classical theories is prerequisite to understanding of the state-of-the-art technologies.

A person must demonstrate the following to become an engineer in true sense:

    (a) an ability to apply knowledge of mathematics, science, and engineering
    (b) an ability to design and conduct experiments, as well as to analyse and interpret data

(c) an ability to design a system, component, or process to meet desired needs

(d) an ability to function on multi-disciplinary teams

(e) an ability to identify, formulate, and solve engineering problems

(f) an understanding of professional and ethical responsibility

(g) an ability to communicate effectively

(h) the broad education necessary to understand the impact of engineering solutions in a global and societal context

(i) a recognition of the need for, and an ability to engage in life-long learning

(j) a knowledge of contemporary issues

(k) an ability to use the techniques, skills, and modern engineering tools necessary for engineering practice.

Q.3 What are the different stages of Engineering Education in India?

Ans: Post-Metric Technical Education: Diploma level courses are meant for the training of middle level man-power needed for a wide range of professional duties, for application of knowledge

functions are offered in 291 polytechnics with an annual enrolment capacity of about 50,000 students. They offer a variety of specialisation in engineering and technology as well as in a

institutional instruction is offered and three and the half to 4 years when instruction is on a

part-time education have also been provided in some polytechnics situated in metropolitan cities where the demand for such courses exists.

About two dozen Women Polytechnics with courses of special interest to, and employment potential for women have also been established, particularly to cater to the needs of the socially/ economically inhibited classes who might be reluctant to take advantage of the facilities generally available in the regular polytechnics.

industry.

Degree level – For the professional engineers and technologists, facilities for technical education are available in 1200+ engineering colleges offering courses leading to the award of Bachelor degree in Engineering and Technology. The total admission capacity annually for these courses is

with the new pattern of Secondary Education of 10+2, change over completely by 1981-82 to a duration of four years (except architecture).

Post-Graduate Courses
as also for undertaking research and development activities in engineering and technology, post-graduate courses have been offered widely in the various selected institutions offering degree courses. The number of the institutions offering such post-graduate courses is about 100 with an annual intake capacity of about 2,000+. These courses normally lead to the Master's degree in the concerned discipline and are of two years/one and half-year duration. Facilities also exist at

these centres offering part-time courses at the Post-graduate level for those who are already in service. Duration of such courses normally is three years.

Institutional Framework

As has been mentioned above, the Vocational Training/Craftsmen Courses are offered at the Industrial Training Institutes. The Diploma courses are offered in the Polytechnics which are

Boards of Technical Education who lay down in general the levels and standards of the courses and guide the system of evaluation of the students appearing at the examination. Degree and Post-

Departments, and institutions declared as of national importance or as deemed Universities.

Indian Institutes of Technology: These are our apex institutions for engineering education and research. Each Institute conducts a First degree course and Master's degree course in a wide range

the Institutes is on the Post-Graduate studies and Research with an inter-disciplinary approach. To this end each Institute has developed good departments of Physics, Chemistry, Mathematics, and Social Sciences which interact with the departments of Engineering and Technology. The student enrolment at the Institutes at the Undergraduate level is limited to 1250 and admission at the Post-Graduate level is designedly kept at about the same order as in the under-graduate courses. The Institutes are in various stages of consolidation and development. As part of the national plan of

Indian Institute of Science, Bangalore: The Indian Institute of Science, Bangalore is the oldest and leading post-graduate and research centre in Science and Engineering and has facilities in special

and Power Engineering, High Voltage Engineering, Power Engineering, Bio-Chemistry, Chemistry, Physics and Mathematics. A major Centre in Automation and Control Systems and another in Electronics Design Technology are in the process of establishment.

The National Institutes of Technology (NITs) is an engineering, science, technology and management school system in India comprising thirty autonomous institutions located in one each major state/territory of India. Since their inception decades ago, all NITs were referred as Regional Engineering Colleges (RECs) and governed by their respective state governments. A parliamentary legislation in 2002 brought them under the direct purview of India's federal government. In 2007, through legislation, the Indian government declared these schools as Institutes of National Importance at par with the Indian Institutes of Technology. NITs were founded to promote regional diversity and multi-cultural understanding in India. Therefore, in the NIT school system, half of the student population in each batch is drawn from the respective state of the NIT and the other half is drawn from the rest of India on a common merit list. This is different than the Indian Institutes

India as the IIT admission criteria is based only on the performance of a student in an entrance examination. NITs offer degree courses at bachelors, masters, and doctorate levels in various branches of engineering and technology. Various nationwide college surveys rate most of the

NITs over other colleges in India, except for the IITs and a few other institutions. NITs function autonomously, similarly to IITs, sharing only entrance tests. The autonomy enables the NITs to set up their own curriculum, thereby making it easier to adapt to changing industry requirements.

State Colleges and University Departments: In addition to the above institutions offering courses at degree and post-graduate level, there is a wide network of engineering colleges established and administered by the State Governments, Universities and private agencies; they are also

Some of them are more than a century old and have been pioneers in engineering education in

Special Institutions: In additions to the above institutions there are certain specialised institutions

National Institute for Training in Industrial Engineering, Bombay — offers a two years post-graduate programme in Industrial Engineering as also a number of Executive Development Programmes and

National Institute of Foundry and Forge Technology, Ranchi — offers a special post-graduate training programme of 12-18 months duration in Advanced Foundry and Forge techniques for personnel from the industry.

Indian School of Mines, Dhanbad — which has been declared a deemed University is a specialised Centre for Undergraduate and Post-graduate studies and research in Mining, Applied Geology, Petroleum Technology and Geo-Physics.

Other Institutions: There are also other institutions offering courses in architecture and town planning (such as School of Planning and Architecture at New Delhi which offers degree course in Architecture and Post-graduate course in Town Planning with specialisation in Urban Design,

Institute of Industrial Design, Ahmedabad), Marine Engineering (College of Marine Engineering, Mumbai), etc.

Q.4   What is All India Council of Technical Education (AICTE)?

Ans: The All India Council for Technical Education (AICTE) was set-up in November 1945 as a national level Apex Advisory Body to conduct survey on the facilities on technical education and to promote development in the country in a coordinated and integrated manner. And to ensure the same, as stipulated in, the National Policy of Education (1986), AICTE be vested with statutory authority for planning, formulation and maintenance of norms and standards, quality assurance through accreditation, funding in priority areas, monitoring and evaluation, maintaining parity of

of technical education in the country.

The purview of AICTE (the Council) covers programmes of technical education including training and research in Engineering, Technology, Architecture, Town Planning, Management, Pharmacy, Applied Arts and Crafts, Hotel Management and Catering Technology, etc., at different levels.

Q.5 Why should I choose Engineering as a Career?

Ans: Engineering is the most versatile profession one can opt as a career. In fact engineering degree is so versatile that you can enter any area of economy whether it is banking, administrative service, tourism, defense service and many more in addition to mainstream engineering profession. Unlike other professions, knowledge of the nature of engineering, and the role of engineers, is concerned with the design and production of so many objects, devices, and systems which are an integral part of our environment and day-to-day life. These systems are as vital to society as are our school, health care, and legal systems. Engineers probably have a wider choice of environment in which to work, and a greater variety of jobs, than is possible in any other profession.

The purpose of engineering is to design and manufacture the hardware of life and make it comfortable. From bicycle to aeroplane; to television to computer; all adds to the quality of life we are living today. Moreover engineering profession is rewarding — socially as well as economically. An engineer has a place of pride in the society and country. Engineers are always among the highest paying executive in any industry or organisation. There are ample opportunities for growth and innovation in the engineering profession. So if you are interested in innovating new things which have practical and commercial utility certainly engineering is your profession.

accelerating technology. There are a record 2 million engineers in the United States, making the engineering profession the second largest in the nation. And companies are hiring! In short, it a seller's market for engineers.

Employment opportunities in engineering are expected to be plentiful through the year 2011 and beyond. That's because employment is expected to increase about as fast as the average for all occupations while the number of degrees granted in engineering is expected to remain near present levels. An engineering degree also opens doors to other careers. Engineering degree is the most versatile degree available in the present day education system in country like India. New generation careers like IT, Biotechnology, Bioinformatics, and Genetic Engineering, etc., are more suitable to students with engineering background than any other background. Many engineering graduates move into other professions, such as administrative service, medicine, law and business, where an engineering background is a valuable asset.

Q.6 How can one become an Engineer in India?

Ans:

from any of the recognised institution. As discussed earlier there are three levels of engineering courses available at engineering institutions in the country.

> Degree (BE/B.Tech) and postgraduate degree courses offered by engineering colleges (both in government and private sector), universities, National Institute of Technology (NIT) and Indian Institute of Technology (IIT)
>
> Diploma courses offered by polytechnics
>
> Training in engineering skills offered by Industrial Training Institutes (ITI)

Over and above the BE/B.Tech. programmes conducted by engineering colleges/ NITs/IITs and other central institutes, there are professional bodies recognised by the Government of India to award AMIE (Associate Member of Institution of Engineers) equivalent to any degree in engineering to cater mainly to working people in the private and public sectors. Students who cannot join a engineering college due to any reason can complete a diploma in engineering from any of the polytechnics and then join an engineering college through lateral entry scheme or can complete AMIE to become equivalent to a BE/B.Tech degree holder in engineering. However our discussion in the book shall be limited to degree level courses (BE/B.Tech) in engineering.

To join an engineering college in our country, a student has to opt for science stream after High

with subjects such as Physics, Chemistry, Mathematics, Computer Science, Biology, Biotechnology and Engineering Drawing, etc. Though majority of the branches of engineering colleges needs Mathematics, Physics and Chemistry as compulsory subjects at (10+2) level, some of the branches also admit student having Mathematics and Physics as compulsory subject and any one of Chemistry/Computer Science/ Biology/ Biotechnology /Engineering Drawing as the third subject.

A science student after completing B.Sc. with major in Physics/Chemistry/ Mathematics can also join any of the 3 years B.Tech programme in engineering offered by some institutions/ universities. Moreover students can also complete M.Sc. in electronics/ radio physics/ Information Technology, etc., and join the engineering profession. However entering the engineering college after (10+2) and acquiring the B.Tech/B.E to join the engineering profession is the most popular route to become an engineer.

Q.7   What is Aeronautical Engineering?

Ans: Aeronautical engineering is the branch of engineering that deals with study or practice of

or military aircraft; develop more powerful but also more eco-friendly jet engines.

Some of the elements of aeronautical engineering are:

Aerodynamics:
wind tunnels.

Propulsion: The energy to move a vehicle through the air (or in outer space) is provided by internal combustion engines, jet engines, or rockets.

Control engineering: The study of mathematical modelling of systems and designing them in order that they behave in the desired way

Structures:

Materials science: Related to structures, aerospace engineering also studies the materials of

Aero elasticity:

programming of any computer systems on board an aircraft or spacecraft and the simulation of systems.

Q.8 What is Aerospace Engineering?

Ans:

engineering. Aerospace engineers are concerned with the design, analysis, construction, development, testing and manufacture of commercial and military aircraft, missiles and spacecraft. Aerospace engineers have specialties in aerodynamics, propulsion, thermodynamics, structures, celestial mechanics, acoustics and guidance and control systems. For aerospace engineers employment is available with Air India, Indian Airlines, Pawan Hans, Helicopter Corporation of

get employment in organisations such as HAL, Defence Research and Development Organisation and laboratories, National Aeronautical Lab, Aeronautical Development Establishment & Civil Aviation Department, to name a few. With the rise in the number of air taxis and liberalisation of airspace, avenues for aeronautical engineers have seen upward swing.

Q.9 What is Agricultural Engineering?

Ans: This is the branch of engineering that deals with design and development of farm machineries and other implements related to agriculture, processing of agricultural products, etc. With entry of high-tech entering the agricultural engineering, Satellites will improve agriculture, resource management and you can think of it as micromanagement from the heavens. Global positioning systems, says Bernie Engel, a Purdue professor in agricultural and biological engineering, use satellite signals to help determine where we are on the ground. When used with geographical information systems, these systems can provide a tremendous amount of detail about soil, air,

of acres or even square feet. By combining various data about soils, for example, farmers can predict where they may need to apply fertilizer or pesticide or where they're likely to have an

implications in agriculture and natural resources management," Engel says, "Forests, grasslands and ranges can be monitored this way, too."

A large percentage of agricultural engineers works in academia or for government agencies such as the States Department of Agriculture or state agricultural extension services. Agricultural engineers work in production, sales, management, research and development, or applied science.

Q.10 What is Automobile Engineering?

Ans: Automobile engineering is the branch of engineering that deals with design, development, manufacture and repair of automobiles. Matthew Franchek, a Purdue University professor of mechanical engineering, says he believes that engines in the future will be able to continuously monitor their own health. Within 10 years, he predicts, an automobile will communicate with its driver and with service personnel to request maintenance. Furthermore, relying on global positioning satellites, individual cars will be able to communicate on-the-road emergency needs during vehicle failures. Emergency road crews will be able to pinpoint the stalled vehicle and know precisely what parts are needed to repair it.

Q.11 What is Architectural Engineering?

Ans: Architectural engineering is the application of engineering principles to the design of technical systems of buildings. The profession of architectural engineering includes practicing engineers designing, managing and constructing mechanical, electrical or structural systems for buildings. Architecture combines technicality with aesthetics and creativity. An architect's job is to create landscapes and design buildings, roads and bridges or even townships. Needless to say, architects play an important role in society's development.

Q.12 What is Bioinformatics?

Ans: Bioinformatics is an engineering discipline at the convergence of computing and the life sciences aimed at development of technologies for storing, extraction, organising, analysing,

The potential employers for bioinformatics graduate includes:

Specialised bioinformatics companies, Pharmaceutical and biotech companies employ bioinformatics technology in all stages of the drug discovery process. A biotech/ industrial biotech company using bioinformatics for study of crops and livestock.

The computing companies building specialised hardware and software for bioinformatics.

Other potential employers include academic research groups, Govt agencies such as patent

methods, while the latter focuses more on hypothesis testing and discovery in the biological domain. Although this distinction is used by National Institutes of Health in their working

of developments and knowledge between the more hypothesis-driven research in computational biology and technique-driven research in bioinformatics. Computational biology also includes lesser known but equally important subdisciplines such as computational biochemistry and computational biophysics.

A common thread in projects in bioinformatics and computational biology is the use of mathematical tools to extract useful information from noisy data produced by high-throughput

biology in this regard). A representative problem in bioinformatics is the assembly of high-quality DNA sequences from fragmentary "shotgun" DNA sequencing, while in computational biology, a representative problem might be statistical testing of a hypothesis of common gene regulation using data from mRNA microarrays or mass spectrometry.

Q.13 What is Biomedical Instrumentation Engineering?

Ans: With the introduction of sophisticated diagnostic and life support medical equipment currently used for medical investigations, during open heart surgery, dialysis, etc., in modern hospitals throughout the country, the need was felt for well-trained personnel with knowledge of both the human system and technology of the instruments used, and who would thus understand and

technology and its use and intelligent operations.

Q.14 What is Biotechnology?

Ans: Biotechnology is the industrial and pharmaceutical application of cell and molecular biology. It is a major growth industry worldwide, with exciting new developments in medicine, agriculture, horticulture, forensic science and microbiology, and it offers increasing opportunities for graduates with biotechnology knowledge and skills. Applied biotechnology involves introducing new genes into organisms, breeding organisms to form new variants or treating organisms with

Q.15 What is Biological Engineering?

Ans: It is a broad-based engineering discipline that deals with bio-molecular and molecular processes, product design, sustainability and analysis of biological systems. Generally, bioengineering encompasses other engineering disciplines when they are applied to living organisms (e.g., prosthetics in mechanical engineering). Bioengineering is often synonymous with biomedical engineering, though in the strict sense the term can be applied more broadly to include food engineering and agricultural engineering. Biotechnology also falls under the purview of the broad umbrella of bioengineering. Biological Engineering is the same thing as Agricultural Engineering, whereas Biomedical engineering (also known as bioengineering) is related with the

engineering is called Bioengineering by others. Therefore, people could easily get confused.

Q.16 What is Biochemical Engineering?

Ans: Biochemical engineering is a branch of chemical engineering that mainly deals with the design and construction of unit processes that involve biological organisms or molecules. Biochemical engineering is often taught as a supplementary option to chemical engineering due to the similarities in both the background subject curriculum and problem-solving techniques used by both professions. Its applications are used in the pharmaceutical, biotechnology, and water treatment industries.

Bio-chemical engineering has two central domains: (i) processing of biological materials and (ii) processing using biological agents as living cells, enzymes or antibodies. Biochemical engineering

and as well as (ii) of chemical engineering methodology and strategies.

This branch captures the information and technologies from both areas and accomplishes new synthesis for bioprocess design, operation, analysis and optimisation. Classic topics of biochemical engineering are design and analysis of bioreactors, biomass production in cell cultures, instrumentation and control of bioprocesses and bio-product recovery. Recent developments are metabolic engineering and bio-systems technology.

Q.17 What is Biomedical Engineering?

Ans: Biomedical Engineering is the application of engineering principles and techniques to the

It is a less known discipline than other specialties such as electrical engineering or mechanical engineering. An increasing number of universities with an engineering faculty now have a biomedical engineering programme or department from the undergraduate to the doctorate

after completing an undergraduate degree in a more traditional discipline of engineering or science. However, undergraduate programmes are becoming more widespread.

Research and development is the most commonline of work for biomedical engineers and covers a processing, biomechanics, biomaterials, systems analysis, 3-D modelling, etc. Examples of concrete applications of biomedical engineering are the development and manufacture of prostheses, medical devices, diagnostic devices and imaging equipement, laboratory equipment, drugs and other therapies as well as the application of engineering principles to biological science problems.

Clinical engineering is a branch of biomedical engineering for professionals responsible for the management of medical equipment in a hospital. The tasks of a clinical engineer are typically the acquisition and management of medical device inventory, supervising biomedical engineering technicians (BMETs), ensuring that safety and regulatory issues are taken into consideration and serving as a technological consultant for any issues in a hospital where medical devices are concerned. Clinical engineers work closely with the IT department and medical physicists.

Q.18   What is Chemical Engineering?

Ans: Chemical engineering applies principles of chemistry and physics to the design and production of materials that undergo chemical changes during their manufacture. Chemical engineer also

to preserve our natural resources.

technology, processing of food and agricultural products, synthetic food, petrochemicals, synthetic

Chemical engineers will be needed to develop new polymeric materials for medical devices, light-weight alloys for aircraft and solid-state materials that allow electronic miniaturisation and further development of the computer industry. Improved health care also will require new manufacturing processes for pharmaceutical products.

Chemical engineering largely involves the design and maintenance of chemical processes for large-scale manufacture. Chemical engineers in this branch are usually employed under the title of process engineer.

Chemical engineers are aiming for the most economical process. This means that the entire production chain must be planned and controlled for costs. A chemical engineer can both simplify and complicate "showcase" reactions for an economic advantage. Using a higher pressure or temperature makes several reactions easier; ammonia, for example, is simply produced from its component elements in a high-pressure reactor.

Three primary physical laws underlying chemical engineering design are Conservation of mass, Conservation of momentum and Conservation of energy. The movement of mass and energy around a chemical process are evaluated using Mass balances and energy balances which apply these laws to whole plants, unit operations or discrete parts of equipment.

In doing so, Chemical Engineers use principles of thermodynamics, reaction kinetics and transport phenomena. The task of performing these balances is now aided by process simulators, which are complex software models (such as Pro II and Hysys) that can solve mass and energy balances and usually have built-in modules to simulate a variety of common unit operations.

The modern discipline of chemical engineering encompasses much more than just process engineering. Chemical engineers are now engaged in the development and production of a diverse range of products, as well as in commodity and specialty chemicals. These products include high performance materials needed for aerospace, automotive, biomedical, electronic,

and composites for vehicles, bio-compatible materials for implants and prosthetics, gels for

properties for opto-electronic devices. Additionally, chemical engineering is often intertwined with biology and biomedical engineering. Many chemical engineers work on biological projects such as understanding biopolymers (proteins) and mapping the human genome.

Q.19   What is Civil Engineering?

Ans: Civil engineering is the oldest branch of engineering and incorporates the design and construction of roads, airports, tunnels, bridges, water supply and sewage systems, dams harbours, railroad systems, docks, power supply systems, building and even nuclear power plants. Civil engineering offers areas of specialisation such as structural engineering, highway engineering and water management.

habitable place to live in.

Engineering has developed from observations of the ways natural and constructed systems react and from the development of empirical equations that provide bases for design. Civil engineering

Sub-disciplines of civil engineering are:

    General civil engineering
    Structural engineering
    Geotechnical engineering
    Transportation engineering
    Environmental engineering
    Hydraulic engineering
    Construction engineering
    Urban engineering

land (real property) divisions. General engineers spend much of their time visiting project sites, developing community/neighbourhood consensus, and preparing construction plans.

Structural engineering is concerned with the design of bridges, buildings, offshore oil platforms, dams, etc. Structural design and structural analysis are components of structural engineering and a key component in the structural design process. This involves computing the stresses and forces at work within a structure. There are some structural engineers who work in non-typical areas, such as designing aircraft, spacecraft and even biomedical devices. Major design concerns are sense, structural engineering is largely the application of Newtonian mechanics to the design of structural elements and systems: such as buildings, bridges, walls (including retaining walls), dams, tunnels, etc.

Structural engineers ensure that their designs satisfy a given design intent predicated on safety

and building sway are not uncomfortable to occupants). In addition, structural engineers are

new building, including calculating the loads on each member and the load capacity of various building materials (steel, timber, masonry, concrete). An experienced engineer would tend to

building components.

and structural engineering for buildings. Additionally, structural engineers often further specialise into special structure manufacture or construction, such as pipeline engineering or industrial structures.

occupants and furniture in a building, the forces of wind or weights of water, the forces due to seismic activity such as an earthquake, dead loads including the weight of the structure itself and all major architectural components and live roof loads such as material and manpower loading

like winds, earthquakes and Tsunamis. In recent years, however, reinforcing structures against sabotage has taken on increased importance.

Geotechnical engineering also known as soil mechanics is concerned with soil properties, mechanics of soil particles, compression and swelling of soils, seepage, slopes, retaining walls, foundations, footings, ground and rock anchors, use of synthetic tensile materials in soil structures, soil-structure interaction and soil dynamics. Geotechnical engineering covers this

The importance of geotechnical engineering can hardly be overstated: buildings must be supported

an important subject of geotechnical engineering.

Transportation engineering is primarily concerned with motorised road transportation. This

Other specialised areas of transportation engineering deal with the designs of non-road transportation facilities, such as rail systems, airports, and ports.

Environmental engineering deals with the treatment of chemical, biological, and/or thermal

prior waste disposal or accidental contamination. Among the topics covered by environmental transport. Environmental engineers are also involved in pollution reduction, green engineering, and industrial ecology. Environmental engineering also deals with the gathering of information on the environmental consequences of proposed actions and the assessment of effects of proposed actions for the purpose of assisting society and policy makers in the decision making process.

Environmental engineering is the contemporary term for sanitary engineering. Some other terms in use are public health engineering and environmental health engineering.

area of engineering is intimately related to the design of pipelines, water distribution systems, drainage facilities (including bridges, dams, channels, culverts, levees, and storm sewers), canals, and to environmental engineering. Hydraulic engineers design these facilities using the

Construction engineering involves planning and execution of the designs from transportation, site development, hydraulic, environmental, structural and geotechnical engineers.

Urban engineering is a subset of the general practice of urban planning. It is limited to civil engineering in an urban setting and does not include designing buildings or their functions.

Q.20   What is Computer Science and Engineering?

Ans: This course is concerned with theoretical and engineering aspects of computer architecture, system and application software, computer networks, VLSI, internet technology and applications. Adequate emphasis is also given to programming, algorithm design and analysis, formal languages and automata theory, and theoretical computer science.

Computer Engineering is a discipline encompassing electronic engineering and computer science. This hybrid of electronic engineering and computer science allows the computer engineer to work on both software and hardware, and to integrate the two. Computer engineers are involved on all aspects of computing, from the design of individual microprocessors, personal computers, and supercomputers, to the integration of computer systems into other kinds of systems (a motor vehicle, for example, has a number of subsystems that are computer and digitally oriented).

Electronic equipment today relies very heavily on computer technology and so electronic engineers and computer engineers may work together to design and manufacture electronic equipment which requires both hardware and software design. Common computer engineering tasks include writing embedded software for real-time microcontrollers, designing VLSI chips, working with analog sensors, designing mixed signal circuit boards, and designing operating systems.

Computer engineering will draw an increasing number of students who have an interest in the design of computer hardware and software. According to the Bureau of Labour Statistics

Q.21   What is Ceramic Engineering?

Ans: This branch of engineering deals with composition and behaviour of materials. The strength of materials under different kind of load conditions is studied. New materials can be produced as per requirement by combining different materials and their properties.

The multibillion-dollar ceramic industry converts processed materials and raw materials taken directly from the earth (clay, sand, etc.) into such useful products as spark plugs, glass, electronic components, nuclear materials, abrasives, rocket components, and even tableware.

High-temperature processing is the key to ceramic engineering, and the products are always inorganic, nonmetallic solids. From a single chemical source, ceramic engineers make useful materials in many forms. Carbon as diamond is used as an abrasive for grinding; carbon in the

cables, etc.

Q.22 What is Dairy Technology?

Ans:
of diary technology. Dairy Technologists apply the knowledge of various other sciences such as bacteriology, chemistry, physics, economics and engineering to the production, preservation and distribution of dairy products.

Q.23 What is Electrical Engineering?

Ans: Electrical engineers are concerned with the generation, distribution and use of electrical power and power control. Electrical engineers work with equipment that produce and distribute electricity such as generators, transmission lines, transformers, lighting and wiring in buildings. In fact, electrical engineers are involved in the practical application of electrical energy.

job opportunities in industries like the railways, construction, civil aviation and all types of manufacturing plants.

More than a quarter of all engineers concentrate in electrical engineering. The demand for electrical engineers is expected to remain high due to projected growth in the aerospace, telecommunications and microelectronics industries.

Q.24 What is Electronics Engineering?

Ans: Branch of engineering that deals with the behaviour of electron and application of this in developing equipments. Electronics engineer study and use systems that operate by controlling

semiconductors. The design and construction of electronic circuits to solve practical problems is

engineering.

Q.25 What is Environmental Engineering?

Ans: Environmental engineering is the branch of interdisciplinary engineering which deals with the protection of environment and developing equipments for reducing air, water pollution and instruments for monitoring pollution, etc. Negative environmental effects can be decreased and controlled through public education, conservation, regulations, and the application of good engineering practices.

Q.26   What is Energy Engineering?

Ans:
services, facility management, plant engineering, environmental compliance and alternative energy technologies. Domain of Energy Engineering expertise combines selective subjects from

which has relativity with electrical, mechanical and chemical engineering. Energy minimisation is the purpose of this growing discipline. Often applied to building design, heavy consideration

of current systems. Energy Engineering is increasingly seen as a major step forward in meeting carbon reduction targets. Energy Technology refers to the knowledge of and usage skills required for conversion, production, transfer, distribution and use of energy. This leads to the mastering of technology based on the laws of nature, as a result of which different forms of energy can be used to serve the needs of mankind in such a way that nature is spared and the economic resources of society are taken into consideration.

Q.27   What is Food Technology?

Ans:
industry has responded positively to this by developing new technology to cater to the new needs of the consumer market. Food technologist develops new methods for processing, preservation and packaging of foodstuffs and evaluating their nutritional value.

Q.28   What is Food Processing Technology /Food Processing & Preservation Technology?

Ans: This is the latest area where lot of manpower is needed these days. World is fast moving towards processed, ready to eat food products. Tinned or packed food is the example of those opportunities of employment exists in Food processing Industries' supply of packed / tinned food to Airlines, Defence and other places besides local market.

Food Science and Technology is the Application of Science, Technology and Engineering to the

of study to encourage education, investigation and research in all aspects of food science and technology and also to support improvement of the food supply and its use through science, technology and education. Job Opportunities are available in various food concerns like Pepsi foods, Pepsi Co India, Nestle, etc.

Q.29   What is Fire Engineering?

Ans:
equipment and process, etc. It involves the study of the behaviour, compartmentalisation,

development, production, testing and application of mitigating systems. In structures, be they land-based, offshore or even ships, the owners and operators are responsible to maintain their facilities

code, which are enforced by the Authority Having Jurisdiction. Buildings must be constructed in accordance with the version of the building code that is in effect when an application for a building permit is made. Building inspectors check on compliance of a building under construction with the building code. Once construction is complete, a building must be maintained in accordance with

Q.30   What is Information Technology (IT)?

Ans:

the rapid development of computing. Communication and Internet based technologies and their tremendous impact on our daily lives. In contrast to the more traditional information systems discipline, information technology deals with the development, utilisation, inter-relation and

in the context of the global Internet. As we enter the information Age of the 21st century, society will be increasingly dependent on information technology, and demand for IT professionals will remain high throughout the decades to come.

In particular, IT deals with the use of electronic computers and computer software to convert, store, protect, process, transmit, and retrieve information. For that reason, computer professionals are often called IT specialists, and the division of a company or university that deals with software technology is often called the IT department. Other names for the latter are information services (IS) or management information services (MIS), managed service providers (MSP).

Information technology (IT) or Information and communication(s) technology (ICT) (also Infocomm) is a broad subject concerned with technology and other aspects of managing and processing information, especially in large organisations.

Q.31   What is Industrial Engineering?

Ans: It studies the production resources of an industry, i.e. people, materials, information, fuel, energy, etc., and ensures the effective utilisation of these in the production process. The Industrial engineer interfaces between the management and operations sectors in order to ascertain the proper use of available industrial resources. Industrial engineering draws upon the principles and methods of engineering analysis and synthesis, as well as mathematical, physical and social sciences together with the principles and methods of engineering analysis and design to specify, predict and evaluate the results to be obtained from such systems. Industrial engineers work to eliminate wastes of time, money, materials, energy and other resources.

Industrial Engineering is also known as Operations Management, Production Engineering, Manufacturing Engineering or Manufacturing Systems Engineering; a distinction that seems to depend on the viewpoint or motives of the user. Recruiters or Educational establishments use the names to differentiate themselves from others. In healthcare Industrial Engineers are more commonly known as Management Engineers, or even Health Systems Engineers.

is applied in virtually every Industry. Examples of where industrial engineering might be used include shortening lines (or queues) at a theme park, streamlining an operating room, distributing products worldwide, and manufacturing cheaper and more reliable automobiles.

The name "industrial engineer" can be misleading. While the term originally applied to manufacturing,

research, systems engineering, ergonomics and quality engineering. The unicist approach to engineering considers industry as a complex system.

to make products more manufacturable and consistent in their quality, and to increase productivity.

Q.32   What is Instrumentation Engineering?

Ans: Instrumentation Engineering is concerned with the development and maintenance of

and control. An instrument is a device that measures and/or regulates physical quantity/

contrivances that can be as simple as valves and transmitters, and as complex as analyzers.

vehicles. The control of processes is one of the main branches of applied instrumentation.

Instrumentation can also refer to handheld devices that measure some desired variable. Diverse handheld instrumentation is common in laboratories, but can be found in the household as well. For example, a smoke detector is a common instrument found in most western homes. Output instrumentation includes devices such as solenoids, valves, regulators, circuit breakers, and relays. These devices control a desired output variable, and provide either remote or automated

remotely or by a control system.

Q.33   What is Mechanical Engineering?

Ans: Mechanical engineering applies the principles of mechanics and energy to the design of machines and devices. These engineers are concerned with the design, operation and maintenance of machines, their components, machine tools, manufacturing systems and processes. Perhaps the broadest of all engineering disciplines, mechanical engineering is generally combined into three broad areas: energy, structures and motion in mechanical systems, and manufacturing.

large technical or manufacturing company has a need for mechanical engineers. Manufacture's

are expected to lead the revolution taking place in manufacturing processes, in which defects

engineering mechanics, and manufacturing. Depending on the colleges and the universities, some mechanical engineering programmes offer more specialised programmes, such as mechatronics, robotics, transport and logistics, cryogenics, and biomechanics, if a separate department does not exist for these subjects.

Modern analysis and design processes in mechanical engineering are aided by various

computer-aided design (CAD) and computer-aided manufacturing (CAM). In system design and controls, a mechanical engineer may apply CAD/CAM systems to feed "instructions" to computer numerically-controlled (CNC) machines such as robots, milling machines, and lathes. In this way the engineer could automate the manufacturing process without the need for intermediate

itself, such as a fan to cool an electrical system, a turbine to power a submarine, or a spray gun to apply chemical coatings.

Given the wide range of subjects, students preparing to study mechanical engineering should consider the programmes available in their respective colleges and universities. Most mechanical engineering programmes offer the major subjects of study. Fundamental subjects of mechanical engineering include: statics, dynamics, strength of materials, solid mechanics,

(including robotics), manufacturing technology, mechatronics and control theory. Mechanical engineers are also expected to understand and be able to apply concepts from chemistry and electrical engineering. At the smallest scales, mechanical engineering becomes nanotechnology and molecular engineering — one speculative goal of which is to create a molecular assembler to build molecules and materials via mechanosynthesis.

Q.34   What is Mining Engineering?

Ans: Mining provides the raw materials and energy resources needed to sustain modern civilisation. The mining curriculum combines basic engineering subjects, topics in geology and essential courses in mining to prepare graduates to discover, evaluate and develop mineral deposits. Graduates of the programme design, operate, manage and reclaim mines and mining facilities in a

a strong background in mathematics, computer applications, economics, communication skills and physical sciences, particularly geology, physics and chemistry. A strong global and domestic economy requires innovative well-trained engineers to meet the ever-increasing demand for energy and mineral resources.

Materials recovered by mining include bauxite, coal, diamonds, iron, precious metals, lead, limestone, nickel, phosphate, rock salt, tin, uranium, and molybdenum. Any material that cannot be grown from agricultural processes must be mined. Mining in a wider sense can also include extraction of petroleum, natural gas, and even water.

Q.35   What is Printing Technology?

Ans: With advent of science and technology, computers, lasers and microprocessor, printing has become no longer a craft. It is a multi-disciplinary profession dealing with nitration of text and

manufacturers and in packaging industries, etc.

Q.36   What is Plastic & Rubber Technology?

Ans: Plastic is now a household goods and Plastic Technologist works for design, development and utilisation of plastic in industrial as well as domestic sector. The plastic industry is an expanding one with new products and applications being developed all the time. Plastic goods are used throughout the world with everything from household goods to the most advanced aircraft using the latest technology. The range of use is endless because plastic is so versatile. Plastic has many

but promising beginning by commencing production of polystyrene in 1957. The potential Indian market has motivated entrepreneurs to acquire technical expertise, achieve high quality standards and build capacities in various facets of the booming plastic industry.

Rubber is useful in many industries as an ingredient in the manufacturing process, including various automobile and its components. Rubber and recycled rubber have a variety of applications

industries. Specialisation include products for high technology companies such as health care, military, aerospace, electronics and food processing industries including rubber-to-metal bonded parts.

The plastic and rubber sector is considered a sunrise industry and has been exhibiting a consistent export growth rate in the past. The top ten trading partners of India's plastic products include

Q.37 What is Textile Technology?

Ans:
equipment and processes. Textile engineers design, research, develop and implements automated

R&D production control, technical sales, quality control and corporate management through the production supervisory route.

Q.38 What is Leather Technology?

Ans: It deals with processing of leather obtained from various sources. After processing various products are made depending on its properties of the leather. Various types of suitcases, Jacket, Bags, etc., are made from leather. Various methods to preserve it for a longer period are also taught. Job opportunities exist in the industries dealing with above-mentioned products.

Q.39 What is Marine Engineering?

Ans: It is the branch of engineering, which operate and maintain the propulsion and electrical generation systems on board a ship. They also can help with the design, build, and repair of these complicated systems. New design is mostly included within the naval architecture or ship design.

is closely related to mechanical engineering, although the modern engineer requires knowledge (and hands on experience) with electrical, electronic, pneumatic, hydraulic, chemistry, control engineering, naval architecture, process engineering,gas turbines and even nuclear technology on military vessels.

Marine Engineering staff also deal with the "Hotel" facilities on board, notably the sewage, lighting, air conditioning and water systems. They deal with bulk fuel transfers, and require

tasks — especially with cargo loading/discharging gear and safety systems. A ship's crew is divided into two distinct sections — those who 'drive' the ship and those who maintain it. The drivers are the deck department whose manager is the Captain, and those who maintain and look after the technical side are the engineers, whose manager is the Chief engineer. Also on board are

maintenance and operation of the ship.

The original term, engineer, on a ship meant the people who dealt with the engines ("The black hand gang"), as opposed to the Consulting Engineer concept. Marine Engineers are generally much more hands on, and often get dirty, sweaty and hot doing their jobs. Care and thought is required, however, especially with heavy machinery in a seaway, and in managing the rest of the engine-room crew.

Q.40 What is Metallurgical Engineering?

Ans: Metallurgical Engineering is indispensable activities in supplying materials to any industrialised nation. Curriculum is designed to provide fundamental knowledge of basic engineering and extensive

is extremely diverse, and it offers a wide variety of career opportunities for young people who have an interest in technology, science and engineering. Metallurgical engineers are employed in

products. You have probably heard many times that modern societies cannot function without a plentiful supply of every conceivable type of metal and alloy and that people who are skilled in the use or production of metals and metallic materials of all kinds are highly valued.

reduced either chemically or electrolytically.

In production engineering, metallurgy is concerned with the production of metallic components for use in consumer or engineering products. This involves the production of alloys, the shaping, the heat treatment and the surface treatment of the product. The task of the metallurgist is

toughness, hardness, corrosion resistance and performance in extremes of temperature.

Common engineering metals are aluminium, chromium, copper, iron, magnesium, nickel, titanium and zinc. These are most often used as alloys. Much effort has been placed on understanding one

as steel. Normal steel is used in low cost, high strength applications where weight and corrosion are not a problem. Cast irons, including ductile iron are also part of this system.

Stainless steel is used where resistance to corrosion is important. Aluminium alloys and magnesium alloys are used for applications where strength and lightness are required.

Most engineering metals are stronger than most plastics and are tougher than most ceramics.

applications require high tensile strength with little weight. Concrete rivals metals in applications requiring high compressive strength and resistance to the effects of water. Wood rivals metal in applications requiring low cost and availability of materials and low cost of construction, as well as in applications requiring certain aesthetics.

This is indeed true, and metallurgical engineers command good salaries, and young metallurgical graduates can expect to be able to choose from some exciting career alternatives. Opportunities for employment exists in Research Institutions / Public Sectors Heavy Steel Plants / Laborites where search is going on for new materials to be used in space technology, Automobile Industry, Food processing, Nuclear Industries, etc.

Q.41   What is Naval Architecture?

Ans: Naval architecture is an engineering discipline dealing with the design, construction, maintenance and operation of marine vessels and structures. Naval architecture involves basic and applied research, design, development, design evaluation and calculations during all stages of the life of a marine vehicle.

Preliminary design of the vessel, its detailed design, construction, trials, operation and maintenance, launching and dry-docking are the main activities involved. Ship design calculations are also

Naval architecture also involves formulation of safety regulations and damage control rules and

Q.42   What is Ocean Engineering?

Ans:

Oceanographic engineering, also called marine electronics engineering, concerned with the design of electronic devices for use in the marine environment, such as the remote sensing systems used by oceanographers.

Offshore construction, also called offshore engineering or maritime engineering, concerned with

wind farms.

The goal of Ocean Engineering is to develop the knowledge and technology to foster and enable the wise and effective use, development, and preservation of the ocean, its natural resources and environment.

Q.43   What is Robotics/Robotic Engineering?

Ans:

computer science, dealing with intelligent behaviour in machines.

all roughly convey the same idea:

Conventional AI (symbolic AI / logical AI / neat AI): distinguished by formalism, statistical analysis,

includes expert systems and case based reasoning.

Computational Intelligence (CI) (non-symbolic AI / scruffy AI, soft computing): recognised for its informal, non-statistical and often trial-and-error approaches. Learning is usually an iterative process of connectionist system parameter tuning, based on empirical data. CI subdivides into 3 main sections: Neural networks, Fuzzy systems and Evolutionary computation. This research overlaps with a life, cognitive science, cybernetics & robotics. Many hybrid intelligent systems have also appeared.

Q.44   What is Materials Science?

Ans:

and all applications to its micro, nano, and atomic-structure, and vice versa. It is closely related to applied physics, chemical engineering and chemistry, bio-engineering and biology, mechanical engineering, civil engineering and electrical engineering; it is one of the most multidisciplinary

science. Because of this, in recent years materials science has been propelled to the forefront at many universities, sometimes controversially: many academics feel that the nano buzzword is bringing in large amounts of funding at the cost of detracting from the teaching of fundamental materials science by putting too much emphasis on devices and applications which may or may not see fruition as working products.

Q.45   What is Engineering Physics (EP)?

Ans: Engineering Physics is an academic degree, usually at the level of Bachelor of Science. Unlike other engineering degrees (such as aerospace engineering or electrical engineering), EP does not necessarily include a particular branch of science or physics. Instead, EP is meant to provide a more thorough grounding in applied physics of any area chosen by the student (such as optics, nanotechnology, control theory, aerodynamics, or solid-state physics).

Q.46   What is Micro Technology?

Ans: Micro technology is technology with features near one micrometre (one millionth of a

microscopic transistors on a single chip, microelectronic circuits could be built that dramatically improve performance, functionality, and reliability, all while reducing cost and decreasing volume. This development led to the Information Revolution. More recently, scientists have learned that not only electrical devices, but also mechanical devices, may be miniaturised and

technology has given to the electrical world. While electronics now provide the 'brains' for today's advanced systems and products, micromechanical devices can provide the sensors and actuators — the eyes and ears, hands and feet — which interface to the outside world. Today, micromechanical devices are the key components in a wide range of products such as automobile airbags, ink-jet printers, blood pressure monitors, and projection display systems. It seems clear that in the not-too-distant future these devices will be as pervasive as electronics.

Q.47   What is Nanotechnology?

Ans: Nanotechnology comprises technological developments on the nanometer scale, usually 0.1 to 100 nm (1/1,000 µm, or 1/1,000,000 mm). A possible way to interpret this size is to take the length of a hair, and imagine something ten thousand times smaller. The term has sometimes been applied to microscopic technology. Nanotechnology is any technology which exploits phenomena and structures that can only occur at the nanometer scale, which is the scale of several atoms and small molecules.

is the understanding and control of matter at dimensions of roughly 1 to 100 nanometers, where

can result in different electromagnetic and optical properties of a material between nanoparticles and the bulk material; the Gibbs — Thomson effect, which is the lowering of the melting point of a material when it is nanometers in size; and such structures as carbon nanotubes.

materials science departments at universities around the world in conjunction with physics, mechanical engineering, bioengineering, and chemical engineering departments are leading the breakthroughs in nanotechnology. The related term nanotechnology is used to describe

in nanotechnology. Nanoscience is the world of atoms, molecules, macromolecules, quantum dots, and macromolecular assemblies, and is dominated by surface effects such as Van der Waals force attraction, hydrogen bonding, electronic charge, ionic bonding, covalent bonding, hydrophobicity, hydrophilicity, and quantum mechanical tunneling, to the virtual exclusion of macro-scale effects such as turbulence and inertia. For example, the vastly increased ratio of surface area to volume opens new possibilities in surface-based science, such as catalysis.

Q.48 What is Nuclear Technology?

Ans: It is the technology that involves the reactions of atomic nuclei. It has found applications from smoke detectors to nuclear reactors and from gun sights to nuclear weapons. There is a great deal of public concern about its possible implications, and every application of nuclear technology is reviewed with care.

Major current applications:

Nuclear weapons of various designs can release tremendous destructive power. Some have been designed to level cities (up to the largest, Tsar Bomba), while other designed have looked at smaller nuclear weapons, for nuclear artillery, nuclear land mines, and nuclear bunker-busting missiles. International agreements attempt to regulate nuclear testing and limit nuclear proliferation. Nuclear medicine is the application of nuclear technology to medicine. This includes the use of radiation to obtain images of the inside of a living body, as well as to destroy cancer. Radioactive tracers are used to probe the motion of elements on the body.

Nuclear power is the application of nuclear technology to generate power. This includes both large nuclear power plants and smaller, safer, nuclear batteries. The latter have been used on a number of spacecraft as compact, light, long-term energy sources and to power cardiac pacemakers.

Ionising radiation is readily generated by radioactive decay. Nuclear technology is often used to construct gamma ray or neutron sources. This ionising radiation can be useful in killing cancerous cells, or in sterilising food and water (this process is generally known as irradiation).

A number of consumer items use nuclear technology:

Smoke detectors often contain americium; they detect smoke because it reduces the ability of alpha radiation to ionize air in the detector's ionisation chamber.

Glowing watch dials and gun sights (now) often contain tritium, whose decay triggers phosphorescence in a pigment on the dial. During World War II they often contained radium instead.

Q.49 What is Optical Engineering?

Ans:

Optical engineers design optical instruments such as microscopes, telescope and other equipment that utilises the properties of light, including optical sensors and measurement systems, as well as

Since optical engineers want to design and build devices that make light do something useful, they must understand and apply the science of optics in substantial detail, in order to know what is physically possible to achieve (physics and chemistry). But they also must know what is practical

engineering computers are important to many (perhaps most) optical engineers. They are used with instruments, for simulation, in design, and for many other applications. Engineers often use general computer tools such as spreadsheets and programming languages, and they also make

Optical engineering metrology uses optical methods to measure micro-vibrations with instruments like the laser speckle interferometer or to measure the properties of the various masses with instruments measuring refraction.

Q.50 What is Financial Engineering?

Ans:

make trading, hedging and investment decisions, as well as facilitating the risk management of those decisions. Utilising various methods, practitioners of Financial Engineering aim to precisely

Investment banking
Corporate strategic planning
Securities trading and risk management
Derivatives trading and risk management
Investment management

Q.51 What is Manufacturing Engineering/Production Engineering?

Ans:

means of tools and a processing medium, and including all intermediate processes involving the

and of secondary production. Some industries, like semiconductor and steel manufacturers use the term "fabrication".

Although handicraft production has been with us for many millennia, modern-style manufacturing is generally regarded as beginning around 1780 with the British Industrial Revolution, spreading thereafter to Continental Europe and North America, and subsequently around the world. Originally, the term applied to commodities or artifacts which were "made by hand".

Q.52   What is Telecommunication Engineering?

Ans: It is the branch of engineering that deals communication of information over a distance. The term comes from a contraction of the Greek tele, meaning 'far', and communications, meaning "the discipline that studies the principles of transmiting information and the methods by which it is delivered (as print or radio or television etc.)"

The term is most used to refer to communication using some type of signalling, such as the aldis lamp or the transmission and reception of electromagnetic energy. This covers many media and

and computer networking, although other types of signalling are also included.

Q.53   What is Paper Engineering/Technology?

Ans: Paper technology encompasses the design and analysis of the equipment and processes that

treatment of the sheet with coating, calendering, and other mechanical processes. Paper making is not chemical engineering. On the contrary, the paper industry is a client of the chemical industry.

Q.54   What is Nuclear Engineering?

Ans: It is the practical application of the atomic nucleus gleaned from principles of nuclear

nuclear safety, heat transport, nuclear fuels technology, nuclear proliferation, and the effect of radioactive waste or radioactivity in the environment.

Q.55   What is Petroleum Engineering?

Ans: Petroleum Engineering is involved in the exploration and production activities of petroleum as an upstream end of the energy sector. Upstream, refers to the source of the petroleum, the

as a river supplies the ocean. The diverse topics covered by petroleum engineering are closely related to the earth sciences. Petroleum engineering topics include geology, geochemistry, geomechanics, geophysics, oil drilling, geopolitics, knowledge management, seismology, team building, team work, tectonics, thermodynamics, well logging, well completion, oil and gas production, reservoir development, and pipelining.

It is an increasingly technical profession that involves procuring reserves from places that

prices. While not thought of as highly technical in some circles, this is a fallacy. The use of high technology equipment, high speed computers, innovative materials, team management philosophies, statistics, probability analysis, and knowledge management, is usually coupled with the reality of only indirect measurement of most essential facts due to being buried under miles of earth. One look at the number of patents held for use in the industry is testimony to the

One key aspect of this profession is excellence. Where mistakes are measured in millions of dollars petroleum engineers will be held to a higher standard. Deepwater operations can be compared to space travel in terms of technical challenges. Arctic conditions and conditions of extreme heat have to be contended with. High Temperature and High Pressure (HTHP) environments that have become increasingly commonplace in today's operations require the petroleum engineer to be savvy in topics as wide ranging as thermohydraulics, geomechanics, and intelligent systems.

Petroleum engineers must implement high technology plans with the use of manpower, highly coordinated and often in dangerous conditions. The drilling rig crew and machines they use become the remote partner of the petroleum engineer in implementing every drilling programme. Understanding and accounting for the issues and communication challenges of building these teams remain just as vital to the petroleum engineer as ever.

The Society of Petroleum Engineers is the largest professional society for petroleum engineers and is a good source of information. Petroleum engineering education is available at dozens of universities in the United States and throughout the world – primarily in oil producing states.

Petroleum engineers have historically been one of the highest paid engineering disciplines; this is offset by a tendency for mass layoffs when oil prices decline. Petroleum engineering offers a challenging blend of earth sciences, geology, operations, politics, advanced mathematics and the opportunity to risk massive amounts of money. The rewards for successful engineers range from high paying jobs to the opportunities to start oil companies.

Q.56   What is Software Engineering?

Ans: It is the profession of people who create and maintain software applications by applying technologies and practices from computer science, project management, engineering, application

traditional engineering disciplines. Some software applications contain millions of lines of code that are expected to perform properly in the face of changing conditions, making them comparable in complexity to the most complex modern machines. For example, a modern airliner has several million physical parts (and the space shuttle about ten million parts), while the software for such an airliner can run to 4 million lines of code.

Q.57   What is Safety Engineering?

Ans: Safety engineering is an applied science strongly related to systems engineering. Safety engineering assures that a life-critical system behaves as needed even when pieces fail.

Safety engineers distinguish different extents of defective operation: A "fault" is said to occur when some piece of equipment does not operate as designed. A "failure" only occurs if a human being (other than a repair person) has to cope with the situation. A "critical" failure endangers one

Safety engineers also identify different modes of safe operation: A "probabilistically safe" system has no single point of failure, and enough redundant sensors, computers and effectors so that it is very unlikely to cause harm (usually "very unlikely" means, on average, less than one human life lost in a billion hours of operation). An inherently safe system is a clever mechanical arrangement that cannot be made to cause harm — obviously the best arrangement, but this is not always possible. A fail-safe system is one that cannot cause harm when it fails. A "fault-tolerant" system can continue to operate with faults, though its operation may be degraded in some fashion.

These terms combine to describe the safety needed by systems: For example, most biomedical equipment is only "critical", and often another identical piece of equipment is nearby, so it can be merely "probabilistically fail-safe". Train signals can cause "catastrophic" accidents (imagine chemical releases from tank-cars) and are usually "inherently safe". Aircraft "failures" are "catastrophic" (at least for their passengers and crew) and aircraft are usually "probabilistically fault-tolerant". Without any safety features, nuclear reactors might have "catastrophic failures", so real nuclear reactors are required to be at least "probabilistically fail-safe" and some like pebble-bed reactors are "inherently fault-tolerant".

Q.58   What is Space Technology/Engineering?

Ans: Space technology/engineering is a term that is often treated as a different category of engineering. Outer space (as commonly used, the universe exclusive of Earth, see also extraterrestrial) is such an alien environment attempting to work with it leads inevitably to new leading edge techniques and knowledge. New technologies originating with or accelerated by space-related endeavours are often subsequently exploited in other economic activities. This has

investment of public funds in space activities and programmes. Political opponents counter that

For example: Computers and telemetry were once leading edge technologies that might have been considered "space technology" because of their criticality to boosters and spacecraft. They existed prior to the Space Race of the Cold War but their development was vastly accelerated to meet the needs of the two major superpowers' space programmess. Though still used in spacecraft and missiles, their more prosaic applications are remote monitoring (via telemetry) of patients, water plants and highway conditions, etc., the widespread use of computers outweighs their space applications in quantity and variety of application.

Q.59   How can one take admission in an Engineering College?

Ans: Different Boards (central or state) conducts 10+2 or Higher Secondary Examination in science stream throughout the country, which is the minimum educational eligibility criterion for admission into an engineering college. In order to keep parity of admission and give every student equal opportunity irrespective of the board from where he/she has passed the qualifying examination, most of the reputed engineering colleges conduct admission test for admitting

at National Level as well as State Level. The most important engineering entrance test at the national level is the IIT-JEE and All India Engineering Entrance Examination (AIEEE). Admission to all the Indian Institute of Technology is through IIT-JEE and all the National Institute of Technology (NIT) is through AIEEE only. Given below is a list of some important engineering admission tests

01.	IITs/ISM/BHU(IIT-JEE)	Sept/Oct
02.	Birla Institute of Technology, Mesra	Jan/Feb
03.	National Institute of Foundry & Forge Technology	January
04.	College of Architecture, Chandigarh	January
05.	Department of Chemical Engg & Tech(Panjab University)	January
06.	Punjab Engineering College(All India Seats)	January
07.	University of Delhi(all India Seats)	Fan/Feb
08.	Jamia Millia Islamia, New Delhi	May
09.	School of Planning & Architecture, New Delhi	April/May
	1, Main Road, Gandhi Nagar, Bangalore-560009	Feb/March
12.	National Institute of Design, Ahmedabad-380007(GDPD courses)	Oct/Nov
14.	National Fire Service College, Nagpur	March
15.	Sir J.J. College of Architecture, Dr. D.N.Road, Mumbai-400001	April
16.	Pondicherry University(All India Seats)	April/May
17.	Thapar Institute of Technology(All India Seats)	Jan/Feb
18.	BITS, Pilani	April
19.	Indian Institute of Information Technology, Hyderabad	Jan/Feb
20.	Indian Institute of Information Technology, Allahabad	Jan/Feb
21.	Anna University, Chennai(All India Seats)	Jan/Feb
22.	AMU, Aligarh	Jan/Feb
23.	Dayalbagh Educational Institute, Agra	April/May
24.	GB Pant University(All India Seats)	April/May
26.	University of Roorkee	November
27.	Rohilkhand University	January
28.	All India Engineering Entrance Examination(AIEEE)	Nov/Dec

Q.60 What is IIT-JEE?

Ans: The Indian Institutes of Technology are Institutions of national importance established through an act of Parliament. These Institutes play a leading role in technological manpower development and research programmes comparable with the best in the world. Admissions to Undergraduate Programmes for all Indian and Foreign nationals at these institutions are made through the Joint Entrance Examination (JEE).

Institute of Technology, Banaras Hindu University, Varanasi is one of the oldest institutions devoted to education in various engineering disciplines. Indian School of Mines, Dhanbad, a deemed university, is the oldest institution of its kind in India. The admissions to the Undergraduate Programmes at these institutions are also made through JEE.

research in frontier areas. The environment at all these Institutions is highly conducive for:

Building of solid foundation of knowledge

Development of personality

Pursuit of excellence and self-discipline

Enhancement of creativity through motivation and drive, which helps to produce professionals well trained for the rigours of professional and social life.

Today, alumni of these institutions occupy key positions in industry/academia in India and abroad.

Each Institute has well-equipped modern laboratories, a state-of-the-art library and computer networks. The selected candidates live in a pleasant and intellectually stimulating environment. The teaching methods rely on direct personal contact between the teacher and the students. Living in such an environment with people having similar goals and aspirations is an exciting experience during one's academic life.

pace. A minimum level of performance is necessary for satisfactory progress. The medium of instruction is English. These institutes offer courses leading to Bachelor's degree in a number of engineering, technology and science disciplines.

M.Sc. integrated courses in pure and applied sciences and M.Tech. (Integrated) courses in a few disciplines are also offered by some of these Institutes. In addition, some IITs offer dual-degree M.Tech. programmes, wherein both B.Tech. and M.Tech. degrees are awarded at the end of the programme.

The current pattern, which has been followed since 2006, consists of two objective type papers each containing maths, physics and chemistry sections. The syllabus of the examination is predominantly based on topics covered by the CBSE Board Examination (AISSCE) and the ISC Board Examination. The pattern of questions in JEE is deliberately variable so as to minimize the chance of students getting selected by cramming up the probable questions. As it is objective type questions, Optical mark recognition answer sheets has been adopted since 2006. In previous years, there were separate maths, physics and chemistry papers, each of two hours' duration that contained both subjective and objective Questions. The current pattern is adopted so as to reduce the students' stress.

Given the importance attached to the JEE by students all over India, the IITs follow a rigorous procedure while conducting it every year. The exam is set by the JEE Committee (consisting of a group of faculty members drawn from the admitting colleges) under the tightest security. Multiple sets of question papers are framed and the set that is to actually be used on the day of the exam is

The age limit for appearing in IIT-JEE is 25 years. For candidates belonging to SC, ST and PD categories, the relaxed age limit is 30 years. From 2007, a candidate is allowed to take the JEE two times at the most. This has been done mainly to reduce stress on students and discourage the concept of "cram schools". Furthermore, from 2007 on, students who are selected for admission to an IIT cannot attempt the examination again in the future. From 2008 six new IITs have been opened with 120 seats each increasing the total number of seats to almost 7000. For 2009, admissions have been made to two more IITs, namely IIT Indore and IIT Mandi (Himachal Pradesh) taking the seat count to almost 8300. As of 2011, with additional courses in several old and new IITs, the total seat count has crossed 9600.

Candidates applying for JEE should have either completed or appearing in any one of the following qualifying examinations:

Board, such as Central Board of Secondary Education, New Delhi; Council for Indian School

Intermediate or two-year Pre-University Examination conducted by a recognised Board/ University.
Final Examination of the two-year course of the Joint Services Wing of the National Defence Academy.

Advanced (A) level.

Any Public School/Board/University Examination in India or in any foreign country recognised by the Association of Indian Universities as equivalent to 10+2 system.
H.S.C. Vocational Examination.
Senior Secondary School Examination conducted by the National Open School with a

3 or 4-year Diploma recognised by AICTE or a State Board of Technical Education.

In case the relevant qualifying examination is not a public examination, the candidate must have passed at least one public (Board or Pre-University) examination at an earlier level. The candidates belonging to the general category must secure a minimum of 60 percent marks in aggregate in their Qualifying Examination. Candidates belonging to SC, ST and PD categories must secure a minimum of 55 percent in aggregate in the Qualifying Examination. If any Board awards only letter grades without providing an equivalent percentage of marks on the grade

Physical Fitness
Registered Medical Practitioner in the prescribed format that will be made available to them at

study at the participating Institutes.

Websites and IVRS for JEE

Institute	Websites	STD code	Number
IIT Bombay	http://www.iitb.ac.in/jee	022	25767062
IIT Delhi	http://www.iitd.ac.in/jee	011	26581064, 26582002
IIT Guwahati	http://www.iitg.ac.in/jee	0361	2692788

	http://www.iitk.ac.in/jee	0512	2597236
	http://www.iitkgp.ernet.in/jee	03222	281881, 278241
IIT Madras	http://jee.iitm.ac.in/	044	22578223
IIT Roorkee	http://www.iitr.ac.in/jee	01332	279805, 279806

Q.61 What is All India Engineering Entrance Examination (AIEEE)?

Ans: The All India Engineering Entrance Examination (AIEEE) is an examination organised by the Central Board of Secondary Education (CBSE) in India. Introduced in the year 2002, this national level competitive test is for admission to various under-graduate engineering and architecture

Technology (IIITs) and thirty National Institutes of Technology (NITs). The examination is generally

week of June. Candidates are ranked on an all-India basis and state basis. Thus, they have an All India Rank (AIR) and a State Rank (SR).

The examination consists of two papers: Paper 1 and Paper 2. Paper 1 has three sections: Mathematics, Physics and Chemistry with equal weight for each subject. Each section consists of multiple choice objective-type questions each of which has four choices. Out of the four choices for a given question, only one choice is correct. Paper 1 has a negative-marking scheme wherein an incorrect answer is negatively marked with one fourth of the maximum marks allotted to the question. Paper 2 has three sections: Mathematics, Drawing, and Aptitude. Mathematics, and Drawing sections have multiple choice objective-type questions and the Aptitude section has drawing-based questions. The duration of each paper is three hours. Candidates are not allowed to carry any textual material, calculators, logarithmic tables or electronic devices into the examination hall. The number of questions and their maximum marks has been variable through the years. The questions are based on a syllabus that is common to syllabi of all the state boards in India and the Central Board of Secondary Education. Candidates can opt for question papers either in English or in Hindi language. For admission to B.Tech or B.E. courses in the participating institutes the candidate is required to take the Paper 1; for admission to B.Arch or B. Planning courses the candidate is required to take Paper 2. Students can opt to take any one or both the papers. The examination was conducted in

candidates who opted for the same, while the remaining students took the examination in the conventional pen and paper mode. The number of attempts which a candidate can avail at the examination is limited to three in consecutive years.

Q.62 What is IISc (Indian Institute of Science, Bangalore)?

Ans: Jamsetji Nusserwanji Tata (1839-1904) was one of the extraordinary men, who towards the end of the nineteenth century was convinced that the future progress of the country depended crucially on research in Science and Engineering. He envisaged this Institute to promote original

After consulting several authorities in the country, he constituted a Provisional Committee to prepare the required scheme for the setting up of the Institute. On 31st December 1898, a draft prepared by the Committee was presented to Lord Curzon, the Viceroy-designate. Subsequently, upon the request of the Secretary of State for India, the Royal Society of London asked for the help of Sir William Ramsay, Nobel Laureate. Ramsay made a quick tour of the country and reported Bangalore to be the suitable place for such an Institution.

With the establishment of the University Grants Commission in 1956, the Institute came under its purview as a deemed university.

uniqueness in its character. It is neither a National Laboratory which concentrates solely on research and applied work, nor a conventional University which concerns itself mainly with teaching. But the Institute is concerned with research in frontier areas and education in current technologi
innovative Integrated Ph D Programmes in Biological, Chemical and Physical Sciences for science graduates.

During the past eight decades many are the alumni and faculty who have gone out from this Institute to direct science and technology in the country, to create and nurture other laboratories

Sarabhai, J C Ghosh, M S Thacker, S Bhagavantam, S Dhawan, C N R Rao and scores of others

closely associated with the Institute.

contributions to frontier areas of research. The number of students in the institute is kept deliberately small in order to focus on quality. It has been able to innovate and introduce (a) new systems of imparting knowledge; and (b) educational reforms such as offering courses under unit system.

the Integrated Ph.D Programmes in Biological, Chemical, Physical and Mathematical Sciences for

the + 2 level; and (iv) IISc Young Engineering Fellowship programme for merited III year BE/ B Tech students.

involved in several areas of national importance: space science and technology, nanoscience and engineering, environmental and atmospheric sciences, endocrinology, genetic engineering, rural technology and energy problems.

been transferred to industries. Transfer of technology has also taken place in areas such as low-

available at the Institute such as low and high speed wind tunnels, water tunnel, high speed computers and sophisticated instruments have been helping public and private sector industries and defence. There has also been a certain amount of social utilisation of work in biosciences, for instance, (i) in plant tissue culture of sandal wood, eucalyptus and teak wood, (ii) disease control in silk worms, and (iii) on nutritional value enhancement of rice strains.

Some recent projects include the development of cryogenic equipment and vessels for advanced aircraft, fracture analysis of industrial and space launch vehicle components, thermo-metallurgical modelling of steel industries, acoustic absorbers to reduce acoustic pollution in industrial environment and automobiles, and microbial techniques for gold extraction from

and ferroelectric materials. It has also launched a major new initiative, called Sustainable Transformation of Rural Area (SuTRA).

In all these endeavours, the Institute, with a keen awareness of its noble tradition and the need

and technological goals of our country.

Whatever may be your natural skill and interests — mathematics, frontier research areas in the theoretical sciences, experimental work in biology, physics and chemistry, new areas in engineering

Research Programmes

Science Faculty (Ph D only):

> Astronomy & Astrophysics
> Biochemistry
> Ecological Sciences
> High Energy Physics
> Inorganic & Physical Chemistry
> Materials Research
> Mathematics
> Microbiology & Cell Biology
> Molecular Biophysics
> Molecular Reproduction Development and Genetics
> Organic Chemistry
> Physics
> Solid State & Structural Chemistry

Engineering Faculty (M. Sc [Engg] & Ph D):

> Aerospace Engineering
> Atmospheric & Oceanic Sciences
> Chemical Engineering
> Civil Engineering
> Computer Science & Automation
> Electrical Engineering
> Electronics Design & Technology
> Electrical Communication Engineering
> High Voltage Engineering

Instrumentation
Management Studies
Materials Research
Mechanical Engineering
Metallurgy
Supercomputer Education & Research

Use Programmes

ME in following branches

Aerospace, Chemical, Civil, Computer Science & Engineering, Electrical, High Voltage, Internet Science & Engineering, Mechanical, Metallurgy, Microelectronics, Signal Processing, Systems Science & Automation and Telecommunication.

M TECH

Instrumentation, Electronics Design and Technology, and Computational Science.

M DES

Product Design & Engineering

Integrated Ph D Programmes (after B.Sc. in 10+2+3 system)

(i) Biological, (ii) Chemical, (iii) Physical and (iv) Mathematical Sciences.

Q.63 What is National Institute of Design (NID)?

Ans: The National Institute of Design (NID) is internationally acclaimed as one of the foremost

and international awards since it was established in 1961 as an autonomous institution under the Ministry of Industry, now known as Ministry of Commerce & Industry, Government of India. NID has been a pioneer in industrial design education after Bauhaus and Ulm in Germany and is known for its pursuit of design excellence to make 'Designed in India: Made for the World a reality.' NID's graduates have made a mark in key sectors of commerce, industry and social development by taking role of catalysts and through thought leadership. NID has been recognised as a Science and Industrial Research Organisation by the Department of Science & Technology, Government of India.

Graduate Diploma Programme in Design (GDPD) commences with a two-semester Foundation Programme. This programme is geared to assist in developing attitudes and sensorial skills,

awareness of the environment and to arouse the students' creative faculties. The primary concern of the Foundation Programme is to introduce the students to the Fundamentals of design, to inculcate them to design as a problem solving process and to develop a highly evolved aesthetic sensitivity, and 'design' attitude.

In the foundation programme, basic design courses are augmented by related studies of science and liberal arts, to help and develop an understanding of the Indian milieu and the relevance of design. The foundation programme is geared to inculcate the development of values, attitudes and sensorial skills; necessary for any design specialisation. It aspires to create an awareness of the changing environment by constantly relating the students learning to real life situations. The programme provides the necessary direction, stimuli, facilities and experience to foster creativity and thereby help each individual discover their own identity, ability and potential.

The foundation programme is the basis on which the remaining design curriculum is built. It also makes students appreciate the multidisciplinary nature of design. This 4-year intensive professional UG programme is offered in the following three Faculty streams (possible areas of design specialisation through projects are given in brackets):

Industrial Design: Product Design, Furniture and Interior Design, Ceramic & Glass Design

Communication Design: Graphic Design, Animation Film Design, Film & Video Communication, Exhibition Design

Textile and Apparel Design: Textile Design

Admission is open to students who have passed or who will appear for qualifying examinations under the Higher Secondary (10+2) or equivalents like AISSCE/IB/ICSE, etc. It is understood that individual students, who have passed the Institute's admission tests/interviews will be admitted provisionally to the education programme subject to passing their qualifying examinations before they join the Institute.

Competence in technical and related subjects will normally be considered an advantage. The medium of instruction at NID is English. Upper age limit for candidates is 20 years (relaxable by 3 years for SC/ST candidates) as on 1 June of the year of admission.

Admission announcements are issued in the leading national dailies in the last week of September every year. Application forms along with the prospectus for admission is available on request from the second week of October on payment of requisite fees by Demand Draft of any scheduled bank drawn in favour of the National Institute of Design payable at Ahmedabad. Forms are also available at selected branches of Bank of India across the country. Forms downloaded from NID's website <www.nid.edu> along with required amount of DD drawn in favour of National Institute of Design payable at Ahmedabad is also accepted.

Admission is on the basis of NID's method of selection which extends beyond the students'

the perception, attitudes, aptitudes, and achievement motivation essential for a challenging and satisfying design career. The objectives of the tests and the interviews are to ascertain these. The tests at the various centres consist of design aptitude tests. Based on scores obtained from these tests, shortlisted candidates are called for second phase of admission procedure.

The second phase of the admission procedure includes studio tests followed by interviews at Ahmedabad. All those called for the second phase are required to attend the studio tests and interview, which completes the process of selection. The procedures, grades and weightage for each year will be decided by the Admission Committee for the year.

The norms for the selection are the sole prerogative of the Admission Committee and the decision of the Admission Committee and the Management in any of the matters concerning the admission

The Graduate Diploma Programme students are admitted only into the Foundation Programme and their entry into different design domains is not automatic. On successful completion of the

by the Semester Jury. All students are required to be present for the Orientation Programme and no exceptions can be made. Failure to be present at the Orientation programme may mean an automatic withdrawal by NID of its admission offer. Students who leave the Institute after joining will forfeit the entire tuition fees and other charges and will get only the refundable deposit.

seats are reserved for Scheduled Caste and Scheduled Tribe candidates. 3% seats are reserved for persons with disabilities as per the Persons with Disability Act, 1995. The qualifying candidates need to meet the eligibility and admission requirements of NID.

Number of Seats: Intake into the Graduate Diploma Programme is 60 and for the Post-Graduate Diploma Programme are 165. The number of seats available for PGDPD in different disciplines is as under:

Product Design	15
Furniture & Interior Design	10
Ceramic & Glass Design	10
Toy Design & Development	10
Apparel Design & Merchandising	15
Lifestyle Accessory Design	10
Textile Design	15
Animation Film Design	10
Film & Video Communication	10
Graphic Design	10
New Media Design	10
Software & User Interface Design	10
Information & Digital Design	10
Strategic Design Management	20

Important Dates

Issuing of Forms starts from — October

Issuing of form by post from NID — November

Obtaining forms from BOI — November

Receiving completed forms at NID — December.

Test for PGDPD — January

Test for GDPD — January

Q.64 How can one take admission at BITS Pilani?

Ans: The Birla Institute of Technology & Science (BITS), Pilani is an all-India Institute for higher education. The primary motive of BITS is to "train young men and women able and eager to create and put into action such ideas, methods, techniques and information".

The Institute is a dream come true of its founder late Mr G.D.Birla, an eminent industrialist, a participant in Indian freedom struggle and a close associate of the Father of Indian Nation Mahatma Gandhi. What started in early 1900s as a small school, blossomed into a set of colleges for higher education, ranging from the Humanities to Engineering until 1964 when all these colleges amalgamated to culminate into a unique Indian University of International standing. This university was christened as the Birla Institute of Technology and Science, Pilani, known to many as BITS, Pilani.

Over the years, BITS has provided the highest quality technical education to students from all over India admitted on the basis of merit. Its graduates may be found throughout the world in all areas of engineering, science and commerce. BITS symbolises the maturing of Indian technical ability and "can-do" entrepreneurial spirit, especially as derived from the private sector. BITS is located in the Vidya Vihar campus adjacent to the town of Pilani in Rajasthan.

First Degree Programmes

(Hons.), M.M.S (Master of Management Studies), M.Sc. (Hons.), M.Sc. (Tech.) and M.A. (Hons.). These are level wise equivalent degrees. These are called integrated degrees for two reasons: (i) there are several common courses like basic math and science amongst these degrees, and (ii) no intermediate degree, like B.Sc., B.Sc. (Hons.), B.A., B.A. (Hons), etc., is awarded. These degrees are based on a modular structure and their academic requirements are spelt out in respect of the number of courses rather than the number of years. All these programmes are structured in a

For admission to any of the above Integrated First degree programmes candidates should have passed the 12th examination of 10+2 system from a recognised Central or State board or its equivalent with Physics, Chemistry, and Mathematics. Further the candidate should have obtained a minimum of aggregate 80% marks in Physics, Chemistry and Mathematics subjects in 12th examination, with at least 60% marks in each of the Physics, Chemistry, and Mathematics

In order to apply for admission to the Integrated First degree programmes, the candidates have to appear in the online computer based test (BITSAT) as per the announcement made by the Institute through advertisement and brochures. Admissions are made purely on merit. The merit position of the candidate for admission will be based on the score obtained by the candidate

minimum marks in 12th examination, as mentioned above. The Institute considers only the latest performance through a public examination for admission. If the results of the latest examination are not available within the due date for submission of application, the candidate will not be considered even if there are some earlier performances of 12th class or its equivalent or any higher examination available with him/her. If a candidate has taken more than one attempt in 12th class or its equivalent, only his latest performance is considered, provided this attempt has been for the full component of subjects/courses prescribed.

all the central and state boards to the programme of their choice, irrespective of their BITSAT score.

Eligibility criteria for admission under 'Direct admission to Board toppers' scheme:

To be eligible for admission under the 'Direct admission to Board toppers' scheme, the candidate should be the topper from the science stream having taken Physics, Chemistry, Mathematics subjects in 12th. To identify the topper, the following criteria will be adopted.

(a) has taken Physics, Chemistry, and Mathematics subjects in 12th and

(b) has obtained the highest aggregate percentage of marks in 12th among all the students who have taken Physics, Chemistry, and Mathematics subjects from the Board. For the purpose of calculating the aggregate percentage, the aggregate marks should include the marks of Physics, Chemistry, and Mathematics subjects in addition to other subjects which are required to pass the 12th examination from the Board under consideration. Further, the Physics, Chemistry, Mathematics subject marks should be included in the aggregate,

main/optional/elective in his marksheet(s).

Applicants under the scheme should attach documentary proof in support of their claim, along with

stream. The Institute will also make efforts to get these data from the different boards on its own. In all cases, the Institute will be guided by the data provided by the concerned Board. In cases where

Q.65 How can one take admission in Delhi College of Engineering?

Ans: The admission to B.E. courses in both the reputed engineering institutions in Delhi, namely, Delhi College of Engineering (DCE) and Netaji Subhas Institute of Technology (NSIT), is done centrally by Delhi College of Engineering on the basis of the Combined Entrance Examination, CEE held in May.

Eligibility conditions for admission

A candidate passing any one of the following examinations (termed hereafter as the Qualifying Examination) and securing 60% or more marks in the aggregate of Physics, Chemistry and Mathematics shall be eligible for admission to the First Semester of Bachelor of Engineering Programme provided he/she has passed in each subject separately:

Education (C.B.S.E.) New Delhi.

(iii) B.Sc. (Gen.) Group A' Final Examination of the University of Delhi or an equivalent examination.

(iv) Must have passed B.Sc. (Hons.) examination in Physics, Chemistry and Mathematics of the University of Delhi with a combination of Physics, Chemistry and Mathematics having equal weightage to the subsidiary subjects, or an equivalent examination.

of the C.B.S.E. by the University of Delhi.

A candidate must additionally have passed English as a subject of study either at the 10th Class level or 12th Class level (core or elective).

Note:

(i) An applicant who has to leave an Engineering degree Course, or an equivalent Course, after exhausting the permissible number of chances in any other University/Board in India, will not be eligible for admission to Bachelor of Engineering Course.

(ii) Candidates who have appeared at the Annual Examination in the year and placed in compartment will not be eligible for admission for the year.

(iii) Candidates who have appeared at the Annual Examination of the year and are to reappear for the improvement to acquire the eligibility will not be considered for admission for the year.

(iv) No admission will be made directly to the second or any subsequent semester of the Course.

(v) No change of branch will be permitted after the commencement of the second semester, even if some seats fall vacant in some of the branches during the Course of second-semester.

(vi) No admission will be made after 31st August. The University of Delhi may, however, condone the delay in exceptional cases.

Relaxation in Marks for Reserved Category: Candidates belonging to the following categories, who apply for seats reserved for them shall be allowed a concession in the minimum eligibility requirements as detailed below:

(i) Scheduled Castes/Scheduled Tribes Candidates shall be allowed 10% concession of marks in the minimum eligibility/requirements.

(ii) Defence Quota: The children and/or widows of Personnel of Armed/Para-Military forces killed/disabled in action during hostilities who apply for seats reserved for them shall be allowed relaxation of 5% marks in the minimum eligibility requirements.

(iii) Physically Handicapped (PH): The candidate belonging to Physically Handicapped category shall be allowed 5% concession of marks in the minimum eligibility requirements. Applicant must be 17 years of age on or before the 1st October of the year in which he/she seeks admission. Relaxation in age up to one year only, with the approval of the Vice-Chancellor, is permissible (Such candidates should apply for relaxation only at the time of admission).

Q.66 How can one take admission in engineering courses of Guru Gobind Singh Indraprastha University, Delhi?

Ans: Guru Gobind Singh Indraprastha University, established by the Government of NCT of Delhi under

University that aims to facilitate and promote studies, research and extension work in emerging areas of higher education with focus on professional education in the disciplines of engineering, technology, management studies, medicine, pharmacy, nursing, education, law, etc.

Various full time/weekend professional programmes offered in the University Schools of Studies, University maintained Indira Gandhi Institute of Technology, Government Institutions, Centres of

Common Entrance Test (CET) held for admission into

Bachelor of Architecture (B.Arch.)

B.Tech./M.Tech. (Dual degree)

Bio-Technology

The eligibility criteria and all other details for Admission/ CET are available in the Admission Bulletin.

With a view to make hassle-free environment during the admission and thereby providing the requisite convenience to the applicants as well as their parent/guardians, the University is also providing On-Line Registration/Submission of Application Form. For detail visit www.ggsipu.nic.in.

Q.67 Which are the best engineering colleges in India?

Ans: Top 100 engineering colleges of India

Rank	College Name	Govt./Private
1		Government
2		Government
3	Indian Institute of Technology IIT Bombay, Mumbai	Government
4	Indian Institute of Technology IIT Madras, Chennai	Government
5	Indian Institute of Technology IIT Delhi, Delhi	Government
6	BITS Pilani, Pilani	Private
7	IIT Roorkee, Roorkee	Government
8	IT-BHU, Varanasi	Government
9	IIT-Guwahati, Guwahati	Government
10	College of Engg , Anna University, Guindy	Government
11	Jadavpur University, Faculty of Engg & Tech, Calcutta	Government
12	Indian School of Mines, Dhanbad	Government
13	NIT- National Institute of Technology, Warangal	Government
14	BIT, Mesra, Ranchi	Private
15	NIT- National Institute of Technology, Trichy	Government
16	Delhi College of Engineering. New Delhi	Government
17	Punjab Engineering College, Chandigarh	Government
18	NIT- National Institute of Technology, Suratkal	Government
19	Motilal Nehru National Institute of Technology, Allahabad	Government

20	Thapar Inst of Engineering & Technology, Patiala	Private
21	Bengal Eng and Science University , Shibpur, Howrah	Government
22	MANIT, Bhopal	Government
23	PSG College of Technology, Coimbatore	Government
24	IIIT, Hyderabad	Government
25		Government
26	Malviya National Institute of Technology, Jaipur	Government
27	VNIT, Nagpur	Government
28		Government
29	Dhirubhai Ambani IICT, Gandhinagar	Private
30	Osmania Univ. College of Engineering, Hyderabad	Government
31	College of Engineering , Andhra University, Vishakhapatnam	Government
32	Netaji Subhas Institute of Technology, New Delhi	Government
33		Government
34	NIT- National Institute of Technology, Rourkela	Government
35	SVNIT, Surat	Government
36	Govt. College of Engineering, Pune	Government
37	Manipal Institute of Technology, Manipal	Private
38	JNTU, Hyderabad	Government
39	R.V. College of Engineering, Bangalore	Private
40	NIT- National Institute of Technology, Jamshedpur	Government
41	University Visvesvaraya College of Engg., Bangalore	Government
42	VJTI, Mumbai	Government
43	Vellore Institute of Technology, Vellore	Private
44	Coimbatore Institute of Technology, Coimbatore	Government
45	SSN College of Engineering, Chennai	Private
46	IIIT, Allahabad	Government
47	College of Engineering, Trivandrum	Government
48	NIT Durgapur, Durgapur	Government
49	SIT, Calcutta	Government
50	Mumbai University Institute of Chemical Technology, Mumbai	Government
51	Sardar Patel College of Engineering, Mumbai	Private
52	P.E.S. Institute of Technology, Bangalore	Private
53	Maharashtra Institute of Technology, Pune	Private
54	Amrita Institute of Technology & Science, Coimbatore	Private
55	National Institute of Engineering, Mysore	Private
56	B.M.S. College of Engineering, Bangalore	Private
57	Laxminarayan Institute of Technology, Nagpur	Government

58	Nirma Institute of Technology, Ahmedabad	Private
59	IIIT, Pune	Government
60	Amity School of Engineering, Noida	Private
61		Government
62	S.J. College of Engineering, Mysore	Private
63	Chaitanya Bharathi Institute of Technology, Hyderabad	Private
64	IIIT, Bangalore	Government
65	SRM Institute of Science and Technology, Chennai	Private
66	SASTRA, Thanjavur	Private
67	Bangalore Institute of Technology, Bangalore	Private
68	The Technological Institute of Textile & Sciences, Bhiwani	Government
69	III, Gwalior	Government
70	JNTU, Anantpur	Government
71	M.S. Ramaiah Institute of Technology, Bangalore	Private
72	Gitam, Vishakhapatnam	Private
73	NIT- National Institute of Technology, Hamirpur	Government
74	NIT- National Institute of Technology. Jalandhar	Government
75	SV University Engineering College, Tirupati	Government
76	NIT- National Institute of Technology, Raipur	Government
77	Vasavi College of Engineering, Hyderabad	Private
78	The ICFAI Inst of Science and Technology, Hyderabad	Private
79	NIT- National Institute of Technology. Patna	Government
80	Cummins Colleges of Engg of Women, Pune	Government
81	VIT, Pune	Private
82		Private
83	Muffakham Jah Engineering College, Hyderabad	Private
84		Private
85	D.J. Sanghvim, Mumbai	Private
86	Sathyabhama Engineering College, Chennai	Private
87		Private
88	Mepco Schlek Engineering College, Sivakasi	Private
89	Guru Nanak Dev Engineering College, Ludhiana	Government
90	Hindustan Inst of Engineering Technologym, Chennai	Private
91	SDM College of Engineering, Dharwad	Private
92	R.V.R. & J.C. College of Engg, Guntur	Private
93	Jamia Millia Islamia, New Delhi	Government
94		Private
95	Dharmsinh Desai Institute of Technology, Nadiad	Private

96	S.G.S. Institute of Technology & Science, Indore	Government
97	Jabalpur Engineering College, Jabalpur	Government
98	Sree Chitra Thirunal College of Engineering, Trivandrum	Private
99	G.H. Patel College of Engg & Technology, Vallabh Vidyanagar	Government
100		Private

Q.68 How can I test my aptitude towards Engineering Education/Vocation?

Ans: Take the following Vocational Aptitude Test — Engineering and see your score.

There are 15 questions in this test and time allotted is **10 minutes**. Do the test in one sitting. The

Full Marks: 70

Study the following passage carefully and answer the relevant questions:

Applicants should have at least a high second class degree in mechanical or electrical engineering

Design & Development. Relevant postgraduate specialisation is preferable for Foundry, Quality control and Industrial Engineering.(From a Trainee Engineers advertisement.)

01. Applicants should be: 2
    a. Civil Engineers
    b. Mechanical Engineers
    c. Chemical Engineers
    d. Agricultural Engineers

02. It is preferable that applicants should have post-graduate specialisation for the following branches of engineering:
    a. Chemical   2
    b. Civil
    c. Industrial
    d. Foundry
    e. Quality Control.

03. For Industrial Engineering and Design & Development, it is necessary that the candidate should have a: 2
    a. First class degree
    b. First class diploma

    d. First class MBA
    e. First class CA

04. The method of inquiry in modern experimental science includes which of the following basic steps:
    a. A statement as to what investigator will personally gain from such inquiry?

b. A statement as to the purpose of inquiry?

c. An evaluation as to how it will serve human progress?

d. Determining what can be presupposed?

e. Steps to be taken in solving the problem?

a. 45 and 18

b. 43 and 61

c. 36 and 32

d. 32 and 36

e. 38 and 36

A, D, II, ___, ___, Z ? are they:

a. P and O

b. M and D

c. O and P

e. M and S

a. The heart

b. The eyes

c. The stomach glands

d. The mammary glands

e. The urinary bladder

08. Given below are some chemical names. By what are they commonly known?   5

a. Calcium Carbonate

b. Aluminium Potassium Sulphate

c. Sodium Bicarbonate

d. Methane

e. Calcium Oxide

09. What is an Atomic Pile? Is it: 6

a. Atom bombs kept in a pile

b. Heavy water

d. A device or machine used to produce controlled atomic energy

e. Piled up atoms

10. Answer the following: 10

a. What great astronomer was born at Thorn (Poland) in 1473?

    b.   Why is so famous?

    c.   What is the full form of NASA

    d.   Name the Indian Astronaut who died in space shuttle STS-07 accident

11. Which of the following are metals?   4

    a.   Pallium

    b.   Palladium

    c.   Vasculum

    d.   Spectrum

    e.   Vanadium

12. Which of the following are poisonous gases: 6

    a. Thermite   b. Phosphorite   c. Lewisite

    g. BBC   h. Phosgene   i. OED

    m. Arsenic   n. DB   o. CAD

    a.   Ampere

    b.   Ohm

    c.   Volt

    d.   Coulomb

    e.   Farad

14. What is Avagardo's law? What is Avagardo's number?   5

15. Answer the following: 3

    b.   Who invented computer

    d.   What is the full form of NAAC and AICTE

    e.   What is the full form of IIT, NIT and AIEEE

Score Chart:

10

ENVIRONMENTAL SCIENCE

Q.1 What is Environmental Science & Environmental Studies?

Ans:

biological sciences, (including but not limited to Ecology, Physics, Chemistry, Biology, Soil Science, Geology, Atmospheric Science and Geography) to the study of the environment, and the solution of environmental problems. Environmental science provides an integrated, quantitative, and interdisciplinary approach to the study of environmental systems. Related areas of study include environmental studies and environmental engineering. Environmental studies incorporate more of the social sciences for understanding human relationships, perceptions and policies towards the environment. Environmental engineering focuses on design and technology for improving environmental quality.

Environmental scientists work on subjects like the understanding of earth processes, evaluating alternative energy systems, pollution control and mitigation, natural resource management, and the effects of global climate change. Environmental issues almost always include an interaction of physical, chemical, and biological processes. Environmental scientists bring a systematic

scientist include the ability to relate space, and time relationships as well as quantitative analysis.

Q.2 What is Atmospheric Science?

Ans: Atmospheric science focuses on the Earth's atmosphere, with an emphasis upon its interrelation to other systems. Atmospheric sciences can include studies of meteorology, greenhouse gas phenomena, atmospheric dispersion modelling of airborne contaminants, sound propagation phenomena related to noise pollution, and even light pollution. Taking the example of the global warming phenomena, physicists create computer models of atmospheric circulation and infra-red radiation transmission, chemists examine the inventory of atmospheric chemicals and their reactions, biologists analyse the plant and animal contributions to carbon dioxide

understanding the atmospheric dynamics.

Q.3 What is Ecology?

Ans: Ecology is an interdisciplinary analysis of an ecological system which is being impacted by one might examine an estuarine setting where a proposed industrial development could impact certain

chemists would analyze the transport of water pollutants to the marsh, physicists would calculate air pollution emissions and geologists would assist in understanding the marsh soils and bay mud.

Q.4. What is Environmental Chemistry?

Ans: Environmental chemistry is the study of chemical alterations in the environment. Principal areas of study include soil contamination and water pollution. The topics of analysis include chemical degradation in the environment, multi-phase transport of chemicals (for example, evaporation of a solvent containing lake to yield solvent as an air pollutant), and chemical effects upon biota. As an example study, consider the case of a leaking solvent tank which has entered the habitat soil of an endangered species of amphibian. As a method to resolve or understand the extent of soil contamination and subsurface transport of solvent, a computer model would be implemented. Chemists would then characterise the molecular bonding of the

plants, and ultimately pond-dwelling organisms that are the food of the endangered amphibian.

Q.5 What is Geosciences?

Ans: Geosciences include environmental geology, environmental soil science, volcanic phenomena

including oceanography. As an example study of soils erosion, calculations would be made of surface runoff by soil scientists. Fluvial geo-morphologists would assist in examining sediment

transmission in the receiving waters. Biologists would analyze subsequent impacts to aquatic

Q.6 What is Hydrology?

Ans: Hydrology is the study of the movement, distribution, and quality of water on Earth and other planets, including the hydrologic cycle, water resources and environmental watershed

environmental science, physical geography, geology or civil and environmental engineering.

Domains of hydrology include hydrometeorology, surface hydrology, hydrogeology, drainage basin management and water quality, where water plays the central role. Oceanography and meteorology are not included because water is only one of many important aspects within those

Branches of hydrology: Chemical hydrology is the study of the chemical characteristics of water. Ecohydrology is the study of interactions between organisms and the hydrologic cycle. Hydrogeology is the study of the presence and movement of ground water.

Hydroinformatics is the adaptation of information technology to hydrology and water resources applications. Hydrometeorology is the study of the transfer of water and energy between land and water body surfaces and the lower atmosphere. Isotope hydrology is the study of the isotopic signatures of water. Surface hydrology is the study of hydrologic processes that operate at or near Earth's surface. Drainage basin management covers water-storage, in the form of reservoirs, pollutants and natural solutes.

Applications of hydrology

> Determining the water balance of a region.
> Determining the agricultural water balance.
> Designing riparian restoration projects.

> Designing irrigation schemes and managing agricultural productivity.
> Part of the hazard module in catastrophe modelling.
> Providing drinking water.
> Designing dams for water supply or hydroelectric power generation.
> Designing bridges.
> Designing sewers and urban drainage system.
> Analysing the impacts of antecedent moisture on sanitary sewer systems.
> Predicting geomorphological changes, such as erosion or sedimentation.
> Assessing the impacts of natural and anthropogenic environmental change on water resources.
> Assessing contaminant transport risk and establishing environmental policy guidelines.

Q.7 What is Meteorology and what are the different areas of Meteorology?

Ans:

eighteenth century. The nineteenth century saw breakthroughs occur after observing networks developed across several countries. After the development of the computer in the latter half of the twentieth century breakthroughs in weather forecasting were achieved. Meteorological phenomena are observable weather events which illuminate and are explained by the science of meteorology. Those events are bound by the variables that exist in Earth's atmosphere; temperature, air pressure, water vapour, and the gradients and interactions of each variable, and how they change in time. Different spatial scales are studied to determine how systems on local, region, and global levels impact weather and climatology. Meteorology, climatology, atmospheric physics, and atmospheric chemistry are sub-disciplines of the atmospheric sciences.

between Earth's atmosphere and the oceans are part of coupled ocean-atmosphere studies.

transport, agriculture and construction.

Meteorologists are scientists who study meteorology. Meteorologists work in government agencies, private consulting and research services, industrial enterprises, utilities, radio and television stations, and in education. Meteorologists are best-known for forecasting the weather. Many radio and television weather forecasters are professional meteorologists, while others are merely reporters (weather specialist, weatherman, etc...) with no formal meteorological training.

management. It is important for air crews to understand the implications of weather on their of ice on aircraft are cumulative — thrust is reduced, drag increases, lift lessens, and weight increases. The results are an increase in stall speed and a deterioration of aircraft performance. In extreme cases, 2 to 3 inches of ice can form on the leading edge of the airfoil in less than 5 minutes. It takes but 1/2 inch of ice to reduce the lifting power of some aircraft by 50 percent and increases the frictional drag by an equal percentage.

Agricultural meteorology: Meteorologists, soil scientists, agricultural hydrologists, and agronomists are persons concerned with studying the effects of weather and climate on plant

the energy balance of managed and natural ecosystems. Conversely, they are interested in the role of vegetation on climate and weather.

Hydrometeorology: Hydrometeorology is the branch of meteorology that deals with the hydrologic cycle, the water budget, and the rainfall statistics of storms. A hydrometeorologist prepares and issues forecasts of accumulating (quantitative) precipitation, heavy rain, heavy snow, and

required overlaps with climatology, mesoscale and synoptic meteorology, and other geosciences.

Nuclear meteorology: Nuclear meteorology investigates the distribution of radioactive aerosols and gases in the atmosphere.

Maritime meteorology: Maritime meteorology deals with air and wave forecasts for ships operating at sea. Organisations such as the Ocean Prediction Centre, Honolulu National Weather Service forecast

Q.8 What is Natural Resource Management?

Ans: Natural resource management refers to the management of natural resources such as land, water, soil, plants and animals, with a particular focus on how management affects the quality of life for both present and future generations (stewardship). Natural resource management deals with managing the way in which people and natural landscapes interact. It brings together land use planning, water management, biodiversity conservation, and the future sustainability

and their livelihoods rely on the health and productivity of our landscapes, and their actions as stewards of the land play a critical role in maintaining this health and productivity. Natural

principle that forms a basis for sustainable global land management and environmental governance

of those resources. Environmental management is also similar to natural resource management.

Q.9 What is Oceanography?

Ans:

coastal waters, shelves and the ocean bed. As such it is an interdisciplinary science that integrates principles of Biology, Chemistry, Geology, Meteorology and Physics.

it provides opportunity to those with intrinsic curiosity and a desire to venture into the vast realm of the unknown, which exists within our oceans. The work involves collecting samples, conducting surveys, analysing data using sophisticated equipment in the sea for long hours. Oceanographers apply the basic sciences to study the world's oceans and coastal waters. They study the motion and circulation of the ocean waters and their physical and chemical properties, and how these properties affect coastal areas, climate, and weather. Often, they are chemists, physicists, biologists, or geologists who bring their special skills to ocean studies. Being essentially a research-oriented profession, long periods are spent at the sea with all its challenges and

biology, geological oceanography, physical oceanography and chemical oceanography.

Q.10   What is Marine Biology?

Ans:

bodies of water. Given that in biology many phyla, families and genera have some species

environment rather than on taxonomy. Marine biology differs from marine ecology as marine ecology is focused on how organisms interact with each other and the environment, and biology is the study of the organisms themselves.

Q.11   What is Biophysics? What are the major areas of Biophysics?

Ans: Biophysics is an interdependent science discipline that employs unique methods of physics and physical chemistry to acquire knowledge on the biological systems present in our world. It applies the principles of Physics and Chemistry and the methods of Mathematical Analysis and Computer Modelling to understand how biological systems work. Biophysics explains biological function in terms of the molecular structures and their properties. Biophysics is a bridge between biology and physics. This discipline is concerned with applications of the principles and methods of physical sciences to biological problems.

because it deals with humans. Biophysics has a great importance in all our lives today. Biophysics

biology, nanotechnology, and agro physics. It can be said that Biological systems is the very root of all our existence. Biophysics incorporate the study of all levels of biological organisation, from molecules to ecosystems. The main aspect of biophysics is the use of the ideas and methods of physics and chemistry to study and explain the structures of living organisms and the mechanisms of life processes.

was the discovery of the double helix structure of the DNA molecule in 1953. Biophysics helped create powerful vaccines against infectious diseases. Biophysical methods are increasingly used to serve everyday needs, from forensic science to bioremediation. Medical imaging technologies including MRI (Magnetic Resonance Imaging), CAT (Computed Axial Tomography) scans, etc., are the invention of Biophysics.

from atoms and molecules to cells, organisms and environments. Biophysicists attempt to explain why our biophysical environment behaves as it does. Biophysicists study how organisms develop, see, hear, think and live. They investigate how the brain processes and stores information, the heart pumps blood, muscles contract, plants use light in photosynthesis, genes are switched on and off and many other questions. Biophysicists usually work with groups or teams of other scientists and professionals with other backgrounds to collaborate on solving common problems.

various problems they come across.

The major areas of biophysics are the following:

Molecular biophysics is the study of large molecules and particles of comparable size which play important roles in biology.

Radiation biophysics consists of the study of the response of organisms to ionising radiations, such as alpha, beta, gamma and x-rays and to ultraviolet light.

Physiological biophysics called by some as Classical biophysics, is concerned with the use of physical mechanisms to explain the behaviour and the functioning of living organisms or parts of living organisms and with the response of living organisms to physical forces.

Mathematical and theoretical biophysics- deals primarily with the attempt to explain the behaviour of living organisms on the basis of mathematics and physical theory.

Medical biophysics - deals with the study that uses physics to describe or effect biological process largely for the purpose of medical application. The areas of research combining Physics and physiology include medical imaging such as MRI, computed tomography and PET (Positron emission tomography); oncology and cancer diagnosis using radiolabelling and molecular imaging; and vasculature and circulatory system function.

Eligibility for those who intend to pursue biophysics career is that they must basically have an undergraduate degree with Physics, Biology and Chemistry. Some institutes also offer undergraduate programmes with special attention given to biophysics.

In India, however there are only few universities that offer courses in biophysics at the undergraduate level. Most biophysicists begin their career with a four-year Bachelor of Science degree in Biophysics, and then go on to earn a master's and a PhD in physics or a sub-discipline of physics. Biophysicists who wish to do research generally need to obtain a PhD and spend

biophysics, one to two years of post-degree clinical (residency) training is required.

Course areas of Biophysics include molecular biophysics, membrance biophysics, neuro-biophysics, biophysical techniques, bioenergetics, medical biophysics.

or government organisations in various academic grades for research oriented programmes. A faculty in a university, medical or dental college offering a programme in biophysics. Forensics laboratories, chemical companies, food-processing plants, drug manufacturers, cosmetic industry, and manufacturers of agricultural chemicals (fertilizers, pesticides, etc.) also employ biophysicists. There is a wide range of opportunities abroad in Biophysics, to carry on higher studies and to work.

Some of the world class organisations that hire biophysicists are National Institute for Research in Reproductive health (NIRRH), Mumbai; All India Institute of Medical Sciences, New Delhi; Institute of Microbial Technology, Chandigarh; Indian Institute of Science (IISC), Bangalore and National Institute of Virology (ICMR), Pune.

Q.12   What is Geosciences?

Ans: Geoscientists study the composition, structure, and other physical aspects of the Earth, and the Earth's geologic past and present by using sophisticated instruments to analyze the composition of earth, rock, and water. Many geoscientists and hydrologists help to search for natural resources such as groundwater, minerals, metals, and petroleum. Others work closely with environmental and other scientists to preserve and clean up the environment.

geology, geophysics, and hydrology. Geologists study the composition, processes, and history of

formation. They also study the evolution of life by analysing plant and animal fossils. Geophysicists use the principles of physics, mathematics, and chemistry to study not only the Earth's surface, but also its internal composition, ground and surface waters, atmosphere, oceans, and magnetic, electrical, and gravitational forces. Hydrologists study the quantity, distribution, circulation, and physical properties of water and the water cycle.

geologists map the subsurface of the ocean or land as they explore the terrain for oil and gas deposits. They use sophisticated instrumentation and computers to interpret geological information.

offering advice on major construction projects and assisting in environmental remediation and natural hazard-reduction projects. Mineralogists analyze and classify minerals and precious stones according to their composition and structure, and study the environment surrounding rocks in

alteration of sediments, such as sand, silt, and mud. These sediments may contain oil, gas, coal, and many other mineral deposits. Paleontologists study fossils found in geological formations to trace the evolution of plant and animal life and the geologic history of the Earth. Stratigraphers examine the formation and layering of rocks to understand the environment which formed them. Volcanologists investigate volcanoes and volcanic phenomena to try to predict the potential for future eruptions and hazards to human health and welfare. Glacial geologists study the physical properties and movement of glaciers and ice sheets. Geochemists study the nature and distribution of chemical elements in groundwater and earth materials.

Geophysicists specialise in areas such as geodesy, seismology, and magnetic geophysics. Geodesists interpret data from seismographs and other geophysical instruments to detect earthquakes and

measurements taken over the past few centuries to devise theoretical models that explain the Earth's origin. Paleomagnetists interpret fossil magnetisation in rocks and sediments from the

Other geophysicists study atmospheric sciences and space physics.

Q.13 What are the courses available in Environmental Science and what is the Career and Job Prospect?

Ans: Undergraduate and Post-graduate courses in environmental science are offered by several institutes across the country. Career in Environmental Science starts with a B.Sc/B.E degree

Science subjects. The duration of this course is three years. For M.Sc in Environmental Science which is of two year duration, B.Sc Environmental Science or in any science subject is must. The two year M.Tech in Environmental Science course is also offered by some technical institutes for which B.E/B.Tech students are eligible. There are also short term PG Diploma courses in Environment Management and Environmental Science. At the higher level there are doctoral and post-doctoral courses like M.Phil and PhD courses in Environmental Science.

Environmental science graduates have multiple career options. They can work with different government departments and agencies like Forest and Environment, Pollution Control Boards, Urban planning, Industries, Water resources and Agriculture, etc. Now NGOs working for environmental protection are a good option for environmental scientists. Private industries

processing industries and textile mills employ environmental scientists. Environmental scientists also can be involved in research activities in public and private sector institutions. Environmental scientists also can seek employment in media as environment journalists. Teaching in collages, universities is also a good option available for environmental scientists.

Many universities and technical institutions offer B.Sc/ M.Sc/ B.E/ B.Tech/ M.Tech courses in Environmental Science. Some names are given below:

    University of Delhi, Delhi
    Delhi College of Engineering, Delhi
    Jawaharlal Nehru University, New Delhi

    Jamia Milia Islamia, New Delhi
    University of Mumbai
    University of Chennai, Chennai
    Indian Institute of Environment Management (SIES), Mumbai
    University of Mysore, Mysore
    University of Pune, Pune
    Visveswariah Technological University, AIT, Chikmagalur

Bharathiar University, Coimbatore
Rajiv Gandhi Proudyogiki Vishwavidyalaya, Indore (MP)
UP Technical University (Instt of Engg & Tech) Lucknow
Centre for Environment Education, Nehru Foundation for Development, Ahmedabad
Andhra University, Waltair
Aligarh Muslim University, Aligarh
Guru jambheshwar University, Hisar

The Profession: The efforts towards clean air, water protection, noise abatement, waste management, pollution control and the like requires new goods and services, creating many more fresh jobs. Environmental science as a profession promises tremendous employment opportunities. Environmental science is a composite of both natural and social sciences. Resource management

environmental biologists, environmental modelers and environmental journalists.

Environmental science is a broad term, incorporating various different activities. In can be

Industry
Research and Development
Social Development
Environmental Journalism
Environmental Modelling

Work of Environmental Scientist: An environmental scientist's job is to utilise the knowledge of various principles and concepts of science and engineering disciplines, in order to protect and preserve the environment. Environmental scientists also conduct research studies in order to develop theories or methods of abating and controlling the sources of environmental pollution. So the major tasks performed by environmental scientists consist mainly of proactive and research-oriented work. It may involve tasks like:

Administrative Tasks
Advisory Tasks
Protective Tasks

Environmental Science Jobs

A habitat garden educator in the neighbourhood
The roles and functions of an environmental health specialist
Health and safety manager — a great job for a highly motivated individual
Green career opportunities for environmental health specialists
Get a green job as an environmental health specialist
Environmental health specialists: ensuring a healthy environment for everyone

Erosion control specialists make the study of soil their life's work

Be your own boss — be a beekeeper

A wilderness ranger is a great career choice for those who love the great outdoors

Trail coordinator — great job for those who love to hike and enjoy the wilderness

Water analysts hold positions of responsibility to protect our water supply

Pollution control design

Recycle coordinator — good for the environment, and little college education

Park ranger jobs are scarce — if you love the outdoors, take a shot

Marine biologists help ensure survival of all species on earth

Land managers will spend much of their time outside, loving nature is important

Land surveyors perform many duties and command good salaries

Field science educators help students develop an interest in the environment

Environmental technicians research the problem of pollution

Environmental research assistants gain valuable experience for future endeavors

Environmental restoration planners make positive changes to the environment

Environmental, health & safety analysts: keeps employees safe and healthy

Entomologists lead to surprising conclusions about history, disease, or solving crimes

Botanists are in demand and have many career paths to choose

Bird bander jobs are scarce and seasonal, but interesting for nature lovers

Archaeologists study history and past civilisations — for history buffs, it's the perfect choice of vocations

Our storm chasers — meteorologists

Environmental systems analyst — a career that's both demanding and rewarding

Fish hatchery technicians have a variety of duties

Ecologist — a constantly changing profession for a constantly evolving science

Why green educators are a growing job

Environmental lobbyist

Environmental educator

Climatologist

Air quality specialist

Fisheries technician

Ecologist

Forester

Science teacher

Q.14 How is the life of an Environmental Scientist?

Ans: On a typical day an environmental scientist's tasks might include:

Collecting, synthesising, analysing, managing and reporting environmental data, such as pollution emission measurements, atmospheric monitoring measurements, meteorological and mineralogical information, and soil or water samples.

correlations between human activities and environmental effects.

sessions or public hearings.

governmental agencies, environmental programmes, industry or the public.

Processing and reviewing environmental permits, licenses and related materials.

Reviewing and implementing environmental technical standards, guidelines, policies and formal regulations that meet all appropriate requirements.

11

FASHION DESIGNING & MODELLING

Q.1 What is fashion designing?

Ans: Fashion design is the art of application of design and aesthetics or natural beauty to clothing

time and place. Fashion designers work in a number of ways in designing clothing and accessories. Some work alone or as part of a team. They attempt to satisfy consumer's desire for aesthetically designed clothing and because of the time required to bring a garment onto the market, must at times anticipate changing consumer tastes. Fashion designers attempt to design clothes which are functional as well as aesthetically pleasing. They must consider who is likely to wear a garment and the situations in which it will be worn. They have a wide range and combinations of materials to work with and a wide range of colours, patterns and styles to choose from.

Q.2 Tell me in detail career opportunities in fashion designing?

Ans: Fashion is what we wear, through a constant process of selection, adoption and change. Fashion is triggered by people, events and social, economic and technological change. No wonder, Fashion and apparel designing have become one of the fastest growing professions in India in recent years. The world of clothes and accessories has expanded into a giant industry, both for domestic requirements and for export. Today, the Fashion industry in India is a high growth sector.

There is an ever-growing demand for more designers who can come up with the innovative designs that are commercially viable in the export market. With fashion becoming a big business and India emerging as one of the major players in the global garment market, the need for

opportunities for those who are good at it. The status and income of the person goes up as he establishes a reputation of his own. Exposure to the fashion industry abroad may help in widening horizons since Indians still tend to copy western styles. With beauty pageants, fashion shows, foreign labels and a public that is increasingly becoming fashion conscious, you as a fashion designer have enough chances to exhibit your talent. If you are enterprising, you can set up

lucrative job in the textile industry. A fashion designer is no longer an anonymous entity — designer labels give him an identity. As long as people feel the urge to dress well, there will always be a need for more designers to provide a variety of clothing that is appealing, fascinating and up-to-date. Export houses, domestic markets and manufacturing units throw up ample opportunities for you to work as a fashion designer in textile designing. It involves working with different fabrics and material. Textiles account for a major chunk of exports. The textile industry calls for technically skilled executives who are specialists in designing interpretation, pattern creation, garment construction, grading, product development, marketing and computer aided design. So

a job in accessory designing — designing anything from hair clips and sunglasses to footwear and luggage. There are a lot of opportunities for you in designing leather accessories.

Q.3   What are the attribute and qualities required to become a Fashion Designer?

Ans: The fashion industry demands the vision to see beyond what is already there and the ability

manual dexterity, organisational skills, a sensibility for colours, textures and style and business

as on talent and creativity. Styles and tastes keep changing all the time and a good designer needs to be on his toes to give the consumer the best and the latest. In the realm of designing, fashion is a business and it must not be misunderstood for an art form. Its dynamics are guided by commerce. Unlike popular belief, fashion design does involve a certain amount of technical knowledge, of types of material, their adaptability to weather, wear and tear, etc. Production

made in design, production, merchandising and marketing. As a designer, your job is to forecast fashion and translate the requirements of the market into saleable designs. It calls for a rare

of creativity. You should be able to withstand the stress of failure, deadliness, and long and

Q.4   What are the different categories/types of fashion in fashion designing?

Ans: The garments produced by clothing manufacturers fall into three main categories, although

Haute couture: Until the 1950s, fashion clothing was predominately designed and manufactured on a made-to-measure or haute couture basis (French for high-fashion), with each garment being

is usually made from high-quality, expensive fabric, sewn with extreme attention to detail and

cost of materials and the time it takes to make.

Ready-to-wear: Ready-to-wear clothes are a cross between haute couture and mass market. They are not made for individual customers, but great care is taken in the choice and cut of the fabric. Clothes are made in small quantities to guarantee exclusivity, so they are rather expensive. Ready-to-wear collections are usually presented by fashion houses each season during a period known as Fashion Week. This takes place on a city-wide basis and occurs twice a year. The main seasons of Fashion Week include, spring/summer, fall/winter, resort, swim and bridal.

Mass market: Currently the fashion industry relies more on mass market sales. The mass market caters for a wide range of customers, producing ready set by the famous names in fashion. They often wait around a season to make sure a style is going to catch on before producing their own versions of the original look. In order to save money and time, they use cheaper fabrics and simpler production techniques which can easily be done by machine. The end product can therefore be sold much more cheaply.

Q.5   I want to know about Global fashion design industry?

Ans: Fashion today is a global industry, and most major countries have a fashion industry. Some

Spain, Germany, Brazil and India. Five countries have established an international reputation in

American fashion design: The majority of American fashion houses are based in New York,

of high fashion clothing manufactured in the US is actually made. There are also burgeoning industries in Miami, Chicago and especially San Francisco and New York. American fashion design

lifestyles of American city-dwellers. A designer who helped to set the trend in the United States

designs have been revived in recent decades.

British fashion design:
wide range of foreign designs which have integrated with modern British styles. Typical British design is smart but innovative yet recently has become more and more unconventional, fusing traditional styles with modern techniques. Vintage styles play an important role in the British fashion and styling industry. Stylists regularly 'mix and match' the old with the new, which gives British style that unique, bohemian aesthetic that many of the other fashion capitals try to

Britain.

French fashion design: Most French fashion houses are in Paris, which is the capital of French

smart accessories. Although the Global Language Monitor placed it 3rd in the Media, after Milan and New York, French fashion is internationally acclaimed.

Italian fashion design: Milan is Italy's capital of fashion. Most of the older Italian couturiers are in Rome. However, Milan and Florence are the Italian fashion capitals, and it is the exhibition venue for their collections. Italian fashion features casual elegance and luxurious fabrics.

Swiss fashion design: Most of the Swiss fashion houses are in Zürich. The Swiss look is casual,

dance club scene.

Japanese fashion design: Most Japanese fashion houses are in Tokyo. The Japanese look is loose and unstructured (often resulting from complicated cutting); colours tend to the sombre and new way of cutting (comparable to Madeleine Vionnet's innovation in the 1930s).

Q.6 What is the scope of Fashion education globally?

Ans: There are a number of well-known art schools and design schools worldwide that offer degrees in fashion design and fashion design technology. Some colleges also offer Masters of Fashion courses. Though it is not a requirement to have a Masters level, it is recommended by those already working in the industry to study at this level. The most notable of design schools in Europe include London College of Fashion, Central Saint Martins College of Art and Design, University of Westminster and

Fashion Design courses in Ireland. Istituto Marangoni, Domus Academy, Politecnico of Milan, NABA - Nuova Accademia di Belle Arti Milano, Istituto Europeo di Design, University Iuav of Venice in Italy, the Fashion Federation PARIS] European Fashion Accreditation www.Fashion-Board.com, Antwerp Fashion Academy in Belgium. There is Parsons The New School for Design, Creative Business House, Fashion Institute of Technology and the Pratt Institute in New York City. Elsewhere in the United States there is the Academy of Art University in San Francisco, Savannah College of Art and Design, Virginia Commonwealth University, Otis College of Art & Design, and Fashion Institute of Design & Merchandising in Los Angeles, School of the Art Institute of Chicago and Columbia College Chicago in Chicago. The National Institute of Fashion Technology in India, Haryana Technical Institute Rohtak in

fashion design courses.

The only Ivy League University having a Fashion Design undergraduate programme is Cornell University in Ithaca, NY. The programme is offered by the department of Fiber Science & Apparel Design. Cornell University also offers a Ph.D programme in apparel design. An updated list of fashion design masters and Ph.D programmess can be found at ITAA.org. The programmess are intended to address the needs of academia, industry and research by considering apparel design as an applied science that embraces design, technology, physical sciences, the humanities and social sciences in order to meet the human needs for clothing. There are many universities that offer fashion design throughout the United States. The major incorporating fashion design may have alternative names like Apparel and Textiles or Apparel and Textile Design and may be housed in departments such as Art and Art History or Family and Consumer Studies.

Q.7 What are the different jobs available in Fashion Design industry?

Ans: Some of the jobs available in fashion industry are:

Fashion designer: Conceives garment combinations of line, proportion, colour, and

of successful fashion design. Most fashion designers are formally trained or apprenticed.

Technical designer: Works with the design team and the factories overseas to ensure

changes to make before mass producing the garment.

Pattern maker (or pattern cutter): Drafts the shapes and sizes of a garment's pieces. This may be done manually with paper and measuring tools or by using a CAD computer software programme. Another method is to drape fabric directly onto a dress form. The resulting pattern pieces can be constructed to produce the intended design of the garment and required size. Formal training is usually required for working as a pattern marker.

Tailor: Makes custom designed garments made to the client's measure; especially suits (coat and trousers, jacket and skirt, et cetera). Tailors usually undergo an apprenticeship or other formal training.

Textile designer: Designs fabric weaves and prints for clothes and furnishings. Most textile designers are formally trained as apprentices and in school.

Stylist: Co-ordinates the clothes, jewelry, and accessories used in fashion photography and catwalk presentations. A stylist may also work with an individual client to design a coordinated wardrobe of garments. Many stylists are trained in fashion design, the history of fashion and historical costume, and have a high level of expertise in the current fashion market and future market trends. However, some simply have a strong aesthetic sense for pulling great looks together.

Fashion buyer: Selects and buys the mix of clothing available in retail shops, department stores and chain stores. Most fashion buyers are trained in business and/or fashion studies.

Seamstress: Sews ready to wear or mass produced clothing by hand or with a sewing machine, either in a garment shop or as a sewing machine operator in a factory. She (or he)

Teacher of fashion design: Teaches the art and craft of fashion design in art or fashion school.

Custom clothier: Makes custom-made garments to order, for a given customer.

Dressmaker: Specializes in custom-made women's clothes: day, cocktail, and evening dresses, business clothes and suits, trousseaus, sports clothes, and lingerie.

Illustrator: Draws and paints clothing designs for commercial use.

Fashion forecaster: Predicts what colours, styles and shapes will be popular ("on-trend") before the garments are on sale in stores.

Model: Wears and displays clothes at fashion shows and in photographs.

Fit model:
their design and pre-manufacture. Fit models need to be a particular size for this purpose.

Fashion journalist: Writes fashion articles describing the garments presented or fashion trends, for magazines or newspapers.

Alterations specialist (alterationist):
ready-to-wear, and sometimes re-styles them. NOTE: despite tailors altering garments to

Image Consultant, wardrobe consultant or fashion advisor: recommends styles and

Q.8 I want to know about NIFT (National Institute of Fashion Technology)?

Ans: National Institute of Fashion Technology (NIFT) was set up in 1986 under the aegis of the Ministry of Textiles, Government of India. It has emerged as the premier Institute of Design, Management and Technology, developing professionals for taking up leadership positions in fashion business in the emerging global scenario. NIFT has been granted statutory status under the act of Parliament of India in 2006, empowering the Institute to award degrees and other academic distinctions. The Institute is a pioneer in envisioning and evolving fashion business education in the country through a network of twelve professionally managed domestic centres at New Delhi,

and Shillong. NIFT has further spread its wings globally with the opening of an international centre at Mauritius. NIFT has set academic standards and excelled in thought leadership by providing a pool of creative genius and technically competent professionals. The Institute provides a common platform for fashion education, research and training. The curriculum at NIFT allows students to easily blend into a global network, as well as acquire a greater appreciation of local industry trends. The multidisciplinary and broad-based structure aims at an all-round development of students. Deriving from the changing paradigms of industry and commerce, its content as well as the methodology is constantly reviewed by academia and industry experts.

Q.9 What are the different types of programmes NIFT offers?

Ans: NIFT offers B.Des. (Fashion Design), B.Des. (Leather Design) B.Des. (Accessory Design),

discipline at undergraduate level and M.Des. (Master of Design) at mmaster level. NIFT offers B.F.Tech. (Apparel Production) in the technology discipline at undergraduate level and M.F.Tech. (Master of Fashion Technology) at the master level. NIFT also offers M.F.M. (Master of Fashion Management) in the management discipline at master level.

Q.10 How many centres NIFT has?

Ans: NIFT has 13 centres at present in India and one international centre. They are located in Bengaluru,

Q.11 What is the general calendar of admission process in NIFT?

Ans:

Announcement of Admission	November
Application Form Available	November to December
Written Entrance Examination	First week of February
Declaration of Written Examination Result	Mid March
Situation Test / GD / Interviews	April - May
Declaration of Final Results	End of May

Q.12 What is the admission test pattern?

Ans:

BACHELOR PROGRAMMES	TEST	WEIGHTAGE
Design	GAT (General Ability Test)	40%
	CAT (Creative Ability Test)	40%
	Situation Test	20%
Apparel Production	GAT (General Ability Test)	60%
	(MAT) Managerial Ability Test	40%

MASTER PROGRAMMES	TEST	WEIGHTAGE
Design	GAT (General Ability Test)	40%
	CAT (Creative Ability Test)	40%
	GD (Group Discussion)	10%
	Interview	10%
Management	GAT (General Ability Test)	40%
	MAT (Managerial Ability Test)	40%
	GD (Group Discussion)	10%
	Interview	10%
Technology	GAT (General Ability Test)	40%
	MAT (Managerial Ability Test)	40%
	GD (Group Discussion)	10%
	Interview	10%

Q.13   What are the eligibility criteria for various programmes of NIFT?

Ans: Eligibility for Bachelor Programmes — Design

Fashion Communication)

The +2 level examination in the 10+2 pattern of examination of any recognised Central/ State Board of Secondary Examination, such as Central Board of Secondary Education, New

Advanced (A) level. OR

Any Public School/Board/University Examination in India or in Foreign countries recognised by the Association of Indian Universities as equivalent to 10+2 system. OR

A pass grade in the Senior Secondary School Examination conducted by the National Open

3 or 4-years diploma recognised by AICTE or a State Board of Technical Education.

Eligibility for Bachelor Programme — Technology

B.FTech. (Apparel Production)

The +2 level examination in the 10+2 pattern of examination of any recognised Central/ State Board of Secondary Examination, such as Central Board of Secondary Education, New

Chemistry and Maths. OR

advanced (A) level with Physics, Chemistry and Maths. OR

Any Public School/Board/University Examination in India or in foreign countries recognised by the Association of Indian Universities as equivalent to 10+2 system with Physics, Chemistry and Maths. OR

A pass grade in the Senior Secondary School Examination conducted by the National Open

3 or 4-years diploma recognised by AICTE or a State Board of Technical Education (Engineering background).

(Candidate must be pass in Physics, Chemistry & Mathematics)

Please note that the upper age limit for applying in bachelor programmes is restricted to 23 years as on 1st November.

Eligibility for Master Programme — Design

M.Des. (Master of Design)

> Graduation degree from a recognised University in any discipline* OR
>
> Bachelor in Applied Arts (Fashion Design / Visual Communication / Graphic Design / Industrial Design / Interior Design / Multimedia Design / Product Design / Textiles & Accessories. OR
>
> B.A. (Fine Arts) or B.Sc. (Textiles & Clothing) OR
>
> B.Arch. OR
>
> Design Diploma / Degree from NIFT / NID only

Candidates having relevant industry experience in areas of Fashion / Textile / Communication Design would be preferred.

*If a candidate possessing Graduation Degree in any discipline applies for the course, then he / she has to compulsory undergo 2 months (i.e. 8 weeks) training programme to develop the desired skills before taking on the course itself.

Eligibility for Master Programme — Management

M.F.M. (Master of Fashion Management)

A three years Bachelor's Degree or equivalent in any discipline recognised by the Association of Indian Universities or Diploma in Accessory / Fashion Design / FIT from NIFT only. For foreign Bachelor's

Body constituted in the country concerned for granting equivalence will have to be produced.

Eligibility for Master Programme — Technology

M.FTech. (Master of Fashion Technology)

B.E. / B.Tech. (Textiles / Apparel / Mechanical / Industrial / Production / Electronics / Computer / Information Technology)

Q.14   Is the NIFT degree recognised worldwide?

Ans: Yes. NIFT has been granted statutory status under the act of Parliament of India in 2006, empowering the Institute to award degrees and other academic distinctions.

Q.15   Does NIFT offer any other course other than the full time programme?

Ans: NIFT has developed a range of Continuing Education Programmes, which have been developed in consultation with reputed academicians and industry practitioners. These programmes professional growth, and are relevant to individuals at different stages of their careers.

industry professionals with formal technical education in their respective areas of work. The

professional activities. With focus on interactive learning, the programmes provide a congenial

successful completion of the programme.

For any further detailed information kindly visit www.nift.ac.in

Q.16 What are the other good institutions offering courses in Fashion Design?

Ans: National Institute of Design, Ahmedabad

Paldi, Ahmedabad, Gujarat, 380 007

Phone (079) 663 9692 / 660 5243

Fax (079) 662 1167

e-mail : academic@nid.edu

Undergraduate Programme: 4 year Graduate Diploma Programme in Textile and Apparel Design (GPD

Admission: open to students who have passed or who will appear for qualifying examinations under the Higher Secondary (10+2), or equivalents like AISSCE/IB/ICSE etc + Entrance Examination + Interview.

Postgraduate Programme: 2 and 1/2 year Post-Graduate Diploma Programme in Textile Design, Apparel Design & Merchandising and Lifestyle Accessory Design (PGPD)

Admission: open to graduates of B.F.A, Applied Arts, B.Arch. Interior Design, graduates with

Home Science (with Textile & Clothing)+ Entrance Examination + Interview.

Central Leather Research Institute, Chennai

Adyar, Chennai 600 020

Phone: 91-44-24915238

email: clrim@vsnl.com

Programmes: B Tech, M Tech, Ph D Degree programmes in Leather Technology and 1 year diploma programme in Leather Processing, Leather Goods, Footwear, etc.

Admission: Degree programmes as per admission norms of Anna University, diploma programme open to students who have passed or who will appear for qualifying examinations under the Higher Secondary (10+2) with 50% marks

National Institute of Fashion Design, Chandigarh

NIFD House, SCO. 32-35, Madhya Marg, Sector 8 C, Chandigarh 160 009

Phone : +91- (172) - 2784 980-81

Fax: + 91 - (172) - 2547095

e-mail : corporate@nifd.net

Programmes: 3 year B.Sc. Bachelor of Science in Textile Design and Fashion Design, 2 year Advance Diploma in Textile Design and Fashion Design + 12 months and 6 month courses

Admission: open to students who have passed 10+2 Examination or an equivalent examination

J D Institute of Fashion Technology, Mumbai, New Delhi, Ludhiana, Chandigarh, Nagpur
JD, Hemu Archade,
Opp Vile Parle Station West, Mumbai 400056
Tel: 022-2615 4949
email: jdinstitute@vsnl.com

Programme: 3 year degree course and 1 year diploma course in Fashion and Design, Jewelry design, Fashion Illustration and Fashion Photography

Admission: after 12th standard

Srishti School of Design, Bangalore
Srishti School of Art, Design and Technology, P.O. Box No. 6430, Yelahanka New Town,
Doddabalapur Road, Opp. Wheel & Axle plant, Bangalore-560 064
Phone: 91.80.28462506/07/08, 28560238.
TeleFax: 91.80.28560240
E-mail: srishtischool@vsnl.net

Programmes: 2 + 2 year Professional Diploma in Textiles Design

Admission: open to graduates or diploma holders in Art and /or Design, Architecture or related disciplines, or students with at least 2 years of study successfully completed

Symbiosis Centre of Design, Pune
Symbiosis Institute of Design [SID], Viman Nagar, Pune 411 014, Maharastra
Phone: +91 20 2663 4547 / 48
Contact: info@symbiosisdesign.ac.in

Programmes: Graduate Diploma Programme in Communication Design, Product Design, Fashion Communications and Fashion Design

Admission: open to students who have passed or who will appear for qualifying examinations under the Higher Secondary (10+2)

Pearl Academy, Delhi, Jaipur

A - 21/13, Naraina Industrial Area - Phase II, New Delhi - 110028.

Tel. No. : 51417693-94; 25703451/5478/8506

Email : info@pearlacademy.com

Programmes: 4 year Undergraduate Degree Programmes in Fashion Design, Textile Design and Communication Design

1½ year Master's Degree Programme in Fashion Design, 2 year Postgraduate Degree Programmes in Fashion Design and Apparel and retail Management

Admission:

Arch Academy of Fashion, Art & Design, Jaipur

Tel. No. : 091-141-329 6203

Email : info@archedu.org

Programmes: 4 year Undergraduate Degree Programmes in Fashion Design, Textile Design , Jewellery Design, Visual Merchandising and Accessory Design

1½ year PG Degree and PG Diploma in garment production & export management.

Admission:

Wigan & Leigh College, Delhi, Mumbai, Bangalore, Kolkata, Hyderabad, Pune, Indore, Lucknow, Ahmedabad, Chennai

Tel: 011-51617053/4/5/6, 9818479333

Email : delhi@wiganindia.org

Programmes: 3 year Advanced Diploma and B.A. (Hons.) in Fashion Technology and 2 year Postgraduate Diploma in Fashion Technology (PGDVC)

Admission:
considered + Aptitude Test + Interview

Apeejay Institute of Design, New Delhi,

54 Tughlakabad Institutional Area, Meherauli-Badarpur Road, New Delhi-110062

Phone : 011-29955459 , 29957050

Email : aid.del@apj.edu

Programme: 4 year Bachelor in Design in Fashion Design and Textile Design, 1 year Postgraduate Diploma in Design and 2 year Master in Design

Admission: 12th Pass with 45% marks from CBSE, CSC, Punjab Board or equivalent for Bachelor in Design and Graduation in Fine Arts, Engineering, Design for Master in Des

Sophia Polytechnic, Mumbai

Phone: 022- 2351 3157, 2351 4147
Email: sophia@bom2.vsnl.net.in

Programmes: 3 year professional course in Dress Designing and Garment Manufacturing

Admission: 10th Pass with minimum 50%

Raheja Centre, Linking Rd & Main Avenue, Santacruz (W) Mumbai 400 054
Tel: 022-5572 6711, 5502 9522, 98190 24429

Programmes: 3 year Bachelor of Arts (hons) Fashion degree programme in Fashion Design, Fashion Marketing and Management

Admission: 12th Pass with TOEFL scores

Northeast Institute of Fashion Technology, Guwahati
Bora Service Bylane G.S. Road Guwahati 781007 Assam
Tel:. 9864018094, 9864026772, 9864033255
Telefax: 0361 2462444
E-mail neiftghy@gmail.com, info@neift.com

Programmes: 2 year diploma programme in Fashion Design, Fashion Marketing and Management, Life Style & Accessories Design, Textile Designing, Jewellery Designing, Fashion Merchandising, Fashion Photography & Modelling

Admission: 12th Pass

Army Institute of Fashion Design, Bangalore
(A Unit of Army Welfare Education Society)
ITI B Area, Doorvani Nagar, Old Madras Road, Bangalore – 560016
Tel: 080-25617309, 080-25617559
Fax: 080- 25618014
Web: www.aifdonline.in
E-mail: aifdonline@gmail.com

Programmes: UG: 3 year degree programme in Fashion and Accessory Design

Admission: 12th Pass

2G: 2 year diploma programme in Fashion Design and in Apparel Merchandising & Logistics Management

Admission: open to any graduate

Creative-i College of Creative Arts, Pune

Ganga Dham Comm. Phase I, Sr. No. 612 - 615, Lullanagar Bibwewadi Road, Market Yard, Pune 411 037.

Phone: 020 – 2420 9166 / 88, 30917340

Email: info@creativei.info

Programmes: 3 year Graduate Degree Programme in Fashion Design.

IILM School of Design, Gurgaon

Plot 69-71, Sector 53, Near DLF Golf Course, Gurgaon - 122003 (NCR-Delhi.)

Phone: 011-33330132, 0124-3096874

Contact: adm@iilminstitute.org

Programmes: 4 year graduate programme in Product Design, Communication Design, and 2 year Postgraduate programme in Communication Design, Product Design, Interior and Furniture Design, Animation Design, Exhibition Design and Textile Design

Admission: Undergraduate programmes open to students who have passed 10+2 Examination

Bangalore Institute of Fashion Technology (BIFT), Bangalore

6, Bilekahalli Gate (near IIM-B), Bannerghatta Main Road, Bangalore-560 076.

Phone : 91-80-32721283 / 41109966

E-Mail : info@biftindia.com

Programmes:
Design, Fashion Management, Apparel Marketing, etc.

Admission: Undergraduate programmes open to students who have passed 10+2 Examination

Arch Academy, Jaipur, Rajasthan

Plot No. 9, Govind Marg, Opp. Block A, Malviya Nagar Institutional Area, Jaipur-302017

Phone: 91-141-2520551, 2521074, 3296203

Contact: info@archedu.org

Programmes:
of Fashion Design, Textile Design, Jewellery Design, and Interior Design

Admission: Undergraduate programmes open to students who have passed 10+2 Examination and PG diploma to any graduate student

International Institute of Fashion Technology, Delhi

H-12, South Extension Part - I, New Delhi, India.

Phone: 91-11-24620430, 24629370

Contact: rdlal_iift@hotmail.com

Programmes:
Design, Retail Management, Textile Design, Jewellery Design, and Interior Design, Accessory

Design, etc.

Admission: Undergraduate programmes open to students who have passed 10+2 Examination and PG programmes to any graduate student

Government Institute of Garment Technology (GIGT), Amritsar

Majitha Road Byee Pass, Amritsar, Punjab, India

Phone: 91-0183-2421763

Email: principal@gigtasr.org

Programmes:

Admission: open to students who have passed 10+2 Examination

Gemmological Institute of India (GII), Mumbai

29, Gurukul Chambers, 187-189, Mumbadevi Road, Mumbai - 400 002

Phone: 91-22-2342 0039 / 2341 3785

Email: gemforum[at]giionline.com and gemforum[at]gmail.com

Programmes:

Admission: open to students who have passed 10+2 Examination

Gandhi Institute of Fashion & Textile Design, Ahmedabad

White Cross Building, 15, Patel Society, Gulbai Tekra Road, Panchwati, Ellisbridge, Ahmedabad-380006

Phone: 91- 79 - 6463702

Contact: info@gift-india.com

Programmes:
Jewellery Design, and Interior Design

Admission: Open to all

Q.17 What is Modelling?

Ans: A model (from Middle French modèle), sometimes called a mannequin, is a person who is employed to display, advertise and promote commercial products (notably fashion clothing) or to serve as a subject of works of art.

Modelling (doubled "l" in British spelling, single "l" in American spelling) is distinguished from other types of public performance, such as acting, dancing or mime artist, although the boundary is

a variety of media formats including books, magazines, movies, newspapers, and TV. Models sometimes are featured in movies, reality television shows, or music videos.

As a fashion model you will appear in magazines/newspaper editorials and you might be chosen to be in a catwalk show. Fashion models can promote clothes and accessories to customers, the media and to fashion buyers. Fashion models appear in catwalk shows or in photographs for magazines, advertising campaigns, newspapers and look books. During a catwalk show the fashion models will move along the catwalk, walking and turning to display clothes in front of an audience. In photographic and advertising a fashion model will pose for photographers in a studio or on location and follow directions from the photographer. A fashion model works closely with stylists, hair and make-up artists, producers and directors. However, fashion modelling is not always as glamorous as it seems. A fashion model will also spend much time going to castings for jobs, keeping in contact with the fashion model agency and looking after his/her appearance. Designers, photographers and magazine editors will all choose their models from a fashion model

are self employed and obtain work through their agents. As a fashion model, you will need to spend and invest wisely. For many, the work is irregular, and some models need additional jobs to make a full-time living. Although work opportunities are increasing, modelling is highly competitive with many applicants for each job.

Q.18   What are the different types of models?

Ans: Runway models: Runway models showcase clothes from fashion designers, fashion media, and consumers. They are also called "live models" and are self employed. Runway models work in different locations, constantly travelling between those cities where fashion is well known - London, Milan, New York City, Paris and Mumbai. The demands for runway models include certain height and weight requirements. During runway shows, models have to constantly change clothes and makeup. The models turn and stand to demonstrate the garment's key features. Models also go to interviews (called "go and sees") and must keep a portfolio of their work. They go to

is to be hired for a fashion show. A runway model can work in other areas, such as department store fashion shows, creating product lines, acting, etc.

Supermodels:
celebrities appear on top fashion magazine covers and in fashion shows. Much more importantly,

greater rewards, especially when they conclude deals to advertise a brand exclusively, as "the face" of that brand.

Glamour models: Glamour photography emphasizes the model and the model's sexuality rather than products, fashion or the environment. Glamour modelling focuses on sexuality and its ability to enhance a product's attractiveness. Glamour models are used for mass-produced calendars, pinup and for men's magazines, such as Playboy magazine. Famous glamour models include Pamela Anderson, Jordan, Jodie Marsh, Lucy Pinder, and Louise Glover.

Fitness models: Fitness modelling centres on displaying an athletic physique. Fitness models

body weight is usually similar to (or heavier than) fashion models, but they have a lower body fat percentage due to increased muscle mass and reduced fat mass.

Bikini models:
body shape. Bikini models can usually be shorter, around 5 ft 5 in (1.65 m) to 5 ft 8 in (1.73 m).

Art models: Art models are models who pose for photographers, painters, sculptors, and other artists as part of their work of art. Models are frequently used for training art students, but are also employed by accomplished artists. The most common types of art created using models dominate over the esthetics in advertising, its 'artwork' commonly employs models.

considered the most useful tool in developing the skill of draftsmanship. In some cases, the

and under various lighting conditions.

Alternative models:
model types and may include punk, goth, fetish, tattooed models or models with distinctive attributes. These mix with high fashion and art models. Publishers such as Goliath in Germany introduced alternative models and punk photography to larger audiences.

Body-parts models: Some models are employed for their particularly attractive body parts. For example, hand models may be used to promote products held in the hand and nail-related products. They are frequently part of television commercials. Hand model, Ashly Covington has

Hickey, found fame after being featured on the cover of Twilight. Leg models showcase tights, stockings, socks and leg grooming products. Wrist models display watches or bracelets. Petite models (females under 5 ft 6 in (1.68 m) and do not qualify as fashion models) have found success in body part modelling.

Q.19   How can one become a model?

Ans: Despite the glamour and hype you have seen about the modelling profession, it is hard work.

an 9-6 job. Not all jobs pay well. Unless you are seriously committed about modelling, willing to work at it on your own time, live a healthy life style, etc., you will not succeed as a model. You have to understand that there are many people who want to be models. They are doing everything they can to be successful.

Q.20   Do you have inner stamina to be a model?

Ans: Are you tall and slender and unusually attractive enough that you are as good or better looking than most other models? You also need to have the tenancy, patience, aptitude, interpersonal skills,

try to be a model. Modelling can be fun, exciting, and adventurous. Be sure to maintain realistic expectations, however, the chances of becoming a successful or famous model are less.

The best measurements for modelling are 5'9", 34b bust, 24" waist, 34" hips. If you are within

typically 5'7" to 6' tall and an extremely thin size 7 with 32-35" bust, 22-25" waist and 33-36" hips. They are not necessarily classically beautiful. PETITE measurements would be 5'5" to 5'8" tall and a size 5 to 7. The model MUST have a well proportioned body. PLUS SIZE models are 5'7" to 5'11" tall and wear a size 12 to 14, have a well toned and proportioned body with a thin face, good skin and beautiful hair. Always provide very accurate measurements to the agency and to

The ultimate test for an aspiring Model: Send your photo and resume to reputable co-coordinators.

very busy, if they do not like the photo you will not get an appointment. If they like it you will be invited for an assessment. Then again if you do not have what it takes they will tell you on the spot. If rejected don't give up yet! Each coordinator/agency is different and has different expectations and requirements from their models. Always ask about any immediate physical changes (haircut, weight loss, skin treatment, dental work, etc.) and work on it for the future. Some coordinators/ established models offer good training (in the form of workshops/courses) for local fashion shows

Few steps to be followed to become a Model:

There are many modelling books published and they provide a general knowledge on the modelling industry.

2. As an aspiring model, one of your immediate short term goals is to arrange for photo shoots with a photographer. You need professional pictures to start off your portfolio with. Many aspiring models make the mistake of using unprofessional photos which result in hurting your chances of getting modelling jobs now and in the future. Basically, you want to have professional looking photos for your portfolio. However, you need to have something to show photographers who might be willing to do a test shoot you. Other photos such as pictures from prom night, school pictures, or other special events which you are looking your best will be good for starting off. If you don't have access to a scanner, take your

by, most camera labs provide this service.

3. Find a source on the internet to list your information and pictures. This source may be a friend, college, or you can even get your own free web space and start your own website from a site that gives free web space such as AOL or Yahoo. You should also consider listing with one or more of the modelling services online that host web pages for models and their portfolios.

4. Put your images and HTML documents at one or more of these sites (The more, the more likely you'll be discovered). You may need to recruit some help if you plan to create your own web pages. If you list with one of the online modelling services, they will create the web pages for you. For example, at Model Service.com all you need to do is take ten minutes and create a portfolio automatically online and it will be listed on the site for others to view.

5. While you are adding your portfolio, most sites will ask you what type of modelling you are available for. You need to decide what you like doing. The more types of modelling you put

6. Contact photographers. Let them know who you are, your modelling interest, your personal stats, and it helps to include an image. To make it easier for yourself and the photographer,

have an online portfolio. Do this to more than one photographer to make your name and photos more famous in the modelling industry. The more photographers you contact, the better it is for your career.

7. Spend some time looking at other modelling websites. Look at the models, their experience, their interests, and look at how you compare to some of them. You should also spend time

you measure up.

8. Contact those offering JOBS!!! If you join an online modelling agency, they will contact you as the jobs come.

Some important tips on Modelling: You should be able to accept rejection. Like any other art or talent profession, you will face rejection from agencies and those who are casting. Do not take it personally; your look may not be right for the current moment, but it may be perfect in a few months or in other agencies! Never give money upfront to an "agency" that asks for it. Legitimate agencies are licensed and bonded; they make their money from commissions from bookings they get their models (usually 15 to 20 percent). Don't waste time and money on modelling schools

agents will usually have to "retrain" you – at no cost to you. Spend the money developing a personal website, better photos, comp cards, cosmetics, and other items needed to invest in your career. Never go to a photo shoot alone. Reputed photographers usually encourage someone to accompany their models to a photo shoot. Models under 18 are encouraged to take a parent or guardian with them to all photo shoots and bookings.

Q.21 Name some institutions offering courses in Modelling?

Ans:

College / Institute	State	Eligibility
Face 1,797, Jesia Building, Jam-e-Jamshedji Road, Parsi Colony,Dadar, Mumbai- 400 014, Ph: 414 9968, 412 6878	Maharashtra	
	Delhi	
Platinum Models, A 276, Shivalik, New Delhi	Delhi	
Glitz, F-100 Lajpat Nagar II, New Delhi - 110 024, Ph: 683 0921	Delhi	
Oz1 Models Management, Gamdevi Phiroze Shah Road, Santa Cruz (W),Mumbai	Maharashtra	
The Ramp, A 22,Gulmohar Park, New Delhi - 110 049	Delhi	
The Tina Factor,C-31 Defence Colony, New Delhi- 110 024	Delhi	
YSG Worldwide Model and Promotion Agency Orient House, 4th Floor, Adi Marzban Path, Mumbai - 400 038 Ph: 261 6732. 261 5029	Maharashtra	
Aditi Modelling Service, 324, Upper Palace Orchard, Bangalore - 560 080, Ph: 334 2518		
Ph: 359 3502, 334 6319	West Bengal	
Colony, Srinagar	Jammu &	

	Andhra Pradesh	
Mayrose Management Services, 302, Radha Mukund, B.P. Road, Dahisar-West, Mumbai, Ph: 91 22 8911187; Fax: 91 22 8927861	Maharashtra	
The Bridge,201, Bhanot Trade Centre, Paschim Vihar, New Delhi,Ph: 91-011-56017119	Delhi	
New India Models.Com,201, Mayur Plaza, LSC Opp. ASN School, Mayur Vihar Phase-1, New Delhi, Ph: 91-11-2712222	Delhi	
Mayhar Bhasin Academy [contact E-186, Greater	New Delhi	
The Model Shoppe at Talwalkar's Fitness Club(Juhu), Gulmohar Society, Gulmohar Road No. 1, Mumbai- 400049	Maharashtra	
New Delhi-110-51552222.	Delhi	
Elite Model Managament India, Nariman Bhavan 9thFloor,Mumbai- 400021 Ph: 022-256303666	Maharashtra	

Hotel Management and Hospitality Management

Q.1 What is Hospitality Management?

Ans:
management of hotels, restaurants, travel agencies, and other institutions in the hospitality

needs. People who are interested in careers in hospitality management may opt to pursue it

is vast and very diverse. Any time people travel, stay in a hotel, eat out, go to the movies, and engage in similar activities, they are patronising establishments in the hospitality industry.

enough to anticipate and meet a wide variety of needs. They must also handle tasks such as training employees, handling staff, setting standards, and so forth. Some people develop careers in hospitality management by working from the ground up. They get experience in various low level positions before gradually being promoted into supervisory positions, and eventually attain managerial status. For people who plan to work with a single organisation for life, this method can be a great way to advance, as it familiarizes them with all of the nuances of the organisations they work for and gives them a better idea of the amount of work involved at all levels to run a facility like a busy resort.

Q.2 What are the career prospect for Graduates in Hospitality/Hotel Management?

Ans: Global growth and development of tourism have opened up innumerable openings; as a result graduate in Hotel/Hospitality Management can look forward to career opportunities as:

Management Trainee in Hotel and allied hospitality industry

Indian Navy Hospitality services
Guest/ Customer Relation Executive in Hotel and other Service Sectors
Management Trainee / Executive in international and national fast food chains

Opportunities in Hospital and Institutional Catering

Faculty in Hotel Management/ Food Craft Institutes(after requisite work experience)

Opportunities in Shipping and Cruise lines

Marketing/ Sales Executive in Hotel and other Service Sectors.

Opportunities in State Tourism Development Corporations

Opportunities in Resort Management

Self employment through entrepreneurship

Opportunities available in multinational companies for their hospitality services

Opportunities for commissioned job in Indian Navy

Q.3   I want to know about National Council for Hotel Management & Catering Technology (NCHMCT).

Ans: National Council for Hotel Management & Catering Technology is an autonomous body under Ministry of Tourism, Government of India. The Council centrally regulates academics for B.Sc. Hospitality and Hotel Administration and other eleven structured courses of studies that are imparted at the existing 21 Central Institutes of Hotel Management, 12 State Govt. Institutes

operational area. All Institutes uniformly follow standardised course curricula prescribed by the Council for the different professional program. Quality of education and training provided

and other allied service sectors. The Council has till date trained more than 45000 Hospitality

occupy key positions in hospitality industry as well as in teaching institutions both in India and abroad.

The Bachelor of Science programme in Hospitality and Hotel Administration is offered jointly by the National Council for Hotel Management and the India Gandhi National Open University. The Three-Year (Six Semesters) programme equips students with all the required skills, knowledge

programme also involves in-depth laboratory work for students to acquire required knowledge and skills standards in the operational areas of Food Production, Food and Beverage Service,

Food Safety and Quality, Human Resource Management, Facility Planning, Financial Management, Strategic Management, Tourism Marketing and Tourism Management.

Q.4   What are the courses offered by institutes affiliated/approved by NCHMCT?
Ans:

Course	Duration		Upper Age Limit	Location of Institutes where Course is available
M.Sc. Hospitality Administration	2 Years	B.Sc. in H.H.A. or 3 Yr Diploma in HM.	NA	IHM- Pusa, Mumbai & Bengaluru

B.Sc.in Hospitality and Hotel Administration	3 years	10+2 or Equivalent	22 (Gen/ O B C / P H) 25(SC/ST)	brochure
Postgraduate Diploma in Accommodation Operation and Management	1½ Years	Graduation in any Stream	25	IHM-Bhubaneswar, Pusa, Guwahati,
Craftsmanship Course in Food Production	1½ Years	10th Class pass of 10+2	22	IHM-Bhopal, Bhubaneswar, Chennai, Pusa, Gangtok, Goa, Guwahati, Gwalior, Shimla, Thiruvananthapuram, Shrishakti Hyderabad.
Craftsmanship Course in Food and Beverage Service	24 weeks	10th Class pass of 10+2	22	Chennai, Goa, Shimla
Hotel and Catering Management	6 Months	Class XII of 10+2 system or equivalent	NA	IHM-Mumbai, Chennai
Diploma in Food Production	1½ Years	10+2 or Equivalent	22	Food Craft Institutes — Ajmer, Aligarh, Faridabad, Darjeeling, Udaipur, Balangir IHMs & SIHMs — Chennai, Chandigarh(AIHM), Hazipur, Jaipur, Shillong, CIHM Chandigarh, Dehradun, Gangtok, Jodhpur, Panipat, Pondichery
Diploma in Food and Beverage Service	1½ Years	10+2 or Equivalent	22	Food Craft Institutes — Ajmer, Aligarh, Balangir Darjeeling, Faridabad, Udaipur, IHMs & SIHMs — Delhi(Pusa), Hazipur, Jaipur, Shimla, Gurdaspur, Panipat, Pondichery, Gangtok, Jodhpur, CIHM Chandigarh
Diploma in Front	1½ Years	10+2 or Equivalent	22	Food Craft Institutes — Ajmer, Darjeeling, Udaipur, Balangir IHM & SIHMs — Jaipur, Jodhpur, CIHM-Chandigarh
Diploma in House	1½ Years	10+2 or Equivalent	22	Food Craft Institutes — Ajmer, Aligarh, Balangir, Udaipur, IHMs & SIHM-CIHM — Chandigarh, Jaipur, Pondichery
Diploma in Bakery and Confectionery	1½ Years	10+2 or Equivalent	22	Food Craft Institutes — Ajmer, Aligarh, IHMs & SIHMs Faridabad, Delhi(Pusa),CIHM-Chandigarh, Panipat

Q.5 What are the minimum qualifications to appear in JEE (Joint Entrance Examination) conducted by NCHMCT and join the course in B.Sc. in Hospitality and Hotel Administration?

Ans:

Secondary education or its equivalent with English as one of the compulsory subject. Those appearing in 10+2 or equivalent examination can also appear in JEE on provisional basis. Provisional admissions will stand cancelled if proof of having passed the qualifying examination (10+2 or its equivalent) is not submitted at the time of counselling or at the time of admission.

to be produced by the candidates at the time of Counselling and at the time of admission in Institute. Even after admission to an Institute, if an applicant is at a later date found ineligible on account of having submitted false information or testimonials or for having suppressed any material information, his/her admission will be cancelled and the fee paid will also be forfeited.

List of approved qualifying examinations for Indian Students

Plus two level examination in the 10+2 pattern of Senior Secondary education of any recognised Central/ State Board, such as Central Board of Secondary Education and Council

Intermediate or two-year Pre-University Examination conducted by a recognised Board/ University.

Advanced (A) level.

Any Public School/ Board/ University Examination in India or in foreign countries recognised by the Association of Indian Universities as equivalent to 10+2 pattern of Senior Secondary education.

H.S.C. Vocational Examination.

Senior Secondary School Examination conducted by the National Open School with a

Q.6 Who is the regulatory authority to approve degree/diploma level course in Hotel Management in India?

Ans: The All India Council for Technical Education (AICTE) is the regulatory authority to approve the diploma and degree level courses in hotel management. Institutions offering degree courses

ensure that the institution and the course in which they are seeking admission are approved by the AICTE. Many institutions are also trying with foreign hotel associations and institutions. Such arrangements provide for additional diploma or for accreditation by relevant authorities, and often facilitate students qualifying from these institutions to enter into institutions abroad. Some foreign collaborators and accrediting organisations are: Education Institute of the American Hotel and Motel Association (AHMA), Council on Hotel, Restaurant and Institutional Education (CHRIE), USA, the Educational Foundation of National Restaurant Association, USA, the Hotel, Catering & Institutional management Association, (HCIMA), London, Australian Hotel Review Panel (AHRP), International Hotel and Restaurant Association, Paris.

Q.7 What are the jobs/career avenue available in a large hotel or star category hotel?

Ans: Some of the jobs available in a large hotel operation are:

General Manager
Director of Room Operations

Front Desk Manager
Front Desk Supervisor
Rooms Coordinator
PBX Supervisor
Guest Services Manager
Concierge Supervisor
Bell Captain
Valet Captain
Executive Housekeeper
Housekeeping Manager
Laundry Supervisor
Custodial Supervisor
Director of Sales & Marketing
Senior Sales Manager
Sales Manager
Marketing Manager
Reservations Manager
Revenue Manager
Director of Food & Beverage
Restaurant Manager
Executive Chef
Room Service Manager
Bar Manager
Director of Events and Catering
Convention Services Manager
Event Manager
Catering Manager
Director of Finance
Finance Manager
Chief Engineer
Director of Human Resources
Director of Security
Information Technology Manager

Q.8 I want to know about Tourism and Travel Management.

Ans: The Ministry of Tourism took the initiative to introduce training programs in tourism and travel management. In 1982, it established the Indian Institute of Tourism and Travel Management

started functioning in New Delhi, and the main campus of the Institute has since been shifted to Gwalior in its own sprawling campus (Govindapuri, Gwalior-4774011). Thereafter, universities started introducing courses in travel management at various levels. Some universities have also constituted Departments of Tourism Studies. Several Polytechnics in some States have also introduces three-year Diploma programs in the subject. The AICTE is the regulatory authority in respect of education and training in tourism and travel. In 1995, the IITTM introduced a full-time Diploma Course in Tourism and Travel Management of fourteen-month duration. The course is also offered at its Eastern Centre in Bhubaneshwar established in 1997.

Eligibility criteria: A graduate degree in any discipline and age not more than 28 years. Selection is made on the basis of an entrance test held in several centres. The test is intended to assess the candidate's general knowledge with particular reference to history, culture, geography and places of tourist attractions in India, reasoning and English. In addition, the IITTM conducts a Diploma in Destination Management (DDM) programme in collaboration with Air India, and National Institute

Thiruvananthapuram.

The Business Management (Calcutta-700073) offers a regular Postgraduate Diploma in Travel and Tourism Management. The course has been designed by the IITM which evaluates the answer scripts, declares the results and awards the diploma. The Thiruvananthapuram Chapter called the

PG Diploma in Tourism and Travel Management of one-year duration. The programme consists of three modules of four months each with emphasis on tour operations and guiding, travel

also offer short-term programmes in foreign languages (French, Spanish and German), Air Travel, Fares and Ticketing, Computerised Reservation System.

University Courses: As of now, as many as 40 universities have introduced travel management

Management course is also offered through distance learning mode. The Bachelor Degree course is of three-year duration leading to the award of Bachelor of Tourism Administration (BTA) or Bachelor of Tourism Studies (BTTM).

The Postgraduate Diploma in Tourism Management (PGDTM) is of one-year duration and is open to graduates in any discipline. The Master's degree programme of two-year duration leads to the award of Master of Tourism Administration (MTA) or Master of Tourism Management (MTM).

the University of Madras is MA (Tourism). The Admission requirement is Bachelor's degree with tourism as one of the subjects or BTA/BTS degree. Sri Chandrasekharendra Saraswathi Viswa

(Indian Culture) of three-year duration. Oriented to tourism, the course covers three areas, viz., Archaeology, Tourism, and Culture. Eligibility is a pass in 10+2 examination. The university also offers a limited number of scholarships for deserving students admitted to the course.

Distance Learning Programmes: Distance learning courses in tourism and travel management

attached to several universities.

Diploma in Tourism Studies (DTS), Advanced Diploma in Tourism Studies (ADTS), Bachelor of Tourism Studies (BTS), and Master of Tourism Administration (MTA), is the most comprehensive one. The CTS (six months), DTS (one year), and BTS (three years) courses are open to candidates

eligible if they have successfully completed the Bachelors' Preparatory Programme (BPP) of six-month duration. Only candidates who have passed the DTS examination are eligible for the ADTS course of one year duration. The MTA course of two year duration is open to two categories of candidates, viz., (i) holders of BTS and BA (Tourism) degrees or PG Diploma in Tourism, and (ii) holders of any Bachelor degree or Diploma in Tourism. However, all candidates in the second category are required to clear four additional courses during the period of study. UP Rajarshi Tandon Open University offers BTS, DTS and CTS courses. The MTA programme is offered only by

Q.9 What are the International Air Transport Associations (IATA) and Universal Federation of Travel Agents' Associations (UFTAA) Training courses?

Ans: Founded in 1945, the International Air Transport Associations (IATA) is the world organisation of scheduled airlines. The IATA, in collaboration with the Universal Federation of Travel Agents' Associations (UFTAA), launched in 1972 an International Travel Agents' Training programme to meet the growing demand for well-trained staff in the travel industry. The IATA/UFTAA Diploma has become a hallmark in the travel industry. It guarantees excellent standards in training and has gained worldwide recognition. The training programme is operated under the authority of Passenger Agency Training Board. IATA's Agency Training Service located in Geneva (Switzerland) oversees general administration, course contents and conducting of examinations. In each country or area, there is a local coordinator who is responsible for the promotion of the course, distribution of training kits and organisation of examinations locally. The Air India is the coordinator in India.

The training programme is basically a self-study course. There are, however, Authorised Training Centres (ATCs) in many countries which prepare students for the examination. The ATCs are authorised to use the IATA-UFTAA course material. Before taking admission to any ATC, the students must verify the authorisation number allotted to it. There are two courses, viz., Standard (Entry level) and Advanced Course. Candidates desirous of taking the Standard Course

in English. They should also have good knowledge of world geography and basic mathematics.

(21/2 hours) and Paper 2: Air Fares and Ticketing (3 hours). Examinations are held every year in

March and September. Students must register themselves three months before the examination. They can take both papers on the same day or separately (e.g., Paper 1 in March and Paper 2 in September). To qualify for the Diploma, the candidates must score at least 75% marks. Information about the courses may be obtained from IATA's website http://www.iata.org/ilc.

Q.10 **What are the different University and Courses in Travel and Tourism Management**

Ans:

Aligarh Muslim University (Aligarh-202002) — MTA

Andhra University (Visakhapatnam-530003) — PG Diploma in Travel and Tourism Management (distance learning mode)

Awdesh Pratap Singh University (Rewa-486003) — MTA, Diploma in Tourism Management Studies

Banaras Hindu University (Varanasi-221005) — MA (Tourism)

Bangalore University (Bangalore-560056) — MTA (offered by the Christ College, Bangalore-560029)

Barkatullah Vishwavidyalaya (Bhopal-462026) — PG Diploma in Tourism and Hotel Management (distance learning mode)

Berhampur University (Berhampur-760007) — PG Diploma in tourism and Indian Monuments

Bharathidasan University (Tiruchirapalli-620024) — PG Diploma in Tourism

Bundelkhand University (Jhansi-284128) — MTTM, PG Diploma in Destination Management,

Devi Ahilya Viswavidyalaya (Indore-452001) — MTA

Dr. Babasaheb Ambedkar Marathwada University (Aurangabad-431004) — MTA

Marketing (distance learning mode)

Dr. Bhim Rao Ambedkar University (Agra-282004) — MTA, PG Diploma in Hotel Management

Dr. Ram Manohar Lohia Avadh University (Faizabad-224001) — BTA

Guru Ghasidas University (Bilaspur-495009) — Diploma in Tourism and Travel Management

Hemwati Nandan Bahuguna Grahwal University (Srinagar-246174) — MTA

Himachal Pradesh University (Shimla-171005) — MTA

Indira Gandhi National Open University (New Delhi-110068) — CTS, DTS, ADTS, BTS and MTS (distance learning mode)

Jai Narain Vyas University (Jodhpur-342001) — MTA, PG Diploma in Tourism and Hotel Management

Jiwaji University (Gwalior-474001) — MTA, PG Diploma in Travel and Tourism Management

(distance learning mode)

learning mode)

PG Diploma in Tourism and Hotel Management (both through distance learning mode)

Studies, Diploma in Tourism Stuides
University of Lucknow (Lucknow-226007) — MTA
University of Madras (Chennai-600005) — MA (Tourism Management)

mode), PG Diploma in Tourism
Magadh University, (Bodh Gaya-824234) — B.Sc (Hons) in Travel & Tourism (offered by the Nalanda College, Biharshariff-803101)
Manonmanian Sundaranar University (Tirunelvelli-627012) — PG Diploma in Tourism

University of Mumbai (Mumbai-400032) — PG Diploma in Travel and Tourism Management
Pondicherry University (Pondicherry-605014) — BA (Tourism), MTA, PG Diploma in Tourism Administration (distance learning mode)
Potti Sreeramulu Telugu University (Hyderabad-500004) — PG Diploma in Travel and Tourism
Sambalpur University (Sambalpur-768019) — PG Diploma in Travel and Tourism Management (distance learning mode)
SNDT Women's University (Mumbai-400020) — PG Diploma in Travel and Tourism Management
Sri Venkateshwara University (Tirupati-517502) — Diploma In Tourism and International Ticketing
Utkal University (Bhubaneshwar-751004) — MTA, PG Diploma in Tourism and Travel Management
UP Rajarshi Tandon Open University (Allahabad-211001) — Bachelor of Tourism Studies(BTS),

Vikram University (Ujjain-456010) — PG Diploma in Tourism.

Q.11 What is Event Management?

Ans: Event Management is a profession in which the person plans and organizes events like Fashion shows, parties, concerts, charity shows, corporate events like seminars, conferences, weddings, etc. Event management involves a lot of planning, budgeting, focusing on the execution and concepts visualising. Event management is the application of project management to the creation and development of festivals, events and conferences. Event management involves studying the intricacies of the brand, identifying the target audience, devising the event concept, planning the logistics and coordinating the technical aspects before actually executing the modalities of the proposed event.

industry. The recent growth of festivals and events as an industry around the world means that the management can no longer be ad hoc. Events and festivals, such as the Asian Games, have a large impact on their communities and, in some cases, the whole country. The industry now includes events of all sizes from the Olympics down to a breakfast meeting for ten business people. Many industries, charitable organisations, and interest groups will hold events of some size in order to market themselves, build business relationships, raise money or celebrate.

The event manager is the person who plans and executes the event. Event managers and their teams are often behind-the-scenes running the event. Event managers may also be involved in more than just the planning and execution of the event, but also brand building, marketing and communication strategy. The event manager is an expert at the creative, technical and logistical elements that help an event succeed. This includes event design, audio-visual production, scriptwriting, logistics, budgeting, negotiation and, of course, client service. It is a multi-dimensional profession. The event manager may become involved at the early initiation stages of the event. If the event manager has budget responsibilities at this early stage they may be termed an event or production executive. The early stages include:

Site surveying
Client Service

Budget drafting

Procurement
Scheduling
Site design
Technical design
Health & Safety

An event manager who becomes involved closer to the event will often have a more limited brief. The key disciplines closer to the event are:

Health & Safety including crowd management
Logistics
Rigging
Sound
Light
Video
Detailed scheduling
Security

Q.12 What is the eligibility to study a course in event management and where can one enroll for a course in event management?

Ans: **Eligibility:** 10+2 education in any stream — Science, Commerce, Arts.

   opp. Lilavati Hospital, Bandra (W), Mumbai-400050
3. Indian Institute of Event Management, 144 Laxmi Plaza, New Likin Road, Andheri West, Mumbai
4. Indian Institute of Management, D-3, Defence Colony, New Delhi-110 048

5. International Centre for Event Marketing, 6/14,II Floor, Sarvapriya Vihar, New Delhi-110 016
6. International Institute of Event Management, SNDT Women's University, Juhu Campus, Juhu Tara Road, Santacruz (W), Mumbai-400 049
7. National Institute of Event Management, Ground Floor, Nandavan Buliding, Corner of Vallabhbhai Road & Ansari Road, Vile Parle (W), Mumbai-400 056
8. Apeejay Institute of Mass Communication — Dwarka, New Delhi — 110 075

Q.13 How can one start an event management company?

Ans: **Step 1: Decide the services you wish to sell**

A service is something which is intangible like: wedding planning, party planning, organising music concerts, fashion shows, conducting MICE (meetings, incentives, conferences and exhibitions), etc.

Choose those services in which you have a strong hold, in which you have majority of your experience and expertise and which can generate maximum revenue for you. Don't try to be jack of all trades and sell all event planning services one can think of. If majority of your experience is in wedding planning, then wedding planning is best for you.

Don't try to get into corporate meetings, just because the market is better. Corporate meetings are different from the weddings in terms of planning, implementation and evaluation. In fact every event is planned, executed and evaluated differently and therefore you can't organise all type of events.

Step 2: Do market research, competitor's analysis and SWOT analysis.

Market Research for Event Management Company

Market means your target audience, i.e. people who may be interested in your events. It also includes those clients who may be interested in hiring your event management services.

If your target audience are least interested in the type of event you organize, then you won't get any audience. Say you want to organise a rock concert in the country of Oman. But people there are least interested in such type of events. It means there is no market for your event in that country. If you organize the event there, it will fail for sure. Similarly if you wish to organize a Christmas Carnival in an area where majority of people are Muslims, then you can't expect many footsteps.

traditions, etc.), where there live and what are their desires and expectations from your event. To do market research you will have to do survey in the area (town/city/state/country) where you wish to organize the event. If you wish to open a wedding planning company and there are hardly two or three weddings in a year in your area, then selling such type of services is not commercially viable.

SWOT Analysis for Event Management Company: SWOT analysis is used to evaluate the strengths, weaknesses, opportunities and threats involved in your event planning venture. In SWOT: 's' stands for strengths, 'w' stands for weaknesses, 'o' stands for opportunities and 'T' stands for threats.

Strengths: Determine your resources and capabilities and how they can be used against your competition and in favour of your target audience. What advantages do you have? What you can do better than the others?

Weaknesses: Determine the resources you lack. Determine the advantages your competitors have. What could you improve? What you should avoid?

Opportunities: Look at your strengths and determine which opportunities are opened for you. Determine how you can open up even more opportunities by eliminating some of your weaknesses.

Threats: Changes in external environment (like changes in economy or market trends) or any unfavourable situation can pose threat to your company or business. Determine all present and possible threats to your business venture. It can be the presence of a very powerful competitor or new or innovative ways of organising events or a heavy tax on entertainment.

Step 3: Prepare business plan for your event management company

You will develop your business plan on the basis of market research, competitors' analysis and SWOT analysis of your event management company. Before developing your business plan, you should keep some points in mind:

2. Don't ignore developing strategies which may come handy in case of adversities in your business.

Following steps can be adopted for developing a business plan for your event management company:

1. Outline your business objectives.

   What do you want to achieve in short term and in long term, i.e. what is the mission and vision of your event planning company? However don't stick too much with long term objectives as they may become meaningless after a long time or changes in market situation.

   Develop the organisational structure of your event management company. Outline your own skills, knowledge and experience and determine how they can be used to achieve business success. Prepare resume of yourself and all of the people who will be involved in your business. These resumes will come handy when you will look for partners/investors later on.

   How you will approach them and how you will sell your services. How you will expand your business? What will be your rules, regulations, policies and procedures regarding payments, reimbursement, penalties, cancellation and behaviour?

4. Estimate your capital requirements for one whole year.

5. Prepare a contingency plan

   What strategies you will adopt in case of capital loss, economic crisis or market downturn.

Step 4: On the basis of your business plan determine your operating cost

The cost to run the business.

Step 5: On the basis of the operating cost, decide your own fees and the staff salary.

Step 6: Get investors/ business partners for your event management company

On the basis of market research, competitors' analysis, SWOT analysis and your business plan.

Step 7: Decide name and logo of your company and its status

Whether the organisation will be a company, partnership or proprietorship.

Step 8: Premises, recruitment and marketing your business

describes your business and services in great detail. Hire an internet marketing professional to promote it.

If you won't promote your website, then nobody will visit your website. So in that case your website will be as good as nothing. Through your website, your business will get global presence, 24 hours a day and 365 days a year. You can also expect to get lot of clients once your website becomes popular.

Step 9: Register your Company

If you have opened a company then get it registered under the Company's Act'. If you have

an establishment, then get it registered under the 'Shops and Establishment Act'. An event management company is just like any other company. So whatever rules and procedures are required to start a company, also applies to an event management company.

Step 10: Register to pay tax

Following taxes are to be paid by an event management company. Income Tax, TDS (Tax deducted at source), service tax, entertainment tax and taxes related to moving goods and merchandise

return. Get registration for service tax.

13

INFORMATION TECHNOLOGY & COMPUTER SCIENCE

Q.1 What is Information Technology (IT)?

Ans: Information technology (IT) is concerned with technology to treat information. The acquisition, processing, storage and dissemination of vocal, pictorial, textual and numerical information by

Review, in which authors Leavitt and Whisler commented that "the new technology does not yet have a single established name. We shall call it information technology (IT)." Some of the

bioinformatics, cloud computing, global information systems, large scale knowledge bases, etc.

IT is the area of managing technology and spans wide variety of areas that include computer software, information systems, computer hardware, programming languages but are not limited to things such as processes, and data constructs. In short, anything that renders data, information or perceived knowledge in any visual format whatsoever, via any multimedia distribution mechanism, is considered part of the IT domain. IT provides businesses with four sets of core services to help execute the business strategy: business process automation, providing information, connecting with customers, and productivity tools.

IT professionals perform a variety of functions (IT Disciplines/Competencies) ranging from installing applications to designing complex computer networks and information databases. A few of the duties that IT professionals perform may include data management, networking, engineering computer hardware, database and software design, as well as management and administration of entire systems. Information technology is starting to spread further than the conventional personal computer and network technologies, and more into integrations of other technologies such as the use of cell phones, televisions, automobiles, and more, which is increasing the demand for such jobs.

Q.2 What is Information and Communication Technology (ICT)?

Ans: Information and Communication Technology, usually abbreviated as ICT, is often used as an extended synonym for information technology (IT), but is usually a more general term that

A Complete Guide to Career Planning

lines and wireless signals), computers, middleware as well as necessary software, storage and audio-visual systems, which enable users to create, access, store, transmit, and manipulate information. In other words, ICT consists of IT as well as telecommunication, broadcast media, all types of audio and video processing and transmission and network based control and monitoring functions.

now also used to refer to the merging (convergence) of audio-visual and telephone networks with computer networks through a single cabling or link system. There are large economic incentives (huge cost savings due to elimination of the telephone network) to merge the audio-visual, building management and telephone network with the computer network system using a single

growth of organisations with the term ICT in their names to indicate their specialisation in the process of merging the different network systems.

Q.3 Who works in the field of Information Technology and what is the nature of job?

Ans:

who maintain large computer networks and database systems. IT professionals maintain databases for organisations and make sure that they are up to date and run smoothly. They resolve problems with the computers on their network by installing and maintaining the programs that run on them, monitoring overall system health and resolving problems such as computer viruses so that they do not spread quickly and cause network-wide system crashes.

Q.4 What kind of Education does one need to work in the field of Information Technology?

opportunities available, and updating one's skills with experience pertaining to the newest technologies out there is extremely important. Formal educational opportunities such as three

abundant. Usually titled associate of science or Bachelor of Science degrees, these courses focus mainly on the majored area of IT. With classes like the principles of computer language, application server programming, enterprise software architecture, and information systems security, students receive a great deal of information regarding the IT industry. In addition to such core classes, these degrees also require courses in mathematics, communications, science, social and behavioural science, as well as some humanities. The length of the programme determines how many classes in each area are necessary for graduation. For those looking to further their information technology degree, many colleges and universities

information communication technology.

various courses available at different institutions. Many diploma and degrees courses are there

Bachelor in Computer Applications (BCA)
Bachelor in Science with Computers (B.Sc)
Masters in Computer Applications (MCA)
M.Sc in computers
Masters in System Management
B.Tech and B.E
M.Tech

Diploma in Computer Applications
Postgraduate Diploma in Computer Applications
DOEACC's O, A, B, C level courses. For Details, check the DOEACC's website:

Q.5   What personal attributes are required to join the field of IT?

Ans:

Flexibility and willingness to learn new things, technologies and adopt new methods of work
Logical thinking
Ability to focus and concentrate
Creativity
Accuracy
Organisational and administrative abilities

Ready to work for long hours and ability to work hard
Ability to take decisions
High intellectual capacity
Ability to gel well with people and good communicational skills

Q.6   What is the Future of Information Technology?

Ans:
devices are shaping the way the world communicates with one another, gets work done, and

the lookout for fresh talent; those who want to play a part in IT's future have no limits on their

Q.7   What are the two main sectors in the field of IT?

Ans: Hardware: This includes the physical elements of the computer system and deals with the designing, manufacturing and maintenance of computers. This area also includes the assembling of the manufactured components of the computers.

Software: This includes the set of instructions by which a computer is programmed for working

various purposes. Programs may be for controlling the functioning of the computers or they may

of packages, which are designed for meeting the different kinds requirements for large number
of people.

Functional areas in Hardware:

    Manufacturing: This involves the work of production and assembly of components of computer systems.

    Maintenance: People in maintenance look after the smooth functioning of the machine and help in rectifying and detecting the breakdown in them. They also help in taking preventive measures so that least amount of damage could be caused to the computer systems and peripherals.

    Research and Development: It involves designing of chips and circuits, computer architecture and integration of peripherals. It also includes improvement and upgrading of the existing systems.

    Management: Managers ensure that the development and production work goes on smoothly. They look after the allocation of resources and planning.

Functional areas in Software:

    Manufacture: This involves preparing the set of instructions or programs to let the computer work. This further needs combining of application of computer science and telecommunications principles and creativity.

    Software development: This involves updating and development of existing operations

    analysis, designing, construction, implementation, etc.

    Data entry: The data for the programs, which are made, have to be fed in computers. So this work is done at data entry level.

    Programmers/Coders: They write and test programs and convert the strategies of the system analyst into working programs.

    Application programmers: They prepare programs either for general purpose or user-

    integrating them.

    Support services: They vary in nature and can range from helping a customers in the purchase of the software, suggesting its right kind of application and providing them with the required training at the initial stage of its use.

    Computer operations: It requires handling of computer peripherals along with other accessories like CD-ROMs, disk drives, printers, etc.

    Database administration: It involves management and maintenance of data.

    Sales and Marketing: The work here involves selling of the computer system and its marketing to different companies or individuals.

Data centre management: It involves management of the dedicated facilities, which houses the critical servers and other networking and backup equipments. Data-centres typically houses those equipment which have to be kept operational 24x7x365.

Q.8 What are the jobs available to IT professionals?

Ans: Software Engineers: They design programs and specialised packages for the required purposes. Their work even involves research and development.

Web developers: They are electronics and computer engineers who are engaged in developing websites for the Internet.

System analysts:
clients on the purchase and installation of the computer systems. They also are responsible for researching the organisational procedures and planning their computerisation.

Consultants: They provide expert guidance to the companies during the purchase of the computer system. System analyst or designers with considerable amount of experience can work as consultants.

Technical writers: they are involved in writing manuals for computers.

E-commerce: They are adept in the net-com business, e-commerce fundamentals and its security issues and assist in developing websites for commercial purposes.

Knowledge engineers: They are expert in designing of the computer systems, which are associated with a human expert, like medical diagnosis or safety systems for industry.

Webmasters:

the hackers and stalkers.

Networking: This work involves designing of networks, implementation of support servicing and management.

Computer education: This job involves giving training to the end users, students or computer professionals in advanced technologies.

Q.9 Which are the important IT Companies in India providing employment?

Ans: Some of the well-known software companies include Accenture, ADP, Apps Associates, Birlasoft, Broadridge, Cap Gemini, Capital IQ, Caritor ,CMC Ltd, Cognizant Technology Solutions, Computer Associates, Cordys, CSC, Cybage Software, Dell, DST Global Solutions, Google, HCL, HP ,IBM, IGate Global Solutions, Infosys, Larsen & Toubro Ltd, NUT Ltd, Microsoft, Oracle, Patni Computer Systems (P) Ltd, Persistent Systems Ltd., Sasken Communications, Sonata Software, Tata InfoTech Ltd, Polaris, Tata Consultancy Services, Verizon, Virtusa Technologies, Wipro Technologies Ltd, and Yahoo, etc. Although the software engineering sector is currency dependant, highly competitive and hectic, it is a lucrative career option. It surely offers a bright future for the IT professionals. Average Salaries for fresher's vary between 3.5 to 4.5 lakhs per annum depending on the recruiting Company

Q.10 What is business process outsourcing (BPO)?

Ans: Business process outsourcing (BPO) is a subset of outsourcing that involves the contracting outsourced large segments of its supply chain. In the contemporary context, it is primarily used

customer-related services such as contact centre services. BPO that is contracted outside a company's country is called offshore outsourcing. BPO that is contracted to a company's neighbouring (or nearby) country is called near shore outsourcing.

BPO is a distinct form of information technology (IT) outsourcing, which focuses on hiring a third-party company or service provider to do IT-related activities, such as application management and application development, data centre operations, or testing and quality assurance. In the early days, BPO usually consisted of outsourcing processes such as payroll. Then it grew to include

"non-core" to the primary business strategy. Now it is common for organisations to outsource

customer service activities and accounting and payroll. These outsourcing deals frequently involve multi-year contracts that can run into hundreds of millions of dollars. Often, the people

also dominate the IT outsourcing business) include US companies IBM, Accenture, and Hewitt Associates, as well as European and Asian companies Capgemini, Genpact, TCS, Wipro and Infosys.

Many of these BPO efforts involve off-shoring — hiring a company based in another country — to do the work. India is a popular location for BPO activities. Frequently, BPO is also referred to as ITES — information technology-enabled services. Since most business processes include some form of automation, IT "enables" these services to be performed.

expertise to handle. For example, whereas an insurance company might outsource data entry

to evaluate new insurance applications based on a set of criteria or business rules; this work would require the efforts of a more knowledgeable set of workers than the data entry would.

well as a number of other business functions. Also coming into use is the term BTO — Business Transformation Outsourcing. This refers to the idea of having service providers contribute to the operation.

Q.11   What is Computer Science?

Ans:
mathematical approach in information technology and computing. A computer scientist is a person who does work at a professional level in computer science.

computer systems and purely theoretical areas. Some, such as computational complexity theory, which studies fundamental properties of computational problems, are highly abstract, while others, such as computer graphics, emphasize real-world applications. Still others focus on the challenges in implementing computations. For example, programming language theory studies approaches to description of computations, while the study of computer programming itself investigates various aspects of the use of programming languages and complex systems, and human-computer interaction focuses on the challenges in making computers and computations useful, usable, and universally accessible to humans.

As a discipline, computer science spans a range of topics from theoretical studies of algorithms and the limits of computation to the practical issues of implementing computing systems in hardware and software. CSAB, formerly called Computing Sciences Accreditation Board, which is made up of representatives of the Association for Computing Machinery (ACM), and the IEEE Computer

science: theory of computation, algorithms and data structures, programming methodology and languages, and computer elements and architecture. In addition to these four areas, CSAB also

communication, database systems, parallel computation, distributed computation, computer-human interaction, computer graphics, operating systems, and numerical and symbolic computation as being important areas of computer science.

Q.12 Which is the nodal department for promotion of IT in India and what are its functions?

Ans: The Department of Information Technology is the nodal department for promotion of IT in India and its functions are:

Policy matters relating to Information Technology, Electronics and Internet.

Initiatives for development of Hardware / Software industry including knowledge based enterprises, measures for promoting Information Technology exports and competitiveness of the industry.

Promotion of Information Technology and Information Technology enabled services and Internet.

Assistance to other departments in the promotion of E-Governance, E-Infrastructure, E-Medicine, E-Commerce, etc.

Promotion of Information Technology education and Information Technology-based education.

Matters relating to Cyber Laws, administration of the Information Technology Act. 2000 (21 of 2000) and other Information Technology related laws.

Matters relating to promotion and manufacturing of Semiconductor Devices in the country.

Interaction in Information Technology related matters with International agencies and bodies.

Initiative on bridging the Digital Divide, Matters relating to Media Lab Asia.

Promotion of Standardisation, Testing and Quality in Information Technology and standardisation of procedure for Information Technology application and Tasks.

Electronics Export and Computer Software Promotion Council (ESC).

National Informatics Centre (NIC)

All matters relating to personnel under the control of the Department.

14

INSURANCE

Q. 1   What are the various opportunities in Insurance sector in India?

Ans: The insurance industry in India offers lot of opportunities for employment in the insurance sector. Some of the opportunities available in the insurance sector are:

Insurance Actuary: Actuary-ship will be one of the most sought after profession in the days to come. In India there is real dearth of actuaries and their number can be counted in hand. The requirement is such that the insurance companies are forced to bring actuaries from outside

and product design are used extensively in the areas of insurance, pensions, investment and

these industries, actuaries perform a wide variety of roles such as design and pricing of product,

in social insurance schemes sponsored by government.

Individual Agent/Advisor: Any person after qualifying the minimum criteria laid down in the IRDA Act can become a insurance agent/advisor. The individual agent processes business in his own name and he can take agency for one life and one non life company. For taking an insurance agency the candidate must directly approach the insurance company where he wishes to join. The insurance companies will bear the cost of the training. On successful passing of the exam

company to work as an agent and procure business for the company. IRDA has issued guidelines for licensing of the insurance agents. www.irdaindia.org

Work as Corporate Agent: As compared to individual agent, only companies can apply to become a corporate agent. The Company processes business in his own name and they can take agency for one life and one non life company. For taking corporate agency the companies must directly approach the insurance company where they wish to join. The insurance companies will bear the cost of the training course. The Corporate Agent may appoint persons for soliciting business on its behalf. The person so appointed must be trained as per IRDA norms. IRDA has issued guidelines for licensing of the corporate insurance agents. www.irdaindia.org

Employment under Brokers: Brokers are the new set of intermediaries which have been allowed to operate in the Indian market. A Broker can work for all the life and general insurance companies at a time. The brokers have to maintain minimum capital as prescribed for different category and have to follow stringent regulations. Brokers are the representatives of the consumers. In India the broking concept is limited and is in its nascent stage. In developed countries the brokers are as big as insurance companies and they undertake all activities from underwriting to settlement of claims. In India the brokers have been given limited role of basically procurement of business

also has underwriting, claims, accounting, marketing department. A person having technical

insurance brokers license.

Employment under TPA's: The Third Party Administrators are also a new concept in India. The TPA's acts as a link between the insurer, consumer and the medical services provider to facilitate

and provides cashless services, i.e. the insured need not pay any money at the time of claim and TPA directly settles the claim with Insurers and the hospitals. A person may get a job under a TPA to administer its operations.

Act as Surveyors: Surveyors are independent professionals licensed by IRDA. As per Insurance Act all the claims above Rs.20000/- must be surveyed by an independent professional. The Insurance Companies on receipt of any claims appoints the surveyor to assess the loss and submit a report quantifying the claim payable under the policy. Any person wishing to become a surveyor must pass an exam, get training for one year under a A or B category surveyor for one year and get himself categorised as per IRDA norms. There are 3 categories of surveyor A,B,C. The categories are being awarded by IRDA depending upon the experience. A surveyor can work with any number of insurance companies.

Join in any Corporate Body as Insurance Manager: The Corporate Bodies having good premium portfolio usually appoint an insurance manager to look after insurance requirements of the company. The job of the manager is to look after the safety measures adopted by the company, procure best possible insurance rates for the company and ensure speedy settlement of insurance claims.

Insurance Faculty: After opening of the insurance sector IRDA prescribed norms for the training of the insurance agents, brokers, surveyors. For meeting the huge demand a large number of

classes on insurance. The faculties are in huge demand and there is a real dearth of good faculties. The faculties are also employed by Insurance Companies to train their advisors about products of their company.

Valuation, Risk Inspection, Supervision jobs: For taking insurance policies the property must be valued to estimate the sum insured. This is usually the job of underwriter but in large insurance proposals the company asks for a valuation report. Similarly persons are required for inspection of risks.

Information Technology Industry: To meet with the IT demands of the insurance companies and the intermediaries the company producing computer software requires technical experts on insurance to help them in developing software on insurance for insurance companies, brokers, agents, surveyors, etc.

BPO Industry: The BPO industry in India is expanding in a big way in India. The Insurance companies outside India are outsourcing their operations into India for servicing of their policyholders. The BPO service providers require technical and experienced person having insurance knowledge to cater to the clients' need.

Insurance Consultant: With multiplicity of insurance companies, intermediaries, the demand for insurance consultants is bound to grow. Any person or company going for insurance will be really confused as to which company or intermediary to select. The consultants will help them to solve the problems and assist them in settlement of insurance claims.

Bancassurance: Bancassurance refers to the process of selling of Insurance by bank. The banks undertake distribution of insurance products through their channels in lieu of commission.

to sell insurance products. Banks are in a better position to advise and pursue its customers to go for requisite insurance as per their needs. Banks will require technical persons in insurance to handle their business.

Q.2   What are the different posts/jobs available with LIC, GIC and other Insurance companies?
Ans:

the candidates joining LIC and GIC on a probation-cum-training period of 6 months. This is to provide exposure about the working of insurance sector. AAOs can choose any of the areas from Administration, Development and Accounts. In Administration AAOs handle policy making, policy

of business, promoting policies, getting contracts, etc. The Accounts AAOs manage the funds including incomes and expenses of the corporation. After 3 years of working as AAOs they can be promoted to AOs. This adds on more powers and authority and they can be posted anywhere in India.

Candidates applying for the post of AAOs should be between 21 and 28 years of age. They should hold a graduate/postgraduate degree in any subject with minimum of 50% marks. Recruitment

objective type and the other is of essay type — test of English. The objective type paper tests intelligence and quickness of response. For the quantitative aptitude test good mathematical knowledge is essential. Logical reasoning, general knowledge, awareness of political, cultural events and happening are also tested. After the written test, selected candidates have to appear for inteviews which are conducted by the Board and are held across the country.

charge of their territory for the development of the insurance policies. They handle recruitment of agents, train them for procurement of new business and servicing of the existing policies. Over years of age and should be graduates. Eligible candidates are then put through written tests in English and Mathematics. On clearing the test, they qualify for the interview which is conducted by the Board. Later on selected candidates have to serve as Apprentice for a period of one year. This is impotant to impart practical training in various areas.

Other Jobs: Apart from the class I and II level, there are other posts such as Assistants, Typists, Machine Operators, Stenographer, Telephone Operators, Clerks, etc. This group comes in the

these posts have to go through a written test and an interview. There are reservations in the jobs for Handicapped persons, SC/ST, ex-servicemen. The age requirement for these posts is between 18 to 25 years.

Q.3 Which are the important institutions that offer courses in Insurance?

Ans: Following institutes offer specialised training and courses in the areas of insurance and reinsurance:

> Insurance Institute of India
> National Insurance Academy, Pune
> Actuarial Society of India

and actuarial sciences which are much in demand.

The Insurance Institute of India (III) formerly known as Federation of Insurance Institutes (J.C. Setalvad Memorial) was established in the year 1955, for the purpose of promoting Insurance

regulator and the industry. In its role as a leading education and training provider The Insurance Institute of India III is closely associated with all the segments of the insurance industry which includes Insurance Regulatory Authority of India, public and private sector insurance companies.

National Insurance Academy (NIA) is an international Academy initially catering to the needs of Insurance Management Education in more than 65 countries in Asia and Africa. NIA was established in 1980, primarily as a training institute for senior executives of insurance industry by the Life Insurance and General Insurance Industry with the active support of Government of India, Ministry of Finance. Over the years, Academy's activities proliferated and now cover training, research, education, consultancy and publication. NIA has been recognised as an Associate Member of the Federation of Afro Asian Insurers and Reinsurers (F.A.I.R.). NIA is also having collaboration with West African Insurance Institute, Banjul, Bimeh Markazi, Iran, Fairfax University, Louisiana & Wharton Business School, USA. NIA has been recognised for imparting training under the Technical Cooperation Scheme of Colombo Plan.

Q.4 What do Actuaries do?

Ans:

(a) **Actuaries Make Financial Sense of the Future:** Actuaries are experts in assessing the

(b) **Actuaries Enable More Informed Decisions:** Actuaries add value by enabling businesses and individuals to make better-informed decisions, with a clearer view of the likely range

project management, banking and health care. Within these industries, actuaries perform

and corporate planning. Actuaries are invariably involved in the overall management of

social insurance schemes sponsored by government. Actuarial skills are valuable for any

Actuaries apply professional rigour combined with a commercial approach to the decision making process.

(c) **Actuaries Balance the Interests of All:** Actuaries balance their role in business

duty of Actuaries to consider the public interest is illustrated by their legal responsibility

profession's code of conduct demands the highest standards of personal integrity from its members.

Q.5 Who can become an Actuary?

Ans: Any person with minimum 18 years of age and having a high degree of aptitude for mathematics

postgraduates in Mathematics, Statistics or Econometrics will be in a better position than others to qualify as actuaries. To qualify as an Actuary, a candidate has to pass all examinations in the prescribed subjects. In addition, he has to comply with other criteria such as experience requirement and attendance at a professionalism course prescribed for the purpose.

Duration of the Course
subjects prescribed are to be cleared before one is awarded the Fellowship, continued and sustained effort is necessary to complete the course. Single-minded devotion, total dedication and a systematic approach to problems are the qualities that will enable a person to qualify as an actuary within a reasonable period of time.

15

LAW

Q. 1 What do Lawyers do?
Ans:

—John Mortimer

At the most basic level, lawyers apply common sense to everyday and extraordinary situations alike. If you're smart, think well on your feet, and love proving your point, the law is for you!

Whether it's an intricate issue of constitutional law that will help preserve our fundamental rights,

people through the application of simple, everyday, common sense. Lawyers do this in various places, and through different means. The most familiar image, of course, if of lawyers screaming their lungs out in courts of law, wearing what looks to some of us like a tacky black bathrobe more than anything else! Litigating lawyers, as these lawyers are called, represent their clients in court. Litigating lawyers are called upon to argue various kinds of issues, ranging from property matters to criminal matters, constitutional issues to matters of family law. Black and white and vociferous, these lawyers argue the law to make sure that their clients' interests are represented in the best possible manner before those that will decide matters of a whole lot of importance

and within the boundaries of the law. Lawyers help business work in the best possible manner, and are an extremely important part of any business transaction. Huge mergers, large stock market issues, and foreign investments are all very cool to talk about, but unless you have someone who understands how these things work, and can get them done in the best possible way, all you'll

struggling to understand how to actually put their ideas in place. Lawyers make it happen! Lawyers are sometimes also referred to as 'social engineers'. As you would know, our society, the way we live, and what we do every day, are all loosely bound by a mesh of rules that we call 'laws'. It is the job of lawyers to understand these rules, and to help people live their lives most meaningfully. Many lawyers help people in distress, advocating areas that they are concerned about, such as child rights, women's issues, or the protection of refugees. If you really want to make a difference to people's lives, if you're actually concerned about something, and if you actually want to go out there and get something done right, this is the way to go for you. Aside from these, lawyers today work with people from every walk of life, interpreting laws, applying legal principles, and, above all, helping people tackle problems on every scale. Simply put, an ideal lawyer is a smart, intelligent person who applies common sense to common and uncommon problems alike, and helps

Q.2   How can one become a Lawyer?

Ans: To become a Lawyer, you have to pass LL.B. degree from a recognised institution and then enroll with Bar Council of India.

Q.3   When can one opt to study LL.B.?

Ans: You can study 5 years LL.B. after (10+2) with Science/ Arts/ Commerce or 3 years LL.B. after Graduation.

Q.4   Is the legal profession financially and socially rewarding one?

Ans: Many individuals choose a career in the law for the wrong reasons. Before embarking on the demanding, time-intensive and expensive journey to becoming a lawyer, make certain that you are making a well-informed decision. Few common myths about life as a lawyer:

1. Becoming a lawyer is a guaranteed path to financial success — The truth is, the most highly compensated attorneys are employed in the world's mega-firms (firms with over 101 attorneys) and such firms represent only 1% of all law firms according to the American Bar Foundation's Lawyer Statistical Report. Furthermore, most mega-firms are extremely selective in their hiring process, choosing only the top students from the most prestigious law schools. The vast majority of lawyers work in lower-paying venues such as small firms, public interest and the government. According to NALP, 83% of all lawyers who work in private practice are employed in firms of fewer than 50 lawyers. The Indian scenario is worse than America. Large law firm lawyers report the least career satisfaction according to a recent survey by the American Bar Association. Billable hour quotas at many large firms require lawyers to work 60-80 hours per week. When you divide your hours worked into your monthly salary, that big-firm paycheck may not look so generous. Attorneys employed in the public sector — which ranks among the lowest paying practice environments — reported the most career satisfaction.

2. As a lawyer, I can eradicate injustice and affect societal change — While you can make a positive impact as a lawyer, litigation has little to do with virtue triumphing over evil and everything to do with advocating your client's position based upon the facts and applicable law. Judicial decisions are not so much about the pursuit of justice or right vs. wrong as about reaching a compromise between all the parties. Judicial policy also affects many case decisions. In the ABA survey cited above, two out of every three lawyers surveyed reported concern that the court system they serve is becoming too political. The same is applicable to India also.

3. I will make myself a great lawyer because I am good at arguing — Although litigation is an adversarial process, legal advocacy is not about "arguing" in the sense of engaging in a verbal battle with your opponent. Instead, it is about persuading your audience — judge, mediator or jury — through a logical, well-researched, well-reasoned discussion

based on the facts and the law. Thus, to succeed as a litigator, a track record of "winning arguments" is not as important as top-notch oral advocacy and writing skills.

4. Litigators lead a thrilling, high-powered and glamorous life – Unlike the lawyers portrayed on television shows, the majority of the work of trial attorneys occurs outside the courtroom. In fact, less than one percent of all civil cases actually proceed to trial. The vast majority of cases are settled out of court or through alternative methods of dispute resolution. The daily life of the average trial lawyer is quite unglamorous. Trial lawyers spend most of their time in the discovery stage of litigation, reviewing pleadings, drafting and answering discovery requests and taking depositions. The work of a trial lawyer is also very research and writing-intensive as much of their work involves drafting briefs, memorandums of law and motions. Litigators spend many long hours engaged in tedious document review, gathering thousands of documents to be produced in litigation and reviewing each document to determine if it must be turned over to the other parties.

5. The work of a lawyer is intellectually challenging – While law practice can be intellectually rigorous, much of the lawyer's work is mundane and repetitive. New lawyers, especially

minute increments throughout the day, a painstaking but necessary task.

Q.5   Where can one study Law?

Ans: Law courses are offered by almost all the Universities across India. Some of the important institutions are:

1. **National Law School of India University**
   P.O. Bag 7201,
   Nagarbhavi
   Bangalore - 560 072
   Phone: 080 - 23213160, 23160532/0533/0535
   Fax: 080 - 23160534
   http://www.nls.ac.in/
   Email: registrar@nls.ac.in

2. **The West Bengal National University of Juridical Sciences**
   NUJS Bhavan
   12, LB-Block, Sector-III

   Phone: 033 - 2335 7379 / 0765 / 0500 / 053
   Fax: 033 - 2335 7422
   http://www.nujs.edu/
   Email: nujs@cal3.vsnl.net.in

3. **NALSAR University of Law, Hyderabad**
   3-4-761, Barkatpura,
   Hyderabad - 500 027
   Andhra Pradesh

Phone: 08418 - 2756 7955
Fax: 08418 - 2756 7310
http://www.nalsar.ac.in
Email: admissions@nalsarlawuniv.org

4. **National Law Institute University, Bhopal**

Pin- 462044,
Phone- 0755-2696717
Tele Fax-0755-2696965,
Email nliu@sancharnet.in
http://www.nliu.com/

5. **National Law University, Jodhpur**
NH-65, Nagour Road, Mandore,
Jodhpur - 342304
Rajasthan
Phone: 0291 - 2577530, 5121594
Fax: 0291-257 7540
http://www.nlujodhpur.ac.in/
Email: nlu-jod@raj.nic.in

6. **Government Law College,**
Mumbai
'A' Road,
Opposite Churchgate Station,
Mumbai - 400 020,
Maharashtra,
Phone: 022 - 2204 1707
Fax: 022 - 2285 1315
http://www.glcmumbai.com
Email: glcstudentscouncil@gmail.com

7. **Faculty of Law (University of Delhi)**
Chattra Marg,
University Enclave,
University of Delhi,
Delhi - 110007
Phone: 011 - 2766 7483, 2766 7725 -Ext. 1511
Phone (Dean) : 011 - 2766 7483
http://www.du.ac.in
Email: dean_law@du.ac.in, lawfaculty@vsnl.net

8. **ILS Pune**
Law College Road,
Pune 411 004
Phone: 020 - 2565 6775, 2567 8678
Fax: 020 - 2565 8665

http://www.ilslaw.edu/
Email: ilslaw@vsnl.com

9. **Amity Law School**
   F-1 Block, Sector 125
   Amity University Campus
   NOIDA - 201303
   Tel: 0120-4392681-82-83
   Fax: 0120-4392690
   E-mail: director@als.amity.edu
   Web: www.amity.edu/als

10. **Hidayatullah National Law University, Raipur**
    HNLU Bhawan,
    Civil Lines, Raipur (C.G.),
    Chhattisgarh - 492001
    Phone: 0771 - 408 0114, 408 0117
    Fax: 0771 - 408 0118
    http://www.hnlu.ac.in/
    Email: registrar@hnlu.ac.in

11. **University Law College, Bangalore**
    No. 1, Palace Road,
    Bangalore University,
    Bangalore — 560 009
    Phone: 080 - 2226 2137

12. **Symbiosis Law College**
    Senapati Bapat Road,
    Pune - 41100
    Phone: 020 -2565 5114, 2565 1495
    Fax: 020 - 2565 1711
    http://www.symlaw.ac.in/
    Email: info@symlaw.ac.in

13. **Faculty of Law, Aligarh Muslim University,**
    Aligarh Muslim University,
    Aligarh — 202 002
    Uttar Pradesh
    Phone: 0571 - 270 2457
    http://www.amu.ac.in/dept/law.htm

14. **Faculty of Law, Banaras Hindu University,**
    Banaras Hindu University,
    Varanasi — 221 005
    Uttar Pradesh
    Phone (Dean): 0542 - 230 7630, 236 9038

    http://www.bhu.ac.in/law.htm

15. **Balaji Law College, Pune**
    Building No. C-2, Bramha Estate,

    Pune - 411 048
    Phone: 020 2683 7545 / 2683 7548
    http://www.balajilaw.com/
    Email: info@balajilaw.com

16. **ICFAI Law School**
    The ICFAI University
    Plot No.1, Nagarjuna Hills,
    Punjagutta
    Hyderabad — 500 082
    Phone: 040 - 2343 0406
    http://www.icfai.org/ils/
    Email: ils@icfai.org

17. **Kishinchand Chellaram Law College (K.C. Law College), Mumbai**
    Churchgate,
    Mumbai - 400 020
    Phone: 022 - 2285 5726
    Fax: 022 - 2202 9092

18. **The Tamil Nadu Dr. Ambedkar Law University**
    "Poompozhil" 5, Greenways Road,
    Chennai - 600 028
    Phone: 044 - 494 1212
    http://www.imsc.res.in/~tandalau
    Email: tandralu@giasmd01.vsnl.net.in

19. **Gujarat National Law University, Gandhinagar**
    Old NIFT Building,
    E-4 GIDC, Electronics Estate,
    Gandhinagar - 382 028,
    Gujarat
    Phone: 079 - 232 43296, 232 43308,
    Fax: 232 43317
    http://www.gnlu.ac.in/

20. **Bangalore Institute of Legal Studies,**
    Vijaya College Campus,
    R.V. Road Basavanagaudi,
    Bangalore - 560 004
    Phone: 080 - 2656 1072

21. **Christ University**
    School of Law,
    Hosur Road , Bangalore 560029
    Tel: 080 4012 9112/ 9100

Fax: 080 4012 9000
E-mail: admission@christuniversity.in
Website: www.christuniversity.in

22. **National University of Advanced Legal Studies, Kochi**

Tel : 0484 - 2337363,
Fax : 0484 2337857.
E - mail : vc@nuals.ac.in
registrar@nuals.ac.in

23. **Rajiv Gandhi National University of Law, Punjab**

Patiala - 147 001
Tel: 0175-2304188
Fax: 0175-2304189
Email: info@rgnulpatiala.org
www.rgnulpatiala.org

24. **Dr. Ram Manohar Lohiya National Law University**

Lucknow - 226 012
Phone: 0522 - 2422841, 2422855
www.nlulucknow.up.nic.in

25. **Chanakya National Law University**
C/o A.N Sinha Institute Campus
Near Gandhi Maidan
Patna - 800001
Telefax : 0612-2205920, 2200789, 6450242
Email : chanakyalawuniv@gmail.com
www.cnlu.ac.in

26. **University of Petroleum & Energy Staff (UPES)**
Campus: Energy Acres,
PO Bidholi Via Prem Nagar,
Dehradun - 248 007 (Uttarakhand)

1st Floor, 55 Community Centre,

Phone: 011-47173400
Email ID: vgupta@upes.ac.in
Website: www.upes.ac.in
Toll Free No.: 1800-102-8737

27. **KIIT LAW SCHOOL**
Patia, Bhubaneswar - 751 024
Tel: +91 674 2725440; 2725440

Mob: + 91 9438303041; 9438304010
Email: query@kls.ac.in, klsat@kls.ac.in
http://www.kls.ac.in

28. **Bharati Vidyapeeth University, Pune**
Bharati Vidyapeeth University,
Erandawane, Pune - 411 038
Tel: 24335510, 24335509, 24331317

29. **Jindal Global Law School, Sonipat**
O. P. Jindal Global University and Jindal Global Law School
Sonipat Narela Road Near Jagdishpur Village
Sonipat, Haryana - 131001
NCR of Delhi, India
Tel: +91-130-3057800, 3057801, 3057802
Fax: +91-130-3057888
Email: info@jgu.edu.in; admissions@jgu.edu.in; registrar@jgu.edu.in
Website: www.jgu.edu.in

30. **MATS Law School, Raipur**

Aarang, Raipur - 493 441 (C.G.)
Email : info@matsuniversity.ac.in
Website : http://www.matsuniversity.ac.in

Q.5 Which are the best Law School/Colleges in India?

Ans:

Law School	India Today Rank (2010)	Rank 2009
NLSIU Bangalore	1	1
Nalsar Hyderabad	2	2
NLIU Bhopal	3	4
Campus Law Centre DU	4	3
Symbiosis Pune	5	6
	6	8
ILS Law College Pune	7	5
NLU Jodhpur	8	7
GNLU Gandhinagar	9	-
Amity Law School Delhi	10	9
HNLU Raipur	11	-
Faculty of Law Benaras, Varanasi	12	11
School of Legal Studies, Cochin University	13	14
	14	18
Army Institute of Law, Mohali	15	21

Faculty of Law, Aligarh Muslim University	16	12
Faculty of Law Rohtak University	17	-
Tamil Nadu Dr Ambedkar Law University	18	24
UCL Bangalore	19	15
Faculty of Law, Osmania University	20	20
	21	13
	22	-
Faculty of Law, University of Mumbai	23	-
Faculty of Law, Jamia Millia Islamnia, New Delhi	24	16
Bangalore University for Legal Studies	25	22

Source: India Today 2010

Q.5 What is Common Law Admission Test (CLAT)?

Ans: The Common Law Admission Test (CLAT) is an all India entrance examination conducted by 14 National Law Schools/Universities for admissions to their under-graduate and post-graduate degree programmes (LL.B & LL.M). The 14 participating NLUs in the order of their establishment are:

1. National Law School of India University, Bangalore (NLSIU)
2. NALSAR University of Law, Hyderabad (NALSAR)
3. National Law Institute University, Bhopal (NLIU)

5. National Law University, Jodhpur (NLUJ)
6. Hidayatullah National Law University, Raipur (HNLU)
7. Gujarat National Law University, Gandhinagar (GNLU)
8. Dr. Ram Manohar Lohiya National Law University, Lucknow (RMLNLU)
9. Rajiv Gandhi National University of Law, Patiala (RGNUL)
10. Chanakya National Law University, Patna (CNLU)

12. National Law University, Orissa (NLUO)
13. National University of Study & Research in Law, Ranchi (NUSRL)
14. National Law University & Judicial Academy, Assam (NLUJA)

that the test should be conducted by rotation in the order of their establishment. Accordingly CLAT-2008 (NLSIU, Bangalore), CLAT-2009 (NALSAR, Hyderabad), CLAT-2010 (NLIU, Bhopal) and

Eligibility for Under-Graduate Programmes — To be eligible to appear in CLAT, a candidate should

a recognised Board with not less than 50% marks in aggregate (45% in case of SC/ST/OBC and PWD). Candidates who have appeared in the 10+2 examination and are awaiting results are also eligible to appear in the test. Age of the candidate should not be more than 20 years in case of General/OBC candidates (22 years in case of SC/ST and persons with Disability) as on 1st July during the year of admission. The candidate must have passed the qualifying examination at the time of his/her admission and be able to submit its proof.

Eligibility for Post-Graduate Programmes — To be eligible for appearing in CLAT, a candidate should have obtained a LL.B/B.L. Degree or an equivalent degree from a recognised University with not less than 55% marks in aggregate (50% in case of SC/ST /OBC and persons with Disability).

Q.6   What is the pattern of CLAT Examination?

Ans: Pattern of the CLAT Paper for Under-Graduate Programme:

Total Marks	200
Total number of multiple-choice questions of one mark each	200
Duration of examination	Two Hours
Subject areas with weightage:	
English including Comprehension	40 Marks
	50 Marks
Elementary Mathematics (Numerical Ability)	20 Marks
Legal Aptitude	50 Marks
Logical Reasoning	40 Marks

The different subject areas of the exam are explained as under:

in English based on comprehension passages and grammar. In the comprehension section, candidates will be questioned on their understanding of the passage and its central theme, meanings of words used therein, etc. The grammar section requires correction of incorrect

March 2011 and March 2012)

3. Mathematics — This section will test candidates only on "elementary" mathematics, i.e. maths that is taught up to the class X.

4. Logical Reasoning — The purpose of the logical reasoning section is to test the student's ability to identify patterns, logical links and rectify illogical arguments. It will include a wide variety of logical reasoning questions such as syllogisms, logical sequences, analogies, etc. However, visual reasoning will not be tested.

5. Legal Aptitude — This section will test students only on "legal aptitude". Questions will be framed with the help of legal propositions (described in the paper), and a set of facts to which the said proposition has to be applied. Some propositions may not be "true" in the real sense (e.g. the legal proposition might be that any person who speaks in a movie hall and disturbs others who are watching the movie will be banned from entering any movie theatre across India for one year). Candidates will have to assume the "truth" of these propositions and answer the questions accordingly. Candidates will not be tested on any

prior knowledge of law or legal concepts. If a technical/legal term is used in the question, that term will be explained in the question itself. For example, if the word patent is used, the meaning of patent ("a legal monopoly granted by the government for certain kinds of inventions") will also be explained.

Q.7 What is the pattern of CLAT for PG programme?

Ans: Pattern of the CLAT Paper for Post-Graduate Programme is as follows:

Total Marks	200
Duration of examination	Two Hours
Multiple-choice Questions (100 questions of 1 mark each)	Pertaining to subject areas, viz, Law of Contracts, Law of Torts, Criminal Law, Constitutional Law and Legal Theory
Short-answer questions (100 Marks)	10 questions of 10 marks each

Q.8 What is AIBE?

Ans: The All India Bar Examination (AIBE) is intended to test an advocate's ability to practice the profession of law in India. The AIBE will assess capabilities at a basic level, and is intended to set a minimum standard for admission to the practice of law; it addresses a candidate's analytical abilities and basic knowledge of law.

Education Committee and the members of the Bar Council of India. The All India Bar Examination

ability to practice the profession of law in India. The AIBE is intended to assess capabilities at a basic level, and is intended to set a minimum standard for admission to the practice of law; it addresses a candidate's analytical abilities and basic knowledge of law. All students graduating from academic year 2009-10 onwards need to clear the AIBE in order to practice law in India. Candidates may apply to appear for the All India Bar Examination only after enrolling as an advocate under Section 24 of the Advocates Act, 1961 and will have to submit suitable proof of such enrolment along with the application form for the AIBE.

Q.9 What are the job options for a Law student/Law graduate?

Ans: Apart from becoming Lawyer / Judicial Magistrate / Judge, the following jobs are also available for Law graduates:

Legal Assistant
File Clerk
Court Messenger
Copy Centre Professional
Mailroom Clerk
Administrative Assistant
Trial Consultant
EDD Consultant

Computer Forensics Professional
Legal Software Consultant
Legal Marketing Consultant
Forensic Scientist
Legal Videographer
Legal Investigator
Accident Re-constructionist
Legal Management Consultant
Document Management Specialist
Legal Publisher
Legal Writer
Legal Editor
Legal Web Manager
Law Firm Administrator
Contract Administrator
Law Firm Marketer
Practice Administrator
Courtroom Deputy
Court Administrator
Court Interpreter
Courtroom Technology Specialist
Court Clerk
Prothonotary
Law Professor
Law School Dean

Legal Career Counselor
Paralegal Instructor
Legal Researcher
Patent Attorney
IP Docketing Specialist
Patent Designer & Illustrator
Patent Agent
Patent Clerk
Attorney General
Public Prosecutor/District Attorney
Legislator
Legislative Aide
Legislative Staffer

Legal Analyst
Lobbyist
Compliance Specialist

Legal Recruiter

16
MANAGEMENT

Q.1   What is Management?

Ans: Management in all business and organisational activities is the act of getting people together

organisation (a group of one or more people or entities) or effort for the purpose of accomplishing

resources, technological resources and natural resources.

including design, to facilitate the production of useful outcomes from a system. This view opens the opportunity to 'manage' oneself, a pre-requisite to attempting to manage others.

Towards the end of the 20th century, business management consisted of six separate branches, namely:

> Human resource management
> Operations management or production management
> Strategic management
> Marketing management
> Financial management
> Information technology management

Q.2   What are the courses offered in the field of Management and which are the good institutions to opt for a course in Management?

Ans: Courses in management are offered generally at undergraduate and postgraduate degree/ diploma levels, by private and government management institutes. Individuals can pursue these courses through correspondence mode also. Usually, a 10+2 pass candidate can take up undergraduate management degree programs, like BBA, BBS, BBM, etc. For post graduation courses, like MBA,

and part-time management courses are conducted at various leading B-schools. Management

information technology, hospitality management, event management, business management,

management, media management, and many more. Almost all reputable management institutions in India admit students through entrance tests, like CET, CAT, SNAP, MAT, etc. For each type of recognised and organised business, there is a management programme made available. A course in management enables one to understand all major and minor aspects of business administration/ management. Besides, planning, organising, leading, monitoring, delegating, and controlling are some other essentials of a management curriculum.

After completing a course in management, one can start his/her own business or aspire to work at managerial and executive levels in corporate houses and multinational companies. There is always

managers, human resource managers, event managers, hospitality managers, and others. For

can enhance their skills and improve their chances of climbing the ladder of hierarchy in their

provides exciting opportunities in the government sector.

Some of the most prestigious institutions for pursuing a management programme in India are: Indian

and Shillong; Management Development Institute, Gurgaon; SP Jain Institute of Management & Research, Mumbai; Xavier Labor Research Institute (XLRI), Jamshedpur; Indian School of Business, Hyderabad; Faculty of Management Studies, University of Delhi, New Delhi; Jamnalal Bajaj Institute of Management Studies, Mumbai; Institute of Management Technology, Ghaziabad; International Management Institute, New Delhi; Narsee Monjee Institute of Management Studies, Mumbai; Symbiosis Institute of Business Management, Pune; Indian Institute of foreign trade, New Delhi; and TA Pai Management Institute, Manipal.

Q.3 What is CAT?

Ans:
the process of seeking admission to the 2 year full time Post-Graduate Degree Programs in Management offered by the IIMs. Currently IIM Ahmedabad, IIM Bangalore, IIM Calcutta, IIM

results of CAT to shortlist the candidates for subsequent part of the Selection Process.

CAT Eligibility: The candidate must hold a Bachelor's Degree, with at least 50% marks or equivalent CGPA [45% in case of the candidates belonging to Scheduled Caste (SC), Scheduled Tribe (ST) and Differently Abled (DA) (It may also referred to as Persons with Disability (PWD) category)], awarded by any of the Universities incorporated by an act of the central or state legislature in India or other educational institutions established by an act of Parliament or declared to be deemed as a University under Section 3 of the UGC Act, 1956, or possess an equivalent

The percentage of marks obtained by the candidate in the bachelor's degree would be calculated based on the practice followed by the university / institution from where the candidate has obtained the degree. In case the candidates are awarded grades / CGPA instead of marks, the

by the university / institution from where they have obtained the bachelor's degree.

In case the university / institution does not have any scheme for converting CGPA into equivalent marks, the equivalence would be established by dividing the candidate's CGPA by the maximum possible CGPA and multiplying the result with 100.

IIMs may verify eligibility at various stages of the selection process, the details of which are

minimum eligibility criteria will not ensure consideration for shortlisting by IIMs.

Prospective candidates must maintain a valid and unique email account and a phone number throughout the selection process.

Admission Process: Please note that each IIM shortlists candidates for second stage of selection which may be independent of each other. The process may include Written Ability Test (WAT), Group Discussions (GD) and Personal Interviews (PI). Performance in CAT examination is an important component in the admission process. IIMs may use previous academic performance of the candidates, relevant work experience and other similar inputs in shortlisting and ranking of candidates at various stages of the admission process. The processes, academic cut-offs and the weights allocated to the evaluation parameters may vary across IIMs. For more information you may refer the admissions policies of IIMs from their respective websites

Test Duration and Pattern
Ability & Data Interpretation; the second section is Verbal Ability & Logical Reasoning. These two sections will be implemented sequentially with separate time limits. The examination will be 140 minutes. Candidates will have 70 minutes to answer 30 questions within each section which will have an on-screen countdown timer. Within the 70 min provided for the section, candidates

section and will no longer be able to go back.

A 15-minute tutorial will be provided before the start of the test, and candidates are advised to go through that carefully before starting the main examination. The total duration will be two

feel of the timed sections, as well as navigation and functionality of the actual test will be made available in the coming weeks. Once again candidates are advised to go though them carefully to familiarise themselves with the screens, layout, and navigation.

At the test venue, each candidate will be seated at a desk with a computer terminal and he/she will be provided with a scratch paper for calculations. After the test, candidates must leave the scratch paper at the desk. Rough work cannot be done on any other paper/sheet, as nothing will be allowed inside the testing room. No breaks will be given during the test.

Q.4   What is XAT?

Ans: XAT stands for Xavier Aptitude Test. To get admission to XLRI, candidates have to appear for XAT.

net.in. Once the candidate logs on to this site, a full set of instructions will appear. The candidate can obtain his/her ID and password by following these instructions. This ID and password are to

A candidate may apply for a maximum of three programmes. Those who apply for multiple programmes may be called for multiple interviews and/or group discussions. The selection criteria for different programmes may differ depending on the nature of the programme. XAT written test will have multiple components and you need to maximize your performance in each of these components. In its pursuit of academic excellence, XLRI actively encourages the students from diverse backgrounds. While preparing the shortlisted candidates for the interview, in addition to XAT performance academic ability and the relevant work experience also count while preparing being out of the country, interviews would be carried out in on-line mode via Internet. XAT has three sections: `English Language Ability and Logical Reasoning' (EL), 'Quantitative Ability' (QA) and 'Decision Making' (DM).

Q.5 Which are the institutions that admit student on the basis of XAT score?

Ans: There are 16 core member institutes and more than 85 associate institutes located in different parts of the country.

S.No	Institute's Name	Place	Website
1.	Acharya School of Management	Bangalore	www.acharya.ac.in
2.	Andhra Loyola Institute of Management	Vijayawada	www.andhraloyolacollege.ac.in
3.	APG Shimla University	Shimla	www.apg.edu.in
4.	Aryans Business School	Punjab	www.aryans.edu.in
5.		New Delhi	
6.	Bengal Institute of Business Studies		www.bibs.co.in
7.	Bharatiya Vidya Bhavan's Usha & Lakshmi Mittal Institute of Management	New Delhi	www.bulmim.ac.in
8.	Bhavan's Centre for Communication and Management	Bhubaneswar	www.bvbbhubaneswar.org
9.	Birla Institute of Management Technology	Greater Noida	www.bimtech.ac.in
10.	BLS Institute of Management	Mohan Nagar	www.blsim.org
11.	Deen Dayal Upadhyaya Institute of Management and Higher Studies		www.dduinstitute.org
12.	Delhi School of Professional Studies and Research	Delhi	www.dspsr.in
13.	Desh Bhagat Institute of Management & Computer Sciences	Amloh	www.deshbhagatinstitutes.com
14.	Disha Institute of Management and Technology	Dist. Raipur	www.dimatindia.com
15.	Driems Business School	Cuttack	www.dbs.ac.in
16.	Entrepreneurship & Management Process International	New Delhi	www.empiindia.com
17.	Entrepreneurship Development Institute of India (EDI)	Gandhinagar	www.ediindia.org
18.	Faculty of Management Studies, Goa University	Goa	www.unigoa.ac.in
19.	Fortune Institute of International Business	Delhi	
20.	Gitam Institute of Management	Visakhapatnam	www.gitam.edu
21.	Gitam School of International Business	Visakhapatnam	www.gsib.org
22.	Globsyn Business School		www.globsyn.edu.in
23.	Goa Institute of Management	Goa	www.gim.ac.in
24.	IBMR - Business Schools	Bangalore	www.ibmrbschool.org
25.	IFIM Business School	Bangalore	
26.	IILM College of Management Studies	Greater Noida	www.iilmcms.ac.in
27.	IILM Graduate School of Management	Greater Noida	www.iilmgsm.ac.in
28.	IILM Institute for Higher Education	Gurgaon	www.iilm.edu

29.	Indian Institute of Finance	Noida	www.iif.edu
30.	Indus Business Academy	Bangalore	www.iba.ac.in
31.	Indus World School of Business	NCR	www.iwsb.in
32.	Institute for Financial Management and Research	Chennai	www.ifmr.ac.in
33.	Institute for Technology and Management	Navi Mumbai	www.itm.edu
34.	Institute of Business Studies and Research	Navi Mumbai	www.ibsar.ac.in
35.	Institute of Management & Information Science	Bhubaneswar	www.imis.ac.in
36.	Institute of Science & Management	Ranchi	www.iismr.org
37.	International Academy of Management & Entrepreneurship	Bangalore	www.iame.org.in
38.	International Institute of Business Studies	Bangalore	www.iibsonline.com
39.	International School of Business & Media	Pune	www.isbm.ac.in
40.	International School of Management Excellence	Bangalore	www.isme.in
41.	Invertis Institute of Management Studies	Bareilly	www.invertis.org
42.	ISBR Business School	Bangalore	www.isbr.in
43.	Jagran Institute of Communication and Management	Bhopal	www.jicm.edu.in
44.	Jaipuria Institute of Management	Indore	www.jimindore.ac.in
45.	Jaipuria Institute of Management	Lucknow	www.jaipuria.ac.in
46.	Jaipuria Institute of Management	Noida	www.jimnoida.ac.in
47.	Jaipuria Institute of Management	Jaipur	www.jimj.ac.in
48.	Jindal Global Business School	Sonipat	www.jgbs.edu.in
49.		Jaipur	www.jklu.edu.in
50.		Ranchi	www.kimds.in
51.		Harihar	www.kiams.ac.in
52.			www.kohinoor.ac.in
53.		Bhubaneswar	www.krupajalbschool.org
54.	Lovely Professional University	Phagwara	www.lpu.in
55.	Loyola Academy	Secunderabad	www.loyolaacademy.ac.in
56.	Loyola Institute of Business Administration	Chennai	www.liba.edu
57.	Management Education & Research Institute	New Delhi	www.meri.edu.in
58.	Mangalvedhekar Institute of Management (MIM)	Solapur	www.mangalvedhekar.org
59.	Mar Athanasios College for Advanced Studies (MACFAST)		www.macfast.org
60.	Marian Institute of Health Care Management	Panaji	www.marianinstitute.in
61.	MATS Institute of Management and Entrepreneurship	Bangalore	www.mats.ac.in
62.	MIT School of Business	Pune	www.mitsob.com
63.	MIT School of Telecom Management	Pune	www.mitsot.com
64.	Mount Carmel Institute of Management	Bangalore	www.mountcarmelinstitute.org
65.	MVRR Institute of Business Management		www.mvrribmgudlavalleru.ac.in
66.	National School of Business	Bangalore	www.nsbindia.org

67.	New Delhi Institute of Management	New Delhi	ndimdelhi.org
68.	Praxis Business School		www.praxis.ac.in
69.	Prin. L.N. Welingkar Institute of Management Development & Research	Mumbai	www.welingkar.org
70.	Pune Institute of Business Management	Pune	www.pibm.in
71.	Ravenshaw Management Centre	Cuttack	www.ravenshawuniversity.ac.in
72.	Regional College of Management Autonomous	Bhubaneswar	www.rcm.ac.in
73.	S P Jain Institute of Management & Research	Mumbai	www.spjimr.org
74.	School of Management Sciences	Varanasi	www.smsvaranasi.com
75.		Bhubaneswar	www.ksom.ac.in
76.	SDM Institute for Management Development	Mysore	www.sdmimd.ac.in
77.	Shiva Institute of Management Studies	Ghaziabad	www.shivaims.edu.in
78.	SIET Institute of Management	Bangalore	www.bsim.in
79.	Siva Sivani Institute of Management	Secunderabad	www.ssim.ac.in
80.	Sri Shrada Institute of Indian Management Research	New Delhi	wwww.srisiim.org
81.	Sri Sri University	Bhubaneshwar	www.srisriuniversity.edu.in
82.	St. Aloysius Institute of Management and Information Technology	Mangalore	www.staloysics.ac.in
83.	St. Berchmans College		www.sbmba.org
84.	St. Francis Institute of Management and Research (SFIMAR)	Mumbai	
85.	St. Joseph's College of Business Administration	Bangalore	www.sjcba.edu.in
86.	St. Joseph's Iinstitute of Management	Trichy	www.jiim.ac.in
87.	Suryadatta Group of Institutes	Pune	www.suryadatta.org
88.	T A Pai Management Institute	Manipal	www.tapmi.edu.in
89.	Taxila Business School	Jaipur	www.taxila.in
90.	The National Management School	Chennai	www.nms.edu.in
91.	The School of Business, Alliance University	Bangalore	www.alliance.edu.in
92.	Training & Advanced Studies in Management and Communications Ltd (TASMAC)	Pune	www.tasmac.ac.in/wales
93.	United World School of Business		www.unitedworld.in
94.	Vanguard Business School	Bangalore	www.vanguardbschool.com
95.	VIT University	Vellore	www.vit.ac.in
96.	WLC College India	Noida	www.wlccollege.org
97.	Xavier Institute of Development Action and Studies	M.P	www.xidas.in
98.	Xavier Institute of Management	Bhubaneswar	www.ximb.ac.in
99.	Xavier Institute of Management & Entrepreneurship	Bangalore	www.xime.org
100.	Xavier Institute of Management & Research	Mumbai	www.ximr.ac.in
101.	Xavier Institute of Social Service	Ranchi	www.xiss.ac.in
102.	Xavier Labour and Relations Institute	Jamshedpur	www.xlri.ac.in

Q.6   What is MAT?

Ans: MAT stands for Management Aptitude Test and conducted by All India Management Association (AIMA) for admission into various management institutions in India. Centre for Management Services (CMS) is the specialised division of AIMA undertaking testing and other management services. The testing services have been in operation since 1988 facilitating academia, industry and governments to screen and select candidates for higher studies, recruitment, promotion, etc. Over hundreds of AICTE approved Institutions & University departments and over lakhs of MBA aspirants having availed AIMA's testing services. MAT is approved by Ministry of HRD, GOI as a National Entrance Test.

Q.7   When & how many times MAT is conducted in a year? What qualification & percentage needed for it?

Ans: MAT is usually conducted 4 times in a year in February, May, September and December. The

B.Sc., B.Com., B.Tech., etc) can also appear provisionally. Usually, there is a minimum percentage requirement in graduation, which is different for different MIs/University. For this refer to the prospectus of the particular MIs/University.

Q.8   What is the mode of test?

Ans: Candidate can choose any one of the two options to take the test: Paper Based Test or Computer Based Test.

Q.9   What are the test dates and timings of the test?

Ans:
September and December from 1000-1230 hours. Whereas the Computer Based Test is being conducted from Saturday onwards (6 days after the Paper Based Test date) and in different Time slots.

Q.10   How many MIs participate in MAT? Do they keep on changing or remain the same? Is there a same admission criterion for each & every Institute? Are they recognised by AICTE?

Ans: The number of participating MIs may vary. The number of MIs keeps on changing from test to test. Admission criteria for every institute are different. All MIs participating in MAT are either AICTE,

contact the MIs/Universities of your choice. The list of various MIs/Universities is available in MAT

the MIs for detailed information.

Q.11   What is the validity of MAT score?

Ans: Validity of the MAT score is for that particular session for most MIs is one year.

Q.12   What is the last date of submitting MAT Registration Form?

Ans: Last date for submission is mentioned in the MAT bulletin. The last date also appears in the

Q.13   Is there any difference between Computer Based Test and Paper Based Test?

Ans: Computer Based Test means the candidate sits in front of a computer and the questions are presented on the computer monitor and the candidate submits the answers through the use of keyboard or mouse. Each computer is connected to a server, which prepares the question set and delivers it to the candidate on the computer. This is unlike the Paper Based Test, which is generally offered on a single day to all candidates. MAT is conducted over a period of time and the candidate can choose the centre, the day and time of his/her convenience to take the test. Computer Based Test assumes that the candidate has basic familiarity with use of computers like use of keyboard and mouse operation. It is the responsibility of the candidate to acquire these skills before appearing in the test and AIMA cannot take responsibility for the same. In traditional Paper Based Test, Candidate is supposed to bring pen, HB-Pencils, erasers and sharper with him/her whereas the Question Paper & OMR Answer Sheet is provided at the Test Centre.

Q.14   Is there any age bar for it? Any Job experience required to appear in MAT?

Ans: There is no age bar. Job experience is not necessary to appear in MAT.

Q.15   What is the nature of MAT test?

Ans: It is an objective type test with multiple-choice answers. The test is designed to measure a person's general aptitudes as the following table indicates:

Section No.	Section	No of Questions	Time Suggested (Minutes)
1.	Language Comprehension	40	30
2.	Mathematical Skills	40	40
3.		40	35
4.	Intelligence and Critical Reasoning	40	30
5.	Indian and Global Environment	40	15
	Total	200	150

Q.16   What is ATMA?

Ans: ATMA is a standard test to assess the aptitude of candidates for Management Education. The test is run by the Association of Indian Management Schools (AIMS), which is a network of over 600 management schools in the country. AIMS represents Indian Management Schools in the international forum and is also associated with many committees of the government or its agencies looking at policies relating to management education. ATMA has nothing to do with the admission process of different management schools, which accept its scores. Candidates who take ATMA do not automatically get considered for admission by the management schools that accept ATMA scores for their admission unless they apply to them directly.

In other words, scores of ATMA test are accessible to those institutions which are members.

Q.17   What is the link between the ATMA and admission process of institutions?

Ans: ATMA is a test essentially assessing the aptitude of students for management education. Around 200 management institutions accept ATMA scores for their admission processes. However, check on the website both lists. Such lists will also be available on ATMA ONLINE portal. It is up to individual management institutes to decide how they will use ATMA scores. Both AIMS and ATMA do not have nor intend to have any information relating to the admission processes of different institutions. This has to be clearly understood. Each student who takes ATMA can apply to any of the schools, which have announced publicly in newspaper announcements or brochure/website that they accept ATMA scores.

Q.18 What are different subjects on which candidates are tested?

Ans: ATMA checks the aptitude of the students for management education through three major elements:

1. Quantitative Skills   2. Analytical Reasoning 3. Verbal Skills

Generally, these are the three areas required to assess the aptitude of a candidate. Other major testing agencies also test students in the same three areas. In ATMA, there are 180 questions, which a student has to answer. It is not really possible even for the best of students to answer all the questions. Exceptions will always be there. If one is unable to answer all the questions, it does not mean that you are not good enough for management education. In each section, the questions focus on different skills considered desirable for admission to good management schools.Reference to the sample of questions given elsewhere in the bulletin or in this website will give you an idea of the kind of questions that are asked in the test.

Q.19 What is the validity period of ATMA?

Ans: ATMA scores are valid for one year. ATMA Paper-based and ATMA Online are administered a few times during an academic year. However, it is up to the institutions to decide scores of which test administration they will utilize. AIMS does not have any say nor does it intend to have any say in this matter. How ATMA scores are utilised in the selection process is left entirely to the institutes or management schools.

Q.20 If I take ATMA, is admission guaranteed?

Ans: ATMA gives you an opportunity to apply to different management schools. Your performance in ATMA will determine your chances of getting admission to the institutes that you are applying to. The ATMA organisation will provide you raw scores and may provide you percentiles in each section when appropriate as well as the total score.

Q.21 What are the areas where a student needs to focus while preparing for ATMA?

Ans: Students should make sure that their fundamentals are clear in each of the three areas in which testing is done. A student with a good record in a good Bachelor's degree should be able to tackle

get some practice from any number of tests that are available in the public domain. A student should brush up his English grammar, meaning of words and comprehension, Mathematics and reading of some basic books on logic. She/he can do some IQ tests as well for practice and speed of response.

Q.22 Which are the best Management Institutions in India?

Ans: The Top management institutions in India are:

1. Indian Institute of Management, Ahmedabad (IIM A): Regarded to be the best of the best business schools in India, IIM Ahmedabad offers four programmes in Management.

PGP — Postgraduate Programme (equivalent to MBA), FPM — Fellowship Programme in Management(equivalent to Ph.D), FDP — Faculty Development Programme for Management teachers and Trainers and MDP — Management Development Programme — a refresher for middle and top level managers.

2. Indian Institute of Management, Calcutta (IIM C): The oldest of the IIMs, IIM Calcutta is amongst the top three B schools in India. The institute offers three full time programs. PGDM — Postgraduate Programme in Management (equivalent to MBA), FPM — Fellowship Programme in Management, PGDCM — Postgraduate Diploma in Computer Aided Management. The institute also offer part time PGDBM — Postgraduate Diploma in Business Management for managers with relevant work experience. In addition, MDP — Management Development Programs are held in regular intervals for middle and top level managers.

3. Indian Institute of Management, Bangalore (IIM B): IIM Bangalore offers two year full time PGP — Postgraduate Programme in Management (equivalent to MBA) and a FPM — Fellowship Programme in Management. Both these programs require the candidate to take CAT. The institute also offers part time non-residential PGSM — Postgraduate Programme in Software Enterprise Management. There is a separate entrance test for this program. This business school is ranked amongst the top three business schools in the country.

4. Indian Institute of Management, Lucknow (IIM L): IIM Lucknow offers a two year full time residential PGP — Postgraduate Programme in Management and a four year FPM program. Both these programs require a candidate to take CAT. The institute also has an interesting student exchange programme where students of this B-School go to premier B-Schools the world over and do part of their education. Students and faculty from these internationally

India.

5. XLRI — Xavier Labour Research Institute, Jamshedpur: Xavier Labour Research Institute, popularly known as XLRI was established in 1949 at Jamshedpur. The institute offers two courses at the post graduation level in management — a postgraduate diploma in Business administration and a postgraduate diploma in Personnel Management and Industrial Relations (PMIR). Online version of the brochure is also available.

6. ISB — Indian School of Business, Hyderabad: Indian School of Business, Hyderabad is emerging as a preferred choice for MBA aspirants who want to pack in the programme into a one year course. As it gradually builds up its permanent faculty base, the ISB has created a unique and sustainable visiting faculty model with some of the world's leading

others. The school offers a one year Postgraduate Programme in Management.

7. FMS — Faculty of Management Studies, University of Delhi: FMS is amongst the top 10 B-Schools in the country and probably one of the two attached to a university amongst the top ten. The full time programme of FMS started in 1967. Generally the demand for students is very high where most of the times students being placed within a day or two.

8. Indian Institute of Management, Indore (IIM I): The Indian Institute of Management, Indore (IIMI) is the latest addition to the IIM community. IIM-I has a two-year postgraduate programme emphasising on Experiential learning, IT orientation, and Social Sensitivity. IIM-I offers the following programs, viz., (a) Postgraduate Programme (PGP), a two year programme (b) Management Development Programme. These are held throughout the year. (c) Faculty Development Programme (FDP) is designed to assist in the development of teachers, researchers, and trainers for management education and (d) Executive Post-Graduate Programme (Exe-PGP) a 18-months programme, designed for working executives.

Its academic programmes encompass a range of long term full time diploma programmes such as Postgraduate Programme in Management, and a number of short duration executive education programmes. The institute also offers an "Interactive Distance Learning Programme."

10. Jamnalal Bajaj Institute of Management Studies, Mumbai (JBIMS): The Jamnalal Bajaj Institute of Management Studies, (JBIMS) was established by the University of Bombay in 1965 in collaboration with the Graduate School of Business, Stanford University with the objective of pioneering and furthering postgraduate management education in India. JBIMS has been ranked in Asia's Top 25 business schools by Asia Inc.

11. S. P. Jain Institute of Management Studies, Mumbai (SPJIMR): The Institute's PGDM programme amongst the best in the country offers the following specialisation in the

Information Management and Manufacturing & Operations Management. Core subjects normally focus on the basic aspects relating to a particular area of specialisation. In addition, each participant can take courses from another specialisation as a 'Minor Specialisation'.

12. Shailesh J. Mehta School of Management, IIT Mumbai (Bombay): The school commenced its operations in 1995 and has been awarding a full time two year masters degree, a doctoral programme in management and Executive Education programs in management. One unique feature of the programme is that apart from the regular courses on Finance, Accounting, Operations and HR, SJM SOM prepares for technology management with core courses like Technology Policy, R&D Management and Managing technology transfer. To secure an admission, you need to take JMET, the Joint Management Entrance Test.

13. Management Development Institute, Gurgaon (MDI): Amongst the top management institutes in India, MDI offers a two year Postgraduate Programme in Management. The curriculum is spread over six terms of about three months each. The core curriculum is spread over

arrangements with Aarus School of Business, Denmark, CBPA, USA; Copenhagen Business School, Denmark; EDHEC, France; ESCP-EAP and Sciences Po, France; Leipzig Graduate School of Management, Germany; McGill University, Canada; Norwegian School of Management, Norway; Queensland University of Technology, Bangkok; Solvay Business School, Belgium; Universita Carlo Cattaneo (LIUC), Itlay and Warsaw School of Economics, Poland.

14. Narsee Monjee Institute of Management Studies, Mumbai (NMIMS): NMIMS offers a two-year full-time programme, spread over six trimesters and leading to the degree in Master of Business Administration. Number of seats: 240. Students are admitted to the programme if they meet the required standards of the two stage selection process — Stage I: A written admission test; Stage II: Candidates who qualify at stage 1 will be required to appear for the second stage of selection process like the Group Discussion and Personal Interview.

15. Xavier Institute of Management, Bhubaneswar (XIM B): XIM Bhuvaneswar offers the following courses: Postgraduate Programme (PGP) in Management, Executive Postgraduate Programme in Management, Postgraduate Programme in Rural Management and Fellow

Institute. The courses impart a generalist perspective, in addition to training the students

production.

16. Symbiosis Institute of Business Management, Pune (SIBM): SIBM, Pune offers a Master's Degree in Business Administration — MBA Dual Specialisation. Specialisations include Marketing, Finance, Human Resource, Manufacturing, and Materials & Logistics Management. A total of 120 students shall be selected for this course.

17. Symbiosis Centre for Management & Human Resources Development, Pune (SCMHRD)

18. Institute of Management & Technology, Ghaziabad (IMT)

19. International Management Institute, Delhi (IMI)

20. Bharathidasan Institute of Management, Trichy (BIM)

21. Mudra Institute of Communications, Ahmedabad (MICA)

22. Indian Institute of Foreign Trade, Delhi (IIFT)

23. T. A. Pai Management Institute, Manipal (TAPMI)

24. Loyola Institute of Business Administration, Chennai (LIBA)

25. Institute of Management Development Research, Pune (IMDR)

17

MASS COMMUNICATION

Q.1   What is Mass Communication?

Ans: Mass communication is the term used to describe the academic study of the various means by which individuals and entities relay information through mass media to large segments of the population at the same time. It is usually understood to relate to newspaper and magazine

advertising. Mass communication research includes media institutions and processes such as diffusion of information, and media effects such as persuasion or manipulation of public opinion. In the United States, for instance, several university departments were remodelled into schools or colleges of mass communication or "journalism and mass communication".

In addition to studying practical skills of journalism, public relations or advertising, they offer programs on "mass communication" or "mass communication research". The latter is often the title given to doctoral studies in such schools, whether the focus of the student's research is journalism practice, history, law or media effects. Departmental structures within such colleges may separate research and instruction in professional or technical aspects of mass communication. With the increased role of the Internet in delivering news and information, mass communication studies and media organisations tend to focus on the convergence of publishing, broadcasting and digital communication. The academic mass communication discipline historically differs from media studies and communication studies programs with roots in departments of theatre,

approaches to communication study. In contrast, many mass communication programs historically lean toward empirical analysis and quantitative research — from statistical content analysis of media messages to survey research, public opinion polling, and experimental research.

Q.2   What are the different fields/areas of Mass Communication?

Ans:

1. **Print Journalism:** In short, journalism is collecting and editing of news for presentation through media. Print journalism has been one of the oldest forms of journalism. Newspapers and magazines, big or small have always been major source of news and information throughout the world and millions of readers go through them daily. Over the years, print journalism has witnessed major transformation; the simple reporting of yesteryears has

factors. The newspapers and magazines today cover a wide range of specialised sections like political events, business news, leisure, cinema, sports, career, health and so many

available courses in that direction.

2. **Electronic Journalism:** Introduction of electronic communication especially through broadcasting has affected the lifestyles and thoughts of masses. Communication mediums like television, radio, audio, video, etc., has made possible news, entertainment, information, education related subjects reach the very far and wide places. It has to an extent sidelined other forms of communication. With the growing network of TV, satellite communication, cable services, radio stations, etc., the future of this industry seems

sound, programme research, script writing, etc.

3. **Films - Producers, Actors, Musicians and Dancers:**
no dearth of available professional career options. Although, it is not all that easy to taste

sanguine and determined, it can be quite rewarding. Films have always earned recognition and fascination of masses. There are so many different groups of people associated with the so-called big screen and one has a variety to choose from the available options from technical professions like directors, producers, soundmen, light-men, cameramen, editors, etc., to artists like actors, dancers, musicians, stuntmen, etc.

in order to hone their skills and make themselves better to compete with the best in the industry.

4. **Advertising:** Advertising is brand building process of a product, idea, thought or a even a service, through effective mediums of communication. From newspapers, magazines, posters, signboards, bills to the commercials on radio, television and even Internet, advertising has come a long way. Business organisations, political organisations, social

Since advertising is a service industry, the reputation of the ad agency depends on the effective work being done and campaign released from time to time. This makes the job even more challenging. With the advent of the multinational companies, more and more Indian agencies are tying up with the foreign agencies to pitch for international clients which is clearly indicative of high growth in coming years in this industry.

5. **Public Relations:** Once, the simple operation of publicity, today has emerged as an important management function. Public Relations, as the name suggests, is used to generate and portray, positive image of an organisation by various means. Business houses, schools, universities, hospitals, government institutions, etc., engage public relations personnel and agencies to cast and present their image, objectives and policies in the best possible light. For somebody to become a successful public relation consultant, it is imperative to have a liking to meet people along with excellent communication skills, ability to interact with, convince people, and build a rapport is important. The other traits should be, quick decision making abilities and good organisational skills.

Q.3   Is Mass Communication the right career for me?

Ans: Answering this question requires a critical self-evaluation. You need to have creativity — a way with words and excellent communication skills as you will be required to explain and inform, about the most complex of issues, in the simplest of terms — to a large number of people.

and quite some time, to make it to the top.

Positives/Negatives: Like any career option, mass communication too has positive features as

of personal time for the sake of staying on front or top, particularly in news industry. A journalist may have to work day in and day out to get breaking news. Similarly, media professionals who are

personal life. However, in a nutshell, mass communication as a career provides job satisfaction, name and fame and a challenge to live with.

Q.4   What would it cost me?

Ans: Courses in mass communication are expensive as tuition fees and charges and expenses

undergraduate courses charge anywhere from Rs 60,000 to Rs 2, 00,000 per year. It means you will have to pay nearly three lakhs for a course of three years duration. Similarly, a PG diploma course from Indian Institute of Mass Communication (IIMC) can cost in the range of Rs 40,000 to Rs 1,00,000 for one year. PG course in Mass Communication from MCRC at Jamia Millia Islamia can cost around one lakh for two years.

Funding/Scholarship: IIMC offers scholarship for candidates in each branch, i.e. print media

Several other memorial scholarships at the institute are based on merit. Other mass communication institutes too provide merit based free-ships and scholarships. Education loans are available from nationalised banks such as Allahabad Bank and Punjab National Bank wherein a student can seek a loan up to Rs 7.5 lakhs at low interest rates.

Q.5   What are the Job Prospects?

Ans:

nutshell, Mass Communication widens up the horizon of career options for a person. Depending upon personal interest and inclination a mass communication professional can choose a job. Attractive and high paying jobs as journalist, actor, director, editor, screenwriter, RJ, producer, VJ are available to the talented and trained individuals.

Pay Packet: Whereas candidates passing out from IIMC, MCRC Jamia, Symbiosis College and many other institutes receive attractive placement after their courses and handsome salaries, students from not-so-well-known institutes have to work hard to get placed. Starting salary for a mass communication professional could be between Rs 12,000 and 25,000. After 5 Years of work experience a professional can expect higher salary in the range of Rs 50,000 to Rs 1,00,000 per month.

Demand and Supply: Demand and supply plays a crucial role in careers of mass communication

graduates of these turbulent times found it extremely hard to get placed. On the contrary, there is a dearth of trained professionals in mass media, new entertainment and news channels and with new launches in the pipeline the demand will only shoot up. Opening up of media sector for

Market Watch: Career opportunities in mass communication are expected to increase as

and entertainment job opportunities are aplenty for trained professionals in various roles

production houses or can make documentaries on their own.

International Focus: News Corporation of Rupert Murdoch, Disney Entertainment, Warner Brothers, CNBC, Guardian Group, BBC, ABC and many others are included among the large media groups which offer attractive jobs in mass communication at different levels and positions. In fact jobs in these organisations are attractive in terms of compensation and offer challenging job

excellent command over English language.

Q.6 I want to Know in detail about Indian Institute of Mass Communication (IIMC)?

Ans: The Indian Institute of Mass Communication (IIMC) made a humble beginning on August 17, 1965, as a department of the Ministry of Information and Broadcasting, Government of India, with a small staff, including two consultants from UNESCO. Later, it was registered as an autonomous organisation under the Societies Registration Act (1860) on January 22, 1966. Over the decades, the Indian Institute of Mass Communication has created a niche for itself in

"Centre of Excellence". It is playing a pivotal role by organising suitable training courses to meet the demand for trained and skilled manpower in today's dynamic media scenario. It provides knowledge and skills to communicators in a variety of disciplines including print journalism, radio and television journalism, photo journalism, development communication, communication research, advertising and public relations.

The Institute has, to its credit, highly acclaimed and experienced faculty members drawn from various streams of media. Visiting faculty, including media stalwarts and industry leaders, too contribute to enrich the quality of the courses offered to the students. Many of the Institute's alumni have risen to high positions in the country's top media houses.

The principal objectives of the Institute, as set out in its Memorandum of Association, are:

> to organise training and research in the use and development of media of mass communication, with special reference to the requirements of socio-economic growth in the country.

> to provide training to the information and publicity personnel of Central and State Governments; to make available facilities for training and research to meet the information and publicity needs of the public and private sector industries.

> to arrange lectures, seminars and symposia on problems connected with mass communication, information and publicity in collaboration with universities, educational and research institutions as well as trade and industry.

to organise refresher courses, summer schools and the like and to invite mass communication experts and research scholars from within the country and abroad for delivering lectures and/or developing research.

In the spirit of these objectives, the Institute conducts training and teaching programmes, develops a framework of research and contributes to the creation of an information infrastructure suitable not only for India but for all developing countries. It provides its expertise and consultancy services to other institutions in the country and collaborates with those abroad.

While the IIMC Regional Centre at Dhenkanal in Orissa has been operating successfully since 1993, two new regional centres opened this year at Amravati in Vidharbha region of Maharashtra and in Mlzoram's capital Aizawl. Two more new regional centres are on the anvil.

Selection of students for both New Delhi and the other campuses is done through a common entrance examination. Students are assigned to the respective campuses based on merit cum choice criteria.

Post-graduate Diploma Course:

General Information

      Journalism (English), New Delhi and Dhenkanal (Orissa)
      Journalism (Hindi), New Delhi
      Advertising and Public Relations, New Delhi
      Radio and Television Journalism, New Delhi
      Journalism (Oriya), Dhenkanal (Orissa)

Eligibility

Nationality: Only Indian nationals are eligible. In addition a limited number of seats are available for NRI sponsored.

Essential: Bachelor's degree in any discipline. Those who have appeared/are appearing for the degree examination are also eligible to apply. If selected, their admission will be subject to their

year applied for, failing which the provisional admission will stand cancelled.

Desirable: 1. Post-Graduate degree in any discipline 2. Media-related work experience

Selection of Candidates: All eligible candidates will be called at their own expense for an

Mumbai/Bangalore/Guwahati. The Institute reserves the right to call any candidates for entrance examination at any centre for administrative reasons. All the candidates who appear in the written examination will be ranked on the basis of the marks obtained by them. A shortlist will be prepared for each of the courses. The shortlisted candidates will be called for Group Discussion/

candidates to be admitted to the courses will be prepared on the basis of the combined marks obtained by the candidates in the written examination and in the GD/Interview. The weightage for written examination and GD/ Interview will be 85:15.

Q.7 What are the various courses available to take a career in Mass Communication?

Ans: You can study B.A.(Journalism); B.A.(Mass Communication); M.A.(Journalism); M.A. (Mass Communication); Postgraduate Diploma (Journalism/Mass Communication), etc., to take up a

The Bachelor of Journalism (B.J.) degree is a professional degree awarded at some universities to students who have studied journalism in a three or four year undergraduate program. In the United States, some schools that do not award the B.J. degree instead confer a Bachelor of Arts, Journalism (B.A.J.), or Bachelor of Science, Journalism (BSJ) that is often part of or in conjunction with a course of study in mass communication. In India, Bachelor of Journalism is of 3 years. Journalism Courses in India are known by various names like B.J. (Bachelor of Journalism), B.C.J. (Bachelor of Communication and Journalism), B.M.M. (Bachelor of Mass Media), B.J.M.C. (Bachelor of Journalism and Mass Communication), B.A.J.M.C (Bachelor of Arts in Journalism and Mass Communication), B.A.- Mass Communication (Bachelor of Arts in Mass Communication). Though the nomenclature differs but these all courses are one and the same with minor changes in content

List of colleges offering B.A Journalism courses

College Name	University	State
Aditi Mahavidyalaya	University of Delhi	Delhi
Administrative Management College	Bangalore University	
Alva's College	Mangalore University	
Apar India Institute of Management and Technology	Sikkim Manipal University of Health Medical & Technological Sciences	Delhi
Bhartiya Jain Sanghatana College	University of Pune	Maharashtra
Bhim Rao Ambedkar College	University of Delhi	Delhi
Chotanagpur Institute of Information Technology & Management,Dhanabad	Makhanlal Chaturvedi Rashtriya Patrakarita Vishwavidyalaya	Jharkhand
CSI Bishop Appasamy College of Arts & Science	Bharathiar University	Tamil Nadu
Delhi College of Arts & Commerce	University of Delhi	Delhi
Delhi Institute of Pharmaceutical	University of Delhi	Delhi
Global Business School	Deemed University/Autonomous colleges	Uttar Pradesh
	Berhampur University	Orissa
	University of Delhi	Delhi
	Guru Nanak Dev University	Punjab
	Guru Gobind Singh Indraprastha University	Delhi
Lady Shri Ram College (LSR College)	University of Delhi	Delhi

18

MEDICINE & HEALTH CARE

Q.1   What are the different Indian Systems of Medicine and what are Educational and Career Opportunities in Indian Systems of Medicine?

Ans: For centuries man has evolved several ways of coping with illness and different societies have looked for different substances and methods that would ease pain and elevate spirits. All

time. With the introduction of the Western systems of medicine, well-known as the "allopathic system" and considered "modern", this ancient system came to be known as the "traditional" or "indigenous" system.

total of all knowledge and practices, whether explicable or not, used in diagnosis; prevention and elimination of physical, mental or social imbalance and relying exclusively on practical experience or observation handed down from generation to generation, verbally or in writing" (American Journal of Pharmacy 1976, 148, 46-52).

With the Western system of medicine, now perceived as the "mainstream system", taking deep roots all over the world, the term alternative medicine was coined to label the diverse assortment

because these therapies could never entirely replace the "mainstream system", and therefore, recommend the term "complementary medicine".

Promotion of Education and Research: Be that as it may, India has a rich heritage of medicine and therapies. The term Indian Systems of Medicine covers both the systems which originated in India as well as outside but got adopted in India in course of time. These systems are Ayurveda, Siddha, Unani, Homoeopathy, Yoga, and Naturopathy. They have become a part of the culture and traditions of India. The National Health Policy (1983) envisaged the necessity for the Indian

Government of India created a new Department of Indian Systems of Medicine and Homoeopathy in the Ministry of Health and Welfare to promote these systems.

The Department has set up four Research Councils, viz., (1) The Central Council for Research in Ayurveda and Siddha, with nearly 90 research centres spread across the country, (2) The Central

Council for Research in Unani Medicine, (3) The Central Council for Research in Homoeopathy, and (4) The Central Council for Research in Yoga and Naturopathy to promote research in the concerned systems of medicine. Seven National Institutions have also been set up to offer

Institute of Ayurveda) (Jaipur), (2) National Institute of Postgraduate Teaching and Research in Ayurveda (Jamnagar), (3) Rashtriya Ayurveda Vidyapeeth, (National Academy of Ayurveda) (New Delhi), (4) National Institution of Unani Medicine (Bangalore), (5) National Institute of Homoeopathy (Calcutta), (6) National Institute of Naturopathy (Pune), and (7) Morarji Desai National Institute of Yoga (New Delhi).

A National Institute of Siddha is also likely to be set up in Chennai. As part of continuing medical education, the government has introduced a scheme to upgrade the knowledge of teachers, researchers, practitioners in Indian Systems of Medicine and Homoeopathy. In order to formulate standards for drugs, Pharmacopoeia Committees for each of these systems were also set up. They are supported by the Pharmacopoeia Laboratory for Indian Medicine, and Homoeopathy Pharmacopoeia Laboratory both located in Ghaziabad.

There are 13 government assisted pharmacies and over 5,000 licensed pharmacists. The total annual turnover of the Ayurvedic drug manufacturing industry is estimated to be around Rs.1,000 crore. Two statutory Councils, viz., the Central Council of Indian Medicine, and the Central Council of Homoeopathy were also established for laying down and maintaining uniform standards

Medicine and Homoeopathy, respectively. The Central Council of Indian Medicine, through a public notice has warned that the courses in electropathy, electro homoeopathy, biochemical, alternative medicine, etc., offered by several institutions and so-called universities are not recognised by it.

Institute of Electropathy (9 New Mahavir Marg, Dew Delhi-110010), (2) Health and Medicine (80 Chowringhee Road, Calcutta-700020), and (3) Medical College of Alternative Medicines (3 Canal Street, Calcutta-700014). The Medical Council of India has also warned that the awards of these

Educational Opportunities: Education in the Indian Systems of Medicine and Homoeopathy is

recognition of the Central Council of Indian Medicine, and the Central Council of Homoeopathy.

Ayurveda:
degree levels leading to Bachelor of Ayurvedic Medicine and Surgery (BAMS), MD (Ayurveda) and

to 48 universities which include one exclusive Ayurved university, viz., the Gujarat Ayurved University (Jamnagar). Many colleges have been established by the State governments. The

capacity is 6,117. Postgraduate courses are of Ayurveda hospitals in the country is 2,203 (with 31,042 beds). Besides, there are 14,048 dispensaries. The number of practitioners is of the order of 3,52,328.

one year of compulsory internship. The entry requirement is a pass in 10+2 class examination with science subjects. In most of the States, the admission is made on the basis of a common entrance test conducted along with the medicine and dentistry courses. The postgraduate course is of three year duration. In Calcutta University, the course of two year duration is also open to MBBS degree holders. A total number of 33 universities have introduced MD study, one of the specialised areas.

Specialised Institutions in Ayurveda: Follwing is a brief account of the educational programmes of the three National Institutes established by the Ministry of Health and Family Welfare. The National Institute of Postgraduate Teaching and Research in Ayurveda located within Gujarat Ayurved University, set up by the Department of Indian System of Medicine and Homoeopathy, imparts education leading to MD (Ay) in 13 specialities of Ayurveda. It has seven teaching departments and six laboratories. The Institute also conducts Ph.D programmes. Gujarat Ayurved University,

and the Institute of Plant Sciences in the area of Pharmaceutical science: (1) Master of Pharmacy (Ayurveda) of two-year duration open to B.Phram degree holders, (2) Bachelor of Pharmacy (Ayurveda) of four-year duration open to candidates who have passed the 10+2 examination with science subjects; (3) Diploma in Pharmacy (Ayurveda) of two-year duration open to candidates who have passed the 10+2 examination, (4) One year PG Diploma in Medicinal Plants, and (5) M.Sc in Medicinal plants are open to graduates in Botany, Pharmacy, Agriculture or Ayurveda.

Rashtriya Ayurved Sansthan (National Institute of Ayurveda) in Jaipur, established in 1976 by the Ministry of Health and Family Welfare, besides BAMS (Ayurvedacharya) course also offers MD

University and provides guidance to Ph.D (Ayurveda) to candidates registered with the University.

The Rashtriya Ayurveda Vidyapeeth (Dhanwantri Bhavan, Road No.66, Punjabi Bagh, New Delhi), an Autonomous institution was established in 1988 with the objective of promoting the knowledge of Ayurveda through acharya-guru-shishya-parampara, and chikitsak-guru-shishya-parampara systems. It has two training programmes, viz., (a) two-year programme leading to the Degree of Membership of Rashtriya Ayruveda Vidyapeeth (MRAV), and (b) one-year training programme

teaching experience. There is a scheme of payment of honorarium to *Gurus* and stipend (Rs.3,500 p/m). to *Shishyas*
Ayurveda degree and having experience in clinical practice.

Three other specialised institutions offering postgraduate programmes are: (1) Institute of Indian Medicine (Pune-411029) — Ph.D (Ay); (2) Institute of Postgraduate Education and Research in Ayurveda (Calcutta-700009) — MD (Ay); and (3) University of Madras — Two-year diploma courses including one on ophthalmology.

Siddha: There are only three Siddha medical colleges in the country, all located in Tamil Nadu, number of seats is 155. The eligibility requirement is a pass in 10+2 examination with Physics, Chemistry and Biological Sciences.

The candidates should have studied in Tamil medium or have passed Tamil as a subject in Class 10. The admission is based on the performance in a combined entrance test conducted by the Directorate of Indian Medicine and Homoeopathy of the Government of Tamil Nadu for admission

at Chennai and Thirunelveli have MD Course in Siddha of three-year duration. Students from neighbouring countries (Sri Lanka, Malaysia, Singapore, etc.,) are also admitted to the course. There are 22 hospitals, all in Tamil Nadu, with 1,636 beds. Siddha medicine is practiced by 12,528 registered practitioners.

Unani:

of compulsory internship. The entry requirement is a pass in 10+2 examination. Those who have

Urdu is desirable. Pune University admits students who have passed the Class 10 examination, and for them the duration is 71/2 years.

Courses offered by the Aligarh Muslim University and Jamia Hamdard (New Delhi), a deemed university, have high reputation. Only three universities, viz., Aligarh Muslim University (Ajmal

(Government Nizamia Tibbi College, Hyderabad-500002) offer MD in Unani Medicine of three-year duration. The Pre-Tibb course is available in Aligarh Muslim University and Jamia Hamdard (New Delhi). The entry requirement is a pass in Fazil (Deoband), Alim (Arabic or Aimyat Nadwa) or Farighul Tehsil from a Dare-e-Nizami Madrasah. There are 183 Unani Hospitals with 3,551 beds. The number of registered practitioners is 41,630.

Homoeopathy:

course leading to Bachelor of Homoeopathic Medicine and Surgery (BHMS) is available in 118

in 10+2 examination in science (including biological science). Like any other course in medicine,

concentration of Homoeopathy colleges (37) is in Maharashtra with 1,937 seats.

National Institute of Homoeopathy (Calcutta-700091) was established by the Government of India as a model institute to provide a high standard of teaching, training and research in all aspects

18 are reserved for candidates from States and Union Territories where no homoeopathic college exists, and two for foreign nationals.

introduced postgraduate course in Homoeopathy — MD (Homy) of three year duration. The eligibility requirement for MD (Homy) is BHMS degree. Six other universities (Calicut University, Maharashtra University of Health Sciences, Mumbai University, NTR University of Health Sciences, Rajiv Gandhi University of Health Sciences and Utkal University) offer MD (Homy) of three year duration. The subjects of study include Materia Medica, Organon of Medicine, Case Taking and Repertorisation, Homoeopathic Philosophy.

Yoga and Naturopathy: Imparting formal university education in Yoga and Naturopathy is a

and Yogic Sciences, Mysore-570073); (2) Tamil Nadu Dr. MGR Medical University (at Tamil Nadu College of Naturopathy and Yoga Research, Salem-636006, and JSS College of Naturopathy and Yoga Research, Ooty-643001); (3) NTR University of Health Sciences at Gandhi Nature Cure

is Bachelor of Naturopathy and Yogic Science (BNYS).

The entry requirement is a pass in 10+2 with biology as one of the combinations. Master's degree programmes are available in three universities, viz., (1) Manipal Academy of Higher Education-M.Sc (Yoga); (2) Mangalore University-M.Sc (Yogic Science) open to graduates in all disciplines; (3)

Sc (Science of Living, Preksha Meditation and Yoga Therapy) open to B.Sc degree holders. More

courses in the subject.

Promotion of Yoga and Naturopathy: The Government of India has set up Morarji Desai National Institute of Yoga (New Delhi) as an autonomous body to propagate Yogic science and also promote facilities for training, teaching and research in the subject. It has a hospital for providing treatment. In 1998, it introduced a diploma programme of one year duration. The Government has also established National Institute of Naturopathy in Pune which, apart from providing treatment, undertakes promotional activities for popularising Naturopathy by holding camps and seminars. The Central Council for Research in Yoga and Naturopathy provides grant-

one-year diploma courses in Yoga and Naturopathy. The Central Council also provides funds to medical and yogic institutions, such as, Defence Institute of Physiology and Allied Science (Delhi), National Institute of Mental Health and Neuro Sciences (Bangalore), Banaras Hindu University, All India Institute of Medical Sciences (New Delhi), to conduct clinical research in physiological and therapeutic aspects of yoga and naturopathy.

Career Opportunities: The Indian systems of Medicine and Homoeopathy are still perceived by many as rural-centric and poor men's panacea for all diseases. The main reason is that compared to the Western system of medicine, the health infrastructure and services of the traditional systems are poorly supported. Only about 4 percent of the national health budget was allocated to the traditional sector. While State government budgets range from less than 1 percent (in

Though the allopathy system continues to dominate the national health care scene, there is

traditional systems. Many newspapers and newsmagazines carry articles on Indian Systems of Medicine and Homoeopathy. Several TV channels also air programmes on it. All these are creating or complementary system of health care. It is only recently that the Government of India has started paying more attention to this sector with the creation of a separate Department in the Ministry of Health and Family Welfare.

While Unani and Siddha systems are more or less restricted to certain regions, the other three, viz., Ayurveda, Homoeopathy and Yoga and Naturopathy are practiced all over the country.

Commission on Health in India's Report (Voluntary Health Association of India, 1997): "Not only

surprising that Ayurvedic practice has been gaining popularity and leading Ayurvedic physicians are setting up clinics or small hospitals and earning as well as, or even more than, their allopathic

and Naturopathy are also fast gaining popularity particularly among those who are victims of stress and strain of the present day hectic life style. The bane of the traditional system is the presence of a large number of quacks who dupe the unsuspecting patients. This has been eroding

of better educational facilities, the things have started changing for the better. Apart from jobs in government and private sectors, the Indian systems provide opportunities for a reasonably good career as private practitioners.

Q.2   What is Allopathy?

Ans: Allopathy is "a system of medical practice making use of all measures proved of value (emphasis added) in treatment of disease." In the present day context, allopathy is the most widely used and accepted system of medicine throughout the world.

The term "allopathy" was invented by German physician Samuel Hahnemann (1755-1843). He conjoined allos "opposite" and pathos "suffering" as a referent to harsh medical practices of his era which included bleeding, purging, vomiting and the administration of highly toxic drugs. These practices were based on the ancient Greek humoural theory which attributed disease to an imbalance of four humours (i.e. blood, phlegm, and black and yellow bile) and four bodily

water). Physicians following the Hippocratic tradition attempted to balance the humours by treating symptoms with "opposites." For instance, fever (hot) was believed due to excess blood

the patient. Hahnemann sought to replace allopathy with his "law of similia" that treated "like

many modern therapies can be construed to conform to an allopathic rationale (eg, using a laxative to relieve constipation), standard medicine has never paid allegiance to an allopathic principle. The label "allopath" was considered highly derisive by regular medicine.

Q.3   What is Homeopathy?

Ans: Homeopathy (Home' - ee - AH' - puh - thee) is a system of healthcare developed and introduced by the German physician Samuel Hahnemann in the late 1700's. At its heart is the phenomenon of cure by similars, where a substance that could produce disease in a healthy person (when given in excess) is used to invite a healing response in someone presenting with a similar disease. Homeopathy takes its name from this phenomenon of cure by similars; from the

This use of cure by similars actually predates homeopathy by several centuries. Hippocrates records

of Delphi, from Indian medical texts as much as 4,000 years old, and from ancient Chinese medical texts. Celsus, a physician of the Greek classical period, and Theophrastus, a Swiss physician of the 16th century, received renown for their effectiveness as physicians relying on this approach.

Hahnemann was trained as a conventional physician, at the University in Leipzig, Germany. Discouraged by the medicine of his day, and distraught at the near demise of his daughter under the care of a conventional physician, Hahnemann left the practice of medicine to write and translate books. In entertaining the question of what a viable system of medicine would involve, he came back to the historical references to cure by similars in the Hippocratic writings. From his own experiments with Chinchona bark (from a Peruvian tree, the source of Quinine), he convinced himself that Chinchona's effectiveness in treating some cases of malaria resulted from its ability to create a similar disease to which the body could respond, with a resulting healing response to both the medicine-induced condition and the malaria.

Hahnemann went on to apply this principal of cure by similars to other conditions, using many other remedies, and came to observe it as a universal law of cure; he coined the expression "Similia Similibus Curentur" ("Let likes cure likes") as the cornerstone of his homeopathic philosophy.

A second cornerstone of homeopathy is the minimum dose. The incredibly tiny doses we use in treatment came about through careful systematic experimentation by early homeopaths. While larger doses could often elicit the healing responses desired, this would often be accompanied by undesirable side effects of the medications. Reducing the dose served to minimise or eliminate these undesirable side effects. Much to the surprise of Hahnemann and his colleagues, these smaller doses also often worked much more effectively in bringing about a healing response. Although the "logic" of using such tiny doses may defy us, we observe it to work in practice, and continue to rely on these minimum doses today.

The third cornerstone of homeopathy is the use of a single remedy at any one time. In inviting a healing response, it can be confusing to the body, with unpredictable results, to invite several responses simultaneously. Although some practitioners have deviated on this point and use combinations of remedies, Hahnemann abandoned this approach after experimenting with it himself.

Homeopathy learns about the properties of remedies through provings. In a proving, a number of healthy people are given excessive doses of a particular remedy, and the symptoms they develop are carefully recorded. These patterns of symptoms have been systematically recorded in books we refer to as materia medica. This remedy could then be used to treat a person presenting with an illness which had a similar pattern of symptoms.

The prescription of a particular remedy will be based upon the totality of symptoms of the individual. In taking a case, the characteristics and behaviour of each symptom of the patient entional medicine, which might consider some symptoms of the individual to be unrelated to the "condition" to be treated, homeopathy views disease as a disharmony of the whole person, and considers the state of the

Homeopathy was a popular system of medical care in the United States during the 19th century. Sociopolitical factors led to its decline in the U.S. in the early 1900's, but it has remained a prominent form of medical care in England, Germany, France, India, and parts of South America.

Advantages: If used properly, Homeopathy is completely safe, free from side effects and is non-toxic and non-addictive. It can be used safely with conventional treatments and you do not need to stop medication before beginning Homeopathic treatment. Homeopathy is safe and effective for all ages, including tiny babies to the elderly.

Q.4   What is Ayurveda?

Ans: Ayurveda is a wholistic system of medicine from India that uses a constitutional model. Its aim is to provide guidance regarding food and lifestyle so that healthy people can stay healthy and folks with health challenges can improve their health.

There are several aspects to Ayurveda that are quite unique:

Its recommendations will often be different for each person regarding which foods and which lifestyle they should follow in order to be completely healthy. This is due to its use of a constitutional model.

Everything in Ayurveda is validated by observation, inquiry, direct examination and knowledge derived from the ancient texts.

forces are called the Tridoshas.

Because Ayurveda sees a strong connection between the mind and the body, a huge amount of information is available regarding this relationship.

Origin: Ayurveda is an intricate system of healing that originated in India thousands of years ago.

In the Rig Veda, over 60 preparatison were mentioned that could be used to assist an individual in overcoming various ailments. The Rig Veda was written over 6,000 years ago, but really Ayurveda has been around even longer than that. What we see is that Ayurveda is more than just a medical system. It is a Science of Life. We are all part and parcel of nature. Just as the animals and plants live in harmony with nature and utilize the Laws of Nature to create health and balance within their beings, we, too, adhere to these very same principles. Therefore, it is fair to say that Ayurveda is a system that helps maintain health in a person by using the inherent principles of nature to bring the individual back into equilibrium with their true self. In essence Ayurveda has been in existence since the beginning of time because we have always been governed by nature's laws.

Meaning: Ayurveda is made up of two Sanskrit words: *Ayu* which means life and *Veda* which means the knowledge of. To know about life is Ayurveda. However, to fully comprehend the vast scope of

is consisted of four essential parts — the combination of mind, body, senses and the soul.

Mind, Body, and Senses: We tend to identify most with our physical bodies; yet, in actuality, there is more to us then what meets the eye. We can see that underlying our physical structure is the mind, which not only controls our thought processes but helps assist us in carrying out day-to-day activities such as respiration, circulation, digestion and elimination. The mind and the body work in conjunction with one another to regulate our physiology for the mind to act appropriately to assist the physical body, we must use our senses as information gatherers. We can think of the mind as a computer and the senses as the data which gets entered into the computer. Smell and taste are two important senses that aid in the digestive process. When the mind registers that a particular food is entering the gastrointestinal tract, it directs the body to act accordingly by releasing various digestive enzymes. However, if we overindulge

the mind to perceive the sweet taste is impaired; and thereby the body becomes challenged in its ability to process sweet foods. Maintaining the clarity of our senses is an essential part in allowing the mind and body to integrate their functions and help in keeping us healthy and happy individuals.

Soul: Ayurveda also sees that before we exist in physical form with the help of the mind and senses that we exist in a more subtle form known as the soul. The ancient seers of India believed that we were composed of a certain energetic essence that precluded the inhabitance of our physical entity. In fact, they hypothesised that we may indeed occupy many physical bodies throughout the course of time but that our underlying self or soul remains unchanged. What we see to help illustrate this concept is what transpires at the time of death. When the individual nears the time to leave the physical body, many of his/her desires will cease to be

particular activity that used to be a great source of satisfaction for that person drops by the wayside. In fact, many individuals have been documented to experience the sensation of being "out of their bodies".

These are just a few examples of how we are made up of these four components that we call life.

Principles: Now that we have a better understanding of what comprises life, let's look at some of the principles of Ayurveda and how they might affect us.

elements are seen to have an ability to combine to create various physiological functions. Ether and air combine to form what is known in Ayurveda as the *Vata dosha*. Vata governs the principle of movement and therefore can be seen as the force which directs nerve impulses, circulation, respiration, and elimination. Fire and water are the elements that combine to form the *Pitta dosha*. The Pitta dosha is the process of transformation or metabolism. The transformation of foods into nutrients that our bodies can assimilate is an example of a pitta function. Pitta is also responsible for metabolism in the organ and tissue systems as well as cellular metabolism. Finally, it is predominantly the water and earth elements which combine to form the *Kapha dosha* the *Kapha dosha*

Vata, *Pitta* and *Kapha*. These ratios of the *doshas* vary in each individual; and because of this, Ayurveda sees each person as a special mixture that accounts for our diversity.

Ayurveda gives us a model to look at each individual as a unique makeup of the three *doshas*

When any of the *doshas*

dosha that has become excessive. We may also suggest certain herbal supplements to hasten the healing process. If toxins in the body are abundant, then a cleansing process known as *Pancha Karma* is recommended to eliminate these unwanted toxins.

Q.5 What is Siddha System of Medicine?

Ans: The Siddha System of medicine is the oldest in the world. There are two ancient system

India. The word Siddha comes from the word Siddhi which means an object to attain perfection or heavenly bliss. Siddha generally refers to Athma Siddha that is the 8th supernatural power. Those who attained or achieved the above said powers are known as Siddhars. There were 18 important siddhars in olden days and they developed this system of medicine. Hence, it is called Siddha Medicine.

Basic Principles: Siddha science considers nature and man as essentially one. Nature is man and man is nature. Man is said to be the microcosm and Universe is the macrocosm because

elements of the various principles which constitute the minerals, vegetables and the animal kingdom. According to Siddha medical science, the Universe originally consisted of atoms which

in the world.

A close relationship is found to exist between the external world and the internal system of man. Siddhars (practitioners of Siddha) maintain that the structure of the human body is a miniature world in itself. Man consumes water and food, breathes the air and thus maintains the heat in

element that gives motion, vigour and vitality to the body. It also helps digestion, circulation and simulation besides respiration and the nervous system. Above all, ether is the characteristic of man's mental and spiritual faculties.

Siddha system of medicine is based on Saiva Siddhantha. Siddha is a Tamil word that is derived from its root 'chit' which means perfection in life or "heavenly bliss".

The fundamental subjects of Siddha methodology are

1. Vadham (Alchemy)
2. Aithiyam (Medicine)
3. Yogam (Yoga)
4. Gnanam Or Thathuvam (Philosophy)

Siddhars, spiritual scientists of Tamil Nadu explored and explained the reality of Nature and its

concept of spiritualism for self improvement and the practices propounded by them came to be known as the "SIDDHA SYSTEM".

Q.6   What is Unani Medicine?

Ans: The Unani system of medicine owes, as its name suggests, its orgin to Greece. It was the Greek philosopher-physician Hippocrates (460-377 BC) who freed Medicine from the realm of superstition and magic, and gave it the status of Science. The theoretical framework of Unani Medicine is based on the teachings of Hippocrates; after a number of other Greek scholars enriched the system considerably. Of them Galen (131-210 AD) stands out as the one who stablised its foundation, on which Arab physicians like Rhazes (850-925 AD) and Avicenna

was best in the contemporary system of traditional medicine in Egypt, Syria, Iraq, Persia,

native medical systems in vogue at the time in various parts of Central Asia. That is why this system is known, in different parts of the world, with different names, such as, Greeco-Arab Medicine, Ionian Medicine, Arab Medicine, Islamic Medicine, Traditional Medicine, Oriental Medicine, etc.

the soil. When Mongols ravaged Persian and Central Asian cities like Shiraz, Tabrez and Geelan,

Tughalaqs and the Mughal Emperors provided state patronage to the scholars and even enrolled some of them as state employees and court physicians. During 13th and 17th century Unani Medicine has its hey-day in India. Among those who made valuable contributions to this system

The scholars and physicians of Unani Medicine who settled in India were not content with the known drugs but they subjected Indian drugs to clinical trials and as a result of their experimentation added numerous native drugs to their own system, thus further enriching its masses and soon spread all over the country and continued to hold an unchallenged sway for a long period even after the downfall of Mughal Empire.

During the British rule, Unani Medicine suffered a setback and its development was hampered due to withdrawal of governmental patronage. But since the system enjoyed faith among

in Delhi, the Azizi family in Lucknow and the Nizam of Hyderabad that the Unani Medicine survived in the British period. An outstanding physician and scholar of Unani Medicine, Hakim

Dawakhana and the Ayurvedic and Unani Tibbia College in Delhi are the two living examples of his immense contribution to the multipronged development of the two Indian system of medicine, Unani Medicine and Ayurveda.

Q.7 How do I know if a career in medicine might be for me?

Ans: First ask yourself what kind of future appeals to you. Do you want challenges, opportunities, or a chance to make a difference? Many bright and motivated college students describe a "dream career" with the following characteristics:

Opportunity to serve: Allows you to help people

Action: Doesn't tie you to a desk all the time

Respect: You are an important part of your community

Security: Allows you a good living with a secure future

Excitement: Changes daily, so it's hardly ever boring

Mobility: You're in demand wherever you choose to live

Flexibility: Gives you lots of career options from the same education base. Few occupations meet all of these standards. None meets them better than a career in medicine

Q.8 How can I know that I am the right kind of person for a medical career?

Ans: Ask yourself some questions:

Do I care deeply about other people, their problems, and their pain?

Do I enjoy helping people with my skills and knowledge?

Do I enjoy learning, gaining new understanding? Do I often dig deeper into a subject than my teacher requires? Do I understand the value of learning beyond just making good grades?

Am I interested in how the human body functions? Am I intrigued by the ways medicine can be used to improve life?

If you answered "Yes" to most of these questions, chances are you have the right kind of personality for a medical career.

Q.9 How do I select the right school for Higher Secondary education (10+2) to enter Medical education?

Ans: Here are some questions to ask while you consider a college or university. Your career

bookstores.

Does the school have a good faculty and a reputation for high academic standards? Is it accredited?

Does it have strong science faculty with good laboratory facilities?

Does it offer all of the required courses I need for acceptance to medical school?

health professions?

Does it have a good track record for having its students accepted to medical school?

Does it offer extracurricular activities that appeal to me? Are there programs to do volunteer work at local hospitals or clinics?

Are there programs where I can demonstrate leadership and compassion?

Does it "feel right" for me? Am I comfortable with its size, location, social life, and general atmosphere?

Q.10 What subjects I should study at Higher Secondary (10+2) to study Medicine and become a Doctor?

Ans: You should study Physics, Chemistry and Biology in 10+2 to study Medicine and become a doctor. Whether you want to study MBBS (Allopathy) or BHMS (Homeopathy) or BUMS (Unani) or BAMS (Ayurvedic) you must study Physics, Chemistry and Biology at 10+2.

Q.11 What is medical school/college really like? I hear it's long and tough. How long? How tough?

Ans: One of the important truths is "things that come easily usually aren't worth much." Medical school/college is challenging. If you want to take responsibility for people's health and well-being, you've got to be serious about learning. Once you've been accepted, the medical school faculty and staff will do everything they can to help you succeed. In fact, more than 97 percent of entering medical students obtain their M.D. degrees.

The curriculum at many medical schools/colleges has changed in recent years. However, here's a

physiology, microbiology, pathology, and pharmacology — as well as behaviourial sciences. You'll also begin learning the fundamental techniques of taking a medical history and examining patients.

Next, you'll go into the hospital and various clinics to observe and work with experienced doctors and begin to learn how to take care of patients. At this time you'll begin to explore the wide variety of career paths within medicine, such as family practice, internal medicine, surgery, psychiatry, obstetrics and gynecology, and pediatrics.

while taking elective courses.

After medical school/college you will spend three to seven years in a residency, where you will gain further experience and training in the specialty you have chosen. You already may have an idea of which specialties interest you; however, it is good to keep an open mind until your third year of medical school.

you study the sciences basic to medicine: anatomy, biochemistry, physiology, microbiology, pathology, and pharmacology, as well as behavioural sciences; introductory patient interviewing and examination techniques; and an introduction to health care. In the third year, you gain

family medicine, pediatrics, obstetrics and gynecology, surgery, and psychiatry. The fourth year is a mix of required and elective courses where you gain additional experience caring for patients. Each medical school differs in how it organizes its educational program.

Medical school/college is tough. A lot will be demanded of you both in the volume of information you will be expected to master and the rate at which you will be expected to learn. You will need good study habits and time management skills as well as a strong academic background. You also will need to be aware of and tap into the tremendous support, guidance, and mentorship that medical school faculty and staff provide to help you succeed. Medical schools are committed to their students and their education. In general, more than 95 percent of all students enrolled succeed in earning their M.D. degree.

Towards the end of medical school you will choose a specialty; after graduation you will spend at least three years in a graduate medical education (residency) programme. During that period you must obtain a license to practice.

Q.12   What is a doctor's career like?

Ans:
with caring for people and continuously learning more about the human body. Every day in

homeless shelters and schools to care for people in need.

But physicians also do many other things. Physician researchers are at work today developing exciting new treatments for cancer, genetic disorders, and infectious diseases like AIDS. Academic physicians share their skills and wisdom by teaching medical students and residents. Others work with health maintenance organisations, pharmaceutical companies, medical device manufacturers, health insurance companies, or in corporations directing health and safety programs. People with medical skills are in demand everywhere.

Q.13   Would medicine provide me with a good living?

Ans:
make about $160,000 a year in the US, but this amount can vary depending on where physicians live and what type of medical specialty they practise. As the American health care system changes, fewer doctors are working for themselves and more are joining health care systems, often as salaried employees. In these organisations, physicians often can command salaries comparable to executives in other occupations. In India a young Doctor with MBBS plus MD/MS can earn minimum Rs. 5,00000.00 per annum and there is no upper limit.

Q.14   What is a primary care doctor? What are their careers like?

Ans: About one-third of the nation's physicians are generalists — "primary care" doctors who provide lifelong medical services for you and all the members of your family. General internists, family physicians, and general pediatricians are all considered generalist doctors. They are the

generalist physicians send them to see a specialist physician.

Specialist physicians differ from generalists in that they focus on treating a particular system or part of the body. Neurologists who study the brain, cardiologists who study the heart, ophthalmologists who study the eye; and hematologists who study the blood are just a few examples of specialists.

medical problems as well as complete and comprehensive care throughout life.

Q.15   What are the specialisation courses available after MBBS?

Ans: MD Anaesthesiology

MD Anatomy

MD Biochemistry

MD Community Medicine

MD Dermatology, Venereology & Leprosy

MD Forensic Medicine

MD General Medicine

MD Hospital Administration

MD Microbiology

MD Paediatrics

MD Pathology

MD Pharmacology

MD Physiology

MD Psychiatry

MD Radio-diagnosis

MD Radio-therapy

MS General Surgery

MS Ophthalmology

MS Obstetrics & Gynaecology

MS Orthopaedic Surgery

MS Otorhinolaryngology

(This is only an indicative list not an exhaustive list)

Q.16 How can one become a Homeopathic Doctor?

Ans: To become a Homeopathic Doctor, you have to complete the course BHMS. Bachelor of Homeo Medicine & Surgery (BHMS) is of 5-years duration course. 10+2 or equivalent examination passed with Physics, Chemistry and Biology is essential eligibility for an aspirant. Admission is either on the basis of marks in qualifying examination or through a competitive entrance examination.

Q.17 How can one become an Ayurvedic Doctor?

Ans: To become an Ayurvedic Doctor, you have to complete the — Bachelor of Ayurvrdic Medicine

equivalent examination passed with Physics, Chemistry and Biology is essential eligibility for an aspirant. Admission is either on the basis of marks in qualifying examination or through a competitive entrance examination.

Q.18 How can one become a Unani Doctor?

Ans: To become a Unani Doctor, you have to complete the course BUMS. Bachelor of Unani Medicine & Surgery (BUMS) is of 5 and half years duration course including internship. 10+2 or equivalent examination passed with Physics, Chemistry and Biology is essential eligibility for an aspirant. Admission is either on the basis of marks in qualifying examination or through a competitive entrance examination. BUMS is offered in almost 25 colleges in the country. Some other courses

Placements of doctors trained in Unani Medicine are in Unani Medical Colleges and hospitals. After post graduation, teaching and research are also good options.

The Central Council for Research in Unani Medicine is an autonomous organisation of the Ministry of Health and Family Welfare Government of India. The Council is engaged in the multifaceted

research, drug research, literary research, survey and cultivation of medicinal plants, and family

through union Ministry of Health & Family Welfare.

Q.19 What is the admission procedure to enter a Medical College for completing the MBBS course and become an allopathic doctor?

Ans: To enter a Medical College in India to become an MBBS doctor, you have to appear in the Medical Entrance Test/ Pre Medical Test (PMT) conducted at National Level or State Level. Any student studying in any part of the country can appear the National Level Entrance Tests, where as the state level entrances are open only to the domicile of the state. The eligibility criteria for domicile for state level tests vary from state to state and not uniform throughout the country.

not a domicile of that state.

The minimum academic eligibility for appearing in the Medical Entrance (State Level/National Level) is generally HS (10+2) with Physics, Chemistry and Biology securing minimum 50% marks.

However, the minimum percentage varies from state to state and exam to exam (50% or 55% or 60%). Some entrance also requires minimum 50% marks in English.

Q.20 Which All India Entrance Exams one can appear for admission into MBBS course?

Ans: The following exams are the All India Entrance Examination for admission into MBBS/BDS courses:

	ALL INDIA ENTRANCE EXAMINATIONS (After 10+2 with science)	
01.	Central Board of Secondary Education, New Delhi(15% All India Seats)	December
02.	All India Institute of Medical Sciences, New Delhi	January
03.	Manipal Academy of Higher Education, Manipal	February
04.	St. John's National Academy of Health Sciences, Bangalore	March
05.	Armed Force Medical College(AFMC), Pune	January
06.	Bharati Vidyapeeth, Pune	April
07.	Mahatma Gandhi Institute of Medical Sciences, Wardha	January
08.	JIPMER	February
09.	CMC, Vellore	February
10.	Sri Ramchandra Medical College & Research Institute, Chennai	March
11.	Jawaharlal Nehru Medical College, AMU, Aligarh	March
12.	BHU Institute of Medical Sciences, Varanasi	January
13.	GGS IP University (VM Medical College), Delhi	December

(This is only a tentative list and not an exhaustive list)

In addition to the All India Entrance Tests, students can also appear in various State Level Entrance Test conducted by state agencies/authorities for admission into MBBS/BDS course in a particular state.

Q.21 What is AIPMT and how can one appear in AIPMT for admission into a good medical college.

Ans: For admission to 15% of the total seats for Medical/Dental Courses in all Medical/Dental colleges run by the Union of India; State Governments, Municipal or other local authorities in India except

(CBSE) conducts All India Pre-Medical/Pre-Dental Entrance Examination. As per the revised scheme of examination the AIPMT examination is conducted in two stages as per the following schedule:

1. Preliminary Examination
2. Final Examination

Pattern of AIPMT

Preliminary Examination: The Preliminary Examination would consist of one paper containing 200 objective type questions (Multiple choice) from Physics, Chemistry and Biology (Botany & Zoology) to be answered on the specially designed machine-gradable sheet using Ball Point Pen only.

The duration of paper would be 3 hours.

Final Examination: Only for those who qualify in the Preliminary Examination.

choice) from Physics, Chemistry and Biology(Botany and Zoology) to be answered on the specially designed machine-gradable sheet using Ball Point Pen only.

The duration of the paper would be 3 hours.

Language of the Question Papers: Candidate can opt for question papers either in English or in Hindi.

Eligibility: The candidate should be at least 17 years of age at the time of admission or will complete the age on or before 31st December during the year of admission. To be eligible to appear in competitive entrance examination, candidate must have passed any of the qualifying examinations as mentioned in the Information Bulletin. Provided also that to be eligible for competitive entrance examination the candidate must have passed in the subjects of Physics, Chemistry, Biology and English individually and must have obtained a minimum of 50% marks taken together in Physics, Chemistry and Biology at the qualifying examination. In respect of candidates belonging to Schedule Caste/Scheduled Tribes or Other Backward Classes the marks obtained in Physics, Chemistry and Biology taken together in qualifying examination be 40% instead of 50% for General Candidates. Those who are taking plus two examinations in the year

Information Bulletin and Application Form: Bulletin containing the Application Form and other

Bank branches. There is provision for submission of application online also. Visit www.aipmt.nic.in for online submission of application. Detail about AIPMT is also available at CBSE website www.cbse.nic.in . To prepare for PMT you have to study your course material well and clear your concepts in Physics, Chemistry and Biology to answer objective type questions and application of various concepts. You can also buy some guidebook for PMT from the market and study these along with your course book. Regular coaching or correspondence course will also help you in this matter.

Q.22   How can I join AIIMS or CMC after completing 10+2?

Ans: In order to join AIIMS you have to appear in the competitive examination after completing your +2 (HS) with physics, chemistry and biology. The competitive entrance Examination will be of 3½ hours duration and will have one paper consisting of 200 objective type (multiple choice and reason-

details of distribution of marks are as follows:

Subject	Total Marks
Physics	60
Chemistry	60
Biology (Botny and Zology)	60
	20
Total	200

The general standard of the Competitive Entrance Examination will be that of 12th class under the 10+2 Scheme/Pre-Medical/Intermediate science or an equivalent. No syllabus for the examination has been prescribed by AIIMS.

Each year 50 seats are available for admission to the graduate medical course, leading to the award of the degree of M.B.B.S. of the All India Institute of Medical Sciences. Out of these, 7 (seven) seats are reserved for the Scheduled Castes, 4 (four) seats are reserved for the Scheduled

the Scheduled Tribes and vice versa. In case suitable candidates are not available from the above

CMC Vallore also conducts an all India Competitive Examination for admission into MBBS course.

The Entrance Examination is conducted on the basis of 10+2 Syllabus. The test is of Multiple choice and contain questions on Physics, Chemistry, Biology and General Ability. The total number of seat for MBBS course in CMC is 60.

plus two' Higher Secondary Examination, taken after a period of 12 years of studies; the last two years of study comprising physics, chemistry and Biology, with English at a level not less than the core course for English as prescribed by the National Council for Educational Research & Training, after the introduction of the 10+2+3 years educational structure as recommended by the National Committee on Education.

Candidates should have passed in English and obtained 50% marks aggregate in Physics, Chemistry and Biology, taken together, both at qualifying and competitive examinations.

Only candidates who qualify the written test are called for the interviews. The duration of MBBS course is of four and a half years and is followed by one year of Compulsory Rotating Residential Internship. The course is taken in three stages, following a short foundation course which provides

months and covers the basic sciences of Anatomy, Physiology and Biochemistry. The next stage is for 18 months and includes Pharmacology, Pathology, Microbiology and Forensic Medicine. The last stage is for 24 months and covers Ophthalmology, Otorhinolaryngology, Community Medicine, General Medicine, Paediatrics, Surgery, Orthopaedic Surgery and Obstetrics & Gynaecology.

For more information on the admission calendar and Prospectus, etc., write to: Registrar, Christian Medical College, Vellore, 632 002, Tamil Nadu.

As both the entrance examinations are highly competitive and few students from this region make it, you have to prepare from the initial stage for the admission test of AIIMS and CMS. The following books may be helpful for preparing AIIMS/CMC admission test along with your (10+2) text books:

(1) Physics by H.C.Verma

(2) Chemistry by O.P.Agarwal and Physical Chemistry by R.C.Mukharjee

(4) Tata McGraw Hill Publication in Physics, Chemistry, Biology

(5) Medical entrance guide by any reputed publisher.

Q.23 What is the admission procedure of Armed Forces Medical College? How can one get admission in AFMC?

Ans: Advertisements for admission/recruitment appear in the leading newspapers of the country in the month of December every year, for MBBS course. Candidates are required to submit their application forms in the prescribed format, along with other necessary documents mentioned therein.

the Medical Council of India.

Admission to MBBS course is based on written examination. The written examination is held on 1st Sunday of May. Successful candidates are called for interview in June for the courses starting

Prospectus Availability: Prospectus is available on sale at all Major City GPOs/ HPOs/POs from the date of advertisement for approximately one month. The present cost of the prospectus is Rs. 250/-.

Course Duration: The duration of MBBS course is four and a half year followed by internship of one year.

Service Liability:
Armed Forces Medical Services. The offer of the type of commission will depend on the vacancies available. The candidates' parents/guardians are required to sign a bond agreement at the time of admission.

A candidate seeking admission to the MBBS course is eligible to take the entrance examination if

A candidate should be a citizen of India or be a subject of Nepal or Bhutan or a person of Indian origin migrated from Pakistan or any other foreign country with the intention of permanently settling in India; must be unmarried. Marrying during the course is not permitted. Should be

Must have attained the age of 17yrs on 31st Dec of the year of application, but must not have attained the age of 22 years on that date(Not more than 24 years in case of candidates who have

attempt of the qualifying examinations as a regular candidate with English, Physics, Chemistry and Biology taken simultaneously and securing not less than 60% of the aggregate marks in these 3 science subjects taken together and not less than 50% marks in English and 50% marks in each of the science subjects. They must have also passed an examination in Mathematics of the 10th standard.

Number of Seats : A total of 130 students (105 boys & 25 girls) will be admitted.

Syllabus for the Examination: The general standard of the entrance examination will be that of 11th and 12th class under the 10+2 scheme/pre-medical/intermediate science or an equivalent examination of the State Education Board/Indian University

Method of Selection: Candidates who are found provisionally eligible as per the criteria of eligibility, will be called at one of the examination centres to appear in the competitive examination on 1st Sunday of May. Issue of admit cards, however, does not necessarily mean acceptance of eligibility which will be further scrutinised at subsequent stages of selection.

The written examination centre will be allotted to candidates depending upon the administrative arrangements for the examination and availability of adequate seating capacity.

The Roll Number of the candidates who qualify for interview based on the above written examination will be published in the leading newspapers.

Interview of Candidate: On the basis of their performance in the written examination selected candidates in order of roll numbers will be called for an interview to be held in the month of June at AFMC, PUNE. The exact date of the above interview will be intimidated to the selected candidates. Request for change of date of interview will NOT be entertained.

time of interview. All candidates will produce result or proof of having appeared in the qualifying examination held, at the time of interview (if the result of such examination has not been declared).

On the basis of the above test and interview two merit lists, one for boys and one for girls, will be drawn up and admissions will be offered only to candidates in accordance with their merit position. Individual letters of admission will be sent only to selected candidates who would be required to join AFMC. The remaining candidates will be on waiting list. The result will be published by the DGAFMS in the newspapers.

SC/ST Candidates: Ten seats are reserved for SC/ST candidates provided

The SC/ST candidates must qualify in the written examination and come within the zone to be called up for interview.

Medical Standards: The candidate must be in good physical and mental health and free from any

visit www.afmc.nic.in for more information).

Q.24 How can one join JIPMER (Jawaharlal Institute of Post-graduate Medical Education and Research)? What is the procedure for admission?

Ans: The various courses offered at JIPMER are as follows:

I. Undergraduates Courses		
1.	M.B.B.S.	98 Seats
2.	B.Sc. (Nursing)	75 Seats
3.	B.Sc. (Medical Laboratory Technology)	30 Seats
4.	B.Sc. (Medical Radiation Technology)	4 Seats
5.	B.Sc. (Operation Theatre Technology)	4 Seats
6.	B.Sc. (Perfusion Technology)	4 Seats
7.	B.Sc. (Dialysis Technology)	4 Seats
8.	B.Sc. (Nuclear Medicine Technology)	4 Seats
II. Postgraduates Courses		
1.	M.D. and M.S.	124 Seats
2.	M.Sc. (Medical Biochemistry)	9 Seats
3.	M.Sc. (MLT-Microbiology)	4 Seats
4.	M.Sc. (Medical Biometrics & Information)	5 Seats
5.	Ph.D	18 Seats
III. Super Specialty Courses		
1.	D.M. (Cardiology)	3 Seats
2.	D.M. (Neurology)	2 Seats
3.	D.M. (Neonatology)	1 Seats
4.	D.M. (Clinical Immunology)	1 Seats
5.	D.M. (Clinical Pharmacology)	1 Seat
6.	D.M. (Clinical Hematology)	1 Seat
7.	M.Ch. (Cardio Thoracic Surgery)	3 Seats
8.	M.Ch. (Urology)	3 Seats
9.	M.Ch. (Neurosurgery)	1 Seat
10.	M.Ch. (Surgical Gastroenterology)	2 Seats
IV.	Fellowship Courses	
1.	Fellowship in Diabetology	3 Seats
2.	Fellowship in Pediatric Critical and Emergency Care	2 Seats
3.	Fellowship in Oncology	2 Seats
4.	Fellowship in Tropical Parasitology	1 Seat
1.		15 Seats

2.	Medical Record Trainee	15 Seats
3.	P.G. Diploma in Public Health Management	20 Seats
4.		4 Seats
5.		20 Seats

Admission Procedure

I. M.B.B.S.

How to apply:

every year in all major Newspapers of India. Application form and prospectus will be available in State Bank of India, JIPMER Campus and can be obtained in person or by post by paying the prescribed fee in cash or by bank demand draft. Online application will be available on the website www.jipmer.edu.in

II. **P.G. Degree Courses**

1. M.D. (General Medicine)
2. M.D. (Anatomy)
3. M.D. (Pathology)
4. M.D. (Microbiology)
5. M.D. (Physiology)
6. M.D. (Pharmacology)
7. M.D. (Pediatrics)
8. M.D. (Anesthesiology)
9. M.D. (Dermatology)
10. M.D. (Biochemistry)
11. M.D. (Community Medicine)
12. M.D. (Radiotherapy)
13. M.D. (Radio-Diagnosis)
14. M.D. (Transfusion Medicine & Immunology Hematology)
15. M.D. (Forensic Medicine)
16. M.D. (Psychiatry)
17. M.D. (Pulmonary Medicine)
18. M.S. (Obstetrics & Gynaecology)
19. M.S. (General Surgery)
20. M.S. (Orthopedics Surgery)
21. M.S. (Ophthalmology)
22. M.S. (Oto-Rhino-Laryngology)

How to apply

in the month of December every year in all major Newspapers of India. Application form and prospectus will be available in State Bank of India, JIPMER Campus and can be obtained in person or by post by paying the prescribed fee in cash or by bank demand draft. Online application will be available on our website also. www.jipmer.edu.in

III. Ph.D (Full Time)

Sl. No.	Subject	Seats
1	Anatomy	2
2	Physiology	2
3	Biochemistry	2
4	Pathology	2
5	Microbiology	2
6	Pharmacology	4
7	Clinical Immunology	2
8	Clinical Pediatrics	2
	TOTAL	18

How to apply

published in the month of May every year in all major Newspapers of India.

IV. M.Ch.

Sl. No.	Subject	Seats
1	Urology	3
2	Cardiothorasic Surgery	3
3	Neurosurgery	1
4	Surgical Gastroenterology	2
	TOTAL	9

How to apply

published in the month of May every year in all Newspapers of India and application form and prospectus available in State Bank of India, JIPMER Campus and can be obtained in person or by post by paying the prescribed fee in cash or by bank demand draft.

V. Para-Medical & Other Courses

be published in the month of May in all Newspapers of India and application form and prospectus will be available in State Bank of India, JIPMER Campus and can be obtained in person or by post by paying the prescribed fee in cash or by bank demand draft.

Candidates are admitted for all the paramedical courses based on Common Entrance Examinations conducted by the Institute.

Q.25 How can one join Manipal Academy of Higher Education (MAHE) to become a Doctor?

Ans: The undergraduate entrance process is based on the candidates rank in the All India MAHE Undergraduate Entrance Test (UGET). Eligibility: General Category — Indian Nationals, pass in 10+2, A level, IB, American 12th grade or equivalent with Physics, Chemistry, Biology and English and 50% in PCB. Admissions are through merit in the entrance test.

Test Pattern: In all there will be three question papers with multiple choice objective type questions.

For detail please visit MAHE website www.manipal.edu .

Q.26 What is the procedure for admission in state Medical Colleges for MBBS in the state of Andhra Pradesh?

Ans: Engineering, Agriculture & Medical Common Entrance Test (EAMCET) is conducted by JNTU or one of the State Universities of Andhra Pradesh (on rotation) for admission to MBBS/BDS/B. Pharm/BAMS/BUMS/BHMS courses in the state of Andhra Pradesh (www.apemacet.org).

Admission is open to Indian Nationals and residents of Andhra Pradesh. The following are considered as State residents:

(i) Candidates who have resided in the State for 10 years excluding periods of study outside the state; (ii) Candidates whose parents have resided in the state for 10 years; (iii) Candidates whose parents/spouses of those in state/central, Public Sector, Local Bodies, Universities employed within the state at the time of application. (iv) Candidates should have passed or appeared for

as optional including practical tests in these subjects, OR any examination (10+2 pattern) with Biology, Physics and Chemistry including practical tests in each of these subjects, recognised as equivalent to Intermediate by the Board of Intermediate Education, A.P. (v) Candidates should complete 17years of age as on 31st December of the year of admission. There is no upper age limit.

Q.27 What is the admission procedure for admission in state Medical Colleges for MBBS in the state of Assam?

Ans:
courses in medical colleges and one dental college of Assam. Admission is open to Indian nationals and native/permanent residents of Assam (20 years). Children of the employees of the State

Services are exempted from the clause. The age limit is 17-24 years on 31st December of the year of admission. Admission is on the basis of merit in the Common Entrance Examination. The CEE consists of 3 papers on the syllabus of Assam Higher Secondary Education Council in Physics, Chemistry and Biology (Botany & Zoology). Each paper carries 100 marks. Exemption from CEE:

of Assam Higher Secondary Education Council securing at least 75% aggregate marks in Physics, Chemistry and Biology.

Q.28 **What is the admission procedure for admission in state Medical Colleges for MBBS in the state of Bihar?**

Ans: Combined Medical Education Entrance Test (CMEET) is conducted for admission to MBBS/ BDS/BAMS/BHMS courses in the state of Bihar. Admission is open to Indian citizens and Bihar native. The following satisfy the Bihar natives: (a) Candidates whose father/mother have been resident of Bihar for 10 years; (b) Children of Central Govt employees serving in the state; (c) Children of State employees/members of All India Services of Bihar cadre; (d) Candidates whose

available for Govt of India, TISCO, Coal Mines Welfare Organisation nominees.

The lower age limit is 17 years and no prescribed upper age limit. Selection is on the basis of merit in the CMEET which is HS (10+2) standard. The test is conducted in Physics, Chemistry and Biology.

Q.29 **What is the admission procedure for admission in state Medical Colleges for MBBS in the state of Delhi?**

Ans: The University of Delhi holds Common Entrance Examination for admission to MBBS/BDS at 3 medical colleges: Lady Hardinge Medical College, Maulana Azad Medical College and University College of Medical Sciences. Govt of India nominees (from Arunachal Pradesh, Andaman & Nicobar Islands, Dadar & Nagar Haweli, Ladakh, Manipur, Meghalaya, Mizoral, Nagaland, Sikkim and Tripura) and children/widow of Armed personnel disabled/killed in action are exempted from CEE.

CBSE, New Delhi (except Patrachar Vidyalaya and Open School) with Physics, Chemistry, Biology and English (Core or Elective) securing minimum 50% aggregate marks in these subjects from the recognised schools conductiong regular classes situated within the Territory of Delhi. The lower age limit is 17 years on 31st December of the year of admission. The CEE consists of two papers of (i) Physics & Chemistry, (ii) Botany & Zoology. Each paper is of generally two and half hours duration and carries 600 marks each. The questions are of objective type.

Q.30 **What is the admission procedure for admission in state Medical Colleges for MBBS in the state of Haryana?**

Ans: MBBS/BDS Entrance Examination is conducted by Maharshi Dayanand University for admission into MBBS/BDS courses in the state of Haryana. Admission is open to Residents of Haryana. Candidates should have studied class X, XI and XII standard from an institution located in Haryana. Govt of India nominees are exempted. The academic eligibility is same with other state level entrance mentioned above and minimum age is 17 years on 31st December of the year of admission. There is no prescribed upper age limit. The entrance test consists of papers on Physics & Chemistry (combined) and Botany & Zoology (combined) of 2 hours duration each with objective type questions of 300 marks. A merit list of candidates (1.5 to 2 times) prepared for interview. Weight age is given for sports participation.

Q.31 **What is the admission procedure for admission in state Medical Colleges for MBBS in the state of Himachal Pradesh?**

Ans: Admission to MBBS courses in Himachal Pradesh is based on merit in competitive examination is 12 years Senior Secondary/ Pre-Medical with Physics, Chemistry and Biology securing 50% aggregate marks including practical and a mere pass in English. BSc degree holders securing 50% marks with any three subjects Botany, Zoology, Chemistry, Physiology, Human Anatomy, Biochemistry and Physics are also eligible. Such candidates should have passed (10+2) exam with Physics, Chemistry and Biology.

Children of Himachalis (15 years stay) and Employees of State Govt/autonomus bodies are eligible for admission. Age limit is 17-25 years on 31st December of the year of admission.

Q.32 What is the admission procedure for admission in state Medical Colleges for MBBS in the state of Karnataka?

Ans: State Level Common Entrance Test (CET) is conducted by the Common Entrance Test Cell,

separate test).

Academic Eligibility:
equivalent exam with Physics, Chemistry & Biology as optional subjects with English as one of the languages of study and obtained at least 50% marks in the PCB group, provided that for Dental course, the candidate must also have secured 50% of marks in English language. (40% in the case of SC / ST / Category-I candidates.) For admission to these courses, the applicant should have completed the age of 17 years on 31st December of the year appearing in the CET.

(a) The candidate should have studied and passed in one or more Government or Government

of seven academic years commencing from I standard to 2nd PUC / 12th standard as on 1st July of the year in which the Entrance Test is held and has appeared and passed SSLC/10th

candidate who had taken more than one year to pass a class or standard, the years of academic study is counted as one year only.

(b) The candidate should have studied and passed I and II year Pre-University Examination or

or recognised by the State Government and that either of the parents should have studied

the year of admission, such candidates should have passed the qualifying examination

also that the candidate shall undergo a test which will be conducted by the CET Cell on to which will be conducted by the CET Cell to establish his ability to speak, read and write

(e) In the case of a candidate who is son or daughter of defence personnel who has worked

June of the year of admission. The candidate should have studied and passed the qualifying examination from any Government or Government recognised educational institution

(f) Son or daughter of serving defence personnel who at the time of joining the defence

of the Defence unit.

(g) In the case of a candidate who is a son or daughter of a defence personnel who had served

qualifying examination from any Government or Government recognised educational

(h) Son or daughter of an ex-servicemen who at the time of joining the defence service had

and produced from the "Deputy Director, Department of Sainik Welfare and Resettlement".

(i) In the case of a candidate being a son or daughter of an employee of the Union Government

Undertaking, who is liable to be transferred anywhere in India as per the terms and

previous year to 30th June of the year of entrance test and such candidate has studied and passed the qualifying examination from any Government or Government recognised

(j) Son or daughter of a working or retired employee of the Union Government or employee

such employee; (a) had declared to the employer at the time of joining service any place

seven years at any time between 1st standard and 12th standard, or Pre-University Examination; and (c) was or is liable to be transferred anywhere in India as per the terms and conditions of his employment.

(l) Son or daughter of serving or retired employee: (a) belonging to All India Service of

outside the State from 1st standard to 2nd PUC or 12th standard examination can be added

NOTE:
means only natural born son or daughter.

Q.33 What is the admission procedure for admission in state Medical Colleges for MBBS in the state of Kerala?

Ans: Common Entrance Examination (CEE) is conducted for admission to MBBS, BDS, B.Pharm,

personnel killed/disabled/missing or Ex-service man/ Anglo Indian Community candidates.

(10+2) with Physics, Chemistry and Biology with 59% aggregate marks. BSc degree holders with Physics, Chemistry, Zoology, Botany/Biochemistry with 50% marks in the main and subsidiary subjects taken together are also eligible. Such candidates should have passed the qualifying exam with Physics, Chemistry and Biology. The minimum age required for admission is 17 years on 31st December of the year of admission. Selection is on the basis of merit in CEE conducted at various centres in the state. The exam is of (10+2)/Pre-university standard and consists of two papers in Physics & Chemistry and Biology (Zoology & Botany). The questions are of objective type multiple choice.

Q.34 What is the admission procedure for admission in state Medical Colleges for MBBS in the state of Madhya Pradesh?

Ans: Pre-Medical Test (PMT) for admission to MBBS/BDS is conducted by Professional Examination Board, Madhya Pradesh, Bhopal for admission into the medical colleges in the state. Admission is

of MP (b) Candidates should have been educated in educational institutions in the state for 3 consecutive years during the 5 years immediately preceding the year of admission (c) Children

Chemistry and Biology. The minimum age required for admission is 17 years on December 31st of the year of admission. Admission is on the basis of merit in the PMT.

Q.35 What is the procedure for admission in state Medical Colleges for MBBS in the state of Tamil Nadu?

Ans: Tamil Nadu Professional Course Entrance Examinations (TNPCEE) is conducted by Anna University, Madras for candidates who seek admission to professional courses in Tamil Nadu offered by Anna University, Government Colleges, Government Aided and Private Professional Colleges

of Indian Medicine & Homeopathy, Tamil Nadu Agricultural University, Tamil Nadu Veterinary & Animal Sciences University for free seats and payment seats.

The candidates selected under the payment seat category have to pay higher tuition fees than the

by the Government of Tamil Nadu. These Entrance Examinations are applicable to candidates

admission to the Professional Courses by the respective admitting authorities.

Other State Candidates are not admitted through TNPCEE to Professional Courses offered by

Homeopathy, Tamil Nadu Agricultural University and Tamil Nadu Veterinary and Animal Sciences University, other State Candidates will not be permitted to appear in the Entrance Examinations for admission to those courses.

12 years Higher Secondary (Academic) or equivalent with Physics, Chemistry, Biology (Botony & Zoology) taken together securing 60% marks in each subject and 70% (140 out of 200) aggregate marks. BC/SC & ST candidates securing 55-60 % and 40% marks in each Science subject are also eligible for admission.

Age: Below 21 years on July1 (24 years for SC/ST) of the year of admission.

Domicile: Candidates whose parents have permanent residence in the State are eligible.

Exemptions: Candidates who have studied from Class 9th to Qualifying Examination in the State; Children of Defence Personnel of TN origin who have passed 10th exam from the State.

Selection: Admission will be made on the basis of the performance of the candidates in the Qualifying Examination (Higher Secondary Course or equivalent) and in the TNPCEE in the ratio 200:100. The Entrance Examination is conducted in the last week of June. It comprises papers on Mathematics, Biology and Physical Sciences (Physics & Chemistry). The candidates have to appear for either two or all the three papers of the Entrance Examination corresponding to the courses to which they seek admission.

How-to-Apply: Prospectus cum Application Form for TNPCEE can be obtained in the month of

from the Secretary TNPCEE, Anna University, Chennai-25

Q.36 What is the procedure for admission in state Medical Colleges for MBBS in the state of Rajasthan?

Ans: A Joint Pre-Medical Test (PMT) for admission to the 1st year MBBS/BDS Course for the Medical Colleges in the state of Rajasthan is conducted by University of Rajasthan.

A pass in the 1st year Science exam of the three year Degree Course (Pass/ Hons) of the University in Rajasthan; Higher Secondary Science (10+2) Exam or any other exam recognised as equivalent therein with English and Medical group of subjects (Physics, Chemistry and Biology). OR BSc Exam of an Indian University recognised by Rajasthan University with not less than three of the following subjects : Chemistry, Botony and Zoology provided further that he/she has passed the earlier Qualifying Examination with English and Medical group of the subjects.

Age: 17 years on December 31 of the year of admission.

Domicile: Candidate who has studied for at least 3 years continuously as a regular student in a recognised institution in the State or whose father/mother has continuously resided in the State for a period of at least 10 years and he/she (candidate) has studied for 5 years in a recognised institution in Rajasthan or whose father/mother is an employee with 3 years' service

Service borne on the State cadre) Undertaking, Corporation, Municipal Boards, Improvement Trust formed under the Act incorporated in Rajasthan, a University or Higher Secondary Board in Rajasthan or whose father/mother is permanent employee of Indian Defence Service and is either of Rajasthan origin irrespective of his place of posting or is posted in Rajasthan at the time of last date of the application for admission.

Selection: All the candidates except those belonging to Govt of India nominees are to appear at the PMT held by the University of Rajasthan, Jaipur in the subjects of Chemistry, Physics, Botony and Zoology. Question Papers in all the subjects are set in English as well as in Hindi. Each paper is of 2 hrs duration and is of 300 marks. The questions are of Multiple Choice Objective-Type. Selection is based on the merit in the test.

The candidates may obtain General Guidelines for PMT and Application Forms in April from the controller of Examinations, PMT, Rajasthan University, RA Podar Institute of Management, Jawahar Lal Nehru Marg, Jaipur-302004 on cash payment or by sending a Bank Draft through Registered post.

Q.37 What is the procedure for admission in state Medical Colleges for MBBS in the state of Punjab?
Ans:
BDS/BAMS courses for the above medical colleges in the State is held by one of the Universities.

New Delhi.

10+2 or equivalent with at least 50% (45% for SC/ST) aggregate marks in the four compulsory subjects English, Physics, Chemistry and Biology. Those awaiting the result of qualifying exam may also apply.

Age: 17 years of age on December 31 of the year of admission.

Domicile: PMT is open to candidates from Punjab only. Exceptions: November 1984 riot affected displaced persons can also apply for admission.

Selection: Selection is based on merit in PMT. The Pre Medical Test is of objective type, multiple choice questions in Physics, Chemistry and Biology of 11/2 hrs duration each. The exam is on the pattern of CBSE. Candidates are also required to appear in the Interview.

How to Apply: Application Form together with Prospectus and Syllabus can be obtained from the University conducting the Entrance Test and the Principals of the Medical Colleges during the month of April of the year of admission on cash payment or by Registered Post.

Q.38 What is the procedure for admission in state Medical Colleges for MBBS in the state of Orissa?
Ans:
above medical colleges in the State is held by one of the College. Fifteen percent of total seats

12 years Senior Secondary/Intermediate Science with English, Physics, Chemistry and Biology (Botony and Zoology) securing at least 50 percent marks in the `Science subjects' taken together. Candidates who have appeared in the qualifying Examination are also eligible.

Age: 17 years of age on December 31 of the year of admission.

Domicile: Permanent residents of Orrisa, Sons/daughters of the employees of the Central/ State/Govt Undertaking/Members of All-India Services (Orissa Cadre) serving in Orisa, Children of Defence personnel serving in the State, Orissa students living in outlying Oriya speaking tract of the neighbouring states of Orissa.

Selection: Merit in the Entrance Examination (2 hours duration – 150 marks). The test consists of one question paper of Multiple Choice Objective-Type Questions covering Physics, Chemistry, Biology and English of Qualifying Examination standard.

Q.39 What is the procedure for admission in state Medical Colleges for MBBS in the state of Maharashtra?

Ans: State level procedure has been formed for admission to all seats in Government/ Municipal Medical Colleges (14 MBBS, 4 BDS) and 'Free Seats' and 'Payment Seats' in Private Colleges (15MBBS/BDS) as per Supreme Court directive. The scheme is applicable to degree courses in the Faculty of Medicine, Dental, Ayurvedic, Homeopathic, Unani and Nursing (MBBS, BDS, BAMS, BHMS,BUMS,BNursing). All seats in Government Colleges and Private Colleges (50% Free and 50%

payment seats on 50:50 basis. The candidates for payment seats have to pay higher fees as

(MBBS, BDS, BAMS, BHMS, BNursing); (2) Municipal Colleges; (3)Pharmacy Colleges.

12 years Higher Secondary with Physics, Chemistry, Biology (Botony & Zoology) and English with 50% of total marks (40% for BC) in single attempt from a school in Maharashtra.

Age: 17 years on December 31 of the year of admission.

Q.40 What is the procedure for admission in state Medical Colleges for MBBS in the state of Gujrat?

Ans: There are common rules and regulations for admission in the Government Medical Colleges of Gujarat for admission to the MBBS/BDS course on the basis of marks obtained in the qualifying examination (10+2).

CBSE, New Delhi.

Higher Secondary Exam (Science Stream) under 10+2 educational pattern of the Gujrat Higher Secondary School Education Board or CBSE from any school in Gujrat with at least 55% (45% for SC/ST/NT/DT) marks in the subject of Physics, Chemistry, Biology, Mathematics and English.

Age: 17 years on December 31 of the year of admission.

Domicile: Candidates should have passed 12 years Senior Secondary exam from the institutions

Gujarat state.Sons/daughters of State Govt employees who have been posted outside the state.

Selection: Admission is made strictly on merit on the basis of marks obtained in the Qualifying Examination.

Q.41   What is the procedure for admission in state Medical Colleges for MBBS in the state of Goa?

Ans: Admission to Goa Medical College is made on the basis of the merit in qualifying examination in Physics, Chemistry and Biology. The candidate should have passed Senior Secondary Examination after a 12 years' study with Physics, Chemistry, Biology and English securing 50% (40% for SC/ST)

should have been residents of Goa for 10 years (5 years for candidates whose parents are of Goa origin) and they should have passed the qualifying (11th and 12th) exam from Goa.

Exemptions: Children of regular State Govt./Central Govt. employees (including Defence Personnel) transferred to and serving/served in the state and Ex-Servicemen; they should have passed the 11th and 12th exam from Goa. The minimum age should be 17 years on December 31 of the year of admission.

Q.42   What is the procedure for admission in state Medical Colleges for MBBS in the state of J&K?

Ans: Admission to MBBS/BDS in Medical/Dental Colleges is made through an Entrance Test. It is

and children of permanent residents of Defence personnal and other paramilitary forces serving in various parts of the country/outside are considered exceptions.

Higher Secondary Exam (Science Stream) under 10+2 educational pattern with English, Physics, Chemistry and Biology with at least 50% (40% for reserved categories: SC, Gujjar

Age: 17 years on or before December 31 of the year of admission.

Domicile: Admission is open to candidates who have passed Qualifying Examination from an

Exceptions:

who are on Deputation to Union Government; Children of permanent resident in Defence and Parliament forcs serving anywhere.

Selection: Admission is made strictly on merit on the basis of marks obtained in the Qualifying examination. The examination is held in Physics, Chemistry and Biology of 11/2 hours duration. In case of tie, candidates obtaining higher marks in Biology/ Chemistry are given preference.

Q.43 What is the procedure for admission in state Medical Colleges for MBBS in the state Uttar Pradesh?

Ans: Combined Pre-Medical Test (CPMT) for admission to the 1st year MBBS/BDS /BHMS/ BAMS /BUMS Courses is held by one of the concerned Universities in the State by rotation and in accordance with

India Entrance Test conducted by CBSE, New Delhi.

Students passed in Intermediate Science Examination or equivalent with Physics, Chemistry and Biology are eligible to appear in the Test. Such candidates as have appeared at the Intermediate Examination of the year of admission can also appear in the test provisionally.

Age: 17 years of age on December 31 of the year of admission.

Domicile:

country, provided the wards have passed the Qualifying Examination from UP.

Selection: A competitive Examination is held in Zoology, Botony, Chemistry, Physics, and Hindi containing Objective-Type questions in English and Hindi medium. The Hindi language paper will be of 1 hour duration and will be of qualifying nature only. All other papers (I: Chemistry and Physics and II: Zoology and Botony) are of 2 hrs each.

Q.44 What is the procedure for admission in state Medical Colleges for MBBS in the state of West Bengal?

Ans: A Joint Entrance Examination (JEE) for admission to MBBS/BDS Courses is held by the Central

on All-India basis through All-India Entrance Test conducted by CBSE, New Delhi.

Passed in Intermidiate Examination of WB council of Higher Secondary education or equivalent exam recognised by concerned University(Calcutta, Burdwan & North Bengal) with

subject having full marks not less than 100 and pass marks not less than 30 in the above subjects.

Age: 17 years of age on December 31 of the year of admission.

Domicile: To be eligible for admission the respective categories of candidates shall be a citizen of India and has been residing in the state of West Bengal uniterruptedly/ continuously for not less than 10 years immediately prior to the date of making application for admission. Candidate who or whose parents are permanent residing in West Bengal having permanent home addresses in the state of WB.

Selection: Admission is made on the basis of merit as determined by the Joint Entrance Examination of eligible candidates. The examination comprises three papers namely Physics, Chemistry of 100 marks each and Biological Sciences of 200 marks.

Q.45 Which are the top 10 Medical Colleges in India?

Ans: The top 10 Medical Colleges in India are:

(i) All India Institute of Medical Sciences, Delhi

(ii) Bangalore Medical College, Bangalore

(iv) Madras Medical College, Chennai

(v) Christian Medical College, Vellore

(vi) Armed Forces Medical College, Pune

(vii) St. John's Medical College, Bangalore

(viii) Osmania Medical College, Hyderabad

(ix) JIPMER, Pondichery

(x) Maulana Azad Medical College, Delhi

(Source: India Today Survey)

Q.46 Who is a Dentist? What are the personal qualities required to become a Dentist?

Ans: Dentists are responsible for the dental and oral healthcare services to the general public and helping those in distress. However, a career in dentistry is not for the faint hearted. General dental practice is recognised as being close to the top of the list of the most stressful occupations around. There is a wide choice in dentistry from being a salaried consultant oral surgeon working in a hospital environment, to the independence and freedom of running a business in private practice.

The personal qualities required by a Dentist:

There are four fundamental personal qualities that are pre-requisites for someone to enjoy a successful career in dentistry. Firstly the aspirant must have a quality that we term as "people's person". That is to say, an outoing personality in someone who genuinely enjoys working with people and is someone who cares.

Secondly and perhaps rather obviously, a high degree of manual dexterity is required in a person with a practical approach to life.

Thirdly, the ability to manage and play the role of team leader is required, along with the business skills needed to manage a successful enterprise.

Finally there must be a strong sense of commitment to the local community and to serve others.

Q.47　How can one become a Dentist? What is the Career prospect?

Ans:

The best course is the BDS (Bachelor of Dental Surgery) offered by Universities/ Dental Colleges. The course is of 4/5 years duration and equivalent to other bachelor degree like MBBS/BE, etc.

Entry requirements: The entry requirement for BDS is 10+2 with Physics, Chemistry and Biology. The entrance is normally through competitive entrance test. Some Dental Schools offer an extra preliminary pre-dental year for those without the necessary science base for entry requirements. In most of the states the entrance test for BDS is combined with MBBS entrance test and hence preparation for MBBS and BDS entrance is same.

The dental curriculum includes a sound theoretical and practical training in all aspects of dentistry against a background of general medicine.

Career Prospects:

General Dental Practice: The vast majority of Dentists will be found in general practice. The

experience in an accredited VT practice.

The opportunity then exists to become an Associate and eventually a practice Principal. All dental practices are privately owned and may be subcontracted by local Health Authorities to provide NHS dentistry under the terms of the General Dental Services.

Practices vary in size, ranging from the small independent practices run by a single-handed practitioner to larger practices staffed by a number of professionals catering for a range of special interests. General practice is very much a home of the self-employed.

Exciting new salaried opportunities for general practitioners are being created in the larger corporate groups such as Boots and Oasis whilst positions in the Community Dental Services provided by local Health Authorities, and roles within the Armed Forces or large commercial companies with in-house dental service also exist and offer salaried careers for those who prefer greater job security.

Community Dental Services (CDS): The CDS provides dental care for those with special needs. In particular the CDS looks after young children who need special help as well as elderly and housebound people and patients with mental or physical disabilities.

The Armed Forces: Although the opportunities to travel abroad are diminishing, a comprehensive

Industrial Dentistry: Some companies with large numbers of employees provide dental services. For example, oil companies and some airlines provide facilities for general dental services as an

Corporate Bodies:

of "Corporates" such as Boots. Boots have introduced dental facilities to a large number of their

Dental Nurses. Adult patients are treated on a private basis and their children under the terms and conditions of the NHS.

Hospital and University careers: Many graduates wish to increase their specialised knowledge with a view to taking up a consultant post later as an Oral and Maxillo Surgeon or perhaps carrying out research and teaching undergraduates. Specialist appointments in areas such as oral medicine, orthodontics, endodontics, paedodontics, are a few of the other career pathways available.

Q.48 What are the courses available for higher studies after completing BDS?

Ans: Master of Dental Surgery (MDS) course is available after BDS in the following subjects:

  (i)   Prosthetics
  (ii) Periodontia
  (iii) Oral and Maxilliofacial Surgery
  (iv) Operative Conservative Dentistry
  (v)   Oral Pathology
  (vi) Orthodontia
  (vii) Oral Medicine and Radiology
 (viii) Pedodontic and Preventive Dentistry
  (ix) Preventive and Social dentistry

Q.49 Who is a Dental Technician? What is the Career Prospect?

Ans: The Dental Technician is an important and often little acknowledged member of the dental team. Working under the prescription of a Dental Surgeon the Technician is responsible for a wide variety of manufacturing operations including making dentures, crowns, bridges, and orthodontic appliances and carrying out numerous other intricate tasks. Some Technicians will decide to remain in a hospital environment working closely with a Consultant Oral/Maxillo facial Surgeon involved in facial reconstruction. In this area, the Technician will be involved in making lifelike prosthetic appliances to replace lost tissues or organs such as the eyes.

Dental Technicians make a wide range of dental appliances including crowns, bridges, orthodontic appliances and dentures, working to the prescription of the Dentist for each patient.

Without the help of a Dental Technician, Dentists would not be able to offer the full range of services to their patients. The Dentist relies on his or her Technician very heavily. The Dental Technician works to a written prescription, but rarely meets the patient for whom he or she is ultimately working.

The majority of dental technicians are employed in commercial dental laboratories, but can also be employed within general dental practices, in hospitals, the community dental service and the armed forces.

Commercial dental laboratories range from single handed businesses, to large multi-site laboratories offering a comprehensive service. Technicians usually carry out work for a number of local practitioners. Some commercial laboratories offer a postal service, dealing with dentists from a wide area.

If a technician works within a dental hospital, it is usually in conjunction with the maxillofacial department. This may involve making large prostheses including eyes, nose and ears. If employed in a hospital, a dental technician may become involved in research, or may teach undergraduates some of the technical aspects of dentistry.

Q.50   What is dental hygienist?

Ans: Dental hygienists remove soft and hard deposits from teeth, teach patients how to practice good oral hygiene, and provide other preventive dental care. Hygienists examine patients' teeth and gums, recording the presence of diseases or abnormalities. They remove calculus, stains, and plaque from teeth; perform root planing as a periodontal therapy; take and develop dental

and periodontal dressings; remove sutures; and smooth and polish metal restorations. Although hygienists may not diagnose diseases, they can prepare clinical and laboratory diagnostic tests for the dentist to interpret. Hygienists sometimes work chair side with the dentist during treatment.

Dental hygienists also help patients develop and maintain good oral health. For example, they may explain the relationship between diet and oral health or inform patients how to select

Dental hygienists use hand and rotary instruments and ultrasonics to clean and polish teeth, x-ray machines to take dental pictures, syringes with needles to administer local anesthetics, and models of teeth to explain oral hygiene.

Q.51   What is dental assistant?

Ans:
chair side as dentists examine and treat patients. They make patients as comfortable as possible in the dental chair, prepare them for treatment, and obtain their dental records. Assistants hand instruments and materials to dentists and keep patients' mouths dry and clear by using suction or other devices. Assistants also sterilize and disinfect instruments and equipment, prepare trays of instruments for dental procedures, and instruct patients on postoperative and general oral health care.

Some dental assistants prepare materials for impressions and restorations, take dental x rays,

anesthetics to gums or cavity-preventive agents to teeth, remove excess cement used in the

Those with laboratory duties make casts of the teeth and mouth from impressions, clean and

payments, and order dental supplies and materials.

Dental assistants should not be confused with dental hygienists, who are licensed to perform different clinical tasks.

Q.52   What is nursing?

Ans:

caring with the science of health care. Nursing places its focus not only on a particular health problem, but on the whole patient and his or her response to treatment. Care of the patient and

Nurses are on the front lines of the health care delivery team. They independently assess and monitor patients, and taking a holistic approach, determine what patients need to attain and preserve their health. Nurses then provide care and, if needed, alert other health care professionals to assist. For instance, emergency department nurses triage all incoming patients, deciding which are the sickest and in what order they require the attention of other health care professionals. Thus, nurses coordinate care delivery by physicians, nurse practitioners, social workers, physical therapists and others. Nurses assess whether care is successful. If not, they create a different plan of action.

Nurses work in many different areas, but the common thread of nursing is the nursing process — the essential core of how a registered nurse delivers care.

This process involves 5 steps:

Assessment: collecting and analysing physical, psychological and sociocultural data about a patient

Diagnosis: making a judgment on the cause, condition and path of the illness

Planning:

Implementation: supervising or carrying out the actual treatment plan

Evaluation: continuous assessment of the plan

Q.53   How to Prepare for a Career in Nursing?

Ans:

sciences, but also how to plan, organise, and educate patients and their families. Students who wish to prepare for a nursing career should give particular attention to math, biology, and chemistry; computer science; and the behavioural and social sciences.

Nursing offers opportunities bedside practice to the president or top administrator of a healthcare organisation. Clinical specialist, nurse practitioner, nurse administrator and nurse educator are just a few examples of the variety of opportunities awaiting you in a nursing career. Nursing involves the care of people throughout the continuum of life and provides an essential service to humankind. As career professionals, nurses improve the quality of health care delivery.

Nursing Education: Registered Nurses must graduate from an accredited school of nursing. Nursing education includes study in nursing theory and techniques, the science and treatment of disease, and several specialty areas. It also includes hands-on clinical practice in hospitals or other settings.

The Bachelor of Science in Nursing (BSN) is a four-year university-based degree. It is strongly recommended as the base for the full range of nursing practice and responsibilities, in the widest number of settings.

Not all people enter nursing studies directly from high school. Today's students often enter

college part-time. For this reason, many nursing schools offer joint degree or ladder programs, or credit for relevant experience. Flexible scheduling is also more common.

The Indian Nursing Council is a statutory body constituted under the Indian Nursing Council Act, 1947. The Council is responsible for regulation and maintenance of a uniform standard of training for Nurses, Midwives, Auxiliary Nurse-Midwives and Health Visitors. The Council prescribes the syllabus and regulations for various nursing courses.

The inspection of Nursing Schools and Examination Centres is done to maintain uniformity and the requisite standard of Nursing Education in the country.

Nursing Specialties: There is a wide variety of nursing specialty areas; you will certainly be

psychiatric, school, public health, nurse-midwives, and others. Note that some specialty areas

Career Opportunities: The rapid changes in our nation's health care system also mean changes in nursing. Some traditional areas of nursing are currently cutting back, while new opportunities arise in others.

Nurses are needed not only in hospitals, but in home health agencies, long-term care facilities such as nursing homes, managed care centres, and in community health. Educating patients & their families in preventive care is highly important. Demands for advanced practice nurses are growing in many areas; some APNs are opening their own practices.

Nurses have never been more important to health care than they are today. They must be well-educated, adaptable, and able to act as patient advocates. Nurses should be prepared for leadership roles in managing resources to promote better health care for their patients, whatever the location or setting.

Q.54   What is pharmacy? How to opt pharmacy as a career?

Ans:

preparing from natural and synthetic sources, suitable and convenient materials for distribution

preservation, combination, analysis and standardisation of drugs and medicines besides synthesis of new drug molecules, manufacturing of various dosage forms, (Liquid orals, powders, tablets, capsules, ointments, injections, ophthalmic products, etc.) quality control, clinical trials, bio-availability, research, side-effects, compatibility, in-compatibility, indications, contra-indications, pharmacokinetics, pharmacodynamics, toxicology, etc.

Pharmacy is a specialised course and the various levels of education in Pharmacy after 10+2 are as under:

Nature of level of education in Pharmacy	Eligibility for admns. to course	Duration of the course
Diploma in Pharmacy (D. Pharm)	10 + 2	2 Years Regular course
Bachelor in Pharmacy (B.Pharm)	10 + 2	4 Years regular course
Master in Pharmacy (M. Pharm)	B. Pharm	2 Years regular course (Minimum 3 semester course)
Doctorate in Pharmacy (Ph.D)	M. Pharm	Regular course but the duration depends upon the completion of the research work.

The curriculum of pharmacy education has been designed to produce the following professional categories of pharmacists having specialised knowledge —

patient and will counsel the patient on various facets of drugs like usage, side effects, indication, contra-indication, compatibilities, in-compatibilities, storage, dosage, etc. Such category of pharmacists will have more opportunity to interact closely with the prescriber, i.e. doctor and hence can promote the rational prescribing and use of drugs. He can also control the hospital manufacture and procurement of drugs to ensure the supply of high quality products.

research, etc.

i.e. manufacture of various dosage forms, analysis and quality control, clinical trials, post-marketing surveillance, patent application and drug registration, sales and marketing.

authorities and pharmaceutical systems.

Q.55   What is Occupational Therapy (OPT)? What an occupational therapist do?

Ans: "Occupational therapists assess occupational performance and modify human and environmental conditions to maintain, restore or enhance occupational performance and health. Occupational performance means the ability to choose, organise, and effectively and safely perform everyday activities necessary for self-care and participation in educational, leisure, home management and work activities." (Occupational Therapists Regulation, BC, December, 1998)

Occupational therapists help people to overcome physical, psychological or social problems arising from illness or disability, by concentrating on what they are able to achieve, rather than

lifestyle and environment. For example, he or she might have problems with everyday tasks such as washing, dressing or cooking, or might need help with getting back to work after an accident. Together with the client, the occupational therapist would write a treatment plan, based on the client's own needs and expectations. They then provide whatever help is needed, whether practical advice about disability equipment, teaching personal coping strategies or using activities to stimulate clients who are de-motivated or depressed.

Occupational therapists work with people of all ages and from all walks of life, and take all aspects of a person's life and environment into consideration. Occupational therapists consult with clients and their families throughout the course of therapy.

(1) They take stock of persons' abilities from physical, mental, emotional, social and environmental points of view.

(2) They identify and prevent circumstances that would make further limit a person's abilities.

(3) They identify challenges and work with clients to set goals to meet those challenges.

(4) They recommend assistive devices and technologies to overcome or compensate for a person's limitations. (www.aota.org)

Q.56   What is Physiotherapy?

Ans: Physiotherapy is an allied health care profession dedicated to allowing patients to achieve the highest level of physical functioning by providing a personalised treatment plan based on individual needs. Physiotherapy in humans is common and well accepted, and more recently

Physiotherapy as the name suggests is the treatment of differing conditions by physical means. This may be by stretching, strengthening, relearning movement patterns, manipulation, massage or by using some electrotherapeutic modalities such as ultrasound or interferential. Whatever is eventually used nothing is done until a comprehensive examination and assessment is carried out. This may take up to an hour. It is usual for people to be taught a little about the mechanism of their problem so that they can see the purpose of various exercises they will almost inevitably be asked to do. In some instances supportive or corrective taping may be used for a time and if this is a long term problem patients will be shown how to do this for themselves. Understanding some basic biomechanics can be extremely helpful in dealing with the endemic spinal problems we all encounter. Advice will be given about the use of various supports, braces, etc., needed by some conditions as well as ergonomic advice for both work, home and sporting environment.

Physiotherapy may be appropriate in the following situations:

Sprains or strains of any joint

Neck or back pain

Following fractures

Following surgery including joint replacement

A physiotherapist has a specialised university education, which focuses intensively in Anatomy, Physiology, Biomechanics, Histology, Orthopedics, Neurology, and Pathology. Specialised training also includes in depth joint biomechanics of the spine and extremities, as well as muscle insertions origins and actions. They are able to assess and treat joint, spine, muscular, and neurological dysfunctions.

Q.57   What is genetics?

Ans: Genes are at the very heart of life. Together they constitute the blueprint of an organism. In computer terms they are the master programme of life. They decide all the properties and all the capabilities of an organism.

Genetics is the study of what make up animals or plants. DNA carries all the information needed for protein synthesis and replication of cells. In living organisms DNA is organised in chromosomes and is located in the nucleus of each cell.

DNA is the genetic material in all known forms of life. DNA contains genes (just as a recipe book contains recipes) that give us many of our physical characteristics. However, we are not simply gene-based machines — the environment we are in also determines our traits.

Q.58   What is Genetic Engineering?

Ans: Genetic engineering is an umbrella term which can cover a wide range of ways of changing the genetic material, "the DNA code" in a living organism. This code contains all the information, stored in a long chain chemical molecule, which determines the nature of the organism, "whether it is an amoeba, a pine tree, a robin, an octopus, a cow or a human being" and which characterises the particular individual. Apart from identical twins, your detailed genetic make-up is unique to you. Individual genes are particular sections of this chain, spaced out along with it, which determine the characteristics and functions of our body. Defects of individual genes can cause a malfunction in the metabolism of the body, and are the roots of many "genetic" diseases.

of genetic engineering, some occur natural and others are man made. Genetic engineering in the current state is a relatively new science and the effects of which are not yet known. This causes controversy as to whether or not genetic engineering is safe or ethical.

The types of genetic engineering that most people would not think of in this way have been

or Survival of the Fittest as it is sometimes known is when the environment in a way chooses the trait that is best suited to the current environment and allows animals with that trait to reproductively mature and reproduce. This is nature's way of ensuring survival and is a form of

spring. An example of this is the domestic dogs all of which descended from the wolf family

The more well-known and controversial genetic engineering is playing round with humans cell in hope of producing cures to diseases or clones, and the insertion of genes into human food to make the food better.

Cloning is a branch of genetic engineering, which is concerned with breeding individuals, which are identical to their parents. This is done by transferring a replication of the DNA of whom you wish to clone into the gamete of the cloned organism. The cloned organism then grows up to be identical to the parent.

The purposes of doing genetic engineering are many and various. These include:

(1) To repair a genetic "defect" (as with the current early trials of gene therapy in humans).

(2) To enhance an effect already natural to that organism and to increase its growth rate.

(3) To increase resistance to disease or external damage from anything in its natural environment.

(4) To enable animal or plant, to do something it would not normally do.

(5) Getting a micro-organism to produce human insulin for diabetics, or a sheep to produce a human blood-clotting protein in her milk.

(6) Getting a tomato to ripen without going squashy, this can be done simply by taking one of its own genes, turning its "pattern" upside down and putting it back again.

The list above simply gives some ideas of what is or might be technically possible. It says nothing of whether that is ethically or socially desirable. Hand-in-hand with technology must go an ethical evaluation. Early trials with growth enhanced pigs revealed disastrous side-effects for the animal. Do we need non-squashy tomatoes? But would it be wrong not to develop a means of producing a vital human therapeutic protein in sheep's milk, if we knew how? Should we develop armies of super warriors, like the warrior in the movie *the Fifth Element*, who had addition genes to make her super human? Should we develop super genius people that may consider everyone else inferior to them, and make the rest of us their slaves? Maybe some one will clone an army of onself, and tried to take over the world. I leave you with these thoughts, is this future science,

Q.59   What is Genomics?

Ans: All the characteristics of a plant, insect or fungus are described in its genome. The relatively

and their function.

Recent advances in genomics are bringing about a revolution in our understanding of the molecular mechanisms of disease, including the complex interplay of genetic and environmental factors. Genomics is also stimulating the discovery of breakthrough healthcare products by revealing thousands of new biological targets for the development of drugs, and by giving scientists innovative ways to design new drugs, vaccines and DNA diagnostics. Genomics-based therapeutics include "traditional" small chemical drugs, protein drugs and potentially gene therapy.

Q.60   I want to take up a career in Biotechnology. Kindly let me know what is Biotechnology?

Ans:

quarter century. It is an interdisciplinary science including not only biology but also subjects like mathematics, physics, chemistry, engineering and many more. It is also a conglomeration of various combined technologies applied to living cells for production of a particular product or enhancing its quality according to our preferences.

Biotechnology is a set of powerful tools that employ living organisms (or part of organisms) to

"Early biotechnology includes traditional animal and plant breeding techniques, and the use of yeast in making bread, beer, and wine."

"Modern biotechnology includes the industrial or pharmaceutical use of recombinant DNA, cell fusion, novel bioprocessing techniques, and bioremediation."

Q.61 What is bioinformatics?

Ans: Bioinformatics is an integration of mathematical, statistical and computer methods to analyze biological, biochemical and biophysical data. It is the science of developing computer databases and algorithms for the purpose of speeding up and enhancing biological research. Bioinformatics is being used most noticeably in the Human Genome Project, the effort to identify the 80,000 genes in human DNA. New academic programs are training students in Bioinformatics by providing them with backgrounds in molecular biology and in computer science, including database design and analytical approaches. Bioinformatics is a combination of Computer Science, Information Technology and Genetics to determine and analyze genetic information.

Bioinformatics is the application of computer technology to the management of biological information. Computers are used to gather, store, analyse and integrate biological and genetic information which can then be applied to gene-based drug discovery and development. The need for Bioinformatics capabilities has been precipitated by the explosion of publicly available genomic information resulting from the Human Genome Project. The science of Bioinformatics, which is the melding of molecular biology with computer science, is essential to the use of

targets for drug discovery.

Q.62 What does a bioinformatician do?

Ans: That varies! Some bioinformatics professionals are adept at using computer software packages that help design experiments, model complex biological systems/pathways/molecules and analyse copious amounts of data. Other bioinformaticians design and develop algorithms, software, and/or database systems to aid in managing biological information, data analysis or

bioinformaticians serve as liaisons (or analysts) between scientists and software engineers. There are also positions that involve training users and supporting commercial biotech/bioinformatics

biological experimental systems are yielding vast quantities of data, and bioinformaticians play a key role in managing this data, and helping sift through the data to produce meaningful biological information.

Q.63 What is a Medical Transcriptionist?

Ans: A Medical Transcriptionist is often also called a "Medical Language Specialist." A Medical Transcriptionist, or "MT" is a person who assists physicians and specialty surgeons usually by transcribing, formatting, and proofreading their dictated medically-oriented reports. Most commonly, MTs transcribe physicians' dictation that outlines a patient's health. In simple words Medical Transcriptionist type (transcribe) what the doctor or medical specialist dictates regarding

handwrite notes on each individual patient, thus dictating a summary is the normal procedure.

subsequent visits and thus relies heavily on their completeness and accuracy.

or as self-employed independent contractors. Working for self is perhaps the most challenging of all the above mentioned medical transcription opportunities. It requires the highest level of determination, discipline, and dependability to do well. The independent contractor must sharply hone his/her medical language skill, as under this situation he/she is working "without a net" when it comes to producing quality work without supervision.

It certainly is helpful to be a good typist but this is not the primary requirement. Medical transcription is not a "keyboard" specialty, but rather a knowledge of medical language. It is essential to possess good English grammar, punctuation, and spelling skills. Likewise, the successful transcriptionist must develop excellent listening abilities and what is "audio acuity".

is the foundation of being a good medical transcriptionist.

Q.64   What all skills do I need to become a Medical Transcriptionist?

Ans: Some of the general skills you will need are: Being able type, or more correctly

good knowledge of general language skills such as your language's grammar, spelling, and punctuation rules, and writing styles; a good knowledge of medical terms, medical phrases,

anatomy and physiology; a knowledge of basic business principles if you are planning to work in your own business at home.

Q.65   Do I need to be formally trained to perform Medical Transcription?

Ans: The job of a medical transcriptionist may seem simple: to take notes on doctor's recordings

education in order to understand the language used by these highly trained personnel. It is for this reason that most employers require a postsecondary degree in medical transcription or an associate's degree, with classes varying from anatomy to punctuation and the English language.

If you are an intelligent person you may be able to learn on your own all the medical knowledge required to become an MT. However, in order to be sure that you are educating yourself in an appropriate manner, it is probably best to at least take a short course in Medical Transcription.

Q.66   Do I need some kind of accreditation, certificate, diploma, or license?

Ans:

require that you have a business license. However completion of one of the professional courses will help prepare you for taking exams for accreditation from an association such as American Association of Medical Transcriptonist (AAMT).

Q.67   What is Microbiology?

Ans: Microbiology is the study of microorganisms. These microorganisms include: bacteria (that's the Latin plural for bacterium); viruses (that's the non-Latin plural for virus-virii sounds weird, so I don't say it); and, fungi (that's the Latin plural for fungus — which by now you have guessed, or already knew, and may not be all that interested to know, anyway). Microbiology is actually made up of several sub-disciplines which individually may stand alone, because there is so much to learn in each. These disciplines include: Immunology (the study of the immune system and how it works to protect us from harmful organisms and harmful substances produced by them); Virology, the study of viruses, and how they function inside cells; Pathogenic Microbiology, the study of disease-causing critters and the disease process; Microbial Genetics, the study of gene function, expression, and regulation ; Microbial Physiology, the study of biochemical mechanisms within bacteria.

agriculture (soil fertility, plant disease, animal health), biotechnology (microorganisms as

introducing them into plants or animals) and food technology (food production and spoilage). Microbiologists are employed in a variety of occupations:

Q.68   How do I study microbiology?

Ans: You can enroll in anyone of a number of different degree programs at undergraduate level and then do further studies in Microbiology at Masters level. Some of the undergraduate courses through which you can prepare a career in Microbiology are:

Q.69   What is applied Microbiology?

Ans: For at least the last 3 billion years, microorganisms have been the dominant habitants on earth. Though invisible to the human eye, microorganisms like bacteria, fungi and viruses inhabit almost every niche on the planet, from hypersaline lakes to subsurface freshwater aquifers, to deep oceanic thermal vents. These tiny, pervasive organisms have a huge effect on life on the planet and have formed the subject of microbiology for about the last three hundred years.

Applied microbiology studies the ways in which the microbial world interacts with our own.

from food production, to pest control, to industrial applications, to medicinal uses.

A major in applied microbiology provides a broad background in the study of microbes and how they relate to agriculture, industry, biotechnology and the environment.

Q.70 What is Human Biology?

Ans: Human Biology is concerned with understanding the human condition from a primarily biological point of view. It takes a holistic view — drawing together all the specialised disciplines that study humans and appreciating that for a full understanding we must do more than merely sum the parts. For convenience, it can be viewed as encompassing three broad areas:

(a) The structure, function & development of the human body

(b) The evolution, variation & ecology of humans

(c) The interrelationships between biology and culture

The distinguishing feature of the discipline is its multidisciplinary approach, with a focus on the interrelationships and interactions between the multitudes of disciplines that study humans.

Sciences can, for convenience, be categorised into two types. Most biological sciences are primarily reductionist in their approach, developing understanding of how things work by examining the components of life in ever-increasing detail.

Human Biology is characterised by a holistic approach, appreciating that life is more than the physical and chemical processes that underlay it. However, these views are relative — chemistry is a holistic science compared to sub-atomic physics — and a holistic approach cannot be effective without detailed knowledge. Human Biology must, like other sciences, have strong reductionist elements.

Human Biologists are specialists — in bringing together the disparate sub-components that contribute to the human condition so that we can more fully understand how humans function and behave, and how these processes arose.

Q.71 What is a Pathologist?

Ans: A pathologist is a medical doctor who examines tissues and is responsible for the accuracy of laboratory tests. Pathologists interpret the results of these examinations and tests-information that is important for the patient's diagnosis and recovery. The pathologist and the patient's other doctors consult on which tests to order, test results, and appropriate treatments. Pathologists play a vital role on the patient's primary health care team.

Pathologists are problem-solvers, fascinated by the process of disease and eager to unlock medical mysteries, like AIDS and diabetes, using the tools of laboratory medicine and its sophisticated

is detected and treated, the greater the chance of a cure and the more cost-effective the treatment. Pathology plays a particularly important role in preventive medicine by ruling out diseases or detecting them early. For example, by reporting a high cholesterol level found with a blood test, the pathologist can help the patient's physician control the condition and prevent a heart attack or stroke.

Thirty years ago, physicians had relatively few laboratory tests to use to detect disease. With

technologists and other laboratory personnel work with pathologists to insure that these tests are available to your physician when and where they are needed, and that the results are accurate. Pathologists often help to determine which test is most effective for a complete diagnosis.

Some tests, such as a glucose test, produce results that are understood by all physicians. Others require specialised professional interpretation by an expert, usually a pathologist. All tissues removed at biopsy or surgery is examined under the microscope by a pathologist who makes a diagnosis. Pathologists assist surgeons during operations by providing immediate diagnoses on biopsies (sometimes called frozen sections) — specially treated tissues removed in surgery and rushed to the lab. The pathologist quickly provides information to help the surgeons complete the operation in a way that assures the best result possible for the patient.

Pathologists work in many areas of the medical laboratory, and a pathologist usually serves as Director of the Laboratory. In the blood bank, pathologists and medical technologists insure that the blood or blood products which you receive are safe for you. In microbiology, microorganisms-

effective drugs to treat a particular infection can be determined.

In clinical chemistry, many hundreds of tests are available which measure the amounts of

In immunology, tests that measure the body's response to infection or disease are performed. Many infections, including hepatitis and AIDS, are diagnosed by detecting the antibodies that the

sclerosis, the body actually makes antibodies against itself.

A popular perception is that the pathologist's major responsibility is performing autopsies. Although an autopsy is an important part of the diagnosis and treatment of deadly diseases and provides valuable information to the patient's doctor and family, it is only a small part of the typical pathologist's practice. Pathologists who specialise in performing autopsies to investigate unexpected or suspicious deaths and determine the causes are known as forensic pathologists or medical examiners.

Some pathologists devote their careers to research in pathology, developing new tests and new instruments to better diagnose diseases.

Pathologists often teach their specialty in medical school pathology programs to educate all physicians, future pathologists, and other students in the medical laboratory professions — medical technologists, cytotechnologists, histotechnologists/histologic technicians, and medical laboratory technicians. After completing four years of medical school, pathologists need four

pathologists also undertake additional training in a subspecialty of pathology.

Q.72   Who is a Psychologist? What is Clinical Psychology?

Ans: Psychologist studies the mind and human behaviour; provides counseling and therapy to those suffering from emotional, learning or behavioural problems, gathers data from tests, observations and interviews with patients and develops a treatment plan.

which applies psychological principles to the assessment, prevention, amelioration, and rehabilitation of psychological distress, disability, dysfunctional behaviour, and health-risk behaviour, and to the enhancement of psychological and physical well-being.

and clinical service, focusing on the study and care of clients, and information gathered from

Clinical psychology is a broad approach to human problems (both individual and interpersonal) consisting of assessment, diagnosis, consultation, treatment, programme development, administration, and research with regard to numerous populations, including children, adolescents, adults, the elderly, families, groups, and disadvantaged persons. There is overlap between some areas of clinical

social work.

Clinical psychology is devoted to the principles of human welfare and professional conduct as outlined in the Code of Ethics for Psychologists. According to this code the activities of clinical psychologists are directed toward: respect for the dignity of persons; responsible caring; integrity in relationships; and responsibility to society.

The training of clinical psychologists requires course work, practical experience, and research, of biological, social, cognitive, and affective bases of behaviour, as well as individual differences, statistics, and research methodology. These areas of psychological knowledge are not unique to clinical psychology, but are generic, and overlap with other areas of professional psychology (such as clinical neuropsychology or counselling psychology), as well as other disciplines, such as sociology and biology.

The knowledge base of clinical psychology is obtained through undergraduate and graduate training,

ability to develop and manage a helping relationship with clients (individuals, couples, groups, organisations, and systems) is an integral part of the knowledge base of clinical psychology.

The knowledge base within clinical psychology is so broad that no individual clinical psychologist can become competent in all areas of clinical psychology. Therefore, clinical psychologists must

expected to clearly acknowledge the limitations of their scope of practice. Clinical psychologists are responsible for referring to others (either within or outside the area of clinical psychology) when they are faced with a task outside of the limits of their knowledge and skill.

Q.73   What is Nutrition and Dietetics?

Ans:
buxom women who were considered healthy. Nowadays, being thin is in. The young girls and

On the other side, the tale is far less romantic. The sedentary lifestyle coupled with stress, strain and tensions of all kinds have given rise to a wide range of ailments and maladies like hypertension, diabetes, cholesterol, spondilitis, angina, heart attacks and so forth. These problems have generated a global awareness about the need to stay healthy by selecting one's daily diet with abundant caution. This is exactly where the nutritionists and dieticians step in to teach people the art of healthy living at no extra cost. A nutritionist:

Assesses nutritional needs and food patterns
Plans and directs the food appropriate for physical and dietary needs
Provides nutrition counseling
Helps to prevent and treat illnesses by promoting healthy eating habits and recommending

Clinical nutritionists provide nutritional services to patients in institutions such as hospitals and nursing care facilities

Q.74 What is Radiography? What does a radiographer do? What is the employment opportunity of a Radiographer and where can one complete a course in Radiography?

Ans:

in November of 1895, a revolution in medical diagnosis was begun. Suddenly the inner realms of the body, hidden and inaccessible but by the knife, became visible and could be recorded on

after it traverses through the body. Today, radiographers are those responsible for the production of radiographs and other types of medical images.

The radiographer, who may also be referred to as a radiologic technologist, is an individual who

who is specially trained in the interpretation of medical images and medical imaging procedures.

The radiographer is responsible for the quality of the images. This includes manipulating the

exposure factors. This also includes placing the patient in the most advantageous position for the demonstration of the anatomy of interest. And, very importantly, the radiographer is responsible for doing this with as little radiation exposure to the patient as possible. The radiographer receives extensive training in human anatomy as well as radiation physics, radiographic exposure,

Most radiographers work in hospital radiology (medical imaging) departments. In this type of setting, modalities such as CT, MRI, ultrasound, nuclear medicine and cardiovascular-interventional procedures are commonly found alongside routine diagnostic radiographic rooms. Diagnostic

GI & urological studies, and will also cover emergency and surgical needs. Radiographers may

The outlook for employment is excellent for radiography graduates today. A nationwide boom of

providing unprecedented options and opportunities for employment.

There is also employment scope in Industrial radiography. Industrial Radiography is the examination of things using radiation, usually either x-rays or gamma rays. Today the term Industrial Radiography normally refers to the radiography of components, welds or castings to check their integrity and assure their safety in use. X-rays have been used for this purpose almost

smaller as time went on and the techniques became of vital importance during the Second World War. Since then, in spite of other, newer methods of inspection now taking over from radiography, the medium is still the best and sometimes the only technique for many applications.

You can study a 3-years B.Sc. course in radiology at University College of Medical Sciences (University of Delhi) & GTB Hospital, Delhi-110095. The eligibility for admission is (10+2) with Physics, Chemistry, Biology and English securing at least 50% marks in aggregate. Admission is through a competitive entrance examination.

Q.75 What is Medical Laboratory Technician? Tell in detail about MLT.

Ans: A medical laboratory technician performs general tests in all laboratory areas. The medical laboratory technician performs general tests in all laboratory areas — Blood banking, Chemistry, Hematology, Immunology and Microbiology. Working with the supervision of a medical technologist, a medical laboratory technician hunts for clues to the absence, presence, extent, and causes of diseases.

Medical laboratory technicians must be accurate, dedicated and skilled. They must also be self-motivated, and take the initiative to do what must be done everyday — to pitch in to help the healthcare team.

All medical laboratory technicians have certain common characteristics. They are problem solvers. They like challenge and responsibility. They are accurate, reliable, emotionally stable,

both in writing and speaking. They set high standards for themselves and expect quality in the work they do. Above all, they are deeply committed to their profession, and are truly fascinated by all that science has to offer.

The challenges and rewards of medicine and science—the medical laboratory technician have the best of both worlds. For someone who chooses a career as a medical laboratory technician, the exploration never ends.

The future long-term employment for medical laboratory technicians looks bright. Employment opportunities are expected to increase through the year 2005 and beyond. Medical laboratory

nursing homes, public health facilities, business and industry currently have positions open for

bright well into the next decade. The need is great everywhere throughout the country.

Career-preparation: To prepare for a career as a medical laboratory technician, you should have a solid foundation in high school sciences — biology, chemistry, math and computer science. You'll need a combination of formal education plus clinical education in a medical laboratory technician

(MLT) program. With a career as a medical laboratory technician, you'll have unlimited choices. Unlike many other careers, your education in medical laboratory technology will prepare you directly for a job. While doing a MLT course, you can work part-time in a laboratory to earn extra money. And you could start working full-time the day after you graduate.

Opportunities for Advancement: The medical technologist performs a full range of laboratory tests, from the most routine to the most complex, with little or no supervision. Medical

exploration.

Different types of courses are available in our country to become a Medical Laboratory Technician. They are:

(1) 3-years B.Sc. (MLT) after 10+2 with Physics, Chemistry & Biology
(2) 2-years Diploma after 10+2 with PCB

Q.76 What is optometry?

Ans: Optometrists examine people's eyes to diagnose vision problems and eye diseases. They use instruments and observation to examine eye health and to test patients' visual acuity, depth and colour perception, and their ability to focus and coordinate the eyes. They analyze test results and develop a treatment plan. Optometrists prescribe eyeglasses and contact lenses, and provide vision therapy and low-vision rehabilitation. They use drugs for diagnosis of eye vision problems and prescribe drugs to treat some eye diseases. Optometrists often provide pre- and post-operative care to cataract and other eye surgery patients. They also diagnose conditions due to systemic diseases such as diabetes and high blood pressure, and refer patients to other health practitioners as needed.

Optometrists should not be confused with ophthalmologists or dispensing opticians. Ophthalmologists are physicians who perform eye surgery and diagnose and treat eye diseases and injuries. Like optometrists, they also examine eyes and prescribe eyeglasses and contact

according to prescriptions written by ophthalmologists or optometrists.

Most optometrists are in general practice. Some specialise in work with the elderly, children, or partially sighted persons who need specialised visual devices to improve their vision. Others develop and implement ways to protect workers' eyes from on-the-job strain or injury. Some specialise in contact lenses, sports vision, or vision therapy. A few teach optometry, do research, or consult.

Most optometrists are private practitioners who also handle the business aspects of running

equipment and supplies. Optometrists who operate franchise optical stores may also have some of these duties.

Requirements for admission to schools of optometry include courses in english, mathematics, physics, chemistry, and biology. A few schools require or recommend courses in psychology, history, sociology, speech, or business. Applicants must take the Optometry Admissions Test, after their sophomore or junior year. Competition for admission is keen.

Employment of optometrists is expected to grow about as fast as the average for all occupations through the year 2008 in response to the vision care needs of a growing and aging population. The demand for optometric services will also increase because of growth in the oldest age group, with their increased likelihood of cataracts, glaucoma, diabetes, and hypertension. Employment of optometrists will also grow due to greater recognition of the importance of vision care, rising personal incomes, and growth in employee vision care plans.

Employment of optometrists would grow more rapidly were it not for anticipated productivity gains which will allow each optometrist to see more patients. These gains will result from greater use of optometric assistants and other support personnel, and the introduction of new equipment and procedures. New surgical procedures using lasers are available that can correct some vision problems, but they remain expensive.

In addition to growth, the need to replace optometrists who leave the occupation will create employment opportunities. Relatively few opportunities from this source are expected, however, because most optometrists continue to practice until they retire; few would transfer to other occupations.

Q.77   What is nuclear medicine?

Ans: Nuclear Medicine involves the use of radioactive isotopes (radioisotopes) to prevent, diagnose, and treat disease. Radioisotopes are utilised in diagnosis as a standard practice worldwide, and have been used for over 60 years. Therapeutic uses (for treating disease) are growing as more treatments are discovered and developed.

Diagnostic Nuclear Medicine: In nuclear medicine diagnosing techniques, very small amounts

organs, bones or tissues, the emissions they produce can provide crucial information about a particular type of cancer or disease. Information gathered during a nuclear medicine technique is more comprehensive than other procedures because it describes organ function, not just structure. The result is that many diseases and cancers can be diagnosed much earlier.

Because nuclear medicine procedures utilise very small doses of short-lived isotopes (ones that only stay radioactive for a few hours or days), the amount of radiation received is generally less than or equal to that of an x-ray. Whole body and healthy tissue doses can be minimised while the radioisotope is targeted toward the affected tissue or organ.

Therapeutic Nuclear Medicine: During the last decade, major progress has been made in the treatment of disease with radioisotopes. Treatments involving the use of medical isotopes are gaining momentum in the race against many types of cancer. Currently the most common therapeutic uses of medical isotopes are for treatment of thyroid and prostate cancer, hyperthyroidism, cancer bone pain, and polycythaemia (abnormal red cell and blood increase). The major use in Europe is for treatment of arthritis.

Some of the most exciting cancer treatments utilising medical isotopes are emerging from current research being conducted on cutting-edge medical applications.

Certain experimental treatments have had such remarkable success that current cancer sufferers should be made aware of their potential. Lives have been saved in numerous cases of patients with fatal brain tumors, lymphomas and leukemias. In several clinical trials testing experimental treatments, very positive results were achieved on patients who had exhausted all other treatment options with no success.

Cancer therapies involving radioisotopes may well lead the way into a new future for millions around the world who would have otherwise been given little or no hope. The Nuclear Medicine Research Council is proud to facilitate greater awareness of these promising developments.

In nuclear medicine, radionuclides—unstable atoms that emit radiation spontaneously—are used

radiopharmaceuticals. Nuclear medicine technologists administer these radiopharmaceuticals to patients, then monitor the characteristics and functions of tissues or organs in which they localise. Abnormal areas show higher or lower concentrations of radioactivity than normal.

Nuclear medicine technologists operate cameras that detect and map the radioactive drug in the

diagnostic imaging equipment, but their equipment creates an image by projecting an x-ray through the patient.

Nuclear medicine technologists explain test procedures to patients. They prepare a dosage of the radiopharmaceutical and administer it by mouth, injection, or other means. When preparing radiopharmaceuticals, technologists adhere to safety standards that keep the radiation dose to workers and patients as low as possible.

Technologists position patients and start a gamma scintillation camera, or scanner, which creates images of the distribution of a radiopharmaceutical as it localises in and emits signals from the

to interpret. Some nuclear medicine studies, such as cardiac function studies, are processed with the aid of a computer.

Nuclear medicine technologists also perform radioimmunoassay studies which assess the behaviour of a radioactive substance inside the body. For example, technologists may add radioactive substances to blood or serum to determine levels of hormones or therapeutic drug content.

Technologists keep patient records and record the amount and type of radionuclides received, used, and disposed of.

associate programs in community colleges; and bachelor's programs in 4-year colleges and in universities. Courses cover physical sciences, the biological effects of radiation exposure, radiation protection and procedures, the use of radiopharmaceuticals, imaging techniques, and computer applications.

and ultrasound technologists wishing to specialise in nuclear medicine. They also attract medical program, a 2-year associate program, or a 4-year bachelor's program.

Technologists may advance to supervisor, then to chief technologist, and to department administrator or director. Some technologists specialize in a clinical area such as nuclear cardiology or computer analysis or leave patient care to take positions in research laboratories. Some become instructors or directors in nuclear medicine technology programs, a step that usually requires a bachelor's degree or a master's in nuclear medicine technology. Others leave the occupation to work as sales

Employment of nuclear medicine technologists is expected to grow about as fast as the average for all occupations through the year 2008. The number of openings each year will be very low because the occupation is small. Growth will arise from an increase in the number of middle-aged and older persons who are the primary users of diagnostic procedures, including nuclear medicine tests. Nonetheless, job seekers will face more competition for jobs than in the recent past. In an attempt to employ fewer technologists and lower labor costs, hospitals have begun to merge nuclear medicine and radiologic technology departments. Consequently, opportunities will be best for technologists who can perform both nuclear medicine and radiologic procedures.

Technological innovations may increase the diagnostic uses of nuclear medicine. One example is the use of radiopharmaceuticals in combination with monoclonal antibodies to detect cancer at far earlier stages than is customary today, and without resorting to surgery. Another is the use of radionuclides to examine the heart's ability to pump blood. Wider use of nuclear medical imaging to observe metabolic and biochemical changes for neurology, cardiology, and oncology procedures, will also spur some demand for nuclear medicine technologists.

On the other hand, cost considerations will affect the speed with which new applications of nuclear medicine grow. Some promising nuclear medicine procedures, such as positron emission tomography, are extremely costly, and hospitals contemplating them will have to consider equipment costs, reimbursement policies, and the number of potential users.

Q.78 What is Prosthetic and Orthotic Engineering?

Ans: Prosthetics is a term derived from the Greek pros (in addition to), tithenai (to put) and tics (a systematic pursuit). Literally, prosthetics is the systematic pursuit of putting one thing (an

Orthotics is a term derived from the Greek ortho (straight, normal) and tics (a systematic pursuit). Literally, orthotics is the systematic pursuit of straightening or correcting limbs or the spine. Orthotics then is the systematic pursuit of straightening or correcting by applying to the body exoskeletal devices that limit or assist motion of any given segment of the human body. Limitation may mean anything from zero degrees (immobilisation) to anything less than the normal range of motion, whereas assistance of motion may be throughout the normal range or and fabricating orthopedic braces and support systems. Prosthetic and orthotic Engineering is combination of medicine, engineering and related sciences that uses technological systems to solve the rehabilitation problems of handicapped people.

Q.79   What is 'The Science and Technology of Speech and Hearing'?

Ans:

the perception of speech and other sounds by humans, and the analysis of speech sounds by machines. We are interested in how speech sounds are made, how these sounds are used to

sounds are analysed by the human hearing mechanism, how humans and machines can recover the linguistic content of speech sounds.

applications, for example: the generation of speech by machine, the recognition of speech by

their voice, the rehabilitation of hearing impairment, etc.

Q.80   What is Linguistics?

Ans: In its broadest sense, Linguistics is the study of human language: how it is structured, how it is used to represent meaning, how it is used to communicate ideas, how it is formed, how it is decoded. Linguistics tries to look for commonality across all human languages, and shouldn't be confused with 'Language Teaching' which aims to teach a single language. It is confusing that an expert in languages is called a 'linguist', since it leaves no name for an expert in Linguistics — maybe he should be called a 'linguistician'!

Syntax: The study of the grammatical form of sentences: what makes the sentence "he gave the book to Mary" have the form of a typical English sentence, while the sentence "gave he book the Mary to" does not?

Semantics: The study of the meaning of sentences: in the sentence "he gave the book to Mary" what was happening? Who was doing the giving? Who was doing the receiving?

Pragmatics: The study of how sentences are used to communicate: what are the rules of discourse that mean we can follow each other's conversations; why when someone asks you "Can you tell me the time?" you don't answer "yes" or "no".

Morphology: The study of the form of words: how groups of words share related meanings through regular patterning: what links "like", "likes", "liked", "likeness", "likely", "likelihood"?

Phonology: The study of the pronunciation of words and sentences: what basic sounds are used by a language, what regular patterning occurs in words; why does the sound used at the end of the word "sing" not occur at the beginning of a word?

Phonetics: The study of the production of speech by the human vocal mechanisms: how are sounds made, how do speakers of different accents differ.

Psycholinguistics: The study of the mental processes by which sentences are constructed and decoded by human beings.

Sociolinguistics: The study of how language variation is related to its use in society to form groups of geographical region, economic class or ethnicity.

Computational linguistics: The study of how computers can be used to analyse and generate sentences.

Other areas include the history of linguistics and the application of linguistic theory in language teaching.

Q.81   What is Phonetics?

Ans: Phonetics is the study of speech. It is concerned with how speech sounds can be categorised, how they are generated in the human vocal tract, why they each sound different to a listener, and how a listener is able to recognise them. The study of the organisation of speech sounds in a language is called phonology, while the study of how humans use their vocal apparatus to speak is called articulatory phonetics. The study of the quality of the sounds used to signal different pronunciations is called acoustic phonetics, while the study of how we perceive

of study in which instruments are used to study speech production and perception is called experimental phonetics

Q.82   What is Audiology?

Ans:
the screening, assessment and diagnosis of hearing disorder, and in the provision of hearing aids and other aspects of rehabilitation.

Q.83   What is Speech Therapy?

Ans:
concerned with disorders of human communication. Speech and Language therapists are involved in the assessment of people with a communication problem, and the provision of therapy. Since communication problems have many causes, a speech and language therapist has to have a wide knowledge of how human linguistic communication works and can fail. Common disorders include: Aphasia — problems in language construction or decoding; Dyspraxia — problems in

stuttering); Dysphonia — problems with the generation of voice in the larynx; and Dyslexia — problems with reading. Common causes of communication disorders include head injury, hearing loss and stroke; although a number seem to have a genetic component.

Q.84   What is medical assistant and what jobs a medical assistant performs?
Ans:
physicians, podiatrists, chiropractors, and other health practitioners running smoothly. They should not be confused with physician assistants, who examine, diagnose, and treat patients under the direct

the location and size of the practice and the practitioner's specialty. In small practices, medical assistants usually are "generalists," handling both administrative and clinical duties and reporting

specialise in a particular area, under the supervision of department administrators.

Medical assistants perform many administrative duties, including answering telephones, greeting

correspondence, scheduling appointments, arranging for hospital admission and laboratory services, and handling billing and bookkeeping.

Clinical duties vary according to State law and include taking medical histories and recording vital signs, explaining treatment procedures to patients, preparing patients for examination, and assisting the physician during the examination. Medical assistants collect and prepare laboratory specimens or perform basic laboratory tests on the premises, dispose of contaminated supplies, and sterilise medical instruments. They instruct patients about medications and special

directed, telephone prescriptions to a pharmacy, draw blood, prepare patients for x rays, take electrocardiograms, remove sutures, and change dressings.

Medical assistants also may arrange examining-room instruments and equipment, purchase and maintain supplies and equipment, and keep waiting and examining rooms neat and clean.

Assistants who specialise have additional duties. Podiatric medical assistants make castings of feet, expose and develop x rays, and assist podiatrists in surgery. Ophthalmic medical assistants help ophthalmologists provide eye care. They conduct diagnostic tests, measure and record vision, and test eye muscle function. They also show patients how to insert, remove, and care for contact lenses, and they apply eye dressings. Under the direction of the physician, ophthalmic medical assistants may administer eye medications. They also maintain optical and surgical instruments and may assist the ophthalmologist in surgery.

Q.85 What is Forensic Science?

Ans: Forensic science is any science used for the purposes of the law, and therefore provides

Forensic science is a multidisciplinary subject, drawing principally from chemistry and biology, but also from physics, geology, psychology, social science, etc.

In a typical criminal investigation, crime-scene investigators, sometimes known as scene-of-crime

and court proceedings, and thus work closely with the police. Senior forensic scientists, who usually specialise in one or more of the key forensic disciplines, may be required to attend crime scenes or give evidence in court as impartial expert witnesses.

Examples of forensic science include the use of gas chromatography to identify seised drugs, DNA

Raman spectroscopy to identify microscopic paint fragments.

The traditional disciplines of forensic science include:

Toxicology (study of alcohol and drugs)

Questioned document examination (examination of documents, handwriting comparison, study of inks, typewriter imprints, counterfeiting, etc.)

Forensic chemistry

Pathology

Odontology (study of bite marks, teeth structure)

Other specialties include

Analysis of lip prints (cheiloscopy)

Forensic engineering

Meteorology (impact of weather on a case)

Voice print analysis

Forensic entomology

Forensic anthropology

Q.86   Why Study Forensic Science?

Ans: Forensic science is a subject that fascinates most of us. What makes forensic science so exciting to study is the nature of the problems to be solved, and this provides its own intrinsic rewards. Great emphasis is placed not only on developing the skills of forensic examination, but

possessing the knowledge and skills for both subject-related employments, such as in a forensic laboratory, or non-subject-related employment in a wider range of careers.

Q.87   What is Toxicology?

Ans: Toxicology is the study of the toxic or harmful effects of chemicals. It is concerned with how toxins act, when their harmful effects occur, and what the symptoms and treatments are for

Q.88   What is Forensic Toxicology?

Ans:

and the need for quality assurance. It also recognised the application of forensic toxicology in

Forensic toxicology is a discipline of forensic science concerned with the study of toxic substances or poisons, of which there are many thousands. Toxicology encompasses theoretical considerations, methods and procedures from many disciplines including analytical chemistry, biochemistry, epidemiology, pharmacodynamics, pathology, and physiology.

Currently, forensic toxicology is the study of alcohol, drugs (licit and illicit) and poisons, including

absorption, distribution and elimination characteristics of such substances in the body, as well as the manner in which the body reponds to their presence and the factors which determine drug safety and effectiveness. To understand drug action one must know where and how the effects occur in the body.

Q.89   Who is an Ophthalmologist?

Ans: Ophthalmologists are physicians who perform eye surgery, and diagnose and treat eye diseases and injuries. They also examine eyes and prescribe eyeglasses and contact lenses. Ophthalmologists are medical doctors, and should not be confused with optometrists or opticians.

Q.90   Who is an Ophthalmic Laboratory Technician?

Ans: Prescription lenses are curved in such a way that light is correctly focused onto the retina of the patient's eye, improving vision. Some ophthalmic laboratory technicians manufacture lenses for other optical instruments, such as telescopes and binoculars. Ophthalmic laboratory technicians

Ophthalmic laboratory technicians should not be confused with workers in other vision care occupations. Ophthalmologists and optometrists are "eye doctors" who examine eyes, diagnose and treat vision problems, and prescribe corrective lenses. Ophthalmologists also perform eye surgery. Dispensing opticians who may also do work described here, help patients select frames

be ground. They place the lens into the lens grinder, set the dials for the prescribed curvature

Next, the technician examines the lens through a lensometer, an instrument similar in shape to a microscope, to make sure the degree and placement of the curve is correct. The technician then

calls for tinted or coated lenses, polishes the edges, and assembles the lenses and frame parts

In small laboratories, technicians usually handle every phase of the operation. In large ones, technicians may specialise in one or more steps, assembly-line style.

Q.91   Who is a Dispensing Optician?

Ans:

by ophthalmologists or optometrists. Dispensing opticians help customers select appropriate recommend eyeglass frames, lenses and lens coatings after considering the prescription and the customer's occupation, habits, and facial features. Dispensing opticians measure clients' eyes, including the distance between the centres of the pupils and the distance between the eye surface and the lens. For customers without prescriptions, dispensing opticians may use a lensometer to record the present eyeglass prescription. They also may obtain a customer's previous record, or verify a prescription with the examining optometrist or ophthalmologist.

Dispensing opticians prepare work orders that give ophthalmic laboratory technicians information needed to grind and insert lenses into a frame. The work order includes lens prescriptions and information on lens size, material, colour and style. Some dispensing opticians grind and insert lenses themselves. After the glasses are made, dispensing opticians verify that the lenses have

broken frames. They instruct clients about adapting to, wearing or caring for eyeglasses.

select the type of contact lens material, and prepare work orders specifying the prescription and lens size. Fitting contact lenses requires considerable skill, care and patience. Dispensing opticians observe customers' eyes, corneas, lids and contact lenses with special instruments and microscopes. During several visits, opticians show customers how to insert, remove and care for

Dispensing opticians keep records on customer prescriptions, work orders, and payments; track inventory and sales; and perform other administrative duties.

Q.92   Who is an Athletic Trainer?

Ans: An Athletic Trainer helps players avoid injuries in sports. They work under the direction of the team physician.

Q.93   What is sports medicine?

Ans: Sports medicine deals with the prevention and treatment of sports injuries, techniques to improve the performance of sports persons and their diet. It takes care of physiological, bio-mechanical, psychological and pathological aspects of exercise and sport.

Q.94   Who is a Gerontologist?

Ans: Gerontologist studies the ageing process from middle age through later life including: physical, mental and social changes in older people as they age. He/She examines changes in society resulting from the aging population and applies this knowledge to policies and programs.

Q.95   Who is a Biomedical Engineer?

Ans: A Biomedical Engineer designs, tests instruments and equipmenst for patient monitoring, computerised scanning equipment, microscopes and laser surgery devices.

Q.96   Who is a biomedical equipment technician?

Ans: A Biomedical Equipment Technician operates, adapts and repairs high-tech medical devices and instrument systems and provides instruction on the use of this equipment.

Q.97   Who is a Clinical Coding Specialist?

Ans: A Clinical Coding Specialist evaluates medical records, codes symptoms, diseases and

reimbursement.

Q.98 Who is an ECG Technician?

Ans: An Electrocardiographic (ECG) Technician prepares patient for electrocardiogram by attaching electrodes to the body and monitors the equipment as the test is run; Records test

Q.99 Who is an Environmental Health Specialist?

Ans: An Environmental Health Specialist focuses on the relationship of physical, chemical and biological factors that affect human health including: air and water quality, hazardous materials management, food sanitation and control of disease vectors.

Q.100 Who is a Health Sciences Librarian?

Ans:
care, education, research and administration; selects books, journals and other reference material and organizes this information into collections.

Q.101 Who is a Radiation Therapist?

Ans: A Radiation Therapist administers ionisation radiation as prescribed for patients with malignant and non-malignant disease; develops treatment plans, observes and evaluates the patient's clinical progression.

Q.102 Who is a Speech-Language Pathologist?

Ans: A Speech-Language Pathologist provides evaluation and therapy to people with speech, language and voice disorders; assists with stuttering problems, those with eating and swallowing problems, and the inability to make proper speech sounds.

Q.103 Who is a Chiropractor?

Ans: A Chiropractor has a holistic view of health, believing the nervous system is essential to the general health of the individual; treats disorders by spinal and joint adjustment in order to promote normal functioning of the nervous system.

Q.104 Who is a Recreational Therapist?

Ans: A Recreational Therapist evaluates, establishes, and coordinates therapeutic recreation programmes for hospital patients and outpatients to meet their physical, social and emotional needs using music, sports, games, art and crafts, and dance.

Q.105 Who is a Respiratory Therapist?

Ans: A Respiratory Therapist specializes in the treatment and care of patients with breathing disorders; administers various types of gases and aerosol drugs, cardiopulmonary resuscitation,

Q.106 Who is a Surgical Technologist?

Ans: A Surgical Technologist prepares for surgery in operating room, provides assistance to physician before and during surgery, maintains/inventories instruments and equipment, cleans the operating room, and returns patients to recovery room.

Q.107 Who is a Sonographer?

Ans: A Sonographer operates ultrasound equipment to produce images revealing the shape and position of internal organs, masses, as well as fetuses; images show gallstones, cysts, tumors, and fetal growth.

Q.108 I want to become a Hospital Administrator. Tell in detail about Hospital Management or Health Management.

Ans: Health Management is among the top ten millennium professions according to a recent survey. As healthcare management is increasingly privatised there is a greater need for not only

If Hospitals have always fascinated you rather than scaring you, you can think of a career in Hospital Management. A large number of private hospitals and clinics have come up all over the country. With increasing emphasis on quality of health care and patient satisfaction there is

Professional courses in Hospital Management / Administration are available for both medical and non-medical persons. You should be in excellent health yourself and have the energy, stamina, patience and tolerance to work for long strenuous hours. Most leading health centres and hospitals have a presence on the net. The others are on the verge of having one very soon. Most of the websites are interactive in terms of content and services. There are computer generated response systems to attend to routine queries. Details of services provided by the organisation are given online with other related information of interest also available. It is essential for you

will be linked to the tools you use.

As a Hospital Administrator you will be responsible for the overall organisation and management of the hospital to ensure its smooth functioning with the objective of ensuring the complete satisfaction of the patient. You will have to co-ordinate between the various departments of

supplies and above all the required standards of cleanliness are maintained. You will also deal highest quality care at the lowest cost. It entails giving 100% of your time to quality in-patient care, lowering the length of stay, decreasing resource utilisation, and working with the medical and administrative staff to co-ordinate all aspects of in-house care.

system.

After completing a professional course in Hospital Management you can avail of challenging job opportunities in medical institutes, hospitals, nursing homes and NGOs operating in the health care sector.

As a fresher, you would be in the Rs. 8000 to Rs. 20,000 slot after which your hard work, efforts and experience will take you up the ladder.

To take admission in undergraduate course (BHM) of Hospital Management, you need to be a Higher Secondary (XII) pass or equivalent with Biology securing minimum 50% marks. For master degree/PG diploma (MHA/MHM) you need to be a graduate in science/arts/commerce with 50% marks. For some institutes an MBBS degree is the criteria for admission.

Q. 109 What is Naturopathy?

Ans: A revolution is taking place in health care. At the frontline of this revolution is naturopathic medicine, a system that focuses on promoting and maintaining health and wellness by the use of natural means and without the use of toxic therapies. Naturopathic doctors are trained specialists in a healing art, which uses non-invasive natural medicine. They are not medical doctors (M.D.s). Naturopathic doctors (N.D.s) are trained in subjects such as anatomy, physiology, counseling, dietary evaluations, nutrition, herbology, acupressure, homeopathy, iridology, exercise therapy, hydrotherapy, oxygen therapy and thermal therapy.

Naturopathic doctors personalise the healing modality to the needs of the individual with methods which are effective for both chronic and acute problems. Naturopathic doctors cooperate with all branches of medical science, referring individuals to other practitioners for diagnosis or treatment when appropriate.

In practice, naturopathic doctors perform lifestyle analysis, nutritional and dietary assessments, metabolic analysis and other evaluative procedures. They are trained to use a wide variety of natural methods, which involve the individual in the healing process. Naturopathy is based on a belief in the body's natural ability to heal itself when given an appropriate internal and external healing environment. Naturopaths are not involved in the practice of medicine and do not use drugs or pharmaceuticals, nor do they perform abortions or surgery. They have traditionally been referred to as "drugless doctors." In reality, naturopathy deals with wellness and relief from conditions, which are the result of stress whether from mental, nutritional, environmental or physical factors.

In summation, naturopathic medicine acknowledges the complex interrelationship of body, mind and spirit, and is based on the following principles:

Each of us is physiologically unique

Nature can provide everything we need to enjoy good health at every stage of life

Illness is a warning sign

Healing must address an illness' underlying cause, rather than just its symptoms

The philosophy of naturopathic medicine is based on seven basic principles:

1. **Do no harm:** Primum non nocere (do no harm) is taken from the Hippocratic Oath. Certainly anybody who is sick does not need any therapy or treatment would harm him or her. As prescription medication has such a potential to make a well man sick, many wonder how it can be expected to make a sick man well. Traditional naturopathy embraces only therapies or procedures which are designed to enhance healing and produce wellness.

2. **Recognise the healing power of nature:** Vis medicatrix naturae means nature has healing powers. The human body is created with the capacity to heal itself and to maintain homeostasis (balance). There is a healing power in nature and this principal is the basis for all of naturopathy. Naturopathy is a system designed to work in harmony with nature, in the restoration and support for the inherent natural healing systems of the body.

3. **Identify the cause:** Tolle causam means identify and treat the cause. In allopathic medicine, the name of the disease is actually the name of the symptom in Greek. The term "arthritis," for example, is made up of two Greek roots "arthro" which means having to do with the

    pain by reducing the joint pain. This can be done with the use of painkillers, nerve blockers or any number of procedures which suppress the symptoms. Naturopaths are committed to

    condition in the body. For naturopaths, the correction of the cause is the most plausible way of eliminating the symptoms and restoring long-term health to the person.

4. **Treat the whole person:** Naturopathic doctors are aware that a person can have a physical or emotional illness. The chosen therapy is determined by what kind of problem the person is experiencing. You cannot be well or healthy if you have a psychological problem even

    biofeedback techniques for those experiencing emotional or behavioural problems.

5. **The physician is a teacher:** Naturopaths are integrative healers, partnering with the client for a team approach in healing. The naturopathic philosophy places the responsibility for wellness with the individual. Man is the steward of his body and the doctor is the teacher or advisor to the individual on how to maintain health. One recognises, for example, that a headache is not

    of health has been violated and the body is responding with pain. Naturopaths should evaluate the connotation and advise or teach their clients what lifestyle; nutritional, emotional, physical or dietary changes should be made to alleviate the condition. The condition is alleviated by the clients desire to make those changes and not by some outside agency.

6. **Prevent disease:** Naturopathic physicians are preventive medicine specialists. Prevention of disease is accomplished through education and encouraging good life habits that support health and prevent disease.

7. **Establish health and wellness:** The primary goals of the naturopathic physician are to establish and maintain optimum health and to promote wellness. Health is the state of optimal well-being. The naturopathic physician strives to elevate the client's state of health and wellness by analysing each aspect of the controllable factors which determine the state of health, those being diet, exercise, thinking, sleep and posture.

Q.110 Is Naturopathy a complete system of medicine?

Ans: No system of medicine or healing is complete but Naturopathy provides us simple means of healing. It offers the society more economical frame work for the medicine of future generations. Naturopathy believes that the patient is treated and not the diseases. It is a drugless therapy and does not use medicine. It is a way of life and hence it can be said to be more preventive than curative.

Q.111 What are the diseases that can be treated by Naturopathy?

Ans: There are wide ranges of ailments that can be treated by Naturopathy. Hyperacidity, Dyspepsia, Obesity, Menstrual disturbance, respiratory problems like Rhinitis, Sinusitis, Bronchitis, Asthma, Gout, Spondylisis, Sciatica, Arthritis, Eczema, etc.

Q.112 Is Naturopathy a recognised system of medicine in India?

Ans: Yes, it is a recognised system of treatment in India. Government of India has already set up Central Council for Research in Yoga and Naturopathy & National institute of Naturopathy in

Q.113 Where can I learn Naturopathy in India?

Ans:
Diploma and Degree courses. Bhavnagar University and Gujarat Ayurvedic University also conduct diploma courses. All India Nature Care Federation, New Delhi also conducts three years diploma course. The All India Nature Care Federation organises nature cure conferences from time to time and engaged in propagation of Naturopathy in India.

started — the Gandhi Nature Cure College — in Hyderabad of Andhra Pradesh. It started with a

Hyderabad. Later on in 1987, the college was taken over by the Government to make it as an

years Degree Course (Bachelor of Naturopathy and Yogic Sciences BNYS) by the addition of one

Dharmasthala Manjunatheswara (SDM) College of Naturopathy and Yogic Sciences — was started

various colleges in India have come up totaling to six, which include two Government Colleges and four Private Management Colleges.

Q.114 What is Medical Council of India?

Ans: The Medical Council of India was established in 1934 under the Indian Medical Council

Act, 1933, now repealed, with the main function of establishing uniform standards of higher

number of medical colleges had increased steadily during the years after Independence. It was felt that the provisions of Indian Medical Council Act were not adequate to meet with the challenges posed by the very fast development and the progress of medical education in the country. As a

in 1964, 1993 and 2001. The objectives and functions of the Council are as follows.

Maintenance of uniform standards of medical education; both at undergraduate and postgraduate levels.

institutions of India or foreign countries.
Permanent registration/provisional registration of doctors with recognised medical

Reciprocity with foreign countries in the matter of mutual recognition of medical

Inspection/visitation with a view to maintain proper standard of medical education in India.
Permission to start new medical colleges, new Courses including P.G. or Higher Courses, increase of seats, etc.

Indian Medical Register: Maintenance of All India Medical Register of persons who hold any

State Medical Councils or Medical Council of India.

Registration:

Q.115 Activities, which are not under the purview of MCI?

Ans: The following activities are not within the purview of MCI:

1. Questions pertaining to drugs, reactions, nonscheduled drugs, etc.
2. Paramedical personnel- Registration, duties, responsibilities of nurses, Pharmacists, Laboratory Technicians, etc.
3. Dental Surgeons — Registration / Practice, etc.
4. Matters relating to Registration and practice of Indian systems of Medicine like Ayurveda , Siddha, Unani and Homeopathy.
5. Queries pertaining to Diplomats of National Board of Examinations and other related matters.
6. Screening test — Scheme of Examination including syllabus, dates of examinations; No of Attempts, etc.
7. Matters relating to Nursing Homes and Hospitals .
8. All India Entrance Examinations for Admission to MBBS courses.
9. All India Entrance Examinations for Admission to PG courses.

Q.116 What is Dental Council of India?

Ans: Dental Council of India is a Statutory Body incorporated under an Act of Parliament, viz., The Dentists Act, 1948 (XVI of 1948) to regulate the Dental Education and the profession of

Family Welfare (Department of Health) through Grant-in-aid. The General Body of the Dental Council of India representing various State Governments, Universities, Dental Colleges, Central Government, etc.

Q.117 What is pharmacy council of India ?

Ans: The Pharmacy education and profession in India up to graduate level is controlled by the Pharmacy Council of India (PCI), a statutory body governed by the provisions of the Pharmacy Act, 1948 passed by the Parliament.

Q.118 What is Central Council for Research in Homeopathy?

Ans: The Government of India after having recognised the need of systematic research for the development of Indian System of Medicine and Homoeopathy in the country, established the Central Council for Research in Ayurveda, Yoga & Naturopathy, Unani, Siddha and Homoeopathy in 1969. This composite Council undertook systematic research in Ayurveda, Siddha, Unani Medicine, Yoga, Nature cure and Homoeopathy and continued to do so till 1978, when it was dissolved to pave way for the formation of four independent Research Councils, one each for Ayurveda and Siddha, Unani Medicine, Yoga and Nature Cure, and Homoeopathy.

The Central Council for Research in Homoeopathy was formally constituted on 30th March, 1978, as an autonomous organisation and was registered under the Societies Registration Act XXI of 1860. It was, however, only in January, 1979 that the Council started functioning as an independent organisation. The policy, directions and overall guidance for the activities of the Council are provided by the Governing Body. The Union Minister of Health and Family Welfare is the President of the Governing Body and has general control on the affairs of the Council and has authority to exercise all the powers.

It is assisted by a Standing Finance Committee for considering the budget proposals and a

The Department of Ayurveda, Yoga & Naturopathy, Unani, Siddha and Homoeopathy in the Ministry of Health & Family Welfare which is headed by a Secretary, administers various schemes for strengthening of research institutions and renders advice on implementation and monitoring of various research programmes.

Objective:
To undertake research or other programmes, the prosecution and assistance in research; the propagation of knowledge and experimental measures relating to the cause and prevention

applied aspects of Homoeopathy. To exchange information with other institutions, associations and societies interested in the objects similar to those of the Central Council and especially in observation and study of diseases.

To promote and assist the institution of research, in the study of diseases, their prevention and cure with focus on the rural population of the country. To prepare, print publish and exhibit papers, posters, pamphlets, periodicals and books for furtherance of the object of the Central Council and contribute to such literature.

Offering prizes and scholarships in furthering the objectives of the Council

Q.119 Which are the books one may study along with textbooks for preparing PMT/ AIIMS/CMC/State Level Medical Entrance Tests?

Ans: students can use the following books as reference book for preparing PMT/AIIMS/CMC/ State Level Medical Entrance:

(i)   Physics by H.C.Verma
(ii) Physics by Tata Mc Graw Hill Publisher
(iii) Chemistry by O.P. Aggarwal
(iv) Physical Chemistry by R.C. Mukherjee
(v)   Chemistry by Tata Mc Graw Hill Publisher

(vii) Physics Today, Chemistry Today & Biology Today by mtg Learning Media

Q.120 What are the different paramedical courses available in India and what is eligibility for admissions?

Ans: Paramedical Courses and Eligibility for Admission:

Sl.No.	Name of Paramedical Course	Duration	Eligibility
01.	Bachelor of Occupational Therapy (BOT)	3.5 years	(10+2) PCB
02.	Bachelor of Physio/Physical Therapy(BPT)	3.5 years	(10+2) PCB
03.	Prosthetic and Orthotic Engineering	3 years	(10+2) PCB
04.	BSc (Audiology & Speech Therapy)	3 years	(10+2) PCB
05.	BSc(Ophthalmic Technology)	3 years	(10+2) PCB
06.	Bachelor of Mental Rehabilitation (BMR)	3 years	(10+2) PCB
07.	BSc(Human Biology)	3 years	(10+2) PCB
08.	BSc(Radiography)	3 years	(10+2) PCB
09.	BSc(Radio Therapy)	3 years	(10+2) PCB
10.	BSc(Nuclear Medicine)	3 years	(10+2) PCB
11.	BSc(Respiratory Therapy Tech)	3 years	(10+2) PCB
12.	BSc(Medical Technology—X ray)	3 years	(10+2) PCB
13.	BSc(Medical Secretarial Service)	3 years	(10+2) PCB
14.	BSc(Operation Theatres)	3 years	(10+2) PCB
15.	BSc(Medical Laboratory Technology)	3 years	(10+2) PCB
16.	BSc(Allied Health Services)	4 years	(10+2) PCB

17.	BSc(Bio Medical Technique)	1.5 years	BSc(BZC)
18.	Bachelor of Speech, Language & Hearing(BSLH)	3 years	(10+2) PCB
19.	Bachelor of Naturopathy & Yogic Sciences	5 years	(10+2) PCB
20.	Dental Hygienist	2 years	(10+2) PCB
21.	Dental Mechanics	2 years	(10+2) PCB
22.	Diploma in Community Health (DCH)	3 years	(10+2) PCB
23.	Diploma in Hospital Aids	2 years	(10+2) PCB
24.		2 years	(10+2) PCB
25.	Radiation Therapy Technician	2 years	BSc(PCM)
26.	PG Diploma in Cardiac Pulmonary Perfusion	2 years	BSc(BZC)
27.	PG Diploma in Cardio Vascular Technique	2 years	BSc(BZC)
28.	PG Diploma in Medical Laboratory Tech	2 years	BSc(BZC)
29.	PG Diploma in Neuro Tech	2 years	BSc(BZC)
30.	PG Diploma in Radiography & Imaging Tech	2 years	BSc(BZC)
31.	Diploma in Anaesthesia Tech	1 year	BSc(BZC)
32.	Diploma in Transfusion Medical Tech	1 year	BSc(BZC)
33.	Diploma in Vascular Surgery Tech	1 year	BSc(BZC)
34.	Diploma in Dialysis Tech	1 year	BSc(PCB/Z/M)
35.	Diploma in ECG Tech	1 year	BSc(PCB/Z/M)
36.	Medical Records Technician	1 year	BA/BSc/B.Com
37.		1 year	BA/BSc/B.Com
38.	Adv. Diploma in Technical & Analytical Chemistry	1.5 years	BSc(Chem)
39.		1 year	HSLC/Matric
40.		1 year	HSLC/Matric
41.		1 year	HSLC/Matric
42.		1 year	HSLC/Matric
43.		1 year	HSLC/Matric
44.		2 years	(!0+2)PCB
45.		2 years	(10+2)PCB
46.	Diploma in Ophthalmic Assistant	2 years	(10+2)PCB
47.		1.5 years	(10+2)
48.	Diploma in Clinical Neuro Technology (DCNT)	1 year	BSc(PCM)
49.	MSc/PG Diploma in Bio-Medical Instrumentation	2 years	BSc(PCM)
50.	PG Diploma in Hospital Management (Eqvt. to MBA)	1.5/2 years	BA/BSc/B.Com
51.	Diploma in Dietetics	1 year	(10+2)PCB

Q.127 How can I test my interest in Medical profession?
Ans:

profession to test your interest in the area of medical sciences. Thirty statements are given below, each followed by four alternative answers (A, B, C & D). Read each statement carefully and marked the appropriate answer (A, B, C or D) before proceeding to the next statement.

01. Genetic information is carried through
    A. t-RNA
    B. DNA
    C. m-RNA
    D. Nucleoproteins

02. The activities of all living cells are controlled by
    A. Chloroplast
    B. Nucleus
    C. Tonoplast
    D. Auxins

03. Cancer cells are more easily damaged by radiation than normal cells because they are
    A. non-dividing
    B. starved by nutrition
    C. different in structure
    D. undergoing rapid division

04. Genes are located in chromosomes in
    A. linear fashion
    B. helical fashion
    C. spiral fashion
    D. circular fashion

05. RNA is important for
    A. synthesis of proteins
    B. cell division
    C. synthesis of carbohydrates
    D. digestion of proteins

06. Activities of all living cells are controlled by
    A. chloroplast
    B. nucleus
    C. tonoplast
    D. chromosomes

07. Qunine, important for the treatment of malaria, is extracted from
    A. cinnamon
    B. chinchona

D.   red ants

08. Viral Dengue fever is caused by

     B.   mosquito

     D.

09. A frog lives in water or near water because
     A.   it gets its food from water
     B.   its hind limbs are webbed and help in swimming
     C.   it respires through the skin
     D.   it can see through its transparent eye lids while swimming

10. Snakes perceives sound through
     A.   ear
     B.   tongue
     C.   skin
     D.   air

11. The venom of cobra affects
     A.   respiratory system
     B.   circulatory system
     C.   digestive system
     D.   nervous system

12. In birds which one is absent
     A.   urinary bladder
     B.   gall bladder
     C.   both A & B
     D.   only A

13. The most intelligent ape is
     A.   chimpanzee
     B.   gorilla
     C.   gibbon
     D.   monkey

14. Formation of fat begins in the body when
     A.   blood sugar level is constant
     B.   glucose is converted into glycogen
     C.   when liver and muscles cannot store any more glycogen

D.   when glucose combines with glycerol

15. Enzymes are essential in our body because the
   A.   supply energy
   B.   catalyze biochemical reactions
   C.   coordinate nervous activities
   D.   are structural component of body

16. Glycogen in our body is stored in
   A.   liver
   B.   liver and muscles
   C.   liver and spleen
   D.   spleen and muscles

17. Metabolic rate is highest in
   A.   man
   B.   elephant
   C.   rat
   D.   monkey

18. Maximum energy is produced by
   A.   minerals
   B.   vitamins
   C.   proteins
   D.   fats

19. The most important food stuff for the body is
   A.   proteind
   B.   carbohydrates
   C.   vitamins
   D.   minerals

20. Mineral responsible for controlling heart beat is
   A.   sulphur
   B.   sodium
   C.   potassium
   D.   iron

21. Vitamin k helps in
   A.   clotting of blood
   B.   maturation of ova
   C.   digestion

D.   neurititis

22. Bile helps in
     A.   digesting fats
     B.   emulsifying fats for digestion
     C.   eliminating waste products
     D.   digestion of proteins

23. Ascorbic acid is
     A.   an enzyme
     B.   protein
     C.   vitamin
     D.   carbohydrates

24. The process of respiration is concerned with
     A.   intake of oxygen
     B.   liberation of oxygen
     C.   liberation of carbon dioxide
     D.   liberation of energy

25. Ciliary muscles are found in the
     A.   eye
     B.   heart
     C.   stomach
     D.   diaphragm

26. During muscle contraction
     A.   chemical energy is changed into electrical energy
     B.   chemical energy is changed into mechanical energy
     C.   chemical energy is changed into physical energy
     D.   mechanical energy is changed into chemical energy

27. The blood bank of the body is
     A.   heart
     B.   bone marrow
     C.   spleen
     D.   liver

28. The person with blood group is universal donor
     A.   A
     B.   B
     C.   AB

D. O
29. Which one is sex-linked disorder?

    A. critinism

    B. beriberi

    C. colour blindness

    D. tylosis

30. The male human is represented by sex chromosomes

    A. XX

    B. XO

    C. XY

    D. YY

KEY:

answers.

1: B	2: B	3: D	4: A	5: A	6: B	7: B	8: B	9: C	10: C
11: D	12: C	13: A	14: C	15: B	16: B	17: C	18: D	19: A	20: B
21: A	22: B	23: C	24: D	25: A	26: B	27: C	28: D	29: C	30: C

COMMENT:

Scores between 21-30: High interest in medicine

Scores between 10-20: Average interest in medicine

Score below 10: Poor interest in medicine

19

MISC CAREER OPTIONS

Q.1 I am a (10+2) student and I want to take admission in "Rail & Transport Management" course. Where can I do this and what are its eligibility? How will this course help me in future?

Ans: You can study one year correspondence diploma course in Rail & Transport Management from Institute of Rail Transport, 17, Rail Bhavan, Raisina Road, New Delhi-110001. The course commences fron June every year. The Ministry of Railway has recognised this diploma as an

Signal Engineering Departments. This course is also very useful to serving employees of Railways, Trade, Industry, and Transport, etc. Persons having a degree in any subject or a minimum two-year diploma in any engineering discipline are eligible for this course.

Q.2 What is Archaeology? What is the job prospect after completing a course in Archaeology?

Ans: Archaeology is the study of ancient cultures through their material remains. The archaeologist's job is to excavate relics and artifacts from ancient sites and infer on their basis the history and customs of the people who lived there. The archaeologist should have a working knowledge of botany, zoology, soil science, geology, history and geography. Archaeologists can

agencies as the Archaeological Survey of India and the National Institute of Oceanography also offer employment to trained archaeologists. Graduate and Postgraduate programs in Archaeology and ancient Indian History and culture are available in many Indian Universities.

Q.3 I am a science graduate. I want to become a professional newsreader in a TV or Radio Channel. What are the eligibility criteria? Is good look extremely essential for a newsreader?

Ans:
English/Hindi/Regional language. Newsreaders also should have good knowledge about current affairs and presence of mind as most of the news coverage now a day becomes live and on real time basis. Though good look is not essential for radio news reading, photogenic, pleasant personality is necessary for TV news reading.

You can try for a short term course in news reading from Film or Television Institute of India, Law College Road, Pune-411004 or Janakidevi Mahavidyalaya, Ganga Ram Hospital Marg, New Delhi-110060 or Indian Television Training Institute, C-41 Gulmohar Park, New Delhi-110049.

In All India Radio, written tests are conducted by the respective stations whenever there is a vacancy for the recruitment of permanent or casual announcers. Those who qualify in the written examination have to pass an audition test followed by an interview.

To join a TV channel begin carefully and critically observing successful news readers; try to identify the genre or programs you would like to present; practice yourd skills after taking a short course in news reading. Armed with this arsenal, you have to go through screen tests, dummy runs and work very hard in order to become a permanent TV newsreader. Good look is desirable but not essential.

Q.4 I would like to know that if students get a B.Tech degree from a private institute whether he will be at par to those students doing B.Tech from govt. institutions.

Ans: A student from a private institute shall be at par with a student from a govt. institute provided his degree is from an university recognised by UGC and the institute and the course is recognised by AICTE. See the NBA rating before you take admission in a private engineering college.

Q.5 What is Forensic Science? What is the prospect in Forensic Science? Where can I study forensic science?

Ans: Forensic science is any science used for the purposes of the law, and therefore provides

Forensic science is a multidisciplinary subject, drawing principally from chemistry and biology, but also from physics, geology, psychology, social science, etc.

In a typical criminal investigation crime-scene investigators, sometimes known as scene-of-crime

and court proceedings, and thus work closely with the police. Senior forensic scientists, who usually specialise in one or more of the key forensic disciplines, may be required to attend crime scenes or give evidence in court as impartial expert witnesses.

Examples of forensic science include the use of gas chromatography to identify seised drugs, DNA

Raman spectroscopy to identify microscopic paint fragments.

The traditional disciplines of forensic science include:

study of inks, typewriter imprints, counterfeiting, etc.)

Other specialties include

Forensic science is a subject that fascinates most of us. What makes forensic science so exciting to study is the nature of the problems to be solved, and this provides its own intrinsic rewards. Great emphasis is placed not only on developing the skills of forensic examination, but also on

individuals possessing the knowledge and skills for both subject-related employments, such as in a forensic laboratory, or non-subject-related employment in a wider range of careers.

Institutes offering courses in Forensic Science

Name of Institution	Course	Duration	Eligibility
Punjabi University, Patiala	M.Sc. (Forensic Science)	2 years	B.Sc./MBBS/ BDS
Department of Criminology & Forensic Science, Dr. Hari Singh Gaur Viswavidyalaya, Sagar (MP)	MA (Criminology) M.Sc. (Forensic Science) M.Sc. (Forensic Toxicology)	2 year	BA/B.Sc./ MBBS/ BDS
University of Madras, Chennai	MA(Criminology)	2 years	BA/B.Sc./B. Com/MBBS/BDS
Banaras Hindu University Varanasi (UP)	MA(Criminology)	2 years	-Do-
Chennai	Degree/Diploma in Criminology & Forensic Science	½ years	-Do-
Department of Criminology & Forensic Sciences,	MA(Criminology) M.Sc.(Forensic Science) M.Sc.(Forensic Toxicology)	2 years	BA/B.Sc/B.Com/ MBBS/BDS, etc.
Department of Forensic Science Dr.B.R. Ambedkar University Agra, Uttar Pradesh	M.Sc.(Forensic Science)	2years	B.Sc./MBBS
Tata Institute of Social Sciences, Deonar, Mumbai	MA (Social Science with specilisation in criminology)	2 years	BA/B.Sc.

National Institute of Criminology and Forensic Science, Ministry of Home Affaitrs, Rohini, Delhi-110085	Training and research program		Govt./Police/ Forensic Laboratory
University of Pune Pune, Maharashtra	M.Sc.(Forensic Science)	2 years	B.Sc. with Physics, Chemistry, Zoology or Botany

Q.6　I am a student class X. I have a strong desire to study sound engineering. Please provide me details about the course.

Ans: You can study 2 years diploma in Sound Recording & Sound Engineering from Film & Television Institute of India, Law College Road, Pune. Eligibility for admission is B.Sc. degree with Physics or Electronics. You can also study 2 year diploma in sound engineering from Satyajit Ray Film &

your B.Sc. try for sound engineering.

Q.7　I am a student of 12th Standard (Commerce). After completing class XII, I want to be a physical trainer completing B.PED and M.PED from Lakshmibai National Institute of Physical Education. What are the eligibility criteria? What is its job prospect?

Ans: Lakshmibai National College of Physical Education, Gwalior offers 3-years B.P.Ed. course.

in recognised sports events at the national level are also eligible. Lakshmibai National College

reputed govt recognised institution for a career in physical education.

Indira Gandhi Institute of Physical Education & Sports Sciences (University of Delhi); B-Block, Vikaspuri, New Delhi-110018 offers 3-years Bachelor of Science (Physical Education, Health

Candidates should be between 17 to 20 years of age and must have passed (10+2)/HS in second division (minimum 40%) of the CBSE, New Delhi or equivalent. Weight age is given to the sports achievement at various levels.

diploma in Physical Education. Manipur University, School of Humanities and Social Sciences, Canchipur, Imphal-795003 offers Physical Education as one of the subjects for 3 years BA course.

Q.8　What is Public Relation? I am a graduate in Arts and I want to complete a Degree/ Diploma course in Public Relation. Where can I do it and what is the eligibility?

Ans: Public Relation is the art of getting along with people we constantly come in touch with. In the corporate world public relation is the link between the corporation and the outer world whether it is the customer, supplier, government, media or general public at large. It is the responsibility of the public relation department in the corporation to build a positive image of the corporation and also to build a good will among people which will help the corporation to achieve it's mission, goal and objective.

The following qualities are needed to become a successful PR Professional:

> Impressive & effective communication skills
> Attractive personality
>
> Good listener
>
> The right i.e. cool temperament
> Tact to deal with people

The best institution to complete a PG Diploma in Public Relation is Indian Institute of Mass Communication (IIMC), Aruna Asaf Ali Marg, JNU New Campus, New Delhi-110067. The eligibility for admission is Bachelor Degree in Science/Arts/Commerce from any recognised university. Admission is through All India entrance examination followed by an interview.

Other institution/university offering Degree/PG Diploma in Public Relation after graduation are:

(i)   Gujrat University, Navrangpura, Ahmedabad-300009
(ii) Indian Institute of Public Relations, B-9, Shivalik, New Delhi-110017
(iii) Makhanlal Chaturvedi National University of Journalism, Bhopal-462016 (MP)
(iv) St. Xavier's College of Communication, Mumbai
(v)   Punjabi University, Patiala
(vi) Devi Ahilya Viswavidyalaya, Indore (MP)
(vii) Aligarh Muslim University, Aligarh
(viii) Bharatidasan University, Tiruchirapalli-620024

Q.9 I am graduate in arts and I want to take a career in insurance sector as an insurance agent/advisor. What is the scope and which are the institutions offering courses in insurance?

Ans: With the opening up of the Indian insurance sector for private players, the future requirement of trained insurance agents is expected to be around 5-8 lakhs by the year 2014. The washout (failure) rate of insurance agents is an high as 70-80%, but with the entry of private players, dramatic changes can be expected, the Post-liberalisation insurance agent may be visualised as a laptop- wielding, number-crunching, smart Alec, who is familiar with all the latest hard-selling strategies. Recognising the need for this sort of a bottom-up grooming, the Insurance Regulatory Development Authority (IRDA) has also made it mandatory for all practicing agents to get their licenses renewed and new agents and intermediaries to obtain formal training from institutes accredited by the authority. According to industry sources, this is a huge untapped market of an estimated insurable 300 million people, the present life insurance coverage is only 24% and our of a retired population of 30 million, the present pension coverage is a meagre one million. The potential of health insurance has not even been scratched. So, it's a sector waiting to be tapped! Certainly you can try for a career in insurance sector. You can contact LIC, GIC, TATA-AIG,

other support to start your business as an insurance advisor.

Q. 10 I am a student of class XI and after completing my 10 + 2 I want to go to the US for further studies. What are the tests I have to take and how should I apply ? Please tell me in detail.

Ans: To be eligible for admission to a U.S. university, you must meet certain minimum entry requirements. These include a secondary school diploma or examination results, English language ability, and in many cases a score from one of the U.S. university admissions tests.

As a part of the application process, most American colleges and universities require scores from one of the U.S. standardised admissions tests. However, some colleges and universities do not require international applicants to take admissions tests, and some schools do not ask for

U.S.-university directories such as the International Student Handbook of U.S. Colleges (The College Board, New York, NY) and Applying to Colleges and Universities in the United States: A Handbook for International Students (Peterson's, Princeton, N.J.). Also note that community colleges do not usually require applicants to take standardised admissions tests.

U.S. standardised admissions tests are primarily multiple-choice aptitude tests that are intended to measure the skills necessary for undergraduate study. American colleges and universities use admissions tests as a means of assessing all applicants (from the United States and other countries)

not an equivalent to admissions tests, and that tests are only one part of the application — good test scores alone do not guarantee admission to the schools of your choice.

There are three main undergraduate admissions tests:

> Scholastic Assessment Test (SAT I)
> SAT II Subject Tests
> American College Testing (ACT) Assessment

Some universities may have their own in-house examinations or additional tests that applicants are required to take. For further information, make a list of the colleges you want to apply to,

The Scholastic Assessment Test (SAT)

Both the SAT I and SAT II are conducted several times throughout the year at locations worldwide.

information about dates, test centres, fees, and registration procedures is available in the SAT registration bulletin or on the SAT test administrators' Website at http://www.collegeboard.org/. You can get copies of the registration bulletin from the College Board in the United States or from your nearest U.S. educational information or advising centre. You may be asked to pay postage costs for these bulletins. U.S. centres also usually have sample questions and other test preparation materials for the SAT tests available for reference use, loan, or purchase.

Content: The SAT I is primarily a multiple-choice test that measures verbal and mathematical reasoning abilities. The test is divided into seven half-hour sections: three verbal; three mathematical; and one additional section, the equating section, which is either verbal or

and does not count toward your score.

The SAT II Subject Tests are also primarily multiple choice, but are only one hour long. They

Many U.S. colleges and universities, especially those that have more competitive admissions criteria, either require or recommend one or more SAT II test scores for admission and/or placement purposes. Be sure to check each institution's requirements before registering for any SAT II test. While some colleges specify which subject tests you must take, others leave the option up to you. In this case, it is advisable to take exams in your strongest areas of study.

Scores: The mathematical and verbal sections of the SAT I are each scored on a 200 to 800 scale. Therefore, the highest possible combined score on the SAT I would be 1,600. Scores are reported separately to colleges for the mathematical and verbal sections. Most college directories and catalogs quote average scaled scores for each institution to give some guidance on relative selectivity. The SAT II Subject Tests are also scored on a 200 to 800 scale.

The American College Testing Assessment (ACT): The ACT is administered by the American College

Unlike the SAT, the number of times the test is offered varies from one test centre to another. As an international student, you may not need to take the ACT. If it is required, however, plan ahead to make sure you do not miss the test date(s) at your nearest centre. Preregistration is required, and deadlines are two to three weeks prior to the exam. Since the ACT is not as widely accepted as the SAT, check to see if the universities where you are applying will accept ACT scores in place of the bulletin, which can be obtained from the test administrators and from many U.S. information and advising centres. Note that the centres may ask you to pay postage costs.

Content: The ACT Assessment is a multiple-choice test that measures English, mathematics, reading, and science reasoning.

Scores: For each of the four subject areas, you receive a raw score, which is the total number of correct responses. The score is then converted into a scaled score from 1 to 36. A composite score is then calculated by adding together the scaled scores and dividing the sum by four. The highest possible composite score is 36, and the lowest is 1. Scores take several weeks to reach universities.

Below is the recommended timetable for applying to universities in the United States. It is sometimes possible to complete the process more quickly, but you may have a much more limited

to the colleges of your choice.

12 TO 18 MONTHS PRIOR to the academic year in which you hope to enroll, begin to consider, research, and do the following:

no later than these deadlines. The tests should be taken in advance of submitting university application forms.

12 MONTHS PRIOR to enrollment, complete the following (months indicated are estimates, based on fall enrollment):

AUGUST

early admission deadlines will be sooner.

travel and expenses on arrival.

and well in advance of your departure date

You should now have a shortlist of colleges that match your needs, interests, and abilities. You

United States, and that you can meet the costs of a U.S. undergraduate education. Now it's time to start putting together your applications. This chapter gives practical information and advice to help you make successful applications to the colleges of your choice.

The entire application process, from obtaining initial information to applying for your student visa, should begin 12 to 18 months in advance of when you want to go the United States. It is

a much more limited choice of colleges.

ENGLISH PROFICIENCY

Foreign Language (TOEFL) as early as possible — at least a year before you plan to enroll. Some institutions accept English language examinations other than TOEFL; check the information you receive from institutions to see which examinations they accept.

requirements for a university, some schools may require you to take courses to improve your mastery of American English, academic or research usage, and study skills. If you studied English

TOEFL Waivers: If you are a non-U.S. citizen and nonnative speaker of English who has been educated in English for most of your school life, your TOEFL requirement may be waived. Allow time in the application process to correspond with U.S. universities about this issue. American universities are unlikely to accept secondary school English language examination results as proof of your language ability.

For detail write to TOEFL or visit their website:
TOEFL
CN 6152
Princeton, NJ 08541-6152
USA

http://www.toe

Q.11 I am a 10 + 2 student and I want to act in theatre after completing a course from National School of Drama or any good university/institution offering a course in drama/acting. Please tell me in detail how I can fulfil my dream?

Ans: National School of Drama, Bahawalpur House, Bhagwandas Road, New Delhi-110001 is the best institution to take a course in Dramatic Arts. The institution is an autonomus institution,

Diploma Course in Dramatic Arts, aims at development of theatre personality by imparting training in acting, design and other disciplines related to theatre. Eligibility for admission is Graduation in any subject from a recognised university in India, participation in at least 10 productions and working knowledge of English and Hindi. Age limit is 18-30 years. Admission is based on the recommendation of the Expert Committee constituted by the school to asses the aptitude and

The following Universities also offer Diploma in Acting for which eligibility is (10+2)/Graduation:

(ii) Andhra University, Visakhapatnam-530003 (Andhra Pradesh)
(iii) University of Hyderabad, P.O. Central University, Hyderabad-500046
(iv) MS University of Baroda, Shastri Bridge Road, Fatehganj, Vadodara-390002 (Gujrat)

Q.12 I am a student of 10+2 standard. I want to take up a career in forestry/wild life. I want to know in detail about it. What are the different aspects of this profession?

Ans: Forests are precious natural wealth for any country. India is blessed with a forest resource that is large in volume and diverse in character. Forestry and Wild Life go together since forests serve as home for wildlife. A large and well-trained work force is needed to operate at various levels for managing and maintaining this natural wealth.

Different aspect of forestry: Social Forestry includes agroforestry (planting trees in agriculture areas), farm forestry (planting trees in farms), community forestry (planting trees in villages), avenue plantation, ornamental forestry and urban forestry.

Wasteland development deals with the effective utilisation and development of land that is infertile. The job sometimes includes optimum utilisation of industrial wastes and residues.

Manufacture of paper and products is also related to this profession. Job opportunities are available in timber factories, paper mills and where paper is produced from bamboo extracts.

research on the history, life span, measuring, grading, classifying the varieties of trees, and studying ways and means of tree improvement through afforestation, etc.

studies and analyses the evolution, behaviour, biological functions, etc., of an organism in its natural environment.

Silviculture is an aspect of Forestry that refers to the growth of plantations that yield periodic harvests.

For the proper maintenance of the energy from forests, expert advice is frequently sought. The advisory task mainly covers this. Besides, the task also involves spreading awareness about natural environment, preservation of forests and prevention of misuse of preservation of forests and prevention of misuse of forest resources.

At an executive level, various policy decisions are made and schemes devised for the conservation of forests and wildlife. The task here, broadly referred to as planning, also includes sanctioning the setting up of sawmill factories and verifying the cutting of trees.

forests and wildlife sanctuaries, with a focus on encouraging tourism. Organising nature camps is also part of the job.

Q.13 What are the attributes one needs to have?

Ans: For Indian Forest Service and State Forest Services, one needs to be physically strong. Men should have a height of at least 165 cms and women should be 150 cms, with corresponding weight. For being a successful forest manager, you must have keen interest in forest resources, wildlife and botany.

inquisitive. The aspirant must also possess a crusading spirit and excellent skills of observation. A very crucial role in the management and supervision of the country's forest reserves and wild life. To join the IFS you should be between the age of 21 and 28 years with graduation in any one of the following: Botany, Chemistry, Geography, Mathematics, Physics, Statistics, Zoology,

by an interview and a rigorous walking test (25 kms in 4 hrs. for men and 14 kms in 4 hrs. for women).

For the successful candidates, training is held at the Indira Gandhi National Forest Academy in

Forest research and education are managed under the aegis of Indian Council for Forestry Research & Education (ICFRE) and Wildlife Institute of India. There are also good openings in manufacturing.

To be in Research, you should at least have a M.Sc. in Forestry, Forest Resources, Agricultural Science, Botany or other related subjects. The Indian Council of Forestry Research and Education (Ministry of Environment and Forests) is an autonomous organisation that conducts research. The Council has branches in Dehradun, Shimla, Jabalpur, Jodhpur, Jorhat, Ranchi, Coimbatore, Bangalore, Hyderabad, Allahabad and Chilwara. Other related programmes are PG Diploma in Forest Management/ Plantation Management/ M.Sc. in Forestry/ M.Sc. in Forest Economics & Management.

B.Sc. (Forestry) is a four-year course which is offered at College of Agriculture, Akola; College of Agriculture, Haryana; Haryana Agricultural University, Hissar; College of Agriculture, Bangalore;

University, Trichur offers a M.Sc. (Forestry), which is a two-year programme.

The Indian Institute of Forest Management, Bhopal, offers a Postgraduate Diploma in Forest Management. The Indian Agricultural Research Institute at New Delhi also conducts Research studies.

For one interested in a harmonious blend of science and wild life and forestry, there are other specialisations like animal cytology, genetics, nutrition, and physiology, and veterinary science. The Aligarh Muslim University, Saurashtra University and the Wildlife Institute of India offer a specialisation in wildlife science.

Academically inclined aspirants interested in research in forestry can work with the Indian Council

The Forest Research Institute, Dehradun; Institute of Social Forestry and Eco- rehabilitation, Allahabad; Institute of Forestry Research and Human Resources Development, Chindwara are some of the institutes working under the aegis of ICFRE.

Q.14 What are the various options and prospects in this profession?

Ans: There are various people who work in forest and wildlife conservation. For example, botanists, mycologists, zoologists, entomologists (study and control of diseases caused by insects and pests), silviculturists (forest propagation and culture), forest statisticians, range forest

There are openings in Forest research institutions, Indian Forest services and State Forest services. Various government undertakings and non-governmental organisations like Society for promotion of

Those in this line can also get into Wildlife biology and management. This would involve protection, preservation and management of wildlife giving special attention to endangered species within the protected area network of National Parks, Sanctuaries and in multiple use areas, management of sanctuaries for education, recreation and captive breeding of endangered species and study of their habitats through research.

Non-governmental organisations and international bodies such as the Food and Agriculture

rise.

Those in this line can also get into Wildlife biology and management. This would involve protection, preservation and management of wildlife giving special attention to endangered species within the protected area network of National Parks, Sanctuaries and in multiple use areas, management of sanctuaries for education, recreation and captive breeding of endangered species and study of their habitats through research.

Non-governmental organisations and international bodies such as the Food and Agriculture Organisation

as there is a rising demand for professionals to prepare environmental impact statements and erosion and sediment control plans, monitor water quality near logging sites, and advise on tree harvesting practices. The academically inclined could also take up teaching or research.

In Forest services, you can start with a salary of about Rs.10, 000/- a month with additional perks and allowances. In research, one can begin as a fellow with stipend of Rs.5000 - 8000 a month or as a Scientist with a salary of about Rs.10, 000/-a month.

Forest Management professionals can get about Rs.12, 000/- or more per month to start with. Their work involves handling resource conservation, utilisation of wastelands and so on.

Forests are a rich source of many natural products like timber, honey, medicinal herbs and natural

Q.15   I want to be an astronaut like Kalpana Chawla. Kindly let me know in detail how I can fulfil my dream?

Ans:
become an astronaut. If you are looking for a career that combines cool technology, interesting science and great adventure, you could hardly make a better choice than becoming an astronaut.

Station, there will be a permanent human presence in outer space and a need for astronauts. But becoming an astronaut in the U.S. space programme is not easy, and the process can take several years.

There are three types of astronauts in the U.S. space program:

The commander is responsible for the mission, the crew and the vehicle. The pilot assists the commander in operating the vehicle and deploying satellites. The mission specialist works with the commander and pilots in shuttle operations, performs space walks and conducts experiments. The payload specialist performs specialised duties as the mission requires. Payload specialists are people other than NASA personnel, and some are foreign nationals.

Astronaut Pilots:
the commander has on board responsibility for the vehicle, crew, mission success, and safety of

the deployment and retrieval of satellites using the remote manipulator system (RMS), referred to as the robot arm or mechanical arm.

Astronaut Mission Specialist: Mission specialist astronauts work with the commander and the pilot and have overall responsibility for coordinating operations in the following areas: systems, crew activity planning, consumables usage, and experiment/payload operations. Mission specialists are trained in the details of the on board systems, as well as the operational characteristics, mission requirements/ objectives, and supporting equipment/systems for each of the experiments conducted on their assigned missions. Mission specialists perform extravehicular activities (EVAs), or space walks, operate the remote manipulator system, and are responsible for payloads and

Payload Specialists: Payload specialists are persons other than NASA astronauts (including foreign nationals) who have specialised on board duties; they may be added to shuttle crews if activities

When payload specialists are required they are nominated by NASA, the foreign sponsor, or the designated payload sponsor. In the case of NASA or NASA-related payloads, the nominations are based on the recommendations of the appropriate Investigator Working Group (IWG).

Although payload specialists are not part of the Astronaut Candidate Program, they must have the appropriate education and training related to the payload or experiment. All applicants must meet certain physical requirements and must pass NASA space physical examinations with varying standards depending on:

an accredited college or university

degree equals one year of experience, and a doctorate equals three years.

examinations.

193 cm) for mission/payload specialists.

which accepts applications continuously. NASA then screens the applications, and you may be asked to go for a weeklong session where you will participate in personal interviews, medical tests and orientations. Your screening performance will be evaluated, and if you are lucky, you may be accepted as an astronaut candidate. NASA announces candidates every two years, selecting about a hundred men and women out of thousands of applicants.

If you are selected, you will report to NASA's Johnson Space Centre in Houston, Texas, for training and evaluations, which last two years. During the training period, you will take classes in basic science (math, astronomy, physics, geology, meteorology, oceanography), technology (navigation, orbital mechanics, materials processing), and space shuttle systems. You will also be trained in land and sea survival techniques, SCUBA, micro gravity, high- and low-pressure environments,

suit and tennis shoes, and tread water for 10 minutes). If you are a pilot, you will train in NASA's

four hours each month.

At the end of the two-year training period, you may be selected to become an astronaut. As an astronaut, you will continue classroom training on the various aspects of space shuttle operations that you started as an astronaut candidate. You will begin training on each individual system in the shuttle with the help of an instructor. After that, you will train in simulators for pre-launch, launch, orbit, entry and landing. Depending upon whether you are a pilot or mission specialist, you will learn how to use the shuttle's robotic arm to manipulate cargo. You will continue generic

shuttle and space station, and underwater training for space walks. The simulations will prepare you for every type of emergency or contingency imaginable.

federal civil service employees (GS-11 to GS-14 grade) with equivalent pay based on experience.

So, you can see that you will need education, hard work and steadfast dedication to become an astronaut. However, the future & career is tremendous!

Q.16   I want to take a career in advertising. What is the potential of advertising as a career? Which universities offer courses in advertising?

Ans:
or services through visual or oral messages. A product or service is advertised to create awareness in the minds of potential buyers. Some of the commonly used media for advertising are T.V., radio, websites, newspapers, magazines, bill-boards, hoardings, etc. As a result of economic liberalisation and the changing social trends advertising industry has shown rapid growth in the last decade.

Advertising is one of the aspects of mass communication. Advertising is actually brand-building through effective communication and is essentially a service industry. It helps to create demand, promote marketing system and boost economic growth. Thus advertising forms the basis of marketing. To enter the career of advertising, you can go for a degree/diploma in advertising/ mass communication/ marketing and then join any advertising agency for on the job training.

Universities/Institutes offering courses in advertising

Q.17 What is interior designing? Who can become an interior designer? What are the career prospects?

Ans: Interior design is the process of shaping the experience of interior space. So it's not just interior decoration but it also involves aspects of environmental psychology, architecture and product design. While some would say it is just the art of putting some furniture together, interior designers beg to differ. Experts say that interior design is a creative process that understands

design document or plan. Many a time, an interior designer works closely with the architect to

different aspects of a home. While your architect will tell you the dimensions of your bathroom

bathroom will compliment your mood. There is quite a big debate on that front. Everyone agrees that you need to be a creative person if you want to be an interior designer. However, some feel

designer," says Parthajeet Sarma, director of iDream Advisory Services Private Limited. Sarma is actually an architect, however, he has been involved in interior design with as much success. He adds, "(Some) One who has an eye for detail and loves solving cryptic puzzles would make a good interior designer. I am not an interior designer but an architect -- however I have been involved in this industry for 12 years now." The key word then is interest. The rest falls in after that. Create

about brick and mortar.

Interior designers are in demand. Industry experts say there is a dearth of good interior designers. "Interior designers are in much demand now due to the retail boom in India," says Shubha Jain who offers interior design courses at the International Institute of Fashion Design (Mumbai).

designer for malls, hotels and design companies. Interior designers are also employed by big

your training, you will need to work hard to get some recognition. "Yes, the career prospects are good," says Sarma, "But be prepared to slog it out during the initial years. If you do that and you are intrinsically good at design, you will surely shine. Be warned however that this is not like doing an MBA from an IIM where you join at the top and retire at the top."

Q.18 What are the vocational/job oriented subjects/courses offered by CBSE?

Ans:

Accommodation Services
Agriculture
Advance Food Preparation
Air-Conditioning and Refrigeration
Applied Physics
Auto Engineering
Auto Shop Repair and Practice
Basic Design (Common to Textile Design-Weaving)
Bakery Science
Beauty Therapy and Hair Dressing
Cash Management and Housekeeping
Clinical Biochemistry
Clothing Construction
Civil Engineering
Confectionery
Cosmetic Chemistry

Commercial Art
Community Health Nursing
Consumer Behaviour and Protection

Dance Odissi
Dance Bharatnatyam
Designing & Pattern Making
Dyeing and Printing
Digital Electronics and Micro Processors
Electrical Appliances
Electrical Machines
Electronics Devices and Circuits
Entrepreneurship
Engineering Science
Establishment & Management of Food Service Unit
Fabrication Technology

Floriculture
Food Science & Hygiene
Food and Beverage Service
Food Preparation
Fundamentals of Nursing
Graphics
India — The Tourist Destination
Laboratory Medicine
Lending Operations
Library Administration and Management
Maternity & Child Health Nursing
Meal Planning & Service
Music Hindustani (Vocal)

Music Hindustani (Instrumental Melodic)
Music Hindustani (Instrumental Percussion)

Marketing
Mechanical Engineering
Microbiology
Ophthalmic Techniques
Optics

Ophthalmic Techniques (Vocational) Biology
Painting
Philosophy
Physical Education
Principles and Practices of Life Insurance
Post Harvest Technology & Preservation
Radio Engineering and Audio Systems
Railway Commercial Working
Reference Service
Radiation Physics
Radiography
Stenography (English)
Salesmanship
Sculpture

Store Accounting

Textile Science
Television and Video Systems
Tourism management and Manpower planning
Travel Trade Management
Transportation systems and Management
 Typewriting (English)
Vegetable Culture
Yoga, Anatomy and Physiology

Q.19   What is data mining?
Ans:

intelligence, machine learning, statistics and database systems. The goal of data mining is to extract knowledge from a data set in a human-understandable structure and involves database and data management, data preprocessing, model and inference considerations, interestingness metrics, complexity considerations, post-processing of found structure, visualisation and online updating.

The term is a buzzword, and is frequently misused to mean any form of large scale data or information processing (collection, extraction, warehousing, analysis and statistics) but also

machine learning and business intelligence. In the proper use of the word, the key term is

mining: Practical machine learning tools and techniques with Java" (which covers mostly machine learning material) was originally to be named just "Practical machine learning", and the term "data mining" was only added for marketing reasons. Often the more general terms "(large

and machine learning are more appropriate.

The actual data-mining task is the automatic or semi-automatic analysis of large quantities of data to extract previously unknown interesting patterns such as groups of data records (cluster analysis), unusual records (anomaly detection) and dependencies (association rule mining). This usually involves using database techniques such as spatial indexes. These patterns can then be seen as a kind of summary of the input data, and used in further analysis or for example in machine learning and predictive analytics. For example, the data mining step might identify multiple groups in the data, which can then be used to obtain more accurate prediction results by a decision support system.

Q.20   What is Narrowcasting?
Ans: Narrowcasting has traditionally been understood as the dissemination of information (usually by radio or television) to a narrow audience, not to the general public. Narrowcasting involves aiming

attributes. Also called niche marketing or target marketing. Narrowcasting is based on the postmodern idea that mass audiences do not exist. The term was coined by computer scientist and public broadcasting advocate J. C. R. Licklider, who in a 1967 report envisioned "a multiplicity of television networks aimed at serving the needs of smaller, specialised audiences. 'Here,' stated Licklider, 'I should like to coin the term "narrowcasting," using it to emphasize the rejection or dissolution of the constraints imposed by commitment to a monolithic mass-appeal, broadcast approach."

The term "narrowcasting" can also apply to the spread of information to an audience (private or

or conference attendees—and requires a localised dissemination of information from a shared source.

Q.21   Who is a knowledge engineer?

Ans:
systems. Receiving information from domain experts, the knowledge engineers interpret the presented information and relay it to computer programmers who code the information in to

construction process of computer systems.

Q.22   What is Graphic Design?

Ans: Ever wondered why do you stay at some websites for a longer time and leave some without spending much time? Ever wondered what is graphic design? Well then you are already on your way to starting a career in graphic design. A graphic designer is a specialist in solving the

in Drawing, Layout, Typography, Lettering, Diagramming and Photography. A graphic designer is someone who can visualise text into pictures and express them through a visual representation. Graphic designers do designing for logos, icons, and make detailed designs and layouts. Graphic designing as a career can be very lucrative, once a person gains experience he can do projects on his own and also start his own venture. As a graphic designer one uses specialised computers and computer software to help you create layouts and design elements and also to programme animated graphics. Initially at the entry level one joins as a graphic designer and then can go on to become creative head of a company.

Q.23   What is Cargo Handling?

Ans: Ever wondered what is cargo handling and how your luggage at the airports is carried, driven and delivered — yes there is a whole science and industry behind it! A cargo handler moves luggage and places them in appropriate locations. He should be physically strong to carry heavy weight luggage. He needs to know how much weight a vehicle can take or a location can handle. Also he needs to

load and unload the luggage from and to the vehicle. They always need to ensure that balance is maintained throughout the journey of the vehicle and no un-forecast incidents happen. If you want to make a career in cargo handling, you can do diploma course after your 12th and be a cargo handler. The training usually deals with logistics, knowledge of supply chain management, maintaining and driving the vehicle. A career in cargo handling can see you not only placed at airport but also at ports.

Q.24   What is Social Work?

Ans:

about each other — families care about their members and friends care about each other. When you do something for your brother, it is not social work, but it's your duty. On the other hand, when you do something for a stranger or for the suffering and the weak, it is called social work. Thus, social work is something that is done for the welfare of a society. It is a professional discipline committed to the pursuit of social welfare and social justice and work toward research and practice to improve the quality of life and potential of each individual, group, and society. As a social worker, you would be working towards organising the NGO sector by channelising resources and funds to the needful. As a social work student you will learn about human rights, child rights, and women rights — you can pick up the sector of your interest and start working with NGOs and Social Groups after gaining a professional degree in social work or psychology. You can travel to other countries as volunteers or paid employees to their NGOs and make a change there too.

IMPORTANT WEBSITES

Career Related websites

01. www.careersindia.com
02. www.egurukool.com
03. www.educationinfoindia.com
04. www.editorial.msn.com
05. www.vuw.ac.nz
06. www.vidyainfo.com
07. www.delhi4students.com
08. www.admissionguru.com
09. www.indiaeducation.info
10. www.indiaedunews.net
11. www.kaptest.com
12. www.ncaa.org
13. www.collegeresource.org

15. www.commonapp.org
16. www.campustours.com
17. www.education.sify.com
18. www.educationinfoindia.com
19. www.rajasthaneducation.net
20. www.studyabroadlinks.com
21. www.roadtocollege.com
22. www.nslijgenetics.org
23. www.directoryofcourses.com
24. www.webindia123.com
25. www.education.sify.com
26. www.aicte.ernet.in   All India Council of Technical Education (AICTE)

27.	www.aieee.nic.in	All India Engineering Entrance Examination (AIEEE)
28.	www.actuariesindia.org	Actuarial Society of India, Mumbai
29.	www.allduniv.edu/hrdm	Allahabad University
30.	www.aadu.org	Allahabad Agricultural Institute (Deemed University)
32.	www.aajivika.com	Ajivika Guidance, Counselling & Training
35.	www.ait.ac.th	Asian Institute of Technology, Thailand
36.	www.asianmedia.org	Asian College of Journalism, Chennai
37.	www.ansalinstitute.org	Ansal Institute of Technology
38.	www.amity.edu	Amity Business School
39.	www.ametindia.com	Academy of Maritime Education and Training
40.	www.aima-ind.org	All India Management Association (AIMA)
41.	www.aiimas.com	All India Institute of Management Studies
42.	www.aimetindia.com	All India Management Entrance Test
43.	www.allayurveda.com	All About Ayurvrdic Education
44.	www.altltd.com	ALT Training College, Bangalore
45.	www.aaft.com	Asian Academy of Film & TV
46.	www.aiuweb.org	Association of Indian Universities
47.	www.atma-aims.org	Association of Indian Management Schools
48.	www.al-ameen.com	AL-Ameen Arts, Science & Commerce College, Bangalore
49.	www.allianceba.org	Alliance Business Academy, Bangalore
50.	www.aiims.ac.in	AIIMS, New Delhi
51.	www.aiims.edu	AIIMS, New Delhi
52.	www.afmcpune.com	AFMC, Pune
53.	www.afmc.com	AFMC, Pune
54.	www.armedforces.nic.in	AFMC, Pune
55.	www.amu.ac.in	Aligarh Muslim University
56.	www.aligmusuniv.cjb.net	Aligarh Muslim University
57.	www.annauniv.edu/ptme.html	Anna University, Chennai
58.	www.annauniv.ac.in	Anna University
59.	www.angrau.net	Acharya NG Ranga Agricultural University
60.	www.apsche.org	Andhra University
61.	www.arunvarsity.org	Arunachal University
62.	www.aau.ac.in	Assam Agricultural University
63.	www.assamuniversity.tripod.com	Assam University, Silchar
64.	www.assamuniversity.nic.in	Assam University, Silchar
65.	www.aec.educations.net	Assam Engineering College, Guwahati

66.	www.aciassam.com	Assam Engineering Institute, Guwahati
67.	www.aurura.ac.in	Aurora's Degree College, Hyderabad
68.	www.aakashinstitute.com	Akash Institute for IIT & PMT Coaching
69.	www.airhostessacademy.org	Air Hostess Academy (AHA)
70.	www.educationandhra.com	Andhra Pradesh Education Detail
71.	www.amsheela.org	AMS Engineering College
72.	www.ayjnihh.org	AYJNIHH, Mumbai
73.	www.anupamainstitutions.com	Anupama College of Management & Science
74.	www.acharyainstitutions.org	Acharya Institutes, Bangalore
76.	www.act.org	ACT details (For US admission)
77.	www.educationbangalore.com	Bangalore Institution Detail
78.	www.onlinebangalore.com	Bangalore Education Detail
79.	www.becollege.org	Bengal Engineering College
80.	www.multiplegroup.com	Bengal Institute of Hotel Management
81.	www.betcoms.com	BET College of Management & Science
82.	www.banasthali.org	Banasthali Vidyapith, Rajasthan
83.	www.badruka.com	Badruka College, Hyderabad
84.	www.bharathiaruni.org	Bharathiar University, Coimbatore
85.	www.bdu.ernet.in	Bharathidasan University
86.	www.bim.edu	Bharathidasan Institute of Management
87.	www.bhavans.ac.in	Bharatiya Vidya Bhavan's College
88.	www.bharatividyapeeth.edu	Bharati Vidyapeeth, Pune
89.	www.engg.bharatividyapeeth.edu	Bharatividyapeeth,s College of Engineering
90.	www.bmcc.ac.in	BMC of Commerce, Pune
91.	www.bhavans.ac.in	Bhavan's College, Mumbai
92.	www.bits-pilani.ac.in	Birla Institute of Science & Technology, Pilani
93.	www.bitmesra.ac.in	BIT Mesra, Ranchi
94.	www.bbaunindia.org	Babasaheb Ambedkar University, Lucknow
95.	www.bhu.ac.in	Banaras Hindu University
96.	www.britishcouncil.org/india	British Council
98.	www.educationuk.in.org	British Education
99.	www.bbclearning.com	BBC Worldwide Learing
100.	www.bbdnitm.edu	BBD National Institute of Technology & Management
101.	www.bundelkhanduniversity.com	Bundelkhand University, Jhansi
102.	www.bundelkhandeducation.org	Bundelkhand University
103.	www.bmccpune@pn3.vsnl.net.in	BM College of Commerce, Pune
104.	www.bmsce.org	BMS College of Engineering

105.	www.bimtechindia.org	Birla Institute of Management Technology, New Delhi
106.	www.bio-campus.com	Bio Campus(For Bio Informatics Education)
107.	www.bioinfo.ernet.in	Bioinformatics Centre, University of Pune
108.	www.bioinformaticscentre.org	Bioinformatics Institute of India, Noida
109.	www.btc.iitb.ac.in	Biotechnology Centre, IIT Mumbai
110.	www.bcwcc.org	Bishop Cotton Women's Christian College
111.	www.sbsec.org	Bhagat Singh College, New Delhi
112.	www.indiaBSchools.com	Business Schools Rating in India
113.	www.indianmba.com	Business School admission help
114.	www.cbse.nic.in	Central Board of Secondary Education (CBSE)
115.	www.cbseresults,nic.in	CBSE Results
116.	www.results.nic.in	CBSE Results
118.	www.clri.org	Central Leather Research Institute

123.	www.herboaltmed.com	Central Calcutta Academy of Medical & Paramedical Tech.
124.	www.careerlauncher.com	Career Launcher
125.	www.ascenteducation.com	CAT coaching
126.	www.civilservicestimes.org	Civil Services Times(For IAS Coaching)
127.	www.cmrims-india.org	CMR Institute of Management Studies
128.	www.smi.ernet.in	Chennai Mathematical Institute
129.	www.chanakya-iasacademy.com	Chanakya IAS Academy, New Delhi
130.	www.cmcl.as	Christian Medical College, Ludhiana
131.	www.cmcludhiana.org	Christian Medical College, Ludhiana
132.	www.cca.nic.in	Chandigarh College of Architecture
133.	www.cmch-vellore.edu	CMC, Vellore
134.	www.vellorecmc.org	CMC, Vellore
135.	www.christcollege.edu	Christ College, Bangalore
136.	www.citycoll@cal3.vsnl.net.in	City College, Calcutta
137.	www.medicalcollegekolkata.org	Calcutta Medical College
138.	www.mpuat.ac.in	College of Tech. & Engineering, Udaipur
139.	www.corvc@rurkiu.ernet.in	College of Engineering, Roorkee
140.	www.annauniv.edu/ceg	College of Engineering, Anna University
141.	www.raifoundation.org	College of Computing & Applied Software Engineering
142.	www.ceptindia.org	Centre for Environmental Planning & Technology
143.	www.cdacindia.com	Centre for Development of Advance Computing(C-DAC)

144.	www.cmd.edu	Centre for Management Development
145.	www.cimindia.com	Centre for International Management
146.	www.annauniv.edu/biotech	Centre for Biotechnology, Anna University, Chennai
147.	www.cssmmarine.com	Chennai School of Ship Management, Chennai
148.	www.cvraman.org	C.V.Raman College of Engineering, Bhubaneshwar
149.	www.cybercollegebir.org	Cyber Institute of Computer Sciences
150.	www.canadorec.on.ca	Canadore College, Canada
152.	www.ccrhindia.org	Central Council for Research in Homeopathy
153.	www.doonparamedicalcollege.org	Doon Paramedical College, Dehradun
154.	www.doe.gov.in	DOEACC Society, New Delhi
155.	www.doeacc.org.in	DOEACC Society, New Delhi
156.	www.dciindia.org	Dental Council of India
157.	www.mst.nic.in/dst	Department of Science & Technology(DST), Govt. of India
158.	www.yas.nic.in	Department of Youth Affairs & Sports, Govt. of India
159.	www.dte.org.in	DTE, Maharashtra
160.	www.ysparmaruniversity.org	Dr. YS Parmar University of Horticulture & Forestry
161.	www.ditddun.com	Dehradun Institute of Technology
162.	www.dayanandsagar.edu	Dayanand Sagar Institutions, Bangalore
163.	www.du.ac.in	Delhi University
164.	www.admissionshelp.com	Delhi University Admission Help
165.	www.brau.com	Dr. B.R.. Ambedkar University, Agra
166.	www.braou.ac.in	Dr. B.R. Ambedkar Open University
167.	www.nitj.ac.in	Dr. B.R. Ambedkar NIT, Jalandhar
168.	www.dce.edu	Delhi College of Engineering
169.	www.dceonline.net	Delhi College of Engineering
170.	www.commdsedu.org	Department of Commerce, Delhi School of Economics
171.	www.daulatramcollege.net	Daulat Ram College, New Delhi
172.	www.dducollege.org	Deen Dayal Upadhyay College, New Delhi
173.	www.dibru.ernet.in	Dibrugarh University
174.	www.da-iict.org	Dhirubhai Ambani Institute of Information Technology
175.	www.dypp.edu	DY Patil Women College of Engineering, Pune
176.	www.darpana.com/darpana.htm	Darpana Academy of Performing Arts, Ahmedabad
177.	www.durgapuriatm.org	Durgapur Institute of Advance Tech. & Management
178.	www.discoveryschool.com	Discovery Channel's science & Math for students
179.	www.engineeringstudies.com	Engineering Study Detail
180.	www.ediindia.org	Entrepreneurship Development Institute of India
182.	www.edcil.co.in	Educational Consultant India Limited, New Delhi

183.	www.eis.ernet.in	ERNET India
184.	www.empiindia.com	EMPI Business School
185.	www.eastwestinstitutions.com	East West College, Bangalore
186.	www.ewit.edu	East West Institute of Technology
187.	www.ethirajcollege.org	Ethiraj College, Chennai
188.	www.ethirajcollege.com	Ethiraj College for Women, Chennai
190.	www.ferguson.edu	Ferguson College, Pune
191.	www.fergusson.edu	Fergusson College
192.	www.fms.edu	Faculty of Management Studies, University of Delhi
193.	www.ftdcindia.com	Foreign Trade Development Centre, New Delhi
195.	www.faeaindia.org	Foundation for Academic Excellence & Access(FAEA)
196.	www.fsm.ac.in	Fore School of Management
197.	www.fddiindia.com	Footwear Design & Development Institute
198.	www.mib.nic.in/FTII.htm	Film & Television Institute of India, Pune
199.	www.gu.nic.in	Gauhati University
200.	www.ggsipu.nic.in	GGS IP University
201.	www.goacom.com	Goa University
202.	www.gnlu.ac.in	Gujrat National Law University
203.	www.gndec.ac.in	Gurunanak Dev Engg College, Ludhiana
204.	www.gmch.nic.in	Govt Medical College, Chandigarh
205.	www.grantmedicalcollege.com	Grant Medical College, Mumbai
206.	www.glc.edu	Govt. College of Law, University of Mumbai
207.	www.gardencitycollege.org	Garden City College of Science & Managt. Studies, Bangalore
208.	www.gsbadelhi.com	Graduate School of Business & Administration
209.	www.giepc.org	Gem & Jewellery Export Promotion Council
210.	www.campus-germany.de	Germany Education Help
211.	www.iitd.ac.in/gate	GATE detail
212.	www.elite-academy.com	GATE coaching (Elite Academy)
213.	www.mba.co	GMAT Detail
214.	www.gre.org	GRE Detail
217.	www.hinducollege.edu	Hindu College, Delhi
218.	www.hinducollege.org	Hindu College
219.	www.hansrajcollege.com	Hansraj College, Delhi
220.	www.hrcollege.edu	HR College of Commerce & Economics, Mumbai
221.	www.hmhiec.com	HMH Education Consultant

222.	www.hindustancollege.com	Hindustan College of Engineering, Chennai
223.	www.homeo.net	Homeopathic Education Detail
224.	www.indiaparenting.com	Help Line for Parents
225.	www.askmeyourproblem.com	Help Line for Students
226.	www.helpteens.com	Help Line for Students
227.	www.expage.com	Help Line for Students
228.	www.10minuteresume.com	Help for your resume writing
229.	www.provenresumes.com	Help for your resume writing
230.	www.resume.com	Help for your resume writing
231.	www.resumezapper.com	Help for your resume writing
232.	www.easymaths.com	Help for Mathematics
233.	www.mathsnet.net	Help for Mathematics
234.	www.mathsisfun.com	Help for Mathematics
235.	www.gomath.com	Help for Mathematics
236.	www.gcsephysics.com	Help for Physics
237.	www.biology-online.org	Help line for Biology
238.	www.gcsechemistry.com	Help for Chemistry
239.	www.chem4kids.com	Help for Chemistry
240.	www.chemistry.co.nz	Help for Chemistry
241.	www.chem4kids.com	Help for Chemistry (For school children)
242.	www.chemhelper.com	Help for Organic Chemistry
243.	www.compusbox.com	Help for+2 Exam (Coaching web site)
244.	www.schoolcircle.com	Help for +2 Exam (Model question & answer)
245.	www.iimahd.ernet.in	Indian Institute of Management, Ahmedabad
246.	www.iimb.ernet.in	Indian Institute of Management, Bangalore
247.	www.iimcal.ac.in	Indian Institute of Management, Calcutta
248.	www.iimidr.ac.in	Indian Institute of Management, Indore
250.	www.iiml.ac.in	Indian Institute of Management, Lucknow
251.	www.iita.com	Indian Institute of Information Technology, Allahabad
252.	www.iita.ac.in	Indian Institute of Information Technology, Allahabad
253.	www.iiitm.ac.in	Indian Institute of Information Tech. & Managt., Guwalior
254.	www.iiitb.ac.in	Indian Institute of Information Technology, Bangalore
256.	www.iisc.ernet.in	Indian Institute of Science, Bangalore
257.	www.iimc.ac.in	Indian Institute of Mass Communication
258.	www.iijnm.org	Indian Institute of Journalism & New Media, Bangalore
259.	www.iihmc.aiol.com	Indian Institute of Hotel Management & Catering
260.	www.iipm.edu	Indian Institute of Planning & Management(IIPM)

261.	www.iipmb.com	Indian Institute of Plantation Management, Bangalore
262.	www.iifm.org	Indian Institute of Forest Management, Bhopal
263.	www.iimt.org	Indian Institute of Medical Transcription
264.	www.iicidindia.org	Indian Institute of Crafts & Design, Jaipur
265.	www.iihmr.org	Indian Institute of Health Management & Research
266.	www.iimmpune.com	Indian Institute of Modern Management, Pune
267.	www.iiem.com	Indian Institute of Export Management, Bangalore
268.	www.iift.edu	Indian Institute of Foreign Trade
269.	www.iif.edu	Indian Institute of Finance
271.	www.icmr.nic.in	Indian Council of Medical Research, New Delhi
272.	www.icssr.org	Indian Council of Social Science Research
273.	www.ibainternational.org	Indian Business Academy, Bangalore
274.	www.diamondinstitute.ac.in	Indian Diamond Institute, Surat
275.	www.ilidelhi.org	Indian Law Institute, Delhi
276.	www.iiace.com	Indian Institute of Aircraft Engineering, Delhi
277.	www.armedforces.nic.in	Indian Army
278.	www.joinindianarmy.nic.in	Indian Army (Careers in Indian Army)
279.	www.nausena-bharti.mil.in	Indian Navy(Recruitment/career)
280.	www.careerairforce.nic.in	Indian Air Force(Recruitment/career)
281.	www.iadcollege.com	Indian Academy Degree College
282.	www.igib.res.in	Institute of Genomics & Interactive Biology
283.	www.imt.edu/dlp	Institute of Management Technology(IMT), Gaziabad
284.	www.imsddun.com	Institute of Management Studies, Dehradun
285.	www.srmscet.edu	Institute of Management Sciences, Bareilly
287.	www.itm.edu	Institute of Technology & Management, Warangal
288.	www.icmr.nic.in	ICMR Institute
289.	www.icrimindia.org	ICRIM
290.	www.ibmr.org	Institute of Business Management & Research, Pune
291.	www.iibr.org	Institute of International Business & Research, Pune
292.	www.iilm.edu	IILM, New Delhi
294.	www.iact.ac.in	International Academy for Creative Teaching, Bangalore
295.	www.iiseindia.com	International Institute for Special Education. Lucknow
297.	www.imi.edu	International Management Institute, New Delhi
298.	www.ibmr.org	Institute of Business Management & Research
299.	www.imtech.res.in	Institute of Microbial Technology

300.	www.iam-cal.net	Institute of Advanced Management
301.	www.inderprastha.com	Indraprastha Engineering College, Gaziabad
302.	www.ibsindia.org	Icfaian Business School
303.	www.icfai.org/isfm	ICFAI School of Finance & Management
304.	www.indrdelhi.com	Institute of Management Development & Research
305.	www.ismindia.org	ITUC School of Management
307.	www.ignou.org	Indira Gandhi National Open University
308.	www.igidr.ac.in	Indira Gandhi Inst. of Development Research, Mumbai
309.	www.ipcollege.com	Indraprashtha College for Women, Delhi
311.	www.icodeindia.org	ICODE Institute
312.	www.immindia.com	Institute of Marketing Management
313.	www.iitb.ac.in	IIT Bombay
314.	www.iitd.ernet.in	IIT Delhi
316.	www.iitm.ac.in	IIT Madras
317.	www.iitg.ernet.in	IIT Guwahati
319.	www.iitr.ernet.in	IIT Roorkee
320.	www.iitr.ac.in	IIT Roorkee
321.	www.itbhu.ac.in	Institute of Technology, BHU
322.	www.irm.ernet.in	Institute of Rural Management, Anand
323.	www.irma.ac.in	Institute of Rural Management, Anand
324.	www.universityofmadras-ice.ac.in	Institute of Correspondence Edn., University of Madras
325.	www.iopb.res.in	Institute of Physics, Bhubaneswar
326.	www.iic.ac.in	Institute of Informatics & Communication, New Delhi
327.	www.imtech.res.in	Institute of Microbial Technology(IMTECH)
328.	www.ibab.ac.in	Institute of Bioinformatics & Applied Biotechnology
330.	www.icai.org	Institute of Chartered Accountant of India
331.	www.icsi.edu	Institute of Company Secretaries of India
333.	www.imagoindia.com	Imago Acting School
334.	www.infy.com	Infosys
335.	www.iimm-delhi.com	International Institute of Mass Media, New Delhi
336.	www.iiit.net	International Institute of Information Technology, Hyderabad
337.	www.isicweb.net	International Students Identity Card
338.	www.ilslaw.edu	ILS Law College, Pune

339.	www.ieccollege.com	IEC College of Engineering & Technology
340.	www.ipsacademyonline.com	IPS Academy
342.	www.isro.gov.in	Indian Space Research Organisation (ISRO)
343.	www.ipr.res.in	Institute of Plasma Research
344.	www.jnu.ac.in	Jawaharlal Nehru University(JNU)
345.	www.jmcdelhi.com	Jesus and Mary College, Delhi
346.	www.jyotinivas.org	Jyoti Nivas College, Bangalore
347.	www.intu.ac.in	Jawaharlal Nehru Technological University
348.	www.sangeetnatak.com/jnmda.htm	Jawaharlal Nehru Manipur Dance Academy
349.	www.jipmer.edu	JIPMER, Pondicherry
351.	www.jbims.edu	Jamnalal Bajaj Institute of Management Studies
353.	www.jaats.com	Jobs & Career
354.	www.jmi.nic.in	Jamia Millia Islamia
355.	www.jamia.net	Jamia Millia Islamia
356.	www.jamiahamdard.edu	Jamia Hamdard
357.	www.jimindia.com	Jaipuria Institute of Management, Lucknow
358.	www.jiitindia.org	Jaypee Institute of Information Technology(JIIT)
359.	www.jdinstitute.com	JD Institute of Fashion Tech
360.	www.jdtiindia.com	Jewellery Design & Technology Institute
361.	www.aicte.org/ASSAM-DIP.doc	Jyoti Chitraban Film & Television Institute, Guwahati
363.	www.jamboreeindia.com	GMAT, GRE, SAT coaching
377.	www.lcbcollege.org	Lalit Chandra Bharali College, Guwahati

378.	www.ladybrabourne.com	Lady Brabourne College, Calcutta
379.	www.lsrcollege.org	Lady Shri Ram College, Delhi
380.	www.loyolacollege.edu	Loyala College, Chennai
381.	www.lbsim.edu	Lal Bahadur Shastri Institute of Management, Delhi
382.	www.primetutor.com	LAW entrance coaching
383.	www.lse.ac.uk	London School of Economics
384.	www.merical.ac.in	Marine Engineering Research Institute (MERI)
385.	www.mit.edu	Massachusetts Institute of Technology, USA
386.	www.monash.edu.au	Monash University, Australia
387.	www.indianmba.com	MBA Institutions & Admission Details
388.	www.justcolleges.com	MBA Admission (Abroad) Details
390.	www.manipal.edu	Manipal Academy of Higher Education, Manipal
391.	www.mpbou.org	Madhya Pradesh Bhoj(Open) University
392.	www.bhojvirtualuniversity.com	Madhya Pradesh Bhoj (Open) University
393.	www.mats.ac.in	Mahaveer Academy of Technology & Science, Bangalore
394.	www.msrit.edu	MS Ramaiah Institute of Technology
395.	www.mlsu.ac.in	Mohanlal Sukhadia University, Udaipur
396.	www.mountcarmelcollegeblr.org	Mount Carmel College, Bangalore
397.	www.makhanlaluniversity.org	Makhanlal Chaturvedi Rastriya Patrakarita Viswavidyalaya
398.	www.mcu.ac.in	MCRPV, Bhopal
399.	www.mrsiit.com	Maharaja Ranjit Singh Institute of IT, Patiala
400.	www.mmcindia.edu	Madras Medical College, Chennai
401.	www.madraschristiancollege.com	Madras Christian College, Chennai
403.	www.msrchm.edu	MS Ramaiah College of Hotel Management, Bangalore
404.	www.msrsas.org	MS Ramaiah School of Advanced Studies
405.	www.msrmc.ac.in	MS Ramaiah Medical College
406.	www.mvjeducation.com	MVJ College of Engineering, Bangalore
407.	www.mdi.ac.in	Management Development Institute(MDI)
408.	www.mastersindia.com	Master School of Management
410.	www.mbs.edu/info/india	Melbourne Business School
411.	www.mica-india.net	Mudra Institute of Communications, Ahmedabad
412.	www.mamc.ac.in	Maulana Azad Medical College, Delhi
413.	www.mciindia.org	Medical Council of India
414.	www.amupmdc.org	Medical Common Entrance Test (Maharashtra AMUPMDC)
415.	www.medistudies.com	Medical Education in Andhra Pradesh & India
416.	www.indiamedicaleducation.com	Medical Education Detail

417.	www.medistudies.com	Medical Education details
418.	www.medicoinfoline.com	Medical Education Detail
419.	www.beadoctor.com	Medical admission detail
420.	www.eduinternational.org	Medical admission in Russia
421.	www.aamc.org	Medical Career Detail
423.	www.mohwfw.nic.in	Ministry of Health & Family welfare
424.	www.mh.du.ac.in	Miranda House, New Delhi
425.	www.mirandahouse.ac.in	Miranda House, New Delhi
426.	www.mithibai.svkm.ac.in	Mithibai College, Mumbai
427.	www.mountcarmelcollegeblr.org	Mount Carmel College, Bangalore
428.	www.pgdoam.com	Morarka Foundation (Courses in Organic Fertilizer)
429.	www.nls.ac.in	National Law School of India University, Bangalore
430.	www.lawentrance.com	National Law School Entrance Guidance
432.	www.nalsarlawuniv.org	NALSAR University of Law, Hyderabad
433.	www.nalsarpro.org	NALSAR University of Law, Hyderabad
434.	www.nlujodhpur.ac.in	National Law University, Jodhpur
435.	www.nlujodhpur.nic.in	National Law University, Jodhpur
436.	www.nliu.edu	National Law Institute University, Bhopal
437.	www.law.nyu.edu	New York University School of Law
438.	www.nips.net	NIPS School of Hotel Management
439.	www.mnrec.ac.in	National Institute of Technology, Allahabad
440.	www.manit.nic.in	National Institute of Technology, Bhopal
441.	www.crec.ker.nic.in	National Institute of Technology, Calicut
442.	www.patra.recham.ernet.in	National Institute of Technology, Himachal Pradesh
443.	www.mnit.ac.in	National Institute of Technology, Jaipur
444.	www.nicj.ac.in	National Institute of Technology, Jalandhar
445.	www.vnitnagpur.org	National Institute of Technology, Nagpur
447.	www.recsurat.ac.in	National Institute of Technology, Surat, Gujrat
448.	www.nitw.ernet.in	NIT, Warangal
449.	www.niftindia.com	National Institute of Fashion Technology(NIFT)
450.	www.nifd.net	National Institute of Fashion Design(NIFD)
451.	www.nifm.org	National Institute of Financial Management
452.	www.niper.nic.in	National Institute of Pharma. Edn. & Research(NIPER)
453.	www.nihfw.org	National Institute of Health & Family Welfare(NIHFW)
454.	www.india-future.com/nioh	National Inst. for Orthopaediacally Handicapped
455.	www.nimhans.kar.nic.in	National Institute of Mental Health & Neuro-sciences

456.	www.schoolofdramaindia.com	National School of Drama, New Delhi
457.	www.nsbindia.com	National School of Banking, Mumbai
458.	www.nicmar.org	National Institute of Construction Mgt. & Research
459.	www.niamonline.com	National Institute of Agricultural Marketing, Jaipur
460.	www.nitie.edu	National Institute of Industrial Engg.(NITIE)
462.	www.nchmct.org	National Council for Hotel Mgt. & Catering Technology
463.	www.nfgcollege.com	National First Grade College, Bangalore
464.	www.niift.com	Nothern India Institute of Fashion Technology
465.	www.nmims.edu	Narsee Manjee Institute of Management Studies, Mumbai
466.	www.nsit.ac.in	Netaji Subhas Institute of Technology, New Delhi
467.	www.ndimdelhi.org	New Delhi Institute of Management(NDIM)
468.	www.niilm.com	NIILM Centre For Management Studies, New Delhi
469.	www.delhihomeo.com	Nehru Homeopathic Medical College, New Delhi
470.	www.nba-aicte.org	National Board of Accreditation (NBA-AICTE)
471.	www.natboard.org	National Board of Examination, Ministry of H & FW, GOI
472.	www.ncte-in.org	National Council of Teachers Education
473.	www.ncert.nic.in	NCERT
475.	www.niit.com	NIIT
476.	www.nid.edu	National Institute of Design(NID)
477.	www.nehu.ac.in	North Eastern Hill University(NEHU)
478.	www.nerist.ac.in	NERIST, Arunachal Pradesh
480.	www.nsit.ac.in	Netaji Subhas Institute of Technology, Delhi
481.	www.nim.ac.in	Nirma Institute of Management, Ahmedabad
482.	www.nursingworld.org	Nursing Education in USA
483.	www.oasisbgn.com	Oasis Pre Medical Test Coaching Institute
484.	www.osmania.ac.in	Osmania University
485.	www.cdeou.org	Osmania University
486.	www.orientalschool.com	Oriental School of Hotel Management
487.	www.theoxford.edu	Oxford Educational Institutions
488.	www.pci.nic.in	Pharmacy Council of India
489.	www.education.nic.in	Pre Medical Test Details (Dept. of Education, GOI)
490.	www.pgimer.nic.in	Postgraduate Institute of Medical Education & Research
491.	www.pec.rdu	Pondichary Engineering College
492.	www.psgtech.edu	PSG College of Technology, Coimbatore
493.	www.pieeducation.com	PIE Education
494.	www.womenpolytechnic.com	Polytechnic for Women, New Delhi

495.	www.ptujal.com	Punjab Technical University
496.	www.pec.ac.in	Punjab Engineering College, Chandigarh
497.	www.puchd.ac.in	Punjab University, Chandigarh
498.	www.pictsitm.com	PICT School of Information Technology & Management
499.	www.pioneerinstitute.com	Pioneer Institute of Professional Studies, Indore
500.	www.pearlacademy.com	Pearl Academy of Fashion
501.	www.presidencycollege.com	Presidency College, Bangalore
502.	www.presidencychennai.com	Presidency College, Chennai
504.	www.coep.org.in	PIET's College of Engineering, Pune
505.	www.primetutor.com	Prime Coaching Institute for NLSIU/NIFT/NID
506.	www.quantum.edu	Quantum Institute
507.	www.queenmarys.net	Queen Mary's College, Chennai
508.	www.raifoundation.org	RAI Foundation, New Delhi
509.	www.indiaresult.com	Rajasthan Pre-Engineering Test(RPET)
510.	www.rcc.nic.in	Regional Computer Centre, New Delhi
511.	www.rehabcouncil.org	Rehabilitation Council of India(RCI)
512.	www.patra.recham.ernet.in	REC, Hamirpur, Himachal Pradesh
513.	www.rect.edu	REC, Tiruchirappalli
515.	www.rlinstitutes.com	RL Institute of Nautical Sciences
516.	www.rcsm.com	Rashtriya Computer Saksharata Mission
517.	www.sriramakrishna.org	Ramakrishna Mission Institute of Culture
519.	www.rurkiu.ernet.in	Roorkee University
520.	www.rauias.com	Rau's IAS Study Circle
521.	www.rimmc.org	Rosary Institute of Media & Mass Com., Pune
522.	www.kalakshetra.org/college.html	Rukmini Devi College of Fine Arts, Chennai
523.	www.ruparel.edu	Ruparel College, Mumbai
524.	www.rvce.ac.in	RV College of Engineering
526.	www.srisathyasai.org.in	Sri Sathya Sai Institute of Higher Learning
528.	www.collegeboard.com	SAT Details & Enquiries
529.	www.sbspgi.com	SBS PG Institute of Biomedical Sciences, Dehradun
533.	www.smu.edu.sg	Singapore Management University

534.	www.skylinecollege.com	Skyline Business School
535.	www.schcpune.com	Symbiosis Centre of Health Care(SCHC)
536.	www.sibm.edu	Symbiosis Institute of Business Management
537.	www.sims.edu	Symbiosis Institute of Management Studies
538.	www.siftpune.com	Symbiosis Institute of Foreign Trade, Pune
539.	www.simc.edu	Symbiosis Institute of Mass Communication
540.	www.scitpune.com	Symbiosis Centre for Information Technology(SCIT)
541.	www.symlaw.ac.in	Symbiosis Law College
542.	www.scdl.net	Symbiosis Centre for Distance Learning(SCDL)
543.	www.sirjjarchitecture.com	Sir JJ College of Architecture, Mumbai
544.	www.sndt.edu	SNDT Women's University, Mumbai
545.	www.indiawatch.org/spa	School of Planning & Architecture, New Delhi
546.	www.scmscochin.com	School of Communication & Mgt. Studies
547.	www.softpune.com	School of Fashion Technology, Pune
548.	www.law.bham.ac.uk	School of Law, University of Birmingham
549.	www.shristiblr.org	Srishti School of Art Design & Technology
550.	www.manipal.edu	Sikkim Manipal University
551.	www.smuhmts.edu	Sikkim Manipal Institute of Medical Sciences
552.	www.smuhmts.edu	Sikkim Manipal Institute of Technology
553.	www.ststephens.edu	St. Stephens' College, Delhi
554.	www.xaviers.edu	St. Xaviers' College, Mumbai
556.	www.sjc.ac.in	St. Joseph's College, Bangalore
557.	www.indiainternet.com/sjcc	St. Joseph's College of Commerce, Bangalore
558.	www.stgeorgecollege.org	St. Gorge College, Bangalore
559.	www.stellamariscollege.org	Stella Maries College
560.	www.sydenham.edu	Sydenham College of Commerce & Economics, Mumbai
561.	www.sliet.org	Sant Longwal Institute of Engineering & Technology
562.	www.polytechnic-sdpw.com	South Delhi Polytechnic for Women
563.	www.cbsdu.org	Sukhdev College of Business Studies, Delhi
564.	www.venkateshwaracollege.edu	Sri Venkateshwara College, Delhi
565.	www.smvit@vsnl.com	Sir M. Visvesvaraya Inst. of Technology
566.	www.srivenkateswaracollege.net	Sri Venkateswara College, Delhi
567.	www.jaincollege.ac.in	Sri Bhagawan Mahavir Jain College, Bangalore
568.	www.srcc.edu	Shri Ram College of Commerce, Delhi
569.	www.rajgurucollege.com	Shaheed Rajguru College of Applied Sciences for Women
570.	www.srmscet.edu	Shri Ram Murti Smarak College of Engg & Technology
571.	www.srmc.edu	Sri Ramchandra Medical College & Research, Chennai
572.	www.spjimr.org	SP Jain Institute of Management & Research, Mumbai

573.	www.sehgalschool.com	Shegal School of Competitions
574.	www.skylinecollege.com	Skyline Business School, New Delhi
575.	www.sams.edu	School Arts & Management Sciences, Gurgaon
576.	www.sambhramgroup.net	Sambhram Institutions
577.	www.sgei.org	Shrada Group of Institutions
578.	www.sndt.edu	SNDT Women's University
579.	www.studyabroadlinks.com	Study abroad detail
580.	www.forumjam.com	SAIT, Canada
581.	www.speechandhearing.net	Speech & Hearing Courses
583.	www.tezu.ernet.in	Tezpur University
584.	www.tnmmu.ac.in	Tamil Nadu MGR Medical University
585.	www.tttichd.ac.in	Technical Teacher's Training Institute, Chandigarh
586.	www.lawentrance.com	Tutorials for Entrance to National Law School, Bangalore
587.	www.thiagarajamanagement.org	Thiagarajar School of Management, Madurai
588.	www.tjohncollege.org	T. John College, Bangalore
589.	www.tiss.edu	Tata Institute of Social Sciences
590.	www.tifr.res.in	Tata Institute of Fundamental Research
591.	www.tiet.ac.in	Thapar Institute of Engineering & Technology
592.	www.tn.gov.in	Tamil Nadu Film & Television Institute, Chennai
593.	www.tnmmu.ac.in	Tamil Nadu MGR Medical University
594.	www.dgshipping.com	T.S. Chanakya for B.Sc. in Nautical Science
595.	www.glc.edu	The Government Law College, Mumbai
596.	www.ugc.ac.in	University Grants Commission (UGC)
597.	www.uvce.in	University Visvesvaraya College of Engineering
598.	www.upsc.gov.in	Union Public Service Commission
599.	www.allduniv.edu	University of Allahabad
600.	www.unipune.ernet.in	University of Pune
601.	www.uohyd.ernet.in	University of Hyderabad
602.	www.unical.ac.in	University of Calicut
603.	www.universityofmadras.ac.in	University of Madras
604.	www.mu.ac.in	University of Mumbai
605.	www.uniraj.com	University of Rajasthan, Jaipur
606.	www.lon.ac.uk	University of London
607.	www.com.ac.uk	University of Cambridge
608.	www.blackwell.co.uk	University of Oxford
609.	www.man.ac.uk	University of Manchester
610.	www.colourado.edu	University of Colourado
611.	www.utkaluniv.org	Utkal University

612.	www.ietlucknow.edu/upseat	Uttar Pradesh State Engineering Admission Test Cell
613.	www.usnews.com	US Study Help
614.	www.justcolleges.com	US Study Help
615.	www.collegeview.com	US Study Help
616.	www.educationusa.state.gov	US Study Help
617.	www.peterson.com	US Study Help
618.	www.ins.gov	US Study Help
619.	www.ttsvisas.com	US Visa Help
620.	www.unanimedicine.org	Unani Medicine Detail
621.	www.vit.ac.in	Vellore Institute of Technology
622.	www.nic.in/dahd/vci.htm	Veterinary Council of India
623.	www.vcetdelhi.com	Vishwesharaiya College of Engg. & Technology
624.	www.viveka.org	Vivekananda College, Chennai
625.	www.nujs.edu	WB National University of Juridical Sciences
626.	www.wii.gov.in	Wild Life Institute of India
627.	www.wiganindia.org	Wigan & Leigh India Ltd
628.	www.wilsoncollege.edu	Wilson College, Mumbai
629.	www.xaviercomm.org	Xavier Institute of Communications, Mumbai
630.	www.ximb.ac.in	Xavier Institute of Management, Bhubaneshwar
631.	www.xlri.edu	XLRI, Jamshedpur
632.	www.xlri.ac.in	XLRI, Jamshedpur
633.	www.ximebangalore.com	XIME, Bangalore
634.	www.zeelearn.com	Zee Interactive Learning Systems

Websites for jobs:

635. www.jobsahead.com
636. www.naukri.com
637. www.jobsadead.com
638. www.humanlinks.com

640. www.careerbuilder.com
641. www.monsterindia.com
642. www.careerspan.com
643. www.careerplanning.com
644. www.groovyjobs.com

21

JOBS IN ALPHABETICAL ORDER

Jobs/Careers in alphabetical order:

A

B

C

D

E

F

G

H

I

J

L

M

N

Jobs In Alphabetical Order

O

P

Q

Quality Control Inspector
Quantity Surveyor

R

S

T

U

V

W

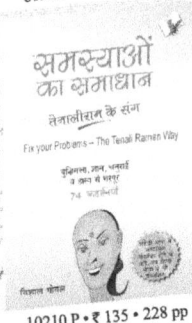

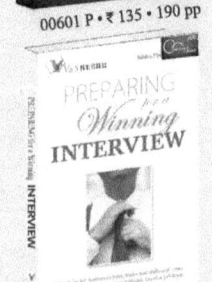

PERSONALITY DEVELOPMENT
(व्यक्तित्व विकास)

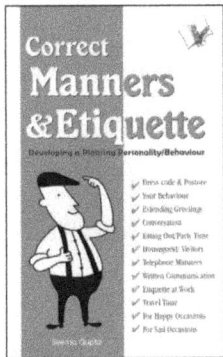

Correct **Manners & Etiquette**
00306 P • ₹ 96 • 156 pp

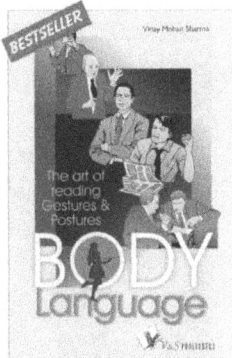

BESTSELLER — The art of reading Gestures & Postures — **BODY Language**
00302 P • ₹ 108 • 120 pp

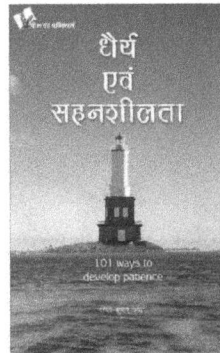

धैर्य एवं सहनशीलता — 101 ways to develop patience
10208 P • ₹ 96 • 152 pp

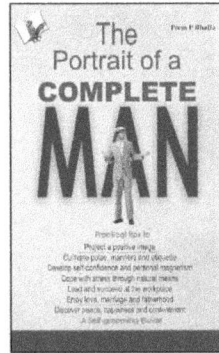

The Portrait of a **COMPLETE MAN**
8995 D • ₹ 110 • 176 pp

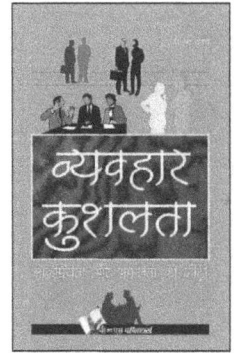

व्यवहार कुशलता
8911 D • ₹ 60 • 128 pp

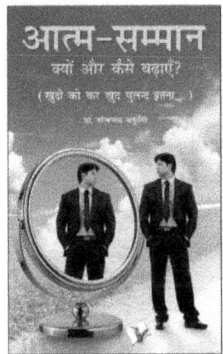

आत्म-सम्मान — क्यों और कैसे बढ़ाएं?
10302 P • ₹ 96 • 112 pp

हां, तुम एक विजेता हो!
10214 P • ₹ 96 • 160 pp

अपना व्यक्तित्व प्रभावशाली कैसे बनाएं
10304 P • ₹ 88 • 142 pp

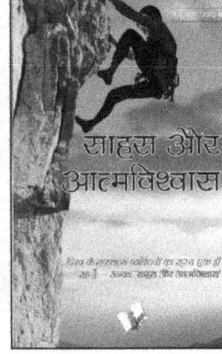

साहस और आत्मविश्वास
10307 P • ₹ 80 • 128 pp

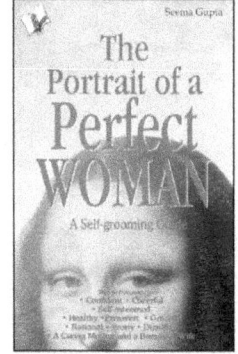

The Portrait of a **Perfect WOMAN** — A Self-grooming
9062 B • ₹ 96 • 136 pp

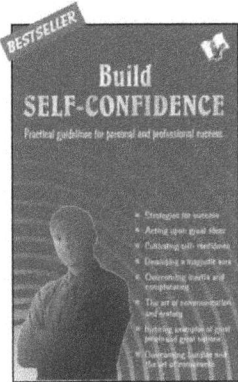

BESTSELLER — Build **SELF-CONFIDENCE** — Practical guideline for personal and professional success
00301 P • ₹ 96 • 120 pp

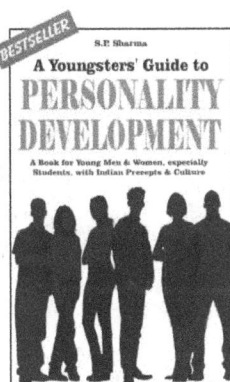

BESTSELLER — A Youngsters' Guide to **PERSONALITY DEVELOPMENT** — A Book for Young Men & Women, especially Students, with Indian Precepts & Culture
00303 P • ₹ 110 • 120 pp

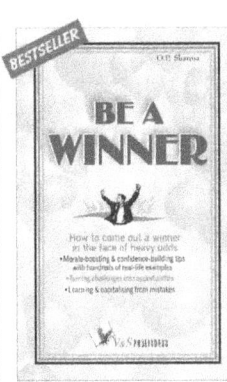

BESTSELLER — **BE A WINNER** — How to come out a winner in the face of heavy odds
00606 P • ₹ 110 • 136 pp

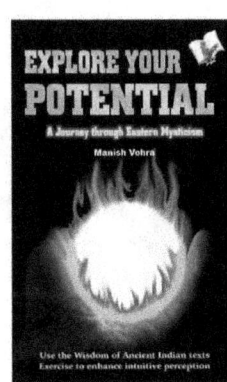

EXPLORE YOUR POTENTIAL — A Journey through Eastern Mysticism — Manish Vohra
02801 P • ₹ 150 • 128 pp

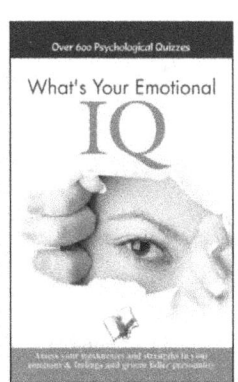

Over 600 Psychological Quizzes — What's Your Emotional **IQ**
00305 P • ₹ 120 • 176 pp

Quick-bite to shake off sloth and lethargy and get cracking on your tasks and goals in life right away for self confidence, success and satisfaction. Liberally sprinkled with stories, anecdotes and events of ordinary people who achieved greatness.

The book provides high-value succinct guidelines on all matters of interest to students and job seeking professionals such as, personality development, etiquette and personal presentation for success in career and life.

Excel in your career! With inputs from hundreds of real-life examples, learn to turn challenges into opportunities, each day, and come out a winner in your social, personal and professional life.

The book helps the reader to get access to wisdom of several scriptures in one piece. Several sutras which are normally only passed on in the oral tradition are documented in the book.

Precise, accurate and to-the-point compilation of 600 psychological quizzes reveal your emotional IQ, an authoritative result which you can use to modify your attitude towards things that need betterment.

SELF-HELP/SELF IMPROVEMENT
(आत्म–सुधार/आत्म–विकास)

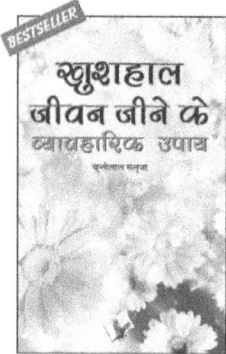

BESTSELLER

खुशहाल जीवन जीने के व्यावहारिक उपाय

10205 P • ₹ 96 • 128 pp

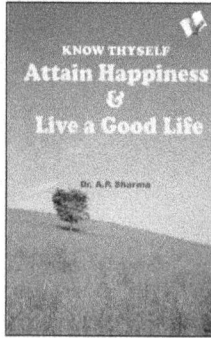

KNOW THYSELF
Attain Happiness & Live a Good Life
Dr. A.P. Sharma

00206 P • ₹ 120 • 121 pp

भयमुक्त कैसे हों
(How to Overcome Fears & Phobias)

10209 P • ₹ 72 • 120 pp

मन की उलझनें कैसे सुलझाएँ

10213 P • ₹ 80 • 128 pp

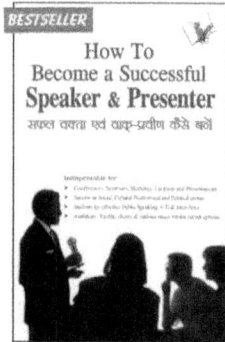

BESTSELLER

How To Become a Successful Speaker & Presenter
सफल वक्ता एवं वाक्-प्रवीण कैसे बनें

00211 P • ₹ 108 • 112 pp

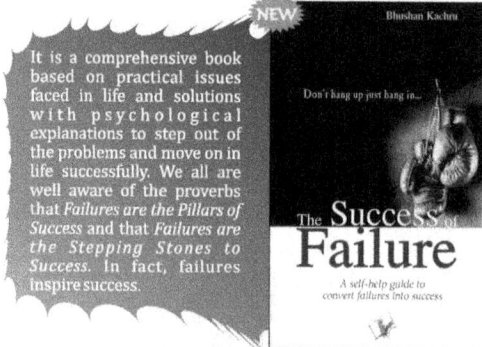

It is a comprehensive book based on practical issues faced in life and solutions with psychological explanations to step out of the problems and move on in life successfully. We all are well aware of the proverbs that *Failures are the Pillars of Success* and that *Failures are the Stepping Stones to Success.* In fact, failures inspire success.

NEW
Bhushan Kachru

Don't hang up just hang in...
The Success of **Failure**
A self-help guide to convert failures into success

00220 P • ₹ 175 • 256 pp

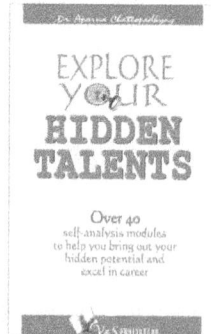

Dr Aparna Chattopadhyay

EXPLORE YOUR HIDDEN TALENTS

Over 40 self-analysis modules to help you bring out your hidden potential and excel in career

8956 M • ₹ 120 • 176 pp

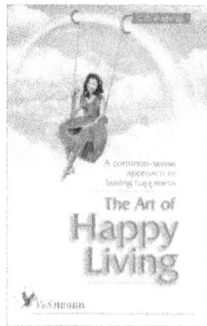

The Art of **Happy Living**

00219 P • ₹ 120 • 165 pp

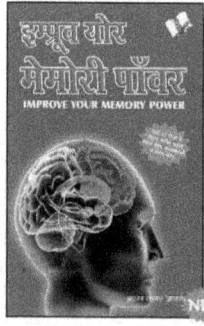

इम्प्रूव योर मेमोरी पॉवर
IMPROVE YOUR MEMORY POWER

10215 P • ₹ 100 • 192 pp

इस प्रतियोगी दुनिया में केवल कड़ी मेहनत से कामयाबी नहीं मिलती। कामयाबी पाने के लिए आपको तरह-तरह की तकनीकों का प्रयोग करना पड़ता है।

प्रस्तुत पुस्तक में इस दिशा में सराहनीय प्रयास किये गये हैं। इसकी मदद से आप न केवल अपनी स्मरण-शक्ति बढ़ा सकते, बल्कि परीक्षा में अच्छे अंक भी प्राप्त कर सकते हैं।

निराशा छोड़ो सुख से जिओ

8918 D • ₹ 60 • 136 pp

स्वेट मार्डेन
जीवन में सफल होने के उपाय

8881 E • ₹ 68 • 143 pp

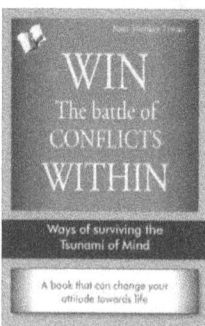

WIN The battle of CONFLICTS WITHIN
Ways of surviving the Tsunami of Mind
A book that can change your attitude towards life

9429 A • ₹ 175 • 260 pp

NEW
जीत निश्चित है!
गया सिर्फ़ श्रेष्ठ है, शेष सर्वश्रेष्ठ है

10216 P • ₹ 96 • 128 pp

सार्थक जीवन जीने की कला
Art of leading a meaningful life

10224 P • ₹ 96 • 124 pp

Quiz Books
(प्रश्नोत्तरी की पुस्तकें)

ENVIRONMENT QUIZ BOOK — 02307 P • ₹110 • 144 pp

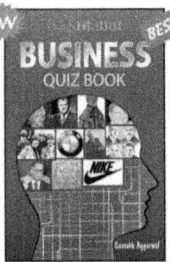

BUSINESS QUIZ BOOK — 02304 P • ₹200 • 256 pp

QUIZ TIME — 02308 P • ₹120 • 128 pp

GLOBAL Quiz Bank — 02302 F • ₹120 • 256 pp

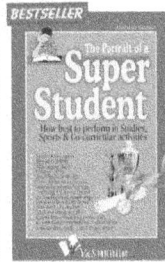

QUIZ TIME HISTORY — 02310 P • ₹120 • 184 pp

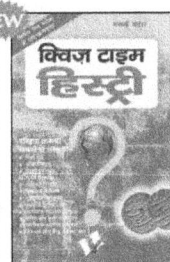

क्विज़ टाइम हिस्ट्री — 12313 P • ₹96 • 168 pp

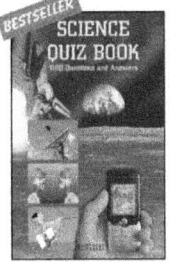

SCIENCE QUIZ BOOK — 02303 P • ₹96 • 192 pp

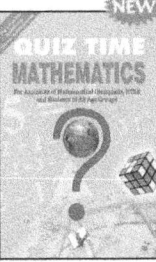

QUIZ TIME MATHEMATICS — 02309 P • ₹96 • 104 pp

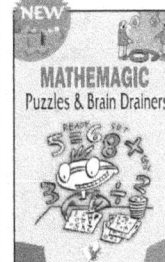

STUDENT DEVELOPMENT
(छात्र विकास)

Super Student — 00503 P • ₹110 • 142 pp

आप भी मेरिट में आ सकते हैं — 10501 P • ₹96 • 152 pp

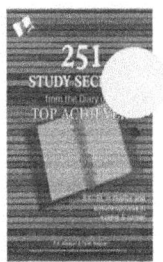

251 STUDY SECRETS — 5645 D • ₹150 • 133 pp

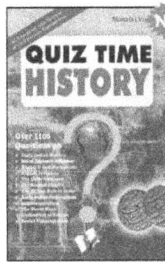

MATHEMAGIC Puzzles & Brain Drainers — 02311 P • ₹96 • 112 pp

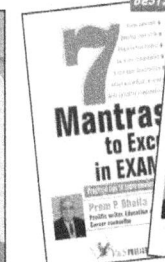

7 Mantras to Excel in EXAM — 9076 D • ₹80 • 144 pp

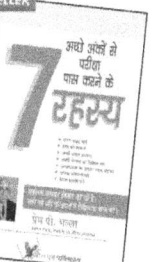

अच्छे अंको से पीछा पास करने के रहस्य — 10502 P • ₹96 • 144 pp

COMPUTERS (कम्प्यूटर्स)

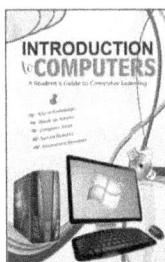

INTRODUCTION to COMPUTERS — 02402 P • ₹100 • 104 pp

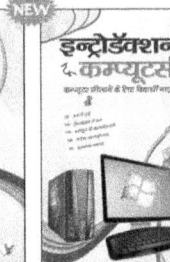

इन्ट्रोडक्शन टू कम्प्यूटर्स — 12403 P • ₹100 • 104 pp

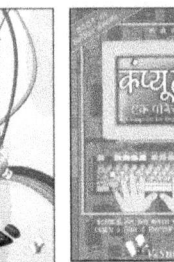

कम्प्यूटर एक परिचय — 12401 P • ₹120 • 164 pp

QUOTES/SAYINGS (उद्धरण/सूक्तियाँ)

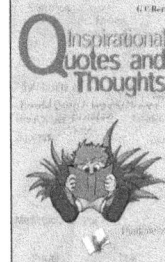

Inspirational Quotes and Thoughts — 00801 P • ₹96 • 132 pp

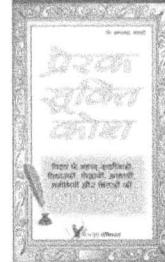

प्रेरक सूक्ति कोश — 10803 P • ₹96 • 144 pp

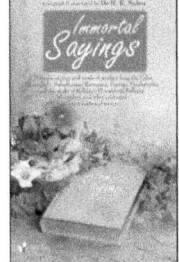

Immortal Sayings — 00804 P • ₹125 • 187 pp

ENGLISH IMPROVEMENT (अंग्रेजी सुधार)

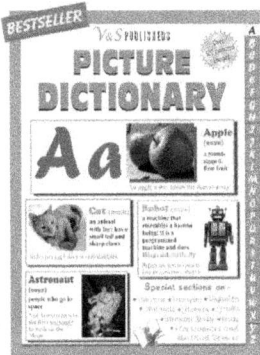

PICTURE DICTIONARY — 03902 P • ₹120 • 64 pp

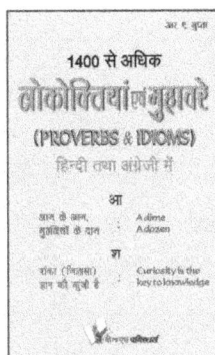

1400 से अधिक लोकोक्तियां एवं मुहावरे (PROVERBS & IDIOMS) हिन्दी तथा अंग्रेजी में — 10802 P • ₹96 • 132 pp

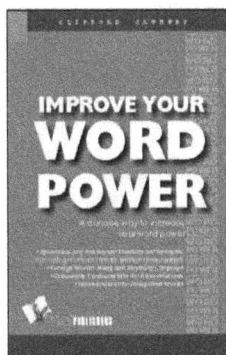

IMPROVE YOUR WORD POWER — 03901 P • ₹88 • 230 pp

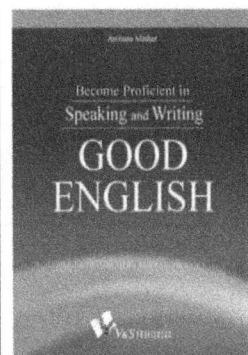

GOOD ENGLISH — Become Proficient in Speaking and Writing — 03907 P • ₹150 • 148 pp

Learn sophisticated style of correct English writing! Polish your communication lines and skill by using effective and attractive words modern readers and writers prefer! Suitable examples for easy application provided.

Contact us at sales@vspublishers.com

www.ingramcontent.com/pod-product-compliance
Lightning Source LLC
Chambersburg PA
CBHW082126210326
41599CB00031B/5886